The Edge of Change

The Edge of Change

Women in the Twenty-First-Century Press

Edited by
JUNE O. NICHOLSON,
PAMELA J. CREEDON,
WANDA S. LLOYD, AND
PAMELA J. JOHNSON

Foreword by
ELLEN GOODMAN

UNIVERSITY OF ILLINOIS PRESS
Urbana and Chicago

©2009 by the Board of Trustees
of the University of Illinois
All rights reserved
Manufactured in the United States of America
1 2 3 4 5 C P 5 4 3 2 1
∞ This book is printed on acid-free paper.

Library of Congress Cataloging-in-Publication Data
The edge of change : women in the twenty-first-century press /
edited by June O. Nicholson ... [et al.] ; foreword by Ellen Goodman.
  p.   cm.
Includes bibliographical references and index.
ISBN 978-0-252-03448-0 (cloth : acid-free paper)
ISBN 978-0-252-07649-7 (pbk. : acid-free paper)
1. Women in journalism. I. Nicholson, June O.
PN4784.W7E34   2009
070.4082—dc22   2009015048

For Bob Nicholson and Bryn
and Christian Rich

For Kelly Reid, Velma Reid, Tom Reid,
and William Bingaman, MD

For Willie and Shelby Lloyd

For Jim Dalton; Matt, Jen, Parker,
and Emma Johnson; Brad Johnson;
Sheila Dalton, Adam Crews,
and Austin James Crews

And for journalists everywhere who
advance a free and vigorous press

If we are to achieve a richer culture, rich in contrasting values, we must recognize the whole gamut of human potentialities, and so weave a less arbitrary social fabric, one in which each diverse human gift will find a fitting place.

—Margaret Mead, 1935

Our republic and its press will rise or fall together. An able, disinterested, public-spirited press, with trained intelligence to know the right and courage to do it, can preserve that public virtue without which popular government is a sham and a mockery. A cynical, mercenary, demagogic press will produce in time a people as base as itself. The power to mold the future of the republic will be in the hands of the journalists of future generations.

—Joseph Pulitzer, 1906

Contents

Part 5. Women Leaders in an Era of Corporate, Legal, and Commercial Pressures

Part 6. Women Making Choices

Part 7. Beyond Gender Diversity

Part 8. The Future: Shifting Paradigms

Photographs follow page 154

Acknowledgments

This book is the result of the contributions of many women and men in the news industry and in universities who provided their support and assistance. These individuals care deeply about the issues for women in journalism and about the future of the press as an institution in American society and in the broader international community. Judy VanSlyke Turk, Jeffrey C. South, Debora H. Wenger, Marcus Messner, Yan Jin, Bonnie Newnan Davis, Ernest F. Martin, and other colleagues in the School of Mass Communications at Virginia Commonwealth University provided enduring support, insights, assistance, and valuable comments on portions of the manuscript. A special thanks as well goes to Laura Moriarty, also of VCU.

The College of Humanities and Sciences at VCU extended its support in the form of a research grant and semester leave for June O. Nicholson, the book's lead editor. The Shorenstein Center at Harvard University, through its conference in November 2007 on "Women and News: Expanding the News Audience, Increasing Political Participation, and Informing Citizens," contributed invaluable research and insight about the links among women in news, politics, and as news consumers in society. Thanks go especially to Ellen Goodman; Shauna Shames, a PhD student at the Kennedy School of Government at Harvard; Nancy Palmer of the Shorenstein Center staff; and the participants in that conference.

Several news industry groups provided assistance, including the Poynter Institute for Media Studies, in St. Petersburg, Florida, one of the nation's leading training and research centers for journalists. We are indebted to Poynter and its president, Karen Dunlap, and female faculty members for their help as this project was conceptualized. Pam Johnson was a faculty member at the Poynter Institute when this book began to take shape. We met several years ago at Poynter to identify issues and plan this project. The proceeds of this book are being donated to the Poynter Institute as support for conferences and seminars at Poynter that will advance women in the news industry and address the issues for the press that we have examined here. We are extremely grateful as well to Mary Glick, associate director of the American Press Institute (API), for her keen interest in the role and impact of women in newspapers, and for her suggestions. Some of the momentum for this book developed out of the J. Montgomery Curtis Seminar at API in 2002, which focused on women in newsroom leadership. Glick and Jan Schaffer, then of the Pew Center for Civic Journalism, spearheaded the research study "The Great Divide," published by API and the Pew Center for Civic Journalism, which was released as part of that seminar.

Other thanks go to LaBarbara "Bobbi" Bowman, diversity director for the American Society of News Editors (ASNE), and to ASNE itself. A number of informal discussions about issues for women in journalism and about this project took place at the annual ASNE conventions, and especially at the Women's Reception at ASNE each year. We also thank the Media Management Center (MMC) at Northwestern University and three dozen participants at the November 2005 conference on "Women and Media: Finding the Leader in You" who informed this project. Thanks go as well to Vivian Valberg and Mary Nesbitt, also of the MMC, and to Regina H. Glaspie.

A number of people read all or portions of the drafts and provided invaluable suggestions or editing assistance. They include Mary Glick, Kay Mills, Karen Jurgensen, Debora H. Wenger, Yan Jin, and Bob Nicholson. We are especially grateful to Jill Hughes, chief copy editor for the project. Thanks go as well to Louise Seals for copy editing assistance, and to Kim Merchant for preparing the index. Other individuals in the industry or in higher education provided extremely valuable insights and suggestions, including Marty Petty, Sandra Rowe, Geneva Overholser, Dorothy Butler Gilliam, Donna Reed, Arlene Morgan, Cathy Henkel, Amanda Bennett, Janet Weaver, Pam Luecke, Judith Clabes, Nora Paul, Pam Fine, Nancy Adler, Venise Wagner, Mi-Ai Parrish, Leila Fadel, Maria Carrillo, Nadiya Abraham, Judith Cramer, Margie R. Fisher, and the late Myrtle S. Barnes. We are deeply indebted to anthropologist Helen E. Fisher of Rutgers University for her research, perspectives, vision, and appearances in recent years at conferences or conventions of API, the Newspaper Association of America, and ASNE. Fisher first came to the attention of the news industry as a result of the 2002 API J. Montgomery Curtis seminar on women in newsroom leadership.

Thanks especially to Bill Regier, editor of the University of Illinois Press, for his continuing support, counsel, and assistance, and to Angela Burton and other members of the UIP staff. This book would not have happened without our families. Their unflinching support of this project, as well as their guidance, humor, and patience, sustained us through the several years as this project was completed. The book originated in large measure because of the presence of young women in our lives, our daughters and daughters-in-law, students and female journalists around the country and the world. The book is an attempt to help create a workplace and society and future for women and men where gender, race, and other differences are no longer a barrier. *The Edge of Change* is perhaps, most importantly, the result of the dedication, professionalism, energy, and sense of pride of the women news executives, editors, and leaders who contributed to this volume. They are the pioneers, the role models, and the visionaries for women in journalism today and for the journalists of the future.

Foreword

ELLEN GOODMAN

Allow me to begin this foreword by looking backward. After all, my generation of women has spent our entire adulthood on the edge of change. As journalists we have not only written the "first rough draft of history," but we have also lived it. In the double helix of social change, we've covered and been a part of the upheaval in women's lives and expectations. We have both chronicled and pushed forward what we call the women's movement.

My own life as a journalist began in 1963 when I was hired straight out of college by *Newsweek* magazine. In those days the newsmagazines sought over-educated young women to be researchers and sought their male peers to be writers. That's the way it was. I repeat this old story not to prove that my generation walked four miles in the snow to school but because I've discovered that young women know we were discriminated against in the bad old days. But they don't know it was legal. It wasn't until the Civil Rights Act of 1964 that sex discrimination became a crime. It wasn't until years later that the women of *Newsweek* filed the first huge lawsuit that blew open the profession. By then I was long gone from *Newsweek*. First to the *Detroit Free Press,* where I was among the first women to have a seat in the newsroom as well as a byline in the news hole. Then to the *Boston Globe,* where I was the only pregnant woman in the days before maternity leave and the only mother of an infant—then toddler and then preschooler—writing in what were still called "the women's pages."

I discovered feminism the way many of us did—on assignment. I was sent out to cover a meeting of a small group of radicals in a Boston church basement. That was in the late 1960s. Soon I began writing about this new movement on the landscape and then began writing columns, making my living by telling people what I think. Much of what I thought about was growing up and living female.

I was sent to my first political convention in 1972, when it was clear that women's issues would be a big story for the Democrats. And when it was also clear that the *Globe* "needed" a woman to cover that story. By 1984, when Geraldine Ferraro was nominated by the Democratic Party to run for vice president, there were finally enough women to talk shop in the ladies' room. And we did. Then, one memorable night in the Moscone Center in San Francisco, a handful of women journalists put aside our credentials and followed our plan to meet on the convention floor at the exact moment Ferraro was officially nominated. We were women with goose bumps as well as deadlines.

Looking backward to the 1970s and '80s, many of us had thought that newspapers would be quickly and fully integrated the same way the help wanted pages had been integrated. It was just a matter of time before we would fill half the slots up and down the masthead and half the jobs across the globe. Half the journalistic "Big Feet" would have a female imprint. But it never quite happened that way.

So now it's time for an assessment. Which way do we view the cup: Half full? Half empty? How do we sum up the state of women, especially at a time when newspapers themselves are in a state? A state of crisis? Decline? Transformation? Every day brings some new concern about declining readership or corporate takeover.

The Edge of Change is a collection of women's voices from pre–baby boomers to Generation Y, from foreign correspondents to sports writers, from print reporters to Internet bloggers. June Nicholson, Pamela Creedon, Wanda Lloyd, and Pam Johnson have included the tales we want to pass on to the next generation and the problems we hope the next generation will solve. As reflected in *The Edge of Change,* women in news are attempting to problem-solve some of the most difficult issues for newsrooms and companies today, among them creating companies and a workplace culture that foster innovation, creativity, new ideas and change, and, yes, even risk. These leaders are tackling credibility and contributing to the debate about First Amendment freedoms in an era when some of those freedoms are threatened.

Some of the women contributors to this volume lead companies today at a time of intense corporate pressure to make a profit and as new business models are being sought. The contributors to *The Edge of Change* are redefining journalism and its role as a "glue" in our changing democracy. Many of the essays are written by women who are card-carrying members of my Beachhead Generation, those who landed uncertainly on the sands of the foreign terrain of newsrooms. They include the beleaguered "firsts," like Dorothy Butler Gilliam, the first full-time black woman at the *Washington Post,* who shares a "tribute to those women who jumped into that ocean with me and swam through often shark-infested waters to reach land and chart new courses for the generations that followed." The redoubtable Nan Robertson revisits the famous lawsuit against the good gray lady, the *New York Times.*

Sandy Rowe, editor of the *Oregonian,* speaks for many of us when she says, "Looking back, I'm amazed we reacted to the absurdities of the time with more acceptance—even amusement—than anger." Today, she adds, just being the editor rather than the "first woman editor" feels like a success. But there are still woes in the locker room, as longtime sports editor Cathy Henkel reports.

The sentiment that runs through many of the pieces is wrapped up in a repeated worry that "we are in a holding pattern." I think that may be our motto in the early years of the new millennium. The pipeline theory—the idea that if enough women filled the pipeline, they would move inexorably, directly, to the top—was too optimistic. There have been leaks, losses, and stoppages in that pipeline.

The narrative line of *The Edge of Change* is that we've made significant strides but we've stalled out. As this book was going to press, only about 20 percent of the editors at the top one hundred newspapers were women, and fewer were in top corporate positions as CEOs, presidents, and publishers. We're stalled out on the op-ed pages, my home turf, stalled out on the mastheads, the sports pages. How do we jump-start the next movement?

Journalism not only describes the world in which women are living but also mirrors it. In corporate America, the women's movement has bumped up against the glass ceiling and has been constrained by the difficulties of balancing work and family. This is also reflected in this status report of the news media.

Some women file dispatches on this from, literally, the combat zone. More women than ever are covering war. But Kirsten Scharnberg Hampton is not reluctant to write honestly and deeply about the special difficulties as well as strengths that come with being a female correspondent in the world's most difficult places. She went up personally against the kind of problems we usually chronicle. "Women—unlike men—tend to view international reporting as a zero-sum career," she writes, "one that can only be successful if they give up any hope of family or personal life." She doesn't shy away from writing about her own experience. Another former editor, Jan Leach, seconds that in her own story on conflicts on the home front, as does Margaret Sullivan of the *Buffalo News.* Carol Guzy of the *Washington Post* writes poignantly of the rewards, difficulties, and emotional impact she has experienced as one of the foremost female news photographers of this generation, while working abroad and in the United States.

There is also a psychological sidebar to the story of change. Women have brought a certain identity consciousness—gender-consciousness, if you prefer—to the newsrooms of America. These days we are all asked less about whether a woman can be as good as a man, but we are asked more about whether having women on the staff makes a difference in the kind of stories that we cover, the perspective we bring. Women on this edge are building a case for change on both the grounds of equality and the grounds of difference. Which will it be? Both? Neither?

Anthropologist Helen Fisher covers some of that terrain in her essay, claiming that those who "deny women's biological uniqueness . . . negate all of the natural talents that women bring to the current business environment." Among those "talents," Arlene Morgan from Columbia University's School of Journalism gives women the special mantle of being "the voice for diversity." She writes, "They are not afraid to use their voice to write with affection and candor about the richness of life that diversity brings to the nation." We have all been enriched by including the voices that we hear on these pages as well, voices from different ethnic groups, racial groups, and sexual orientations.

If looking back brings stories of swift change, if the current narrative is of a movement stalled, what, then, do we see when we look at the news of the news world? Finally this foreword looks forward. As this book was being written, Rupert Murdoch purchased the *Wall Street Journal,* the Tribune Company, which publishes the *Chicago Tribune* and the *Los Angeles Times,* filed for bankruptcy protection, and other newspapers produced online-only editions. Journalists are not paid prognosticators. We don't do windows; we don't do futures. There is a good deal of talk in these pages about both the newspaper crunch and new opportunities from citizen journalists to the blogosphere. At times, it's hard to distinguish the edge of change from the edge of a cliff.

Gloria Steinem, a change agent and optimist by temperament, sees much reason for hope in the evolving landscape of the new media, and Geneva Overholzer finds comfort in the unknown. The unknown, she reminds us, is not the worst thing possible. We can't know yet whether that unknown is fertile territory for women. Much of it depends on another unknown: Will this generation press as much as the last?

How will journalism evolve? Who will lead the change? What is the future for women in news and in society? How does the role of women in news impact the rest of society? *The Edge of Change* raises some of those important questions.

There is a huge open space on the Internet for anyone with a blog. At the same time, I can't help noticing how much of the "new media" looks like a "new boys" club. The online world of news and the political blogs that dot the Internet do not yet seem all that different from the op-ed pages that are overwhelmingly male. At the meeting in August 2007 of the netroots convention the Yearly Kos, one panel was labeled "Blogging While Female." The problems that sometimes silence these women include harassment. The old boys network is alive and well in the blogosphere—a new boys network.

Are we creating the old newspaper online, with mommy blogs forming the old women's pages and with political blogs as a mostly male beat? There are some who believe that the mommy blogs on newspaper sites will entice women into the news pages. Others worry that women readers will stay only on the designated "women's pages" of the Internet. Indeed one of the newest publications, on- and off-line, the much heralded *Politico,* actually has a site labeled

"SHEnanigans," the gossip. There is, in short, much work to be done to fill the other half of the cup.

I remain optimistic, I suppose, because I have seen the first half of the cup filled. I have seen too much change and believe that our daughters simply expect more. They don't regard the limits on their energies and talents with the same amusement that Sandy Rowe remembers. Indeed, those women "blogging while female" are a good updated example.

I applaud the honesty and energy of the women writing in this book. June Nicholson and the other editors have gathered an impressive group, and these pages are both a record of the times we live in and a baseline we can use to measure progress. The next generation will look back through them and see, I hope, how far they have come.

For now, I am reminded that change—real, deep social change—comes slowly. Sometimes I think the beat generation poet Jack Kerouac wrote the best motto for women in journalism way back in the 1950s when he warned us all: "Walking on water wasn't built in a day."

The Edge of Change

Introduction

JUNE O. NICHOLSON

On September 20, 1963, Katharine Graham, then forty-six, was elected president of the Washington Post Company at a meeting of its board of directors, thus succeeding her husband, Philip Graham, a month after his suicide. She wrote in her autobiography, *A Personal History,* which won a Pulitzer Prize in 1998: "What I essentially did was to put one foot in front of the other, shut my eyes, and step off the edge."[1] Over the next four decades, Graham transformed the Washington Post Company, which once had been owned by her father, Eugene Meyer, into a media empire and the *Washington Post* into one of the nation's great newspapers.

As publisher of the *Post* for a decade, CEO and board chairman of the company until 1991, and chairman of the executive committee until her death in 2001, Graham was the first female to head a major media company and to run a Fortune 500 firm. She also was the first female president of the American Newspaper Publishers Association, which preceded the Newspaper Association of America, and the first woman to serve on the board of the Associated Press.

Graham led the *Post* through tumultuous periods for the press and the nation. On June 13, 1971, the *New York Times,* and later the *Post,* began publishing the Pentagon Papers, a classified study about the operation and escalation of the Vietnam War and the government's deception of the American public. The government obtained a restraining order against the *Times* and sought an injunction against the *Post.* In a landmark decision on June 30, 1971, based on the two newspapers' challenges, the U.S. Supreme Court ruled that prior restraints against the press were unconstitutional.

In 1972 Graham and the *Post* again came under intense pressure as two reporters, Carl Bernstein and Bob Woodward, exposed the attempts of top government officials to cover up a robbery of the Democratic National Headquarters and conceal other criminal acts. Graham backed the story and executive editor Ben

Bradlee as the *Post* pursued the scandal known as Watergate. Two years later, in 1974, as the corruption engulfed the Oval Office, Richard Nixon resigned as president.

Graham, who became one of the most powerful women in the history of the press and in the country, wrote of the 1960s and early '70s, "The business world was essentially closed to women."[2] She was then by her own admission skeptical of the fast-growing women's movement. Graham also acknowledged that she was slow in recognizing the need to improve opportunities for women and people of color in America's newsrooms. In an interview in 1969, six years after taking over the *Post*, Graham was asked whether she would appoint a woman to an executive position. She replied, "I think it's a matter of appropriateness. I can't see a woman as managing editor of a newspaper." Graham added, "In the world today, men are more able than women at executive work."[3]

Graham said she changed her mind because of the influence of Gloria Steinem, a leader in the women's movement, and Meg Greenfield, who was then an editorial writer for the *Post*. She was swayed as well by her personal experience as a female executive and by the views of women who worked for both the *Post* and *Newsweek*, which is also owned by the company.[4] These women fought for equal status, an end to discrimination, better pay, and more opportunity.

In 1970, as the civil rights movement gained steam, forty-six women staffers at *Newsweek* filed a sex discrimination complaint with the Equal Employment Opportunity Commission, the first filed by women against a media organization. The same day the action was announced, March 16, 1970, a *Newsweek* cover story appeared titled "Women in Revolt," about the women's movement in the United States.[5] The *Post* also was sued by female staffers. Graham noted that at least at the *Post* and *Newsweek* there were enough women to force change— many other companies in the country had hired few or no women or minorities.[6] Other lawsuits followed against the *New York Times*, the Associated Press, *Newsday*, and NBC News, among other news organizations.[7] These complaints and lawsuits and the momentum of the women's movement began to change the workplace for women in American journalism.

Despite her initial misgivings, Graham gradually helped to remove barriers for women in her newsroom and change company policies to be more accommodating to women and their advancement. She helped break gender barriers in the stuffy business and political circles in Washington and mentored many women who took on positions of influence and leadership.

Women Stepping off the Edge in the Twenty-First Century

The work begun by twentieth-century women trailblazers in the press remains unfinished. More than forty years after Graham took the helm of the Washington Post Company, serious issues remain for women in newspaper journalism and news companies. In recent decades more women have entered journalism, just as they have joined other professions, and the country will experience another huge influx of women into the professional ranks in the next decade.[8] But as *The Edge of Change* describes, the new generation of women in news will encounter many of the same issues that have existed for decades: inequities in salary and advancement opportunities, barriers to top management, and the vexing issue of work-life balance. Graham and others of her generation led the first wave of change for women in the press. Women in news companies and media today are at the edge of another frontier—of change, challenge, but also promise.

This book assesses the progress of women over the past quarter century or more, examines issues for women in contemporary newspapers and media, and looks ahead to the future for women in the news and in society. The book also addresses some of the critical issues for the press in the early twenty-first century, among them credibility and transparency, intense commercial pressures that threaten the solvency of media companies, serious challenges to First Amendment freedoms, and the need for more diversity in newsrooms and in top management in companies.

Each contributor to this volume has written an original essay, and some have contributed additional interviews or materials. Our authors represent various news organizations, points of view, and experience. The women executives, editors, and leaders in this book are shaping contemporary journalism and news companies during a period of seismic change and unpredictability. They include some of the most influential women in U.S. journalism today and over the past quarter century, as well as some relative newcomers. Other authors at universities are educating young journalists and contributing in other ways to the future of news and media.

This volume also includes an essay by Helen E. Fisher, PhD, of Rutgers University, a world-renowned biological anthropologist and an expert on gender and women in the workplace and in cultures around the world. Fisher has worked with the American Press Institute, a premier education center for newsroom professionals, on issues of newsroom leadership and has spoken to other leading newspaper organizations about the role and future of women in the press and in society. Fisher maintains that women have innate natural talents and characteristics that are in demand in the twenty-first-century global marketplace and in leadership. Women bring innovation, imagination, collaboration, differing ways of thinking, and a more contextual view to their work, a trend that will accelerate as more women pile into the workforce around the world, Fisher says. She envisions more equality among the sexes as women take on more leadership roles in companies and in society. In this sense, Fisher says, society is moving back to the lifestyle of a million years ago when men and women had equal status on the grasslands of Africa. Fisher outlined her views and a wealth of scientific evidence in her book *The First Sex,* which was published by Random House in 1999.

The editors and authors of *The Edge of Change* hope to shed light on the views of women in senior leadership in news companies and newsrooms, and as journalists across news and opinion pages. Many journalists and members of the public know little about the experience and contributions of an entire generation of women who have come through the ranks of journalism and news companies in recent decades. *The Edge of Change* examines those women's contributions as innovators and problem solvers, addresses the role of women in shaping news coverage and public opinion, and assesses the leadership style and impact of women at the top ranks of the profession. These women are providing leadership, vision, and a prism through which ideas, public policy, and public opinion are being shaped in the twenty-first century. The book focuses attention on issues for women in journalism and for news organizations as a way to strengthen the press as a foundation of civil society, and as part of examining a new global era in which traditional and new forms of communication and technology play an increasingly important role.

News Industry Imperatives

The Edge of Change challenges the news industry to aggressively address several key issues for women in news that have existed for decades and continue to be identified in news industry and other research. Those include:

- the retention of women in news;
- the necessity for more progressive work-family balance policies and structural change that would allow the news industry to retain the intellectual capital and talents of women;
- bias and discrimination in the news workplace;
- imbalances in pay, job satisfaction, and opportunities for advancement; and
- the lack of diversity in newsrooms and key leadership positions.

Confronting these issues is crucial to improving the workplace for women and men and to the future of the industry. As many of our authors point out, women bring many assets to leadership and to companies, including innovation and differing and unconventional perspectives. Retention of women in news, however, has been an issue for at least three decades, since statistics have been available. Moreover, the news industry lags behind some other professions and industries in retaining and advancing women. News companies are losing a vast amount of talent in women who could bring those leadership skills. Women are one key to drawing new talent and perspectives and bold ideas to the news industry. At the top level of many companies, however, complacency exists about diversity and its implications. In fact, the evidence shows that the existence of more women and people of color in senior leadership and in news-rooms translates into better news coverage of society, larger and more diverse news audiences, and greater corporate success.

The news industry has acknowledged since the 1960s that newsrooms need a diverse staff and leadership so that a variety of perspectives and news interests are reflected in coverage. The industry has not addressed these issues, however, in a way that has produced the changes in coverage that serve diverse contemporary audiences. In addition, approximately 80 percent of newspaper companies studied by Northwestern University's Media Management Center have a "defensive" culture that does not promote innovation or embrace change, according to a 2006 report.[9] The research indicates that more women and people of color in management could help improve the position of companies in the competitive and shifting media environment. A number of CEOs who run news companies are rewarded with corporate bonuses primarily for stimulating higher profits. Too few are rewarded for diversifying senior leadership and are held accountable for results.

Women and men in news companies—and most other companies in America—struggle with work-family responsibilities. Women say they have difficulty balancing the demands of family and their news organizations.[10] Women still are the main caregivers in society and bear the most responsibility for raising children and caring for elderly parents.[11] The news industry overall has been slow to implement family-friendly workplace policies that would address retention and other issues raised by women—these would improve the workplace for everyone. News companies should make it a much higher priority to improve work-family policies that would accommodate both women and men. Society itself and corporate America, however, have not substantially addressed this issue in the ways other countries have, such as those in Scandinavia or in other parts of Europe. One 2007 study argues that high-achieving women leave their jobs in the United States because work-family flexibility is "viewed as an accommodation rather than as part of a standard structure for a workforce."[12] In addition, because they leave, there are too few women at the top who could change the corporate structure.[13] News companies have historically been "traditional," resistant to change and often out of step with more progressive workplace policies in other business sectors. News companies should ensure policies that allow employees more work-family flexibility and that provide equal opportunity for women and people of color to rise to the top.

Challenges and Issues for the Press in the Twenty-First Century

The Edge of Change, very importantly, examines some of the most daunting issues for the press as it moves through a dizzying transformation. Lapses in credibility and ethics have plagued the news industry in recent years and led to an undermining of public trust in the press as an institution. Issues of diversity in newsroom leadership and staffing and coverage of multicultural and diverse communities beg for improvement as the demographics of America change. News companies reeling from competitive commercial forces and changing patterns among news consumers are seeking innovation, new talent, and new ideas and business models.

Contemporary legal challenges to the press and the First Amendment threaten the underpinnings of the free press in the United States. Journalists who cover wars and nations around the world also face unprecedented dangers as they work to inform the public about important international issues and cultures and foreign policy debates that will shape the modern world. This book addresses critical issues for the press as its traditions, values, and freedoms are challenged and as media restructure and undergo change that is unprecedented in modern history. Ways must be found to safeguard the press as rapid changes in technology and news audiences occur in society and media companies.

A Vigorous Press Is Needed

The news industry must provide more meaningful opportunities for women to improve their future as one way of maintaining and building a vigorous press as a centerpiece of public discourse. Women have played a vital role in the press over the course of American history in helping to shape public opinion and perspectives about the United States and the world. Women today lead some of the most innovative and successful newsrooms and news companies in the country, and are leaders in new media. But too little attention has been given to women's contributions and impact, as well as to the issues for women in newsrooms, news companies, and emerging and new media. The strength of the press—and indeed its survival—depends on its ability to adequately reflect the diverse concerns and perspectives of society as a whole, to engage more females as news consumers, to diversify its newsrooms and leadership ranks, and to provide new opportunities for women as media evolve.

A Guide for Women in the Workplace and in Society

The Edge of Change is written for the American public and for young women and men who are considering journalism as a career, as well as for journalists who work to advance the fundamental purpose of the press, which is to inform and educate citizens. But very importantly, in an age when women are becoming more visible in elective office and in the workforce, the book also is for women in the workplace or who aspire to careers in any field. *The Edge of Change* underscores women's issues that cross business, government, the sciences, law, medicine, and other disciplines. Women in news organizations face obstacles that are similar to those described in other fields such as science, law, and medicine.[14] Sadly, journalism is only one of the professions in which women still face substantial gender bias, pay inequity, and barriers to advancement, as a wealth of recent research has shown.[15]

Shorenstein Center Conference: Women and News

This volume also underscores the role of the press in public discourse and public understanding of complex social and global issues. As one example, the future of civic engagement may be linked to the future for women in the news industry. Some one hundred news media leaders, scholars, and journalists participated in the Women and News conference held at Harvard University's Shorenstein Center in November 2007. Among the research highlighted at that conference:

- Some evidence suggests that more women entering politics and seeking office could increase the participation by women in the voting process and their knowledge about politics.
- Women are not as knowledgeable about politics and political figures, which may diminish civic debate and engagement on issues. For example, more women than men continued to believe Saddam Hussein had weapons of mass destruction after it was widely reported that that was not the case. Two weeks before the 2004 election, nearly one-third of men believed there were WMDs but almost half of women. In 2006 only a third of women knew the name of the secretary of state, Condoleezza Rice, but more than half of men did.
- Women and men have different news agendas and interests in news stories. These gender differences have been tracked for two decades by the Pew Research Center for the People and Press and identified in other news research. Women are more interested in news about health, people, crime, culture, and religion, and men are more interested in politics as well as economic and foreign policy stories. Women, however, are just as interested as men in some kinds of stories, including judicial decisions, disasters, and news on the local level.
- Because the news media shape public opinion and knowledge of the world, any lack of engagement in news could have a detrimental effect on public discourse and civic debate in society, as well as participation in the political process.
- Gender gaps in political knowledge or engagement in politics tend to disappear or lessen as more women become involved in politics or run for office. Women tend to be more interested if politics is framed as problem solving rather than represented as a "horse race." One study by the Project for Excellence in Journalism found that early in the 2008 presidential race, only 12

percent of news stories were framed to focus on how citizens would be affected by the outcome, while more than two-thirds, or 86 percent, examined issues that impacted only the political parties and candidates.

- Of the major news outlets, only National Public Radio has women as at least half of its audience, which is considerably higher than a decade ago. Part of the reason may be the way NPR "frames" or presents the news, with a strong narrative component, and/or even the fact that NPR has more of a gender balance in its staff than many news organizations.[16]

Syndicated columnist Ellen Goodman said in her keynote address at the Shorenstein Center conference that much of news today is framed in a way that does not engage women audiences. She said that the "conflict bias" that frames so much political news might be turning off female audiences. Goodman argued that "much of the news content is being deliberately driven by marketing into sex-segregated cul-de-sacs," and that there are too many assumptions about what women want. "I think the best way to connect women and men with politics and civic life is by writing the kinds of stories that journalists, maybe especially women journalists, have always favored, have always taken as the best. These are the stories that contain a compelling narrative, the stories that do indeed draw a line between what matters in our lives and in politics."[17]

A great deal of additional research is needed, but it seems clear that these gender differences in news audiences should be explored and understood and that the news media should seek ways to improve coverage so as to better engage audiences, especially female audiences.

Contributions of Women in the Press

In examining the contributions of women in the news industry, *The Edge of Change: Women in the Twenty-First-Century Press* builds on the excellent work of Kay Mills, a former editorial writer for the *Los Angeles Times,* who wrote *A Place in the News* (Columbia University Press, 1990), and Maurine Beasley and Sheila Gibbons, who wrote *Taking Their Place: A Documentary History of Women and Journalism* (Strata, 1993 and 2003).

In addition to Katharine Graham, many other women laid the groundwork for this generation of female corporate executives and editors. They include Katherine Fanning, Nancy Woodhull, Janet Chusmir, Ellen Goodman, Sandra Rowe, Dorothy Gilliam, Cathleen Black, Judith Clabes, Susan Clark-Johnson, Nan Robertson, Peggy Simpson, and countless others. These women broke barriers for women in the twentieth-century press and today. Each of them had mentors—more often than not, male mentors in the news business—who supported and encouraged their professional careers. In the past several decades, women have made considerable strides in achieving status and influence in newsrooms and news companies. But progress overall has been only incremental.

The press is perhaps the most powerful institution in American society. The people who lead and work in news companies wield enormous power and influence in helping to shape the national agenda as well as public opinion in the United States and abroad. Diversifying newsrooms and the leadership ranks of U.S. news companies is crucial if journalism is to reflect the interests, concerns, and priorities of people across a broad spectrum of society. Diversity, including gender diversity, is also crucial to the success of American businesses.

Women in the Press: Gender and Corporate Success Linked

A significant body of research over the past two decades in business, management, organizational behavior, public policy, the sciences, and the news industry has emphasized the leadership traits and skills that women bring to the workplace. Women have strong interpersonal and listening skills; seek collaboration and consensus; and are more inclusive, flexible, adaptive, and empathetic—all characteristics highly valued in the modern workplace and in news corporations.[18]

In 2004 a study by Catalyst Inc., a leading group that studies women in business, linked gender diversity to the financial performance of companies. U.S. Fortune 500 corporations with a higher percentage of women in the executive ranks had a 35 percent higher return on equity and 34 percent higher return to shareholders than companies with fewer women at the top.[19] In October 2007 Catalyst linked female board representation to financial performance. The study found that Fortune 500 companies with the highest percentage of female board members had better financial performance than companies with the lowest percentages of female directors.[20]

The modern workplace and global economy demand more progress than has been made. The *Economist* magazine reported in April 2006 that women are increasingly driving economic growth around the world, and highlighted the Catalyst findings and other research that indicates women are well positioned for the coming workplace. In that issue the *Economist* cited studies that suggest, for example, that women are often better than men at building teams and communicating.[21]

Newspaper industry research has found that news companies with diverse senior leadership and diverse newsrooms are in a better position to increase readership and successfully adapt to change.[22] A 2004 study by the Readership Institute at Northwestern University found that the newspapers best positioned to increase readership had a greater percentage of diverse employees and leadership. The study said: "Newspapers that get better readership results now and are better positioned to make change for the future tend to have constructive, adaptive cultures. They have better management practices. They tend to have greater diversity in race and/or gender, both in the workforce generally and in positions of influence."[23]

The evidence suggests that the news industry's failure to address gender and other diversity issues in news coverage and in news companies has hindered its ability to capture audiences and talent and to embrace innovation.

News Industry Lags behind Other Professions in Retention

The news industry has lagged behind other professions in addressing reten-tion of women. The percentage of women in journalism has not increased in three decades "despite dramatic increases in women journalism students and increased emphasis on hiring more women in journalism" since the 1980s, ac-cording to a 2007 book, *The American Journalist in the Twenty-First Century: U.S. News People at the Dawn of a New Millennium,* by David Weaver, of Indiana University, and his colleagues.[24] The landmark survey of journalists has been conducted every ten years since the 1970s. Weaver and his research group found that women today constitute about one-third of full-time journalists at daily newspapers and about the same percentage in all news media—that's roughly the same percentage as in 1982.[25] In 2000 women made up more than half of the nation's population and 47 percent of the civilian labor force.[26] Newsrooms remain "a bastion of white male dominance with few inroads made by women and minorities," according to a Project for Excellence in Journalism report ad-dressing Weaver's book.[27]

Since at least 1977–78, women have constituted more than half of the U.S. journalism and mass communications graduates,[28] and for a number of years they have made up approximately two-thirds of the number of graduates of journalism and mass communications undergraduate programs.[29] Many of these women go into public relations or other fields, however.

But women who enter journalism do not stay as long as men do. Since 1992 the percentage of women over the age of thirty-four "remained low, and much below the labor force in general,"[30] suggesting that the "demands of journalism may be more difficult for women who have childbearing responsibilities than are other occupations in general."[31] Fewer than a quarter of journalists from age forty-five to fifty-four are female, a figure largely unchanged since 1971, accord-ing to the Weaver study.[32]

The Weaver research noted that younger women made up the largest percent-age increase since 1992 and now hold 60 percent of the jobs for those under age twenty-five. In fact, for the first time, women constituted more than 40 percent of journalists younger than twenty-five.[33] Those numbers could possibly signal an increase in the number of women in journalism in years to come. But six thousand fewer journalists were working in mainstream news in 2002 than in 1992,[34] and thousands of additional jobs were lost by 2009 because of mergers, buyouts, and downsizing. Young people may not have opportunities to advance. "This will make it difficult to retain the brightest and most ambitious young journalists, especially women and people of color."[35]

In 2002 the gender pay gap in journalism had not changed through the previous ten years: women made about 81 cents for every dollar earned by men,[36] though entry pay was comparable. But women are less satisfied with their jobs than men.[37] In fact, in the past decade a decline has occurred in the relative job satisfaction between men and women in journalism. In the 1980s women and men were about equally satisfied with their jobs, but women are now less satisfied than men. In the latest Weaver study, women also said they had less influence in newsrooms and less autonomy than men.[38] "These gender disparities in pay and job satisfaction will not help to recruit and retain women journalists."[39]

Women Face Obstacles in Advancing in the News Industry

Journalism also lags behind some other professions in advancing women. "The gains women made [in management] during the 1980s appear to largely have been lost by 2002," according to Weaver and his research group.[40] In the workforce overall, women held more than half of professional jobs and 42 percent of management, business, and finance jobs in 2005.[41] In 1970 in the United States, fewer than 10 percent of both physicians and lawyers were female. Women are now 28.7 percent of lawyers,[42] 26 percent of physicians,[43] and about half of law[44] and medical students.[45]

In 1971, approximately 22 percent of daily newspaper journalists were female.[46] In 2009 women made up 34.8 percent of newsroom supervisors and 37 percent of newsroom employees, a slight decrease in each category from the previous year according to the American Society of Newspaper Editors census.[47] The ASNE numbers overall have only inched up in the past decade. The advancement of women in journalism has slowed.

Greater numbers of women have entered journalism and news companies, and some have moved to the top. But many women leave and many who remain say they face many of the same barriers to advancement that their counterparts did a quarter century ago: discrimination, exclusionary social networks, inhospitable newsroom cultures, too few professional development opportunities, and lack of systematic recruitment of women for top jobs.

Status of Women in the Press

Overall, women hold 18 percent of the positions that run companies, such as president, publisher, or CEO.[48] Only about a fifth of top editors of the one hundred largest newspapers are female.[49] The high visibility of some women in recent years in part masks the stagnation for newswomen overall. Susan Bischoff, former associate editor of the *Houston Chronicle,* said, "The success of some women, finally, gives us a sense that women are moving ahead and to the top in newspapers. But the numbers are disappointing."[50]

The successes include women who are now top editors at some of the nation's largest and best newspapers: Sandra Rowe, editor of the *Portland Oregonian;* Julia Wallace, editor of the *Atlanta Journal-Constitution* and ajc.com; and Janet Weaver, vice president and executive editor of the *Tampa Tribune.* Female managing editors are also in place at some of the nation's top newspapers, such as Jill Abramson at the *New York Times.*

Other women lead news companies or are prominent on the corporate side of newspapers, among them Janet L. Robinson, president and CEO of the New York Times Company; Mary Junck, chairman, CEO, and president of Lee Enterprises; Marty Petty, publisher and executive vice president of the *St. Petersburg Times;* Diane McFarlin, publisher of the *Sarasota Herald-Tribune;* and Katharine Weymouth, chief executive of Washington Post Media, publisher of the *Post,* and a granddaughter of Katharine Graham. Jennifer Carroll is vice president for new media content in the Gannett Company's newspaper division. Kathleen Carroll, executive editor of the Associated Press, is a board member of the AP. Three women, Charlotte Hall, editor of the *Orlando Sentinel,* Diane McFarlin of Sarasota, and Karla Harshaw of Cox Community Newspapers, have been president of the American Society of Newspaper Editors since 2000. Harshaw was the first woman of color to head the organization. Only one other female, Katherine Fanning, who was editor of the *Christian Science Monitor,* has been president of ASNE in its 87-year history.

Women on Op-Ed Pages

A few women are running the op-ed pages of major newspapers—Cynthia Tucker of the *Atlanta Journal-Constitution,* Keven Ann Willey of the *Dallas Morning News;* and Renee Loth of the *Boston Globe.* But Gail Collins, who was the first female editorial page editor at the *New York Times,* stepped down in 2006 and her position was not filled by a woman. Overall, female columnists are significantly underrepresented: only 24.4 percent of columnists for the largest syndicates are women.[51] There are only four female editorial cartoonists in the nation who work for mainstream media.[52]

This lack of a voice for women on the op-ed pages has been widely debated in recent years. Some say female columnists do not have as much interest in hard-hitting commentary as men. Others argue that opportunities just are not present for women, given that men largely run most editorial pages and make the decisions about which columns and writers will be used.

Syndicated columnist Ellen Goodman told *Editor and Publisher* in 2005: "Op-ed pages are, of course, a pretty small piece of property. Diversity is measured by subject as well as author. But many pages that have room for five men writing about politics still find that two women are one too many."[53] Patrisia Gonzales of Universal Press Syndicate told *Editor and Publisher,* "There are untold numbers of women and people of color whose ideas are cutting-edge and 'outside of the box'; unfortunately, they rarely make it into the commentary pages on a regular basis."[54]

Far too little progress has been made in recent years for women on the race and ethnicity front in newspapers, particularly in advancing women of color into top positions. While minorities are about 34 percent of the U.S. population, they are 13.41 percent of newsroom employees.[55] The percentage of women of color in newsrooms has increased only slightly in recent years. Only four African American females were editors of U.S. newspapers in early 2009, and one African American female, Edwina Blackwell Clark of Cox Ohio Publishing's Southwest group, was a publisher. Few women of color are in top corporate positions.

Women in Online Media

Women are well suited to seize opportunities in some of the newer media such as blogging and citizen journalism publications as well as online media. Women are good at creating communities of interest because of their strong collaborative and team skills. They like to connect, nurture, and build harmony for a purpose that advances society, according to research and experts across a number of disciplines. Women in newer media such as blogging are gaining some traction and are half of the ninety-six million bloggers, according to columnist Ellen Goodman.[56] But new media already are becoming gendered much like traditional media. Goodman found in her research during spring 2007 as a Shorenstein Center fellow that of the top ninety political blogs, some 42 percent were written only by men and just 7 percent only by women.

One of the most popular female political bloggers is Arianna Huffington, who founded the news and blog site Huffington Post in 2005. Huffington was on *Time* magazine's list of the one hundred most influential people in 2006. The Huffington Post had as many as eleven million unique viewers a day in early 2008. In terms of numbers of Web sites that link to it, the Huffington Post was ranked second. Huffington sees the Web site as a new kind of "Internet newspaper," she told the *New York Times.*[57] The Huffington Post represents a new kind of media empire. Its fewer than fifty full-time staffers do little original reporting. The site mixes blogging and aggregates the work of traditional news organizations. Cofounder Huffington sees the Huffington Post and other sites as complementing mainstream media: "[T]he traditional media that are going to thrive in the brave new world are the ones that incorporate new media in what they are doing. And in the same way, the new media [that] are going to be more and more important players are the ones that incorporate what is best about traditional journalism."[58]

Huffington described several issues for women in new media at the Harvard conference in November 2007. She said that women are more reluctant than men to contribute their voices as bloggers for the Huffington Post and other media, but not because women do not have views. In part, they may hesitate to blog because of the sexist language, name-calling, and harassment that some women around the country have encountered as bloggers, she said. But women also have more "internal obstacles" and fear about putting their views into the public sphere and marketplace of ideas, she said.[59] On the other hand, according to Huffington, blogging holds promise for women because it has easy entry. She said that in her experience with the Huffington Post, women also consume news differently. Women do not see news in the context of labels such as "right" or "left"; rather, they see issues contextually. They are interested not in the "scoring" of who's up and who's down, but in the impact of issues on people's lives, she said.

A few women are playing a significant role in citizen journalism publications, such as Mary Lou Fulton, who is vice president of audience development for the *Bakersfield Californian.* Residents contribute content for this online news operation under a John S. and James L. Knight New Challenge grant. Other women are leaders in providing new online content as part of large mainstream newspapers such as the *New York Times* and the *Washington Post.* Still others are starting their own blog sites or launching new media ventures. But how large a role women will play in online media where growth is occurring is yet to be determined. A decade ago women hoped to get in on the ground floor of this new medium and move to the top of online operations. Research shows, however, that online media did not hold rich opportunities for those women in the early years. An initial surge of women withered, and many of those women in online media left. Now the people in charge are mostly men.

What Will It Take?

Some studies suggest that opportunities will improve for women in news companies and in newsrooms, on the news corporate side and on op-ed pages only when a new generation of executives are in place. Some researchers say the pace of change will quicken when the news industry reaches a "critical mass" of women in top positions, and that women may be nearing that point. But the jury is still out.

The increase of women in newsrooms and companies that occurred during the 1970s and '80s has leveled off. In the past several years, a number of top women in the news profession—with years of experience—have left the industry, and others may do so soon, because of downsizing or ownership or other changes. Among those women are Sue Clark-Johnson, who retired in 2008 as the president of the newspaper division of the Gannett Company; Ann Marie Lipinski, former editor of the *Chicago Tribune;* Carol Leigh Hutton, former vice president of news for Knight Ridder and former executive editor of the *San Jose Mercury News;* Kathleen Waltz, former publisher of the *Orlando Sentinel;* Janis Heaphy, former publisher and president of the *Sacramento Bee;* and Pam Fine, former managing editor of the *Indianapolis Star* and now a Knight professor at the University of Kansas William Allen White School of Journalism and Mass Communication, to name a few.

Media Management Center Research

News industry research indicates that women in newspapers are at a critical juncture and that improvement for them has been minimal in recent years. The research suggests that without changes in the journalism culture and its priorities, the challenges for women in the industry are substantial and may remain so for some time.

The Media Management Center (MMC), part of the Kellogg School of Management at Northwestern University, has conducted research about women in newspapers and media for a decade and has published four reports since 2000. These studies included the 137 daily newspapers with circulations of more than eighty-five thousand. The fourth study by the MMC was published in 2006 and resulted from the November 2005 conference for women media executives at Northwestern. That report focused on issues of newsroom and news company culture and how women can navigate the male-dominated, hierarchal structures in most news organizations.[60]

The 2006 study links diversity and the traits that women bring to management to the ability of news organizations to be viable in a changing and competitive environment. Michael P. Smith, executive director of the Media Management Center, said, "Newspapers that enjoy growth from innovation and development are more likely to have a diverse set of leaders at the top. There are more women and minorities there than at newspapers that are not growing."[61] The report's executive summary says: "The good news for women is that they have an advantage because their management style tends to be more inclusive and responsive, which encourages new ideas and innovation. Because many are relatively new to the power positions, they are not as entrenched . . . Most of the top innovative companies today have women in very senior positions, for their talents and to ensure those companies are meeting the needs of their women consumers."[62]

The study found that most newspapers—approximately 80 percent—have what it terms a "defensive culture" that stymies new ideas and innovation. Only 20 percent of newspaper companies have "constructive cultures" that adapt well to change.[63] Renee Hampton, then publisher of the *Saginaw (Mich.) News* and a participant in the 2005 media conference for news executives at Northwestern, said,

> One of our greatest challenges in the newspaper business is that we are attempting to create a new vision, but we are utilizing old methods. . . . One way to do that is to draw on a diverse pool of leaders and leadership styles. . . . Because most women and men are socialized differently, we see life differently. We can't help but lead differently. One style is not superior to the other. Effective organizations recognize the differences and allow leaders to function comfortably by using the tools that work best for them.[64]

The 2006 MMC report said, "When it comes to career growth, women are in a holding pattern—and not a very favorable one."[65] Moreover, "women executives still lag far behind their male counterparts in both their numbers and the level of position attained." In 2006 women held 29 percent of executive jobs at newspapers.[66] Women are roughly one-fifth of all newspaper group publishers.[67] The publishers are mostly at three of the largest newspaper groups: Community Holdings Inc., Gannett, and Lee Enterprises, while McClatchy and the Tribune Company have the best percentage track records for women publishers.

Almost all of the top six newspapers groups studied had smaller percentages of female publishers in 2006 than in 2003 "due in part to such factors as mergers and acquisitions."[68] And the numbers do not reflect the dismantling of Knight Ridder, which had been the second-largest newspaper group and one of the most aggressive in addressing gender and racial/ethnic diversity.[69] Knight Ridder was sold in March 2006 to McClatchy, and some of its properties were sold to private investor groups.

Only one in ten positions just under the top executives were filled by women in 2006,[70] which suggests few women are in the pipeline for top jobs. On the news side, 39 percent of managing editors are female. However, only about a quarter of the very top of news departments, which include editor, executive editor, and vice president of news, are female.[71]

Women most often hold jobs at the lower end of news companies and in middle management.[72] They particularly have trouble moving up from the position of managing editor.[73] In addition, many women are in marketing, human resources, or community affairs, which are outside the most common lines for advancement in companies.[74]

Gendered Perceptions

The MMC researchers also looked at the differing perceptions men and women have as to why more women do not move to the top of newspaper companies. Men generally said it takes twenty years to "groom" a top executive and that women have not been in the pipeline long enough to advance. Women said, however, that discrimination is at work and that men tend to hire people like themselves. They said women are excluded from the social networks that help men advance.[75]

Studies show that stereotypes of women in leadership play a role in promotions. Men say women cannot make decisions and are not assertive, but women say men do not value or understand their collaboration skills and other assets in the newsroom or in leadership positions.[76]

The Great Divide

"The Great Divide," a research study that was published in 2002 by the American Press Institute and the Pew Center for Civic Journalism, found a "split" in newsrooms—not between males and females, but between two groups of females. The "career-confident" women were satisfied with advancement opportunities, but "career-conflicted" women expressed dissatisfaction with career opportunities and were less happy with the news agendas of the newspapers for which they worked.[77]

Almost half, or 45 percent, of the women in the study said they expected to leave the news business, significantly higher than the 33 percent of men; women were four times more likely to leave newspapers than men. Almost two-thirds of the "career-conflicted" women, or 64 percent in that study, said discrimination—the fact that men tend to promote men—was the main reason for lack of advancement for women. They also stressed that newsrooms did not provide women with sufficient mentoring or career training and planning.

Only one-fifth of women in "The Great Divide" said they wanted to move up in the news industry, compared with 36 percent of men. An overwhelming majority of 72 percent of women, however, said they would reconsider if they felt their presence could lead to change.[78] Clearly some women in newsrooms feel their judgment and perspectives are not valued.

Corporate Boards

The number of women on corporate boards is an important measure of the influence of women in corporate America—and in news companies. Corporate boards determine policy and can change the direction and culture of companies. Among Fortune 500 companies, the movement of women into top corporate positions is slow. Women constituted 15.1 percent of members of corporate boards in 2008; only 3.2 percent of board members were women of color.[79] Catalyst 2005 research found that it would take forty years for women to achieve parity with men in the top executive ranks at the present growth rate, and seventy years for parity to occur on corporate boards.[80]

The MMC's 2003 study found that of all the executive layers, women in news-papers were most underrepresented on corporate boards, following the overall trend in U.S. corporations. Only twenty-two women, or an average of 18 percent of members of boards of directors of fifteen of the nation's newspaper groups that were studied, were women.[81]

Coverage of Women in Society

Women's roles in society and in the professions have changed significantly in the past quarter century. Paradoxically, though, editors and researchers say newspapers as well as other media fall short in covering women in all of their dimensions and in covering issues that are important to women.

Mainstream media see the female audience as important to their success, and some companies have added newer media such as blogs that are attempting to draw more women. Mainstream newspapers are making changes in content to cover issues of more interest to women or even changing the way news is writ-ten or presented.[82] But those efforts have not been successful across the news industry; fewer than half of women read a daily newspaper.[83]

Women do not always see themselves in news coverage. Most news sources are male—and researchers and others have pointed to this as one explanation for some of the decline in female readership. According to a 2005 study by the Project for Excellence in Journalism (PEJ), men are used as news sources more than twice as often as women.[84] The finding is ironic, as the PEJ says in its summary, "given the efforts of many news outlets to increase their audience by reaching out to women—and particularly younger women, a group that generally is underrepresented as news consumers."

While newspapers do a better job than other media in using female news sources, according to the PEJ study only the lifestyle sections of newspapers come close to using a significant proportion of female sources. More diversity—including gender diversity—in newsrooms could enhance the ability of news media to cover women in society more effectively, as Kay Mills detailed in her book *A Place in the News* and later in "What Difference Do Women Journal-ists Make?" in 1997.[85] The same holds true in the twenty-first century. Because of their life experiences, interests, and insights, women often bring differing perspectives to the table and make decisions that differ from men's in assigning and writing news stories and commentary that reflect contemporary society.

A Look Ahead

Women are outpacing men in education. Women make up 58 percent of col-lege students and earn the majority of undergraduate and master's degrees and almost half of the doctoral degrees. By 2015–16, women will earn 22 percent more bachelor's degrees than during 2003–4, and men will earn 14 percent more for the same time period. Women will earn 41 percent more master's degrees, and men 28 percent. For doctoral degrees, the estimated increase is 31 percent for women and 12 percent for men.[86] Women are more successful and seem to work harder in college than men.[87] It is uncertain, though, whether these changes will translate into women doing significantly better in years to come in the job market, or in higher salaries or in other ways. Some researchers say that women's lack of progress is the result of an accumulation of obstacles, and that the gender "dynamic" in society must first be understood before women will advance more quickly.

Economists and researchers have recently pointed to some trends that could limit women. The wage gap has widened recently for college-educated women. According to 2006 labor statistics, women who are thirty-six to forty-five with a four-year college degree earned 74.7 cents for each dollar earned by a male, a decline from 75.7 from the previous decade. Some researchers say the labor wage gap may be attributed to discrimination and to the government's poor enforcement of laws that address gender bias.[88]

Researchers also say the percentage of adult women working outside of the home has leveled off after decades of growth.[89] They say it is unclear whether women who "opt out" will be able to reenter the job market or what financial toll they will experience in their careers as a result. Some economists argue that the number slowed because of a general economic weakening, but others say women are hitting the limits of the work-family balance.

Harvard economist Claudia Goldin said in a speech to the American Economic Association in 2006 that the leveling off across almost all groups of women in the workforce has "led many to wonder if a 'natural rate' of labor force participation has been reached."[90] And in an interview for this book in January 2007, she said, "There is a lot of choice going on [for women] in the workforce. . . . If we go demographically age group by age group and ask what is the maximum labor force participation rate . . . it looks as if things have reached a certain plateau."[91] It is difficult to say overall what corporate America is doing to make the workplace more accommodating for women, Goldin said in the interview. "If companies are not doing something, it is hard to push them." Some pockets of the economy and labor force over decades have shifted to be more accommodating to women, she said, noting veterinary medicine and optometry, and more recently, accounting. "Some of these changes might have occurred anyhow but have been reenforced by the presence of women." She said that these changes "suggest that many other [companies that offer] products and services could be rearranged so that they can serve people with families."

Goldin and Lawrence Katz, also a Harvard University economist, wrote in 2005, "There are many reasons to be concerned that the quiet revolution [regarding advancement of women] has stalled. As economists we are concerned that women's educational investments may be inefficiently used. Universities should be concerned because they are both producers and consumers of educated individuals. All employers need to make career paths more amenable to combining work and family if our nation is not to lose a valuable and growing source of talent."[92] The editors of *The Edge of Change* see little significant movement toward reforming the corporate structure and society to meet these objectives.

The Landing for Women in the Press

The Edge of Change: Women in the Twenty-First-Century Press reflects the contributions of only a small number of the thousands of women who have worked in newsrooms or on the editorial pages or in the corporate side of newspapers in the past quarter century. These individuals have covered stories from community issues to wars abroad—and provided leadership, differing perspectives, creativity, and vision. This book celebrates those achievements and focuses attention on the critical issues that remain for women in journalism and for the companies that employ them in a new era for media. News companies are losing the considerable intellect and talent of many women who aspire to careers as journalists, executives, and managers. It is crucial that the news industry and emerging media address issues for women such as work-family flexibility, pay, advancement opportunities—and make workplace and policy changes that will benefit women and men, news audiences, and the press as an institution.

Katharine Graham wrote in *A Personal History,* "I always thought things would grow better with time, that the atmosphere would become more welcoming of women, particularly when there were more women involved and less notice was given to any single one of us, but it didn't happen that way. For one thing, there never were that many more of us—and still aren't, at least not at the highest levels." When Graham began her *Post* presidency in 1963, she wrote, "The surprise was that I landed on my feet."[93] Women in news and media today are on the edge of yet another wave of change. These women are helping to build the news companies, newsrooms, and audiences of the future. But many women who enter the news industry do not stay, and those who do have not advanced in the numbers they should have. Bias and discrimination still exist, stereotypes are in place, and women who aspire to the top face many of the same structural and hierarchical obstacles they did in the past. Work-family policies and the culture of news companies overall have not changed adequately to address the needs of women in contemporary news. As a result, companies are losing the talent, vision, and perspectives of many women.

The year 2008 and early 2009 were tumultuous for the news media and most other businesses in the United States and around the world. Some of the changes ahead may permanently alter the structure of corporate America and the press. The effect of these changes on gender issues in news and media will require much further study.

The press itself will rise or fall as an institution in the United States, depending on its ability to serve diverse and global audiences, inform the citizenry, and adapt in this period of rapid transformation. Moreover, the future of the press also depends on whether it provides more women in newsrooms and companies and in emerging media with the opportunity to advance and lead that change.

Notes

1. Katharine Graham, *A Personal History* (New York: Vintage Books, 1998), 341.

2. Ibid., 417.

3. Ibid., 418.

4. Ibid., 421–23.

5. Helen Dudar, "Women in Revolt," *Newsweek,* March 23, 1970.

6. Graham, *Personal History,* 424, 426.

7. "A Short History," Newswomen's Club of New York, http://www.newswomensclub newyork.com/index.php?p=about (accessed January 22, 2009).

8. U.S. Department of Labor, Women's Bureau, "Quick Stats 2007." Available at http://www.dol.gov/wb/stats/main.htm (accessed January 22, 2009).

9. Mary Arnold and Mary Nesbitt, "Women in Media, 2006: Finding a Leader in You," Media Management Center, Northwestern University, 2006. Available at http://www.mediamanagementcenter.org/publications/data/wim2006.pdf (accessed January 22, 2009).

10. Mary Arnold Hemlinger and Cynthia C. Linton, "Women in Newspapers: How Much Progress Has Been Made?" Media Management Center, Northwestern University, 2001, 53–54. Available at http://www.mediamanagementcenter.org/research/win.pdf (accessed January 22, 2009).

11. Jane Gross, "Forget the Career: My Parents Need Me at Home," *New York Times,* November 24, 2005. Available at http://www.nytimes.com/2005/11/24/national/24daughter .html (accessed January 22, 2009).

12. Shirley M. Clark and Patricia S. Reed, "Are We Losing the Best and the Brightest? Highly Achieved Women Leaving the Traditional Workforce," final report, U.S. Department of Labor, Employment, and Training Administration, November 2007, 17. Available at http://www.doleta.gov/reports/pdf/AreWeLosingThebest.pdf (accessed January 22, 2009).

13. Ibid., 38.

14. Cornelia Dean, "Women in Science: The Battle Moves to the Trenches," *New York Times,* December 19, 2006. Available at http://www.nytimes.com/2006/12/19/science/19women.html; Timothy L. O'Brien, "Why Do So Few Women Reach the Top of Big Law Firms?" *New York Times,* March 19, 2006. Available at http://www.nytimes .com/2006/03/19/business/yourmoney/19law.html. Both articles accessed January 22, 2009.

15. Joyce K. Fletcher, *Disappearing Acts: Gender, Power, and Relational Practice at Work* (Cambridge, Mass.: MIT Press, 1999); Mary Ann Mason and Eve Mason Ekman, *Mothers on the Fast Track: How a New Generation Can Balance Family* (Oxford: Oxford University Press, 2007); Virginia Valian, *Why So Slow? The Advancement of Women* (Cambridge, Mass.: MIT Press, 1998); Joan Williams, *Unbending Gender: Why Family and Work Conflict and What to Do about It* (Oxford: Oxford University Press, 2000).

16. Shauna Shames and Marion Just, "A Narrative Overview of the Research on Women and News," in "Women and News: Expanding the News Audience, Increasing Political Participation, and Informing Citizens," transcript from Women and News conference, November 29–30, 2007, Joan Shorenstein Center on the Press, Politics, and Public Policy, Harvard University, 2008. Available at http://www.hks.harvard.edu/presspol/publications/reports/women_and_news_transcript_2008.pdf (accessed January 22, 2009).

17. Ellen Goodman, keynote speech, in "Women and News," transcript from Women and News conference (see note 16).

18. See MMC Women in Newspaper studies 2000–2006; "The Great Divide: Female Leadership in U.S. Newsrooms," American Press Institute and the Pew Center for Civic Journalism, September 26, 2002. Available at http://www.pewcenter.org/doingcj/research/r_apipewstudy.pdf; Erika Falk and Erin Grizard, "The Glass Ceiling Persists: The Third Annual APPC Report on Women Leaders in Communication Companies," Annenberg Public Policy Center, University of Pennsylvania, 2003. Available at http://www.annenbergpublicpolicycenter.org/Downloads/Information_And_Society/20031222_Glass_Ceiling/20031222_glass-ceiling_report.pdf; Herb Greenberg and Patrick Sweeney, "How Women Are Redefining Leadership," Caliper, 2005. Available at http://www.caliperonline.com/womenstudy/Leaders6pg.pdf; Helen E. Fisher, *The First Sex: The Natural Talents of Women and How They Are Changing the World* (New York: Random House, 1999). All Web sites accessed January 22, 2009.

19. Catalyst, "The Bottom Line: Connecting Corporate Performance and Gender Diversity," Catalyst, 2004, 2. Available at http://www.femtech.at/fileadmin/femtech/be_images/Publikationen/femtech_Catalyst.pdf (accessed January 22, 2009).

20. Catalyst, "The Bottom Line: Corporate Performance and Women's Representation on Boards," Catalyst, 2007. Available at http://www.catalyst.org/file/139/bottom%20line%202.pdf (accessed January 22, 2009).

21. "A Guide to Womenomics," *Economist,* April 12, 2006. Available at http://www.kennesaw.edu/siegelinstitute/docs/EconomistApril122006Womenandtheworldeconomy.pdf (accessed January 22, 2009).

22. "Reaching New Readers: Revolution Not Evolution," American Society of News Editors, 2004, 13. Available at http://www.readership.org/new_readers/data/overview.pdf (accessed January 22, 2009). Also Arnold and Nesbitt, "Women in Media, 2006." Note: The American Society of Newspaper Editors changed its name to The American Society of News Editors in 2009.

23. "Reaching New Readers," 13.

24. David Weaver, et al., *The American Journalist in the Twenty-First Century: U.S. News People at the Dawn of a New Millennium* (Mahwah, N.J.: Erlbaum, 2007), 6.

25. Ibid., 8, 10. The American Society of News Editors Newsroom Employment Cen-

sus reflects that in 2009, 37 percent of newsroom employees at daily newspapers were female and 34.8 percent of supervisors were female. See ASNE reports at http://www .asne.org/index.cfm?id=7320 and http://www.asne.org/index.cfm?id=5660. Both accessed April 29, 2009.

26. Weaver, et al., *American Journalist*, 8.

27. "The American Newsroom Aging, but Not Diversifying," Project for Excellence in Journalism, October 5, 2006. Available at http://www.journalism.org/node/2281 (accessed January 22, 2009).

28. Weaver, et al., *American Journalist*, 183.

29. Ibid.

30. Ibid., 11.

31. Ibid.

32. Ibid., 184.

33. Ibid.

34. Ibid., 3 (table 1.1).

35. Ibid., 240.

36. Ibid., 194.

37. Ibid., 242.

38. Ibid., 188

39. Ibid., 242.

40. Ibid., 186.

41. U.S. Department of Labor, "America's Dynamic Workforce 2006," news release, August 31, 2006.

42. American Bar Association, "A Current Glance at Women in the Law, 2006," American Bar Association, Commission on Women in the Profession. Available at http://www .abanet.org/women/CurrentGlanceStatistics2006.pdf (accessed January 22, 2009).

43. Mom MD, "Women in Medicine Today," http://www.mommd.com/women.shtml (accessed January 22, 2009).

44. American Bar Association, "Current Glance."

45. American Medical Association, "Table 2—Women Medical School Applicants." See http://www.ama-assn.org/ama/pub/category/print/12913.html (accessed January 22, 2009).

46. Christy C. Bulkeley, "A Pioneering Generation Marked the Path for Women Journalists," *Neiman Reports* 56, no. 1 (2002): 60. Available at http://www.nieman.harvard .edu/assets/pdf/Nieman%20Reports/backissues/02spring.pdf (accessed January 22, 2009).

47. ASNE Newsroom Employment Census 2009. See http://www.asne.org/index .cfm?id=7320 (2009 newsroom census, main news release), and http://www.asne.org/ index.dm?id=5660 (table M for percentage of female supervisors). Both accessed April 29, 2009.

48. Arnold and Nesbitt, "Women in Media, 2006," 28.

49. In early 2005, just over one-fifth, or twenty-two, of the top editor positions at the nation's one hundred largest newspapers were held by women. Margaret Sullivan, "Making a Difference in the Newsroom," *American Editor* (March 2005), 11. Available at http://www.asne.org/files/tae200503.pdf (accessed January 22, 2009).

50. Susan Bishoff, interview with June Nicholson, August 31, 2005.

51. David Astor, "NSNC Prez Writes about Female Op-Ed Columnists," *Editor and Publisher,* April 6, 2005. Available at http://www.allbusiness.com/services/business -services-miscellaneous-business/4674916-1.html (accessed January 22, 2009).

52. Susan F. Walsh, "Taking Humor Seriously: Gender Matters in Political Cartoons of Hillary Clinton in the 2008 U.S. Presidential Campaign," presented to the International Conference on the Arts in Society, July 2008, Birmingham, England. USA female cartoonists available at Daryl Cagle's Political Cartoonists Index (http://cagle.msnbc .com/politicalcartoons) and at Cartoonist Group (http://www.cartoonistgroup/com/ properties/list.php).

53. Quoted in Astor, "NSNC Prez."

54. Ibid.

55. ASNE Newsroom Employment Census 2009.

56. Ellen Goodman, "Angry White Males Rise Once Again," *Richmond Times-Dispatch,* August 11, 2007.

57. Brian Stelter, "Citizen Huff," *New York Times,* March 31, 2008. Available at http:// www.nytimes.com/2008/03/31/business/media/31huffington.html (accessed January 22, 2009).

58. Arianna Huffington, luncheon speech, in "Women and News," transcript from Women and News conference, 29 (see note 16).

59. Ibid., 19.

60. Arnold and Nesbitt, "Women in Media, 2006."

61. Ibid., 8.

62. Ibid., 10.

63. Ibid.

64. Ibid., 43.

65. Ibid., 26.

66. Ibid., 27.

67. Ibid., 26.

68. Ibid., 29.

69. Marina Hendricks, "No Excuses" (interview with Larry Olmstead), *Fusion* (Fall 2006). Available at http://www.naa.org/Resources/Publications/Fusion%20Magazine/ FUSION-Magazine-2006–Fall/Diversity-Fusion-No-Excuses/Diversity-Fusion -No-Excuses.aspx (accessed January 22, 2009). Olmstead, former vice president of staff development and diversity for Knight Ridder, noted that half of the executive editors and 43 percent of the department heads at Knight Ridder were women.

70. Arnold and Nesbitt, "Women in Media, 2006," 28.

71. Ibid.

72. Ibid.

73. Ibid.·

74. Ibid., 26.

75. Mary Arnold Hemlinger and Cynthia C. Linton, "Women in Newspapers, 2002: Still Fighting an Uphill Battle," Media Management Center, Northwestern University, 2002, 21–24. Available at http://www.mediamanagementcenter.org/research/win2002 .pdf (accessed January 22, 2009).

76. Ibid.

77. "Great Divide," 3. That study looked at 40 percent of managers of daily newspapers with circulations of more than fifty thousand.

78. Ibid., 10.

79. Catalyst, "2008 Catalyst Census of Women Board Directors of the Fortune 500," summary, Catalyst, 2008. Available at http://www.catalyst.org/publication/282/2008-catalyst-census-of-women-board-directors-of-the-fortune-500 (accessed January 22, 2009).

80. Catalyst, "2005 Catalyst Census of Women Corporate Officers and Top Earners of the Fortune 500," Catalyst, 2006, 1. Available at http://www.heidrick.com/NR/rdonlyres/30308A4B-614C-439E-8D53-29A073872D2D/0/CTLYST_2005WCOTECensusExecSum.pdf (accessed January 22, 2009); Catalyst, "2005 Catalyst Census of Women Board Directors of the Fortune 500 Shows 10-Year Trend of Slow Progress and Persistent Challenges," news release, Catalyst, March 29, 2006. Available at http://www.catalyst.org/press-release/90/2005-catalyst-census-of-women-board-directors-of-the-fortune-500-shows-10-year-trend-of-slow-progress-and-persistent-challenges (accessed January 25, 2009).

81. Mary Arnold and Marlene L. Hendrickson, "Women in Newspapers, 2003: Challenging the Status Quo," ed. Cynthia C. Linton, Media Management Center, Northwestern University, 2003, 18. Available at http://www.mediamanagementcenter.org/publications/data/win2003.pdf (accessed January 22, 2009).

82. Cory L. Armstrong, "Writing About Women: An Examination of How Content for Women is Determined in Newspapers," *Mass Communications and Society* 9, no. 4 (2006): 448.

83. Ibid., 449.

84. Project for Excellence in Journalism, "The Gender Gap: Women Are Still Missing as Sources for Journalists," May 23, 2005. Available at http://www.journalism.org/node/141 (accessed January 22, 2009).

85. Kay Mills, *A Place in the News: From the Women's Pages to the Front Page* (New York: Dodd, Mead, 1988); Mills, "What Difference Do Women Journalists Make?" *Women, Media, and Politics,* ed. Pippa Norris (New York: Oxford University Press, 1997), 41–55.

86. William J. Hussar and Tabitha M. Bailey, *Projections of Education Statistics to 2015* (NCES 2006-084). U.S. Department of Education, National Center for Education Statistics (Washington, DC: U.S. Government Printing Office, 2006), 13–14. Available at http://nces.ed.gov/pubs2006/2006084.pdf (accessed February 2, 2009).

87. Tamar Lewin, "The New Gender Divide: At Colleges, Women Are Leaving Men in the Dust," *New York Times,* July 9, 2006. Available at http://www.nytimes.com/2006/07/09/education/09college.html?n=Top/Reference/Times%20Topics/Subjects/M/Men (accessed January 22, 2009).

88. David Leonhardt, "The New Gender Divide: Gender Pay Gap, Once Narrowing, Is Stuck in Place," *New York Times,* December 24, 2006. Available at http://www.nytimes.com/2006/12/24/business/24gap.html (accessed January 22, 2009).

89. Eduardo Porter, "Stretched to Limit, Women Stall March to Work," *New York Times,*

March 2, 2006. Available at http://www.nytimes.com/2006/03/02/business/02work.html (accessed January 22, 2009).

90. Ibid.

91. Claudia Goldin, interview with June Nicholson, January 10, 2007.

92. Claudia Goldin and Lawrence F. Katz, "Summers Is Right," *Boston Globe,* January 23, 2005. Available at http://www.boston.com/news/globe/editorial_opinion/oped/articles/2005/01/23/summers_is_right (accessed January 22, 2009).

93. Graham, *Personal History,* 418.

1

The Female Mind

Biology of the Twenty-First-Century Woman

HELEN E. FISHER

You and I are living at a time of massive evolutionary change, a pivotal moment in history when humanity is moving forward to the past—shedding our recent agrarian beliefs and traditions and returning to patterns of business, sex, and love that are highly compatible with our primordial human nature. For millions of years on the grasslands of Africa, women commuted to work to gather fruits and vegetables. They brought home 60 to 80 percent of the evening meal. The double-income family was the rule. And women were just as economically, socially, and sexually powerful as men. Then as our forebears began to settle down on the land some ten thousand years ago and someone eventually invented the plow, men's roles as farmers became more important. Men felled the trees, moved the rocks, plowed the land, and brought their produce to local markets, coming home with the equivalent of money.

Meanwhile, women could no longer wander off the farm to gather vegetables. Instead, they became relegated to secondary jobs—weeding, pruning, picking, preparing meals, and having lots of babies to help on the farm. Across the globe, farming women lost their economic autonomy. With time they lost much of their social and sexual power, too. But with the Industrial Revolution, women's economic power began to reemerge. More and more men (and young women) left the farm for factory jobs. By the end of the 1800s, approximately 16 percent of women worked in the paid labor force. Then after World War I, our modern business economy developed in earnest.

These jobs are still expanding: office work, jobs in the huge health-care industry, those in the travel and leisure business, the service professions, and law, education, and nonprofit companies, and, of course, employment in the news arena. These jobs don't need the physical strength of men. Moreover, as the modern business community has rapidly expanded, women's housework has been shrinking. Washing machines and store-bought clothing are only two of the many conveniences that now help women run their homes. In addition, women are having fewer children, giving them more time to get an education and to enter and remain in the working world. So a myriad of new jobs are available and women have the time and experience to do them. Not surprisingly, UN data on 130 societies indicate that women are moving into the job market in astronomical numbers. And in all but one of these societies, Afghanistan, they are very gradually closing the gap with men in terms of literacy, health, and income. As women assume powerful positions in business, they are returning to the lifestyle they had a million years ago—of economic, social, and sexual equality with men. In fact, we are moving toward what I call a "collaborative society," a global culture in which the talents of both sexes are once again becoming understood, valued, and employed.

Indeed, women's power is likely to escalate, because many of our modern business environments need the skills of women: their verbal skills, their collaborative and nurturing leadership styles, their mental flexibility, and, increasingly, their tolerance for ambiguity. Research shows that corporations with higher percentages of women in the top leadership perform better financially, and they help create an environment that can retain the skills and knowledge of talented women who now pass up management promotions because they deem the price too high. The news industry is just one example of a business sector that requires most workers to be skilled at reading, writing, and verbal abilities, and collaboration. Women, on average, excel at all of these talents.

Women's Way with Words

Little girls speak sooner than boys, with more grammatical accuracy and more words per utterance. By age twelve, girls excel at verbal reasoning, written prose, and verbal comprehension, as well as basic articulation, which is finding the right word quickly. These verbal talents stem from feminine brain architecture and the (predominantly) female hormone estrogen. In fact, a woman's ability to find the right word rapidly increases in the middle of the menstrual cycle, when estrogen levels peak. But even at menstruation, the average woman is better at this, and many other verbal skills, than the average man.

This feminine aptitude for language is seen in societies around the world—for a good Darwinian reason. For millions of years, women held their babies in front of their faces, cajoling, reprimanding, and educating their little ones with words. Words were women's tools. They still are. And words have power. As Mark Twain remarked, "The difference between the right word and the almost right word is the difference between lightning and the lightning bug." At basic articulation, women shine. So as more women break through the glass ceiling in the newsroom and other industries, they will sway minds—with words.

Women's skill with words should give them advantages in positions of top management, too. In the contemporary classroom, we learn largely by patiently sitting, reading, writing, and expressing ourselves orally and on paper. Women excel at all of this, so it is not surprising that today more American women graduate from high school than men. More women graduate from college, too, not only in the United States but in several European countries as well. And 45 percent of American PhDs are women. Today's "gold-collar" jobs need educated people, and it's likely that many of them will be women.

Women's (and Men's) Biological Uniqueness

I find it surprising that some people continue to maintain that the sexes are exactly alike. Even in major universities some women (and men) refuse to acknowledge the huge body of biological data clearly indicating that, on average, men and women have some very different aptitudes. Although our thoughts and behaviors are certainly also shaped by culture and the environment, some of these skills are soft-wired into the gendered brain. Yet these men and women cling to their beliefs for an understandable ideological reason. For centuries, most people in the business establishment regarded women as weaker and dumber than men. In reaction, the "women's movement" of the 1960s focused on the similarities between the sexes. Women, they trumpeted, were just like men.

At that time it was the right thing to say. Scientists knew far less about the human brain, and this was an effective message designed to reduce prejudice against women and enable many of them to enter and prosper in the workforce. But today some individuals remain stuck in their paradigm, fighting the last war. When they deny women's biological uniqueness, they negate all of the natural talents that women bring to the current business environment. Despite their good intentions, these feminists are slowing progress for us all.

They won't stop women's economic growth, however. Moreover, as older managers retire and more and more businesspeople realize that women's aptitudes are valuable in our current business age, women will gradually gain more top positions in corporations and companies—and the economic power they enjoyed in their ancient past.

Women's "Way of Seeing"

Women were probably the first journalists, in fact, sitting around their campfires a million years ago, discussing who did what to whom and then going off to the next campfire to report. Women have probably always been in the news business. So, given women's verbal skills and their savvy in the classroom, it seems odd that more women haven't already reached the top in the newsroom and news companies.

Indeed, women can bring even more natural talents to these top leadership positions. Psychologists report that when women think, they gather more bits of data; they assemble these facts into more complex patterns; they see more relationships between these disparate parts; and they weigh more options and outcomes when they make decisions. Women tend to generalize, to synthesize, to think holistically and contextually. Women think in webs of factors, not straight lines. I call it "web thinking." When men tackle a problem, they tend to get rid of what they regard as extraneous data and focus on what they think is pertinent information. Then they move toward their goal, the solution, in a more linear fashion. I call that "step thinking."

Biology contributes to both styles of cognition. Testosterone, the (predominantly) male hormone, is associated with focused attention. When you inject this hormone into a middle-aged man, his attention becomes even more focused, and more focused on the "here and now." Brain architecture contributes to men's focus and their focus on the present. The male brain is more compartmentalized than the female brain, a process that begins as fetal testosterone builds the male brain in the womb. As a result, men have fewer nerve cables connecting the two brain hemispheres, as well as fewer nerve connections between distant regions of the same hemisphere. So the average male brain is more lateralized, less connected, less integrated than the average female brain.

Many more men than women are geniuses. When the male brain is working, it works very well. But women are, on average, more skilled at seeing "the big picture." This feminine talent for web thinking results, at least in part, from their brain architecture. Women have more nerve fibers connecting the two hemispheres, as well as more nerve cables connecting distant regions within each hemisphere, a brain construction that scientists believe contributes to women's contextual view.

Women's aptitude for web thinking probably stems from millions of years of "multitasking" to rear their young, while men's step thinking most likely helped them focus more narrowly on the hunt. But this brain architecture may contribute to some men's inability to see the far-reaching advantages of hiring women for the top jobs in the news industry or integrating the views of their female writers on the pages and airwaves of the news.

The "Perks" of Web Thinking

Women's web thinking gives them other valuable assets in the news business, as well as many other career paths; among them is mental flexibility. Psychologists report that men are, on average, more "rule-bound" than women, perhaps because women simply grasp more possibilities. This feminine mental flexibility isn't always an asset, of course. Men have long complained that women change their minds too much. Under some circumstances these men are probably correct. In times of economic stability, for example, companies need people who will sustain the status quo. Indeed, during our long farming ancestry, and even during our hunting/gathering past, there must have been enormous ecological and social payoffs for sticking with the "tried and true." As a result, the tendency to follow rules is embedded in the brain, associated with the activities of the neurochemical serotonin. Society is going through a time of monumental transition, however, a time when mental flexibility is paramount. So I suspect that many rule-bound CEOs and other conventional thinkers will gradually be selected out and will be replaced by top managers who are predisposed to see the economic feasibility of hiring women.

For millions of years women had the most difficult job of any animal on earth: raising tiny, helpless babies for many years. Prehistoric women had to think "way down the road." The distaff sex still excels at this long-term view, another valuable asset for those who report, digest, and present the news. Which brings me to ambiguity. Along with women's verbal skills, their web thinking, their mental flexibility, and their long-term view is yet another related female biological talent: women's uncanny ability to embrace ambiguity. If I had to sum up our modern business climate in one word, I would call it "ambiguous." Despite what some politicians tell us, we do not live in a world of "good" and "evil," "right" and "wrong," or "black" and "white." Our world is full of nuance, and effective business managers and journalists (and all others who participate in our global economy) are increasingly obliged to embrace this complexity. Women are built for the job.

Consequences of Short-Term, Inflexible Thinking

In 2003 the Annenberg Public Policy Center did a study of nine hundred managers of top U.S. corporations. The study indicated that "women's effectiveness as managers, leaders and teammates outstrips the ability of their male counterparts in 28 of 31 managerial skill areas." Among these skills was "generating new ideas."[1] In fact, when a group of CEOs of Fortune 500 companies were asked to identify women's greatest contribution to the corporate world, they agreed that it was "women's more varied, less conventional point of view." What is "idea generation" but the ability to reach into the depths of one's stored knowledge, assemble these reams of data in new ways, examine the myriad combinations, and produce new syntheses? All are aspects of web thinking, women's forte.

John F. Kennedy admired imagination. He once said, "The problems of the world cannot possibly be solved by skeptics or cynics whose horizons are limited by the obvious realities. We need men who can dream of things that never were."[2] I think this ability to generate new ideas is a direct result of women's well-connected brains. And this ability affects the bottom line. A study by Catalyst, an organization that tracks women's progress in the business world, found in

2004 that companies with the highest representation of women at the top were better financial performers.[3]

But the inclusion of women at the top continues to be a slow process. Studies by Northwestern University's Media Management Center and the American Press Institute have concluded that men in the male-dominated news industry, and a lot of other sectors of the business world, tend to hire and promote people who think and behave just like themselves. I'm not surprised. For millions of years men went hunting. They needed hunting partners who had a lot of their same skills. But the hiring and promoting of like-minded individuals has become culturally entrenched in many companies. And in our rapidly changing, highly ambiguous, and remarkably varied business climate, this old tradition is no longer productive.

I suspect that natural selection will take its course. Those companies that hire and promote women will triumph, while those that stick to the same old ways will fail.

The "Flat Corporation"

The world is changing in many ways that favor the female mind. Among them is the emergence of the "flat corporation." Many companies are becoming less centralized and less hierarchal because of several trends. As more and more companies expand overseas, each office must make more decisions for itself. Moreover, as a result of the rapidly changing business environment, more office managers are beginning to assemble colleagues in temporary teams that focus on a particular project, and then juggle individuals and projects as circumstances change. This reshuffling of staff tends to create more egalitarian interactions. The revolution in telecommunications contributes to the flattening of the corporate hierarchy, too: Top managers now find it difficult to withhold vital information and connections from those around them. And the trends toward freelance work and work at home are also flattening traditional business strata. So to ride the information highway, and to efficiently manage their expanding business networks, many companies have begun to restructure their organizations, replacing the pyramidal command-and-control model with a more flexible, decentralized, and less hierarchical office structure, as well as more work units composed of team members who see themselves as equals.

This trend toward the less hierarchical corporation is another return to "deep history." For millions of years our ancestors lived in little bands where it was just about impossible to hoard property, networks, or information. So our forebears lived in largely egalitarian societies. Some led with charisma or some other aspect of personality, of course. Some were also better hunters, gatherers, or healers. But by and large, ancestral men and women resided in egalitarian communities. The large, rigidly structured, hierarchical business conglomerates of the Industrial Age are not well suited to the human mind. So as they gradually "flatten" to some degree, we will all benefit.

But women may be the primary benefactors of this slow business trend. Girls form what are called "flat packs"—nonhierarchical, leaderless groups in which individuals are sensitive to one another's needs. Girls take turns. They offer suggestions. They appeal to reason. And they try to persuade. Girls don't like to confront. Instead they seek social stability. If a conflict erupts during an informal game, girls stop their play, change the rules, or make exceptions. They live in a world of "win-win." Girls ostracize. But within the clique, harmony must reign.

Boys live in a world of "win or lose." They sort themselves into large hierarchical packs. And then they spend their time competing to be "top dog." Boys interrupt, give orders, take orders, tease, and barter status to achieve and retain rank. Boys live in a world of "up" or "down" while girls live in a world of "in" or "out." This "male/male dominance hierarchy" is common to all mammalian groups in which several males reside. As the office structure changes toward "flatter," more egalitarian interactions particularly appeal to the female mind.

Certainly hierarchies will remain, particularly in large companies, such as many in the news industry, so smart top managers in these companies might be wise to allocate more power and autonomy at every level of the office. If they can't promote certain female executives to the top, then they could move power down the corporate ladder. People thrive when given responsibility and a voice. It's part of our human nature.

Women on America's Op-Ed Pages

Today roughly a quarter of op-ed writers and columnists are female, which represents a very small increase in recent years. Why are there not more women editors of editorial pages and op-ed writers and columnists in America's newspapers? Some argue that women are just not as combative as men, that they don't want to write hard-hitting, aggressive columns that take a swipe at people or politicians, because women are naturally more nurturing and compassionate. To some extent these naysayers are correct. On average, young women do seek harmony and consensus. They want to be liked. For millions of years, young mothers needed a network of support to rear their young. So it is not surprising that fewer young women make their way to the editorial page, where they are expected to be savagely aggressive. In fact, estrogen, which peaks in young women, is associated with nurturing, not attack.

But as women age, levels of estrogen decline, unmasking women's natural levels of testosterone. And older women show its signs. Like men, they begin to put on more weight around the waist; and middle-aged and older women can become extremely direct, outspoken, and aggressive—not only in the United

States but everywhere in the world. In Japan, for example, older women often dominate the home. In China many are powerful in local politics. In Polynesia they oversee important local trade networks. Many of these middle-aged and older women show an impressive combination of both female and male traits. They are verbal, imaginative, and flexible. They can cope with the ambiguity. They see way down the road. They easily engage their holistic, contextual perspective: web thinking. They are imaginative and creative. They also can be remarkably assertive as well as narrowly focused and inflexible, traits associated with testosterone. I am not surprised that many female columnists are middle-aged and older women.

I think we will see many more female columnists because of two world trends. First, because of world population demographics, we are just about to see a lot more middle-aged and older women in the United States as well as in many other parts of the world. Second, many of these middle-aged women will be productive for many years to come. Some American demographers now say that we should regard "middle age" as up to age eighty-five, because some 40 percent of those in that highest decade—ages seventy-five to eighty-four—have nothing really wrong with them. Ambitious middle-aged men and woman might have another thirty years in the workforce, prompting historian Gerda Lerner to write, "Such a critical mass of older women with a tradition of rebellion and independence and a way of making a living has not occurred before in history."[4]

Surely many from among this tremendous cohort of middle-aged and older women can make comprehensive, imaginative, and, when necessary, acerbic contributions to the op-ed pages of our newspapers. They just need the opportunity.

Women's "Executive Social Skills"

"Tact is, after all, a sort of mind reading," wrote Sarah Orne Jewett. Mind reading has long been regarded as another feminine attribute. Interestingly, the Greek oracles at ancient Delphi were women. Now, though, science can explain many of the skills that women use to "read" people, including "women's intuition." Intuition stems from connecting bits of information in the brain by a process known as "chunking." Chunking is the way we store knowledge. As a person learns to analyze the stock market, run a business, or track a political issue, they begin to recognize a system. They see regularities. And they organize these patterns into blocks of knowledge, "chunking." With more time, more patterns are chunked and stored in long-term memory. Then when a single detail of a specific complex pattern appears, the experienced person instantly recognizes the larger composition, bypassing plodding sequential thought. Both men and women chunk data, of course. But business surveys find that women are somewhat more intuitive. Business reports also show that those who are more intuitive are more successful at their work.

Intuition is one more talent women bring to journalism, and it is one of a suite of related "people" skills that women bring to the office. For example, women in ten countries excel at recognizing emotions in a face. They are better at facial recognition, too. And women in nineteen countries surpass men at reading a person's feelings from their tone of voice, body postures, gestures, and other nonverbal cues. Some of these attributes are expressed in infancy long before culture begins to mold one's behaviors into feminine or masculine patterns. For example, an infant girl projects a bigger smile at a human face than at a blinking light while an infant boy smiles just as much at the flashing light. Moreover, the abilities to read one's emotions, postures, and gestures are all associated with the female hormone estrogen.

Women have better senses of taste, touch, smell, and hearing. On average, they see better in the dark and have better peripheral vision. Women can remember more objects in a room or across a landscape. Women also display more patience than men. These aptitudes all evolved to rear tiny, helpless, prelinguistic babies. But they also enable women to detect more about the people around them. "Executive social skills," as neuroscientists call these attributes, include the awareness of the feelings of others, the ability to pick up emotional expressions in faces, the aptitude to notice and integrate the cues of body language, mental flexibility, and the abilities to make and keep friends, maintain social ties, and override the impulses that distract one from completing one's social goals. All of these social abilities have been associated with a specific gene or gene cluster on the X chromosome that is active in about 50 percent of women but silenced in all men, leading scientists to conclude that women, on average, excel at these executive social skills. Surely women's people skills are an asset in any office where one must interact daily, and often in close quarters, with people of different cognitive and social styles.

I've been called America's last optimist. But when you add up all of women's talents, by far the best business strategy would be to hire women (as well as men), move these women through the pipeline as fast as men, provide one's female executives with a suitable working atmosphere so that they don't leave the company, and use these women's strengths to improve the bottom line. If today's CEOs can't figure this out, tomorrow's bosses will. Natural selection never sleeps. Better business strategies will ultimately prevail.

How Women May Change Office Life

As more women appear in top management, they may change office life, too. Change begets change. As discussed above, women don't thrive as well as men in rigidly hierarchical social pyramids. Clawing competition and the corporate obsession with rank turn many women off. Instead, women tend to work interactively in the office. Women swap information more freely, encourage employees more, and give more praise—and praise is more valuable to women. They also tend to compliment, thank, and apologize more frequently than men, all actions designed to level the social playing field. Women often give suggestions rather than orders. They are more likely to ask for advice, even when they don't want it, in order to include others in the decision-making process. And women can criticize so softly that men sometimes don't realize they have been criticized. Women's management style tends to emphasize shared power, inclusion, consultation, consensus, and collaboration more regularly than men's. Men, on the other hand, tend to assign greater value to titles, office space, and higher salaries, the perks and emblems of rank. Men don't apologize unless they have made a genuine mistake. (But when men do apologize, thank, or compliment another, they are more likely to mean it.)

These gender differences are widely documented and supported by biology. Just inject a fish, lizard, bird, or monkey with testosterone and watch the creature begin to fight for rank. So as women inch their way to the top, we are likely to see even more changes in office structure and office interactions—toward a more egalitarian model. These changes aren't all good, of course; both sexes have their downside. Women, for example, hold grudges, a feminine trait that men often don't understand. Men have been bullied since early childhood. They are used to being knocked around, so they don't take office scuffles as personally as women do. If men hit you in the face, women stab you in the back. So as women make their way to the top, we may see much more subtle office politics.

One interesting fact about women's style of management is that this feminine approach is more effective for keeping a top-level job. A 2004 study by Lominger International reported on the ten top traits that an individual needs to remain in a senior executive position, as opposed to climbing up the ladder.[5] These ten traits are good communication skills, the ability to build teams, the ability to delegate, patience, a smooth interpersonal style, good composure under stress, the ability to handle ambiguity, flexibility, the ability to handle complexity, and the ability to see the big picture. Almost all of these traits are the strengths of women. So those women who actually do get to the top are likely to be highly effective leaders—in the news business and just about everywhere else.

Why Women Leave Top Jobs

I certainly understand, however, why some women leave top jobs or opt out of the pipeline for periods of time. A lot of these senior positions require eighty hours or more of work per week, as well as constant travel. Women, on average, are not as willing as men to jeopardize their spare time, their health, their safety, and their family lives to get ahead. Why are women generally more interested than men in balancing work and family? Probably for several unconscious biological reasons. For at least the past four million years, a woman's primary job was caring for her children, particularly infants. Even in societies in which women have historically been powerful both economically and politically, such as in many traditional West African cultures, they have done the vast majority of rearing of infants. Estrogen has been widely linked with this drive to nurture. Hence, many women are probably biologically predisposed to balance work and family.

On the other hand, men are probably less drawn to balance work and family for genetic reasons, too. For millions of years, men's jobs were to provide meat (essential to the diet) and rarer resources (such as honey), as well as to protect the family and hunting/gathering band. Men still have a tremendous drive to rescue, provide, and protect. In fact, I think one of most men's primary instincts is to be needed by a woman. But men were never primarily responsible for the daily care of the very young. And today men still work hard to acquire the money, status, and other resources that women seek to rear their young. No wonder so many men are willing to endure eighty-hour workweeks, constant travel, and highly dangerous jobs. Indeed, roughly 90 percent of those who die at work are men.

But high-ranking men also get a genetic payoff that high-ranking women don't: "Big men," as they are called in hunting/gathering societies, acquire more wives, more clandestine lovers, and more children. Why? Because women around the world like high-ranking men. In short, men's appetite for rank has been bred into the male mind by women. Many women also want top rank, of course. But climbing up the business ladder can actually have genetic liabilities for them. Women at the top tend to marry less often and have fewer children. High business status doesn't have the same genetic payoffs for women that it often has for men, whereas balancing work and family does. That balance enables mothers to rear healthy babies, infants who will grow up to pass on their DNA. I'm not saying that these genetic motives are conscious. On the contrary, our genetic predispositions are far from our daily thoughts. But across deep history, the sexes developed different strategies for survival, strategies that women unconsciously bring with them as they pour into the contemporary business world.

So, at least in part because of their genetic heritage, women are more likely to shrink from office bullying and seek meaningful work in a harmonious office climate. As a result, if a woman is not happy with her job and future prospects, she's more likely to walk out—unless she depends on this specific position to rear her young. Thus, CEOs are likely to face a lot of costly job shuffling unless they begin to provide for women's needs. In fact, every time a middle-ranking woman walks out of a company because of lack of support or inadequate promotion, her departure costs the company the equivalent of a year and a half of her annual salary. The economically prudent and "politically correct" thing to do is to hire more women, move them through the pipeline as fast as possible, and get them to the top.

Women as a Critical Mass in Corporate America

Where are we headed? Will it take another generation before some of the current CEOs retire and women really achieve their economic and business goals? And how many women must a company install in its highest echelons to experience a tipping point, a genuine collaboration of the male and female mind? Ten percent? Thirty percent? Fifty percent? I think percentages will differ in different industries. Women are likely to dominate specific fields, such as child care, nursing, some branches of medicine and dentistry, education, the service professions, many occupations in the nonprofit world, and some ranks in communications companies.

But some industries will most likely always be dominated by men—among them mechanics, architecture, engineering, surgery, construction, and the mathematical sciences—because men have some exceptional talents, too. Among these, men tend to have superb spatial skills. Many are excellent at understanding and developing complex mathematical and spatial systems, including computers, cell phones, brain-scanning machines, airplanes, bridges, and most of our other new technologies, appliances, and structures. In fact, men have built most of our modern world, bringing joy, convenience, and adventure to just about everyone on earth.

I don't think this will change. But as was said of Wagner's music, "It's not as bad as it sounds." As women regain their economic power in many strata of the business world, global beliefs, customs, and traditions regarding women will continue to change. This new perspective is likely to seep into the male-dominated industries as well, enabling the women who do enter these professions to be appreciated and promoted, too.

The "Networked" Individual

The 2006 Pew Internet and American Life Project showed that people of all ages are using the Internet to build vast networks across communities and cultures, networks they would not otherwise be able to create. And they are using these networks to make major life decisions about career changes, medical care, even whom to vote for. As this study poses, we are entering the age of "networked individualism."[6] I'm a good example. I work alone. But while at my desk, I am connecting constantly with others, through my e-mail, fax, and phone. In the Victorian age, people wrote one another letters. In hunting/gathering societies, people were in contact with at least twenty-five others daily. Today we are simply pursuing this ancient human lifestyle on the Internet. Yet the Internet is dramatically affecting the news business. More and more people are consuming news and information electronically. Some worry that these new sources of news are not verifiable, contextual, or truthful.

As an anthropologist, I am not terribly concerned about this issue. Our forebears always accumulated the news for themselves, through word of mouth; they sifted through it as they pleased and they made up their own minds, albeit swayed by the opinions of those around them. So today, as we sort through the array of news sources for ourselves, we are once again returning to our prehistoric roots. This expansion of news sources may even strengthen our ability to detect nonsense and deception.

But surely we are in the midst of a genuine shakeout in the news industry. According to recent research, some women do not even read newspapers, because they can't find the kinds of stories and issues that interest them. Others leave news companies after a few years of work, unable to get mentorship and support. The news companies that face the many challenges of our dramatically changing times will adapt and some will survive. Among them will be those whose managers have the intelligence to hire and promote women, address the problems and issues of women, and broaden their perspective to include women's "ways of seeing."

Forward to the Past

I see no evidence, however, that women will ever replace men at the top. Instead, as women's roles expand, men's roles are expanding, too. In our agrarian past, men had the sole responsibility for the family finances while women ran the home. Today more women are educated and employed instead, thereby enabling more men to leave unsatisfying jobs for less lucrative but more fulfilling work. With the rise of women in the workforce, men are also going back to school. Still others are retiring early. As women's roles expand, men garner new opportunities as well.

Working women are also changing our patterns of sex, romance, and marriage. Foremost, fewer couples are living in "traditional marriages," in which the husband makes the bulk of the income and the wife works part-time or not at all. Instead, many now reside in what are called "peer marriages." Also known as "companionate marriages" or "symmetrical marriages," these twenty-first-century partnerships are unions between economic, sexual, and social equals. Female sexuality is on the rise, inching forward toward patterns women expressed a million years ago. And around the world more men and women are choosing romantic partners for themselves. Strictly arranged marriages may soon be regarded as a quaint and curious tradition of our farming past.

The Power of the Pen

The news business is still quite traditional. Men are the CEOs of the three historically major American TV networks, and men predominate on their boards.

The top jobs at newspaper companies are also dominated by men, as are their corporate boards. But women are flooding into communications companies, particularly middle management. In the United States, in 2007 about 42 percent of all news analysts, reporters, and correspondents were female and 49 percent of all editors were women.[7] In 2001 women were 38 percent of journalists around the world, according to the International Federation of Journalists.[8] In some forty countries polled by the United Nations in the mid-1990s, more than 50 percent of students in the communications fields were women. Even in India about 30 percent of TV producers were women, and in Japan about 20 percent of TV announcers were women. These female journalists can have a profound effect on people's thinking. Television is the global campfire. We sit around it to form our opinions about the world. We also form our ideas and beliefs from what we read. Speaking of this, Alexander Solzhenitsyn mused, "For a country to have a great writer is to have another government." As women fill influential jobs in the communications industries, they will subtly change the world.

But often a new era develops slowly, at least in part because of cultural inertia. This may be true of business today. For several hundred years, a certain type of personality made it to the top, the kind of person who tended to be traditional, conservative, scheduling, hierarchal, and managerial. More creative, independent, and original personality types were pushed out, probably into academia and entrepreneurial jobs. Sure, some creative geniuses have always made it to the top of the traditional corporate ladder. But then their followers adopted their rules, set these principles in stone, and copied this template decade after decade. In past centuries, this selection process worked because the world moved more slowly. But the modern workplace demands mental flexibility, imagination, and the ability to generate new strategies and ideas. Managers who need these skills will most likely hire and promote women. But how long it will take to get a lot of women into top management, no one knows. I think it will happen, though, in news and in other professions. Women are built for careers in journalism.

But replace men? Never. Women and men are like two feet; they need each other to get ahead. The sexes have been economic and reproductive partners for more than four million years. They will remain partners as long as our species survives on what Shakespeare called "this mortal coil."

Notes

References for all factual data mentioned in this article can be found in Helen Fisher, *The First Sex: The Natural Talents of Women and How They Are Changing the World* (New York: Random House, 1999).

1. Erika Falk and Erin Grizard, "The Glass Ceiling Persists: The 3rd Annual APPC Report on Women Leaders in Communication Companies," Annenberg Public Policy Center of the University of Pennsylvania, December 2003, 8.

2. John F. Kennedy, "Address to the Irish Parliament," June 28, 1963.

3. Catalyst, "The Bottom Line: Connecting Corporate Performance and Gender Diversity," research report, Catalyst, 2004. Available at http://www.femtech.at/fileadmin/femtech/be_images/Publikationen/femtech_Catalyst.pdf (accessed January 21, 2009).

4. Gerda Lerner, *The Creation of Patriarchy* (New York: Oxford University Press, 1986).

5. Michael M. Lombardo and Robert W. Eichinger, "Turning Your Vision into Reality," data presented at conference produced by Lominger International, New York, March 17, 2004.

6. "The Internet Improves Americans' Capacity to Maintain Their Social Networks and Get Help," press release, Pew Internet and American Life Project, January 25, 2006. Available at http://www.pewtrusts.org/news_room_detail.aspx?id=23622 (accessed January 21, 2009).

7. U.S. Bureau of Labor Statistics, 2007, occupation data (table 11: Employed persons by detailed occupation, sex, race, and Hispanic or Latino ethnicity). Available at http://www.bls.gov/cps/cpsaat11.pdf (accessed January 21, 2009).

8. Bettina Peters, "The Varied Pace of Women's Progress: Surveys by the International Federation of Journalists Find Similar Challenges but Contrasting Results for Women in Different Countries," *Nieman Reports* 55, no. 4 (2001): 97–99.

PART 1

Historical and Contemporary Perspectives

2

Starting on the Cusp of Feminism with Dark Brown Skin

DOROTHY BUTLER GILLIAM

As I look back on my career, one admonition continues to echo: "You have so many handicaps, you'll probably make it." Professor John Hohenberg of the Columbia University Graduate School of Journalism said this to me as I sat anxiously in his office on a spring afternoon as graduation drew near. "Being a Negro [as African Americans were called in those days] and a woman, you face a double whammy," he said, shaking his head slightly. Then his voice became inaudible and faded into silence. He didn't need to finish the sentence. I was the only African American woman in a class made up of fifteen women, sixty-four men, and one African American man. He knew that I would be diving into an ocean of white men, where the sparse number of white women were mostly marooned on islands called "women's pages" and the occasional person of color would likely be adrift, clinging to a life raft labeled "novelty." It was a valediction not easily forgotten, despite the fact that he spoke his painful prediction in a kindly tone. At twenty-three in 1961, I had already completed a four-year apprenticeship in the weekly black press. With my master's degree in hand, I was ready to risk the move from the slower pace of weekly publications to the competitive whirl of daily journalism. When I was initially interviewed by a Columbia alumnus in Chicago, where I worked at the time, the white male interviewer included in his letter of recommendation the fact that I had dark brown skin—I guess I was supposed to be the "real thing."

"In the 1960s, on the cusp of feminism," wrote Gloria Steinem in her 2003 essay "The Media and the Movement," "women were identified in print as 'Miss' or 'Mrs.,' 'divorcee' or 'widow,' 'blonde' or 'brunette,' not to mention by what we wore. 'Women's Pages' in newspapers featured social notes often written to please advertisers—a level of journalism that would have been a scandal on the [male] news pages. . . . The rare woman who made news faced a headline like

'Grandmother Wins Nobel Prize.' . . . When African-American women were raped and murdered by European Americans, they were not counted as victims of racially motivated crimes." Such crimes against them were simply ignored by white media; they were "invisible."[1]

As a Southerner, born in Tennessee and reared in Kentucky, I had experienced segregation and racism throughout my life. Perhaps that's why I had never set foot in a daily newspaper office—the *Louisville Courier-Journal* and *Louisville Times* were white and forbidden. My tenure on two African American newspapers and *Jet* magazine had made me aware of how the mainstream daily press had consciously excluded covering and hiring African Americans. Except for the occasional heinous crime committed by an African American that affected whites, we were invisible. That situation had begun to change slowly with the 1954 Supreme Court decision in *Brown v. Board of Education* outlawing segregated schools, and with the advent of the powerful, nonviolent civil rights movement. For the first time, the white-owned media highlighted stories and images of white policemen beating and turning fire hoses on peaceful protesters. The Rev. Martin Luther King Jr. and others had injected themselves into the painful, complex, and enduring racial equation. With no consideration for the fact that I had never learned to swim, I had no idea what awaited me when I jumped into that ocean of white men in the white-male-controlled media.

Swimmers and Women

I'm writing this essay as a tribute to those women who jumped into that ocean with me and swam through often shark-infested waters to reach land and chart new courses for the generations that followed. It is a story of white women and women of color. Some bold, some reserved, some elegant, and some tough. Although these women were—and are—different from one another in numerous ways, in some ways they were quite similar. Their voices were historically left out of decisions on news coverage and how stories were framed. And readers of the nation's daily newspapers often did not know of their contributions as reporters, editors, publishers, and owners.

They had to fight, usually in a ladylike manner, for equal pay, for equal work, and for promotions up the corporate ladder. The advancement occurred more easily for white women than for women of color—though not without legal action and the sacrifice of some of their careers. It is significant that even today, seventy years after the first wave of white women began to push, shove, and fight their way onto the nation's daily newspapers, women of color remain the most left-behind and disillusioned group of journalists. Yet there have been some significant breakthroughs for white women and women of color, and the question this essay poses is this: Given the progress that has already been made, how much further do we push? My answer: a lot further.

In her 1988 history of women in newspapers, *A Place in the News,* longtime *Los Angeles Times* journalist Kay Mills identifies the three phases in which women began moving into the press corps in increasing numbers.[2] First, in the 1930s, with the help of Eleanor Roosevelt; second, during the 1940s, aided and abetted by the war; and, third, in the 1970s and 1980s, supported by an era of social change. And in each of these phases, the twin elements of race and gender combined in surprising ways.

Daring and dynamic, Eleanor Roosevelt was the rare white woman of prominence in the 1930s whose admirers and supporters were not afraid to cross America's deep racial divide. When the Daughters of the American Revolution denied "colored contralto" Marian Anderson the use of their Constitution Hall in 1939, the president's wife resigned from the DAR and used her influence to open the Lincoln Memorial for the famed diva's concert. Black Americans considered the concert one of the great racial milestones of the twentieth century.

When Mrs. Roosevelt barred men from covering her White House press conferences in the 1930s, she practically forced Washington newspapers and news bureaus to hire at least one woman to cover her newsmaking feats. For many women, she opened the daily press corps, which proved to be another of the twentieth century's important moments. Consequently, Mills wrote, a distinguished group of white women reporters began covering Eleanor Roosevelt, women like Lorena Hicks of the International News Service; Beth Campbell Short of the Associated Press; Ruby Black and Beth Cowan of United Press International and later the Associated Press; Beth Furman, who wrote for both the AP and the *Washington Star;* and later Frances Lude, who worked at the *Washington Star.* Other women whose careers took root in the 1930s included Edith Evans Asbury, whose jobs included the *New York Post* and the *New York Times;* Katherine Beebe Harris Pinkham, who worked at the *Oakland Tribune* and later the AP in New York City; Jane Conant, who spent most of her career at the *San Francisco Call-Bulletin,* later the *San Francisco Examiner;* and Mary Ellen Leary of the *San Francisco News.*

Of course, the stellar achievements of these women did not yield lasting change. When Japan bombed the U.S. fleet at Pearl Harbor in December 1941 and the country mobilized, men went to war and more women entered the press corps. When the war was over, most women were forced to give their jobs back to men. The postwar years also found black American soldiers who had fought to protect democracy at home and freedom abroad returning home to racial discrimination and violence against them, their families, and their communities. The 1950s and early 1960s found a small band of trailblazing, mostly white women journalists entering mainstream daily newspapers, enduring bias and humiliation but nonetheless paving the way for other women to enter the profession.

Eileen Shanahan, who began her career with United Press International during the war years, attempted to return to journalism after the birth of her first child.[3] The door was slammed in her face. She was told the same things that women were told into the 1960s. "Your husband has a good job, and you want to leave your baby at home!" A news director at CBS radio said to her, "What on earth makes you think I'd hire a woman?" Fortunately for her, she received a different response from Walter Cronkite, then thirty-two years old. He hired her in 1949 and became one of her most important mentors in the two years she worked for him. Another editor told her that although he liked her work, an economics story under a woman's byline would not have any credibility. After a series of jobs writing for newsletters and journals and a brief stint in government, Shanahan went on to become a star economics reporter in the *New York Times*'s Washington bureau in 1962.

Another pioneer, Peggy Simpson, had never thought much about women's rights in 1960 when she became editor of a countywide weekly newspaper in Texas. "I did have a journalism role model, however," Simpson said. "Pauline Frederick of NBC's *Nightly News,* whom I had listened to on radio since the seventh grade. . . . Her reporting from the United Nations hooked me on news and on the world outside Texas."[4] The *Hondo (Tex.) Anvil Herald* proved to be a great fit for Simpson, who worked eighty-hour weeks and asked for more. Writing about politics, industrial development, sports, rattlesnakes, and even deer hunting, she supervised dozens of community "stringers" and became a stringer herself, for the Associated Press and United Press International.

When the AP hired Simpson for the first of two temporary jobs in early 1962, they didn't credit her previous eighteen months of work as editor at the white weekly newspaper. Instead, AP started her at the minimum seventy-five dollars a week. But she was too focused on the challenge of surviving at the AP to publicly complain, and in 1963 she landed a full-time desk editor's job in Dallas. That November, she helped to cover the Kennedy assassination and was the AP reporter in the jail when Jack Ruby shot Lee Harvey Oswald. "I went on automatic pilot, heading for a telephone to dictate," she recalled.

By then she lived and breathed news and expected to be an AP lifer. She had asked for a transfer to Washington, but at twenty-four, with much experience behind her, she wanted to check out other options as well. One day during lunch with her bureau chief, she asked him what she should be doing differently if she wanted to go overseas as a foreign correspondent or run an AP bureau. Simpson was unnerved when he leaned back and laughed. In fact, her bureau chief not only laughed, but he also said, "Women didn't work in other countries, so the AP couldn't risk sending a woman overseas, because leaders wouldn't talk to her. To land a bureau chief's job," he went on to say, "you first had to sell AP services to radio station managers and newspaper editors. Persuading them to take extra AP photo or newswires usually came after you drank them under the table," he added, "and if the AP sent a woman out to make those deals, their wives wouldn't like it." Nevertheless, Simpson persevered.[5]

Nan Robertson grew up in Chicago and at age eleven decided to become a journalist. After completing her studies at Northwestern University, she worked in Europe for *Stars and Stripes* and the Paris edition of the *New York Herald Tribune,* and was a stringer for the *Milwaukee Journal* and Indiana's *Gary Post-Tribune.* She returned to New York and landed a job on the *New York Times* covering fashion for the women's section. She would go on to become a co-founder of the Women's Caucus of the *New York Times* in 1972 and to write about a discrimination suit in a book titled *The Girls in the Balcony.*[6]

I knew about some of these women when I was hired by the *Washington Post* as its first full-time black woman reporter in the fall of 1961. I joined two black male reporters—Wallace Terry and Luther P. Jackson Jr.—and a number of white women on the city staff, including Eve Edstrom, who covered welfare, and Rasa Gustaitis, who wrote features. Elsie Carper had started at the *Post* during the war and was one of the few women on the national staff. Because it was three years before the first civil rights bill desegregating public accommodations would be passed, and some restaurants did not welcome blacks, the one place where I could be assured of being served lunch was the cafeteria at the YMCA. City editor Ben Gilbert, who had interviewed me at Columbia and was largely responsible for my coming to the *Post,* asked Elsie to be sure to go out to lunch with me. She became an ally, and I was relieved when Elsie and I would occasionally go to the "Y," because many of my *Post* colleagues routinely pretended they did not know me on the streets, and their snubs were sometimes emotionally painful.

It was also tough getting cabs to pick me up when I was on assignment, and tears occasionally formed as I waved in vain for them to stop as the minutes until deadline ticked. I did not complain about these challenges, however, because I feared my white bosses would think I was inventing excuses to mask incompetence. But just covering stories that took me into white neighborhoods in Washington was often an invitation for abuse. One day I was sent to an elegant apartment building to cover the one-hundredth-birthday celebration of a resident. The black doorman, startled to see me, promptly directed me to the maid's entrance. He couldn't believe I was supposed to enter by the front door.

Despite these hurdles, I managed to do some award-winning work, and to this day I'm grateful to Ben Gilbert, the gruff city editor who helped me. He gave me an opportunity to help cover some of the biggest civil rights stories of the era, such as the integration of the University of Mississippi in 1962 by a courageous young black man named James Meredith. Gilbert and his wife embraced my family. After I got married in the fall of 1962, they occasionally invited my husband and me to his home when he and his wife entertained. Then our first daughter was born in 1963. After her birth, I pleaded with the *Post* management for a four-day week in order to spend more time with her, and my request was reluctantly granted. But after a few months, an assistant city editor told me that

I was "lowering the morale in the newsroom" and would have to return to a full-time schedule. He explained that other reporters said they wanted a four-day schedule, too, including men who wanted "to write the great American novel." A woman couldn't be given special privilege for motherhood and child-raising duties. So I returned to a full-time schedule, but by 1965 I was pregnant with my second child. When I went on maternity leave in mid-1965, I terminated my employment at the Post. I suspect an ulterior motive in wanting a second baby was to have an excuse to quit and have more time with my family. On a personal level, the black consciousness era of the 1960s was helping me reclaim the identity that the collective weight of church, state, and society had forced generations of African Americans to surrender. The internalized myths and lies that had produced layers of self-hatred were dissolving.

Women of the African American Press through the Decades

The first African American newspaper began publication in 1827 in New York "to plead our own cause," but the most important woman journalist of the nineteenth century was Ida B. Wells (later Barnett), who in 1889 became part owner of the Memphis Free Speech and Headlight. She crusaded against the lynching of black men until angry whites burned down her newspaper and she was forced to move to Chicago.

During the second half of the last century, however, Ethel I. Payne, who came to be known as "first lady of the black press," was occupying what she would later call her box seat on history, a seat she filled for more than four decades. The granddaughter of slaves, Ethel rose to prominence in a segregated America that forced blacks to attend segregated but unequal schools and women to occupy inferior positions in the male-dominated newspaper business.

Born in Chicago, Payne was the daughter of a Pullman porter and a housewife. In 1948, the year president Harry S. Truman signed an executive order desegregating the armed forces, Payne entered the Army Special Services and became a hostess at the quartermaster depot in Tokyo. She also kept a diary. When a black reporter for the Chicago Defender, L. Alex Wilson, visited Tokyo, he asked her for her notes about black GIs and Japanese women to share with the folks back home. Wilson rewrote Payne's diary notes and the Defender published them emblazoned with the headline "GIs Abused, Amused and Confused." Circulation of the widely published newspaper boomed and the story helped Payne get her first newspaper job, but not before she was investigated by army officials for allegedly disrupting the morale of the troops. In point of fact, Truman's order for armed forces integration was not being carried out, and the article embarrassed the army.

Payne left the military and began her career with the Chicago Defender in 1951. Two years later as the Defender's Washington correspondent, she was the second black woman who worked for the black press to be assigned to the White House press corps. (In 1948, while working for the Associated Negro Press, Alice Dunnigan had traveled with Truman, covering his presidential election campaign, and was the first black woman to cover the White House.) When the Interstate Commerce Commission (ICC) said in 1954 that segregation in interstate travel should be ended, she asked President Eisenhower when an executive order ending the practice would be issued. Eisenhower angrily barked at Payne: "What makes you think I'm going to do anything for any special-interest group? I'm the president of all the people, and I'm going to do what I think is best for all the people." That afternoon, the *Washington Star* carried a box on the front page, "Negro Woman Reporter Angers Ike." The ICC did not ban segregation on buses and trains until 1961.

Payne saw herself as a conduit through which black citizens, whose interests were largely ignored, could have access to presidential thinking about their concerns. Payne covered seven presidents and all of the presidential campaigns from 1955 to 1988. She was the first black female war correspondent, reporting from Korea, Vietnam, and the Nigerian civil war. She also covered major African liberation movements, from Ghana's independence in 1957 to Namibia's freedom from South Africa in 1990, and interviewed heads of state, from Haile Selassie in Ethiopia to Nelson Mandela in South Africa, as well as Uganda's Idi Amin. A commentator on radio and television, she left the *Chicago Defender* in 1978, wrote columns that she self-syndicated, and served as distinguished visiting professor of journalism at Fisk and Jackson State universities. Payne said that although limited resources hampered the black press, it performed the unique role of advocating for African Americans against racism and discrimination. Upon her death in 1991, the *New York Times* called her "the nation's pre-eminent black female journalist."[7]

Changes similar to the ones in which Payne played a pivotal role were occurring in other segments of America. The Supreme Court's 1954 ruling that declared segregated schools are "inherently unequal" and unconstitutional and Rosa Parks's refusal in 1955 to yield her bus seat to a white man inaugurated the historic civil rights movement of the 1950s and 1960s that permanently changed America. That peaceful movement also prompted the 1964 Civil Rights Act, which also led to massive change for women in society overall, an opening of the door that white women took full advantage of. It also opened up educational opportunities for women and minorities, who began going to Ivy League schools and state universities in greater numbers.

The Women's Movement of the 1970s

The women's political movement of the 1970s grew out of those changes and supported the fact that women had the right to file lawsuits to bring about change and, ultimately, justice. Lawsuits were fundamentally important for opening doors for women. Lawsuits by people of color and women in media were the mechanisms that gained opportunities for them, forcing big media companies to hire and promote them. Title IX of the Higher Education Amendments Act opened the door for women to participate in sports, from which they had been largely barred.

Still, it was not until the Kerner Commission issued its 1968 report that I saw clearly the connections between the negative portrayal of blacks in the media, the grinding poverty and discrimination that stifled nearly half of the African American population, and the absence of journalists of color in the newsroom. The Kerner Commission was appointed to investigate the urban riots of the 1960s. The report chided the daily newspaper industry for being "shockingly backward in seeking out, hiring, training and promoting Negroes" and indicated that by such practices the profession had helped to create two Americas—one black and the other white, separate and unequal. It said that racism was still at the center of American life: "Fewer than 5 percent of the people employed by the news business in editorial jobs . . . are Negro. Fewer than 1 percent of editors and supervisors are Negroes, and most of them work for Negro-owned organizations." The commission said the newspaper industry failed to attract young African Americans not simply because of low pay but because they had not been made to feel welcomed by the industry. In the wake of the riots and the Kerner Commission report, daily newspapers began hiring more blacks. It was during that period that I was asked to return to the *Washington Post* as an assistant editor in the style section, thanks in part, I believe, to actions by a group of black reporters who came to be known as the Metro Seven.

In February 1972 this group of black metro reporters for the *Post* sent a three-page memo to executive editor Benjamin C. Bradlee asking a number of questions: Why had there never been more than a single black reporter assigned to the national desk? Why were there no originating black editors in many sections? Why were there no black reporters in sports, and only two in the style section? Why, after an African American reporter obtained an unreleased report on halfway houses in the city, was the assignment taken and given to a white reporter?[8]

Bradlee responded within a week, issuing a five-page memo in which he acknowledged difficulty striking a balance between the paper's "commitment to hire, assign and promote the very best journalists we can find" with its "commitment to hire, assign and promote Blacks." He also stated that the *Post* "now employs more African American editors, reporters and photographers than any newspaper in America." In 1972, of the *Post*'s 396 newsroom employees, 37, or 9.3 percent, were African Americans. Also in that year, African Americans accounted for 2 percent of the staffs of newspapers with circulation of more than ten thousand, and 149 newspapers had none whatsoever. The newspaper would step up its recruitment efforts, Bradlee promised, among other things.

The metro reporters weren't appeased by the response, however, and later that month they demanded that the newspaper implement a strong affirmative action program to increase the number of blacks in virtually every job category to at least 35 percent. The reporters requested that within six months blacks account for between 15 and 25 percent of national and foreign, financial, sports, and editorial desk staffers. Furthermore, they argued, black copy editors also should be hired in virtually every other section, as should assignment editors. Bradlee offered to hire even more black intern reporters, institute an affirmative action plan, add a black reporter to the national staff and a black editor to the metro desk, and initiate a formal coaching system that would pair senior staffers with cub reporters. The metro reporters rejected Bradlee's response, and a series of heated meetings between the reporters and editors ended in an impasse.

On March 23, 1972, the Metro Seven called a press conference to announce that they had filed an Equal Employment Opportunity Commission complaint. It charged the newspaper with "denying Black employees an equal opportunity with respect to job assignments, promotional opportunities, including promotions to management positions, and other terms and conditions of employment." The group's spokeswoman, metro reporter LaBarbara A. Bowman, now director of diversity for the American Society of News Editors, said, "[T]he complaint . . . represents our belief that this discrimination cannot continue to exist at a publication in a city that is 71.1 percent Black." It was the first complaint filed against any American newspaper. Bowman said their action "came after very much thought, very much consideration. We're very sorry we had to take this step. There is no alternative."

In April 1972 I was rehired by the *Post,* promoted to assistant editor in the style section, and given the opportunity to work four days a week to accommodate my young family. The Equal Employment Opportunity Commission voted against pursuing "a staff finding of reasonable cause to believe that discrimination existed at the paper," but gave the plaintiffs a letter entitling them to sue in federal court. For financial reasons, the suit was not pursued. However, the incident inspired a group of white female *Post* staffers to file a discrimination suit, which the newspaper settled in 1980 with five-year hiring goals. The *New York Times* settled a discrimination suit by women in 1978, and one by black staffers in 1980. Newspapers began implementing affirmative action programs in part to thwart the risk of lawsuits.

In 1978 the ASNE urged editors to improve news coverage by employing at least enough journalists of color to reflect their diverse communities. ASNE then began the Newsroom Employment Census to measure the success of its goal of having the percentage of minorities working in newsrooms nationwide equal to the percentage of minorities in the nation's population by 2025. The ASNE cry for parity resulted in minority participation averaging an increase of one-half of 1 percent a year.

By the 1980s women of all races were entering the newspaper industry in greater numbers, but few women of color were being given the opportunity to be the boss. A stellar exception was Pam McAllister Johnson, who in 1981 became the first black female to head a general circulation newspaper in the United States. Twenty-four years later, she explained how it occurred.

> I had been working at Norfolk State University and Gannett would bring people there to interview students for internships. I coached our students and also made sure they were there on time. Gannett liked the way we prepared students. I had been working with Gerald Sass, director of the Gannett Foundation, for years. When I was awarded a fellowship to spend the summer at a newspaper, I asked if I could work on the business side instead of being a reporter. I developed my own program where I spent at least a week in each department. I learned about the management and business benchmarks in each department. So when I was asked, "Would you like to be a publisher?" I blurted out, "Sure." I was to go to New Jersey and work at a Gannett paper for a year or two, so I went, and after four months I attended a meeting, and at the end somebody said, "Your rental car is waiting for you." I didn't know if I was going to Ithaca or Utica. I didn't tell anybody, because I didn't believe it. Then there was all this publicity. People everywhere were talking about this woman who was named publisher at Ithaca. My mother-in-law was on a bus and someone started talking, and she said, "Oh, that's my daughter-in-law." A friend told me, "Someone gave you a job and someone can take it away."[9]

Although Johnson lacked business background, she moved to shore up her weaknesses and relied on the strong business structure that the Gannett Company put around its publishers. "I had a comptroller, a business manager, and others who handled that side as I grew in the job," she said. There were no formal training systems at the time but she later received a great deal of training generated by the company.

Asked how the staff accepted her, Johnson said, "People looked upon me as having three handicaps—black, female, and young. But I was socialized in the 1960s, and I considered myself young, gifted, and black instead of having handicaps. A friend suggested reading management books, and I learned a lot."

She came to realize that some department heads didn't want to work for a young black woman. They "didn't think I had enough clout to promote them. They were thinking, 'I don't know if you're going to have the respect and power so I can get where I want to go in this company.' So I learned corporate politics . . . I defined myself as intelligent, as a firm and fair manager, as someone who could promote my staff, and as a visionary. [Although] I didn't tell anyone how I had defined myself, I carried myself in a certain way."

Johnson served as publisher in Ithaca, New York, for thirteen years.

I really wanted to stay at one paper, because I had two children. I became a "training paper" for Gannett. I had two or three department heads to become publishers and move on to larger newspapers. We were a feeder paper. I went through two recessions, and that was tough. After my kids graduated from high school, I decided it was time to move on. I think there were some questions as to whether I was cutting it, making the bottom line. But overall I felt it was a job well done. When I used to complain to my mother about the job, she said, 'They wouldn't have kept you that long if you weren't doing something right.'"

In its 1999 nationwide study of the obstacles and opportunities for women of color in American media, the International Women's Media Foundation stated a truth that most journalists of color already knew. Despite significant strides in hiring, "the unfortunate reality is that in all but a few rare cases, women journalists of color have established a presence in the newsgathering process, but they have acquired very little influence over news content or product. As a whole, these women are present, yet they are without power and without a voice."[10]

Dorothy M. Bland, another rarity as an African American woman publisher, is a native of Little Rock, Arkansas, who started her career in the 1970s at papers in Arkansas and Tennessee before joining Illinois' *Rockford Register Star*, a Gannett newspaper, in 1980, where she rose from reporter to assistant city editor. One of her major turning points was when she decided to go on loan to *USA Today* when the Gannett Company's new national flagship newspaper was in its start-up stage at the company's headquarters in Rosslyn, Virginia. "Some people join the army; I joined Gannett," she quipped.[11] She worked at *USA Today* from 1983 to 1990, holding a variety of jobs, including states editor, newsmakers editor, and special project editor/reporter. She was promoted to managing editor/library information services in 1989. Her assignments ranged from obituaries and state briefs to investigative and national reporting. While in the Washington, D.C., area, she earned an MBA degree from George Washington University.

Bland then returned to the *Rockford Register Star*, where she worked in every department and also served as assistant to the Gannett Central Newspaper Group president from July 1990 to August 1992. "Some friends thought I had lost my marbles," she said, when she made this move. "I needed to figure out whether I could run a business, and that's why I asked to work through every single department."

She then was named president/publisher of the *Chillicothe Gazette* in Ohio from August 1992 to June 1994. She found that her on-the-ground work in Rockford had made her "a better person and publisher," she wrote in the American Press Institute's "Survival Guide for Women Editors."[12] "From the mailroom to the boardroom . . . I learned things that they never taught me in J-school or the

MBA program. For example, when the press crews saw me nearly neck-deep cleaning the press, my stock went up, and so did my understanding and appreciation of teamwork and press maintenance. In the circulation department, I saw firsthand the consequences of what happens if we miss deadlines or newspapers aren't bagged on a rainy day."

Bland's strategy for upward mobility paid off. She was named president/publisher of the *Fort Collins Coloradoan* in June 1994 and served until September 2005. Under her leadership, the *Coloradoan*'s revenues and profits grew substantially. She also launched the paper's Web site and a variety of nondaily products. She also helped to develop capital expansion plans and oversaw the construction of a new office building, which opened in June 2005.

Along with men of color who have become publishers or top editors of major newspapers against great odds, a few other women of color have also broken racial barriers—some at large newspapers, others at smaller yet significant media outlets. In 2006, twenty-eight years after ASNE began its newsroom census, progress toward increasing nonwhite employment in journalism remained slow. Only 13.62 percent of full-time journalists were people of color. Indeed, newsroom diversity was below its previous peak levels at most daily newspapers in the United States, according to a Knight Foundation study on newspaper employment from 1990 to 2005. Among the two hundred largest newspapers, 73 percent employed fewer nonwhites than they did between 1990 and 2004, despite the fact that the number of journalists of color inched up a half a percentage point in 2004, even as the number of full-time professional journalists dropped.[13]

According to Karla Garrett Harshaw, editor of the *Springfield (Ohio) News-Sun,* and the first woman of color to head ASNE, "It is always good to go forward, especially at a time when demographic change is such a powerful factor in our communities. Because of these changes, we need to measure our progress by full percentage points, and not fractions. We simply must move more urgently. It can be done."[14]

When the quadrennial convention of UNITY: Journalists of Color was held in Washington, D.C., in August 2004, the American Society of Newspaper Editors sponsored a breakfast for top-ranked journalists of color at the nation's newspapers. About 125 people, ranging from assistant managing editors to editors and executive editors, attended, including 34 women of color. Like their white counterparts, these female trailblazers have responded to America's cultural diversity, fast-changing technology, and economic pressures, including the drive for profit margins above 25 percent. The number of women working in newsrooms increased slightly in ASNE's 2004 census—to 37.54 percent—a percentage that has gone up and down since 2001, when women made up 37.35 percent of newsroom professionals, and the percentage of minority women journalists in newsrooms in 2004 increased from 16.27 to 17.20 percent.

Mentors and Role Models

What characteristics are shared among these women of color who have risen to success? Topping the list is having good mentors and role models. Rachel Benavidez, the twenty-nine-year-old editor of the *Brownsville Herald* in Texas, had a meteoric rise from part-time student obituary typist to editor in just five years. She studied at the University of Texas at Austin and later at Brownsville, where she worked under journalism adviser Azenett Connejo, a former journalist who, as Benavidez said, "served as the first example of a Latina journalist that was accessible to me, an aspiring journalist. . . . She still serves as my mentor."[15]

A turning point in Benavidez's career came in 2001 when she left her part-time job as a feature writer and became a full-time writer on the news desk at the *Herald*. Soon after attaining that position, she came under the tutelage of the *Herald*'s first Hispanic editor in chief since the 109 years of its founding, Teclo J. Garcia.

"Young, Texan, and Latino, I identified strongly with him," said Benavidez, "and worked more closely with him than previous editors. He became a mentor and remains very much in that role." Garcia pushed her to study the community where she was born and reared, and demanded that she understand the people's issues and tell the stories that mattered most to them and their families. "What did they want and why?" she recounted. "What did they need and were they getting it? What were their experiences? . . . I learned to reject the stereotypes about the people who live and work here, the image of the poor, uneducated Mexican American that appears in census figures and in the outside press. I learned to recognize the beauty and value of this area."

When Garcia moved on after two years, Benavidez succeeded him as editor in November 2003, becoming the first Latina to hold the job and, at twenty-seven, the youngest person in Texas running a paper of that size. "Teclo continues to challenge me to reject complacency and push for the next level of performance," Benavidez said. She also credits her publisher, R. Daniel Cavazos, the paper's first Hispanic publisher and a champion of Spanish-language journalism in their parent company, Freedom Communications Inc., for naming her editor in chief. "His goal in naming me editor . . . is to continue an era of Hispanic leadership in this 90 percent Hispanic community."

For some of the women of color, their first role models and mentors emerged from their families. That was certainly the case with Renee Hampton, the first African American female editor of the *Akron (Ohio) Beacon Journal.*

> On the personal side, my dearest mentors were my parents. My mother was a wife, college librarian, active in our church and community. She taught me daily, "Treat others the way you want to be treated." That primary lesson became the

foundation of my management style. The ability to get along with and work well with most people is a strength in anyone's career. My father was a God-fearing man and a hard worker. He had a simple and brilliant common-sense approach to life. His mantra, "If you don't know something, ask, and don't stop asking until you understand," was empowering. By his example, he taught us to live our lives with integrity.[16]

Hampton's professional mentors also included a former supervisor who welcomed her questions about the business, about people, about life. "My understanding the 'why' he made the decision that he did," she said, "was vital in developing a career philosophy and work ethic that I could embrace and encourage in others." Hampton left her position in 2006.

Similarly, Mei-Mei Chan, an Asian American and vice president of advertising for the Seattle Times Company, found an important source of strength within the walls of her home. "I was fortunate in that my husband, a former journalist and editor, was my best friend and mentor," she said. "He kept me grounded, gave me the most honest and accurate assessments."[17] She also made the most of professional mentors. "Around 1995, I was paired with Andy Barnes of the *St. Petersburg Times* as part of the Newspaper Association of America Breakthrough Program. Over the years, he has provided me a small glimpse of his world, as well as perspectives on my career decisions." The contacts she made within industry and minority journalist organizations were important resources. Chan would call upon different colleagues from the Asian American Journalists Association, the National Association of Minority Media Executives, or the Newspaper Association of America with specific issues or questions. "I also studied bosses and peers," Chan said. "Like assessing your own parents, you identify traits you want to emulate and traits you don't want to wish upon your worst enemy."

Although these women credit their success to a combination of ambition, skill, opportunity, and good mentoring, all acknowledge that their role as a trailblazing woman of color has advantages and disadvantages. "You certainly stand out," Chan said. "I recall my first job as a cub reporter in the small town of Danville, Illinois. People would actually stop me to applaud my work. The same thing occurred in Idaho. Standing out means more eyes are upon you; the expectations are higher. You cannot be mediocre. You can't just be good. You have to be great. You begin representing an entire segment of the population. You become a role model, like it or not."

Renee Hampton works hard to respect and use her difference for the good of all, but she admitted, "There are times when I think my color screams so loud that others don't hear what I'm saying. Sometimes people seem caught up on the race thing, or maybe it's gender. I never really know. But I sometimes disconnect when there is no obvious other reason. As minorities, we can have the additional burden of wondering, 'Am I the reason we are far apart, even when we are on the same page?'"

Most, like Rachel Benavidez, see their roles as imposing the responsibility to make a way for other people of color in the industry: "As a professional in this industry, I'm very much in the minority. It isn't uncommon for me to be the only woman of color at professional gatherings outside of my region, such as editors' meetings, conferences, et cetera. My first experiences were uncomfortable as I again felt the exposure of being 'different' among my peers. I've embraced my role as a 'first' for Hispanics . . . and am pushing to bring others on board—more women, more women."

But close newspaper industry observers such as Anna Lopez, executive director of UNITY: Journalists of Color, fear that even the slow progress women of color have made is in jeopardy. Although newspapers showed a slight increase in hiring people of color in 2004, she said,

> With all the media consolidation and cutbacks, I think we're going to lose numbers we've gained because people are leaving the industry in frustration. UNITY and their alliance partners—the Asian American Journalists Association, the National Association of Black Journalists, the National Association of Hispanic Journalists, and the Native American Journalists Association—plan to focus on increasing the numbers and reversing the trend. The buyouts, shrinking of newsrooms, and conversions are being driven by the companies' desire to keep their profit margins above 25 or 28 percent—what they were in the 1990s, and that's unrealistic.[18]

Another keen industry observer is Dori Maynard, president of the Robert C. Maynard Institute for Journalism Education, the nation's oldest organization dedicated to training media professionals of color and to helping the news media reflect the nation's diversity in staffing, content, and business operations. Her organization did an assessment that revealed that the media lose people of color after five or six years because they don't see a road to advancement, particularly in management. Responding to this bleak assessment, the Maynard Institute began the Maynard Media Academy in 2005 to train first-time managers. It not only gives them the skills they need to succeed in that first supervisory position but also provides the foundation to rise through the leadership ranks on both the editorial and business sides. Maynard has trained thousands of minorities for the nation's media, including reporters, editors, copy editors, and managers.

Some women of color who rose to positions of power also were mentored by powerful white men and men of color. For Deborah Heard, forty-eight, assistant managing editor for the *Washington Post*'s style section until she took a buyout in December 2008, white men were her only mentors in the early stages of her career as a copy and assignment editor at the *Miami Herald*. But when she arrived at the *Post* at the age of twenty-five, she had a different experience.

> Some of the most prominent people that people listened to were black—columnists like William Raspberry and Dorothy Gilliam. I saw black editors like Milton Coleman, Eugene Robinson, and Herb Denton. I could see a future and it wasn't odd. There were black people in positions of authority. I was able to see a future at an early age. There were people who had done it who could guide me and warn me. . . . The number one message I got from various mentors and some bosses was that I could do it. They supported me even when I made mistakes and even when I didn't know what I was doing.[19]

Heard became one of the highest-ranking black women on newspapers of seven-hundred-thousand-plus circulation. From January 2005 to December 2008, she led a section of sixty people, including the newspaper's best feature writers, arts writers, and critics. "I didn't anticipate how different I would feel," Heard said. "It is so nice to be in charge."

I wrote to showcase just some of the white women and women of color who have blazed new trails in journalism. As I look back on my career now and recall what Professor Hohenberg said to me forty-seven years ago, I have an answer I did not have for him then. Yes, I faced a double whammy, and yes, I had a hard row to hoe. But I was not alone. The army of white women and women of color who followed me continue to break barriers—and they know how to swim competitively.

Notes

1. Gloria Steinem, "The Media and the Movement," in Robin Morgan, *Sisterhood Is Forever: The Women's Anthology for a New Millennium* (New York: Washington Square Press, 2003).

2. Kay Mills, *A Place in the News: From the Women's Pages to the Front Page* (1988; New York: Columbia University Press, 1990). References on women reporters during Eleanor Roosevelt years, 36–48.

3. Ibid. Interview excerpts from Eileen Shanahan, 55.

4. Peggy Simpson, interview with Dorothy Gilliam, September 23, 2005.

5. See Peggy Simpson, "Learning about Discrimination," in the present text, 75.

6. Nan Robertson, interview with Dorothy Gilliam, October 14, 2005.

7. Susan Ware, ed., *Notable American Women: A Biographical Dictionary* (Cambridge, Mass.: Belknap Press, 2004). Ethel Payne entry by Dorothy Gilliam, 502–4.

8. Steven Gray, "The Washington Post's Metro 7," *NABJ Journal* 20, no. 3 (2002): 11.

9. Pam Johnson, interview with Dorothy Gilliam, October 10, 2005.

10. Cynthia Tucker (*Atlanta Constitution*) and Maureen Bunyan, WJLA-TV, quoted in "Women Journalists of Color: Present without Power," International Women's Media Foundation Publications, 1999.

11. Dorothy Bland, interview with Dorothy Gilliam, October 16, 2005.

12. Joyce Gemperlein, "Survival Guide for Women Editors," American Press Institute, November 13, 2002, http://www.americanpressinstitute.org/2002curtis (accessed January 21, 2009).

13. Bill Dedman and Stephen K. Doig, "Newsroom Diversity Has Passed Its Peak at Most Newspapers, 1990–2005 Study Shows," report for the John S. and James L. Knight Foundation, June 1, 2005. Available at http://www.powerreporting.com/knight (accessed January 21, 2009).

14. All material from Karla Harshaw is from an interview with Dorothy Gilliam, October 4, 2005.

15. All material from Rachel Benavidez is from interviews with Dorothy Gilliam, October 4 and October 11, 2005.

16. All material from Renee Hampton is from an interview with Dorothy Gilliam, December 12, 2005.

17. All material from Mei-Mei Chan is from an interview with Dorothy Gilliam, October 10, 2005.

18. All material from Anna Lopez is from an interview with Dorothy Gilliam, October 27, 2005.

19. All material from Deborah Heard is from an interview with Dorothy Gilliam, November 4, 2005.

3

Interview with Gloria Steinem

DOROTHY BUTLER GILLIAM

Dorothy Gilliam: I want to go back to the beginning, to your first feminist article in 1969, "After Black Power, Women's Liberation." Would you summarize the thesis of this article for a new generation?

Gloria Steinem*: I wrote this article after belatedly realizing that there was a sexual caste system that had to be addressed as part of all the other social justice movements. So the first thesis was the recognition of this profound division of human nature and human beings into false categories, not only of masculine and feminine but also of leader and led, subject and object, active and passive, thus depriving everyone. And the second thesis was that if the National Organization for Women, which was more of a reformist group than it is today, and newer, more small-group radical inclusive elements, which were made up mainly of women active in the civil rights and peace movements, could come together, there would be a mass movement.

DG: And it's your sense that's what happened?

GS: Yes. And some of the small-group feminists were too radical to take part in elections, for instance. But eventually these groups recognized the electoral process as an important way of making change, and so they changed as well and also became more practical. Each part of this burgeoning beginning movement was changed by the other and each contributed enormously.

DG: So at the start of the women's movement there was mostly skepticism in the mainstream media?

GS: I would say that the first response was ridicule. I suspect that opposition was a step forward, because ridicule came first.

---

*Gloria Steinem is the founder of *Ms.* magazine and the National Women's Political Caucus.

DG: If you hadn't been stymied by bias against women in your search for a newspaper job early on, would you have begun writing independently?

GS: I did try to find a paying job in media in the very beginning, but frankly I didn't try that hard. Partly it was my own family tradition. My father had two points of pride: He never wore a hat and he never had a job. He was the ultimate freelance person. And it seemed to me better to stay outside an office and become a freelancer. Freelancing seemed more possible, although only marginally more possible.

DG: Who were the other pioneers in journalism?

GS: I believe that Flora Lewis was the single serious woman writing about foreign policy and other serious subjects at the *New York Times*. During Vietnam there were several women covering the Vietnam War. Overall, in terms of working journalists being assigned to serious subjects, there were very, very few women journalists.

DG: Am I right in saying that part of your strategy was to nurture other women as reporters and writers?

GS: Yes, it was clear that we needed to have a place where women could be seen by readers, and that applied not only to journalists, but also to fiction writers and poets. If you look at the first issue of *Ms.* magazine, there were important breakthroughs. We had unpublished work by Sylvia Plath and Virginia Woolf. A few years later the writers we were publishing were very diverse, and included, for example, Alice Walker, who had been published in small magazines before but I don't think in national magazines. So the magazine became a showcase for new or relatively new talent.

DG: How did you find these women writers?

GS: It was a two-way street. Some of them found us. We always tried to read unsolicited contributions, which few magazines did because it's not economically feasible. We also had the advantage of people volunteering as interns. Some things just came in over the transom. Another way was through the editors ourselves. For instance, once Alice Walker became a contributing editor, she told us about authors like Bessie Head and so many African authors that had not been published in this country before but whose work she knew. Each of us had some favorite authors that we could bring to readers as a gift. Talent surfaced in a variety of ways and there was no shortage of it. We could have filled many more magazines.

DG: I understand that you would also occasionally call women reporters and tell them when stories were breaking, or you would alert them to issues that related to women.

GS: Yes, and occasionally, when we weren't sinking below waves of overwork, we'd have a briefing for women reporters and the rest of the press about issues that were coming up in the news, to spread the word and be helpful. A lot of times people would call us as references and sources of information as new issues emerged, such as sexual harassment or battered women, for example. In an odd way, the magazine itself, small as it was, spread its influence more widely because it was a source of information and research for people in the press. I remember at some point along the way—maybe we had been in existence less than a decade—we were all exhausted. We figured out we had published something like four hundred authors. What usually happens in national magazines is that a few stars are published regularly and the magazine has perhaps a stable of a dozen who get more than one or two assignments. So we sort of looked at each other and said, "No wonder we're exhausted." We also tried to do another kind of journalism, which was to interview women, and use these as a diary; for example, a saleswoman, or an activist welfare recipient. So we would interview them and edit a transcript into an article. We regret we did not use more of these.

DG: How large was your staff?

GS: I think the *Ms.* staff, including editorial, art, fact checking, and copy editing, consisted of maybe ten people.

DG: One of the interesting things for me was the role of lawsuits in securing pay equity and promotions for women in mainstream media. What does it say to you that it took lawsuits to make this happen?

GS: It says the media are not a special case in its employment practices but are part of the economic scene. So when Eleanor Holmes Norton was the lawyer for the women at *Newsweek,* for instance, or when the women at the *New York Times* sued the *New York Times,* that was very, very crucial. It's also interesting to look at who did not get sued. Some of the networks were sued, but not CBS. At CBS a group of activist women started an organization and CBS didn't punish them for it. Indeed, CBS gave them a place to meet. So they were able to bring in enough reforms so people didn't feel they had to sue.

DG: This essay is inclusive of women of all races. From your perspective, what were the commonalities and differences between white women writers and journalists and African American women writers and journalists?

GS: The commonality was exclusion, but of course women of color were infinitely more excluded. For instance, Pat Carbine, the founding editor and publisher of *Ms.* magazine, had been editor in chief and vice president at *McCall's.* She had hired the one and only black woman editor there ever. And when she quit, that editor quit. So there were no women of color as editors at any of the women's magazines, for instance. So however excluded white women were, the ante was up for women of color. The internal similarities in terms of discrimination were the deeply rooted ones. That is to say that our reproductive role is the source of our oppression. The desire to control that, to either force us to have or not have children, is a root cause [of oppression] for females altogether, and to maintain us as a cheap labor force is a root cause and pattern. I think some-times the ways the differences work out are not well understood. For instance, the idea that white women and families had inherited wealth and benefited equally was not a realistic idea. In fact, those families were more likely to keep women as ornaments and hostesses. The rate of sexual abuse of little girls was higher in wealthy white families than in the poorer middle-class families. The idea that we had the same degree of power as the men in our families was not accurate at all.

The idea for women of color, and especially black women, that the way to further the power of black communities was for them to be behind their men instead of alongside their men was a problem. It was as if some black men wanted to have all the privileges that white men had had, including the right to boss all women around. And that was very painful. It caused the black community to lose some of its talent from black women. Or as Bella [Abzug] used to put it, "walking around on their knees in order to be shorter than the men they were with." She meant white and black women when she said that. The ways that the problems were interpreted were a problem in and of themselves. It was impor-tant to give women a place where they could speak for themselves—that is to say, how they experienced it [their lives]. Sometimes there were unexpected alliances. I think right before the first issue of *Ms.* magazine, Dorothy Pittman Hughes and I, who had been speaking together [at events] for a while, had been in Alabama. In the community we visited, household workers, who were 100 percent black women, and the employers of domestic workers, who were 100 percent white women, had banded together to say to the husbands, "You have to pay decent wages, and you can't turn women into sexual prey in the household." I remember the meeting because women were just in tears. Both white and black women did band together and for a time raised the wages of the household workers and formed a kind of bond. It happened here in a different way in New York, which was in the struggle to get household workers covered by the minimum wage laws.

DG: What is your assessment of where women in media are now? I'd also like you to take a speculative look forward.

GS: There are certainly many, many more women who are making a living in the media. A group of women and I who have founded the Women's Media Center recently had a meeting of those who book network shows to try to help them find more diverse female experts on more subjects. Every one of those who book for the major networks and CNN were all female and every one of the producers was male, and they were still having a tough time influencing the kind of stories that were done and the kind of experts that were picked.

SheSource.org is a new online reference that has been started by the White House Project, to try to supply female experts in every area. The White House

Project is a nonprofit group that advances women in leadership. That is wonderful, but this group has had to raise money. The networks themselves should pay for this.

There are clearly more women present in the news media, but they are rarely the decision makers. They're present and they're good, smart people doing their best. But if my completely subjective experience is any indicator, of the professional groups I talk with, the women in media are the most depressed and experiencing the most tension. They're the bridge between the outside world and media. They are trying to get more stories in and more facts and more diverse women into newsrooms and news organizations, and to have a kind of journalism that actually says what's accurate. These individuals are trying to investigate what's true instead of presenting two opposing views. They're the bridges and they're trying, but this so rarely works in news and they are having a tough time.

DG: Why do you think that media is a tougher nut to crack than the other industries you mentioned?

GS: There are indeed other professions in which women are less present, but where there is more power it is more difficult to share that power. So many countries around the globe will have a female president before our nation does, because the U.S. presidency is arguably the most powerful position in the world. This country is the media capital of the world and is probably where there is the most competition for influence and control in media.

It's also about advertising and money, and advertising is so much about stereotypes rather than reality. Advertisers want an audience eighteen to thirty-five in spite of the fact that older people have more disposable income. Or they think women don't buy consumer electronics; these all are stereotypes that come with marketing.

DG: Look at the power issue. Is part of it the reluctance?

GS: The media function on image and replicate and manufacture images. One would think that journalism, especially since its job is to reflect reality, would do that less and sometimes that is true. During [Hurricane] Katrina the newscasters finally got to show reality, and they were rewarded for it. They were flooded with letters saying, "Thank God, you're finally showing us what's going on, not just silly stories but important stories." I hope that was a bit of a turning point.

DG: Have you observed a turning point since then?

GS: It does seem that the media are more critical of the administration and a bit more likely to try to say what is accurate and not just repeat what two opposing sides tell them. It's also true that the ultra-right wing in this country have made a concerted electoral and media effort, and it paid off. Some things they just bought—like Fox News. Some things they got rid of—like the Fairness Doctrine. So now news shows that used to be about public service may only be about entertainment because they're a profit center like anything else. So it's partly that ownership of news has changed. I suppose the hope lies in the more populist forms of media—the Internet, blogging, podcasting—because at least those are accessible without a huge outlay of capital. People understandably tend, however, toward the brand names they know, because there's even less guarantee of accuracy in the Internet and blogging than there is in mainstream media.

DG: Also, as you have pointed out, you can cocoon on the Internet, but meanwhile the policies are being made by the articles in the mainstream media.

GS: One survey about two weeks before the last presidential election showed that 60 percent to 80 percent [a majority] of the people who voted for George Bush thought they were voting for the opposite of his real position on many crucial issues. That's what led me to invite all the women I could lay my hands on at the moment in the media to come to lunch in my house and say, "What the hell can we do here?" And that's why other women and I have founded the Women's Media Center.

The Women's Media Center is meant to be an infrastructure for progressive women in media. We're also doing a book and developing a media resource on a Web site called *Unspinning the Spin,* in which we are trying to point out the importance of accurate language. We would not have lost affirmative action in the state of California if it hadn't been called "preferential treatment." The right wing just polled until it came up with a phrase that most people opposed.

The Women's Media Center does a valuable service by being hot-linked to every progressive woman writer in the country that we can find. You can just go there in the morning with your cup of coffee and see what's happening. There will be more as time goes on.

Note: Founded in 2005, the center's goal is to make women visible and powerful in the media. Their mission is to "assure that women and women's experiences are reflected in the media just as women are present everywhere in the real world; that women are represented as local, national, and global sources and that women media professionals have equal opportunities for employment and advancement" (Women's Media Center Web site, http://www.women'smediacenter.com).

4

Interview with Nan Robertson

DOROTHY BUTLER GILLIAM

Dorothy Gilliam: In your book you called the letter that the women dropped on the *New York Times* management's desk in 1972 "a bomb." Could you talk about what it contained and why you characterized it as "a bomb"?

Nan Robertson*: Well, the *Times* is among the smuggest of newspapers. It's always lecturing America on how to be liberal and fair and all that kind of thing, and this letter basically told management of the really sorry lot of its women. There were no women in positions of power, either on the management side or the editorial. On the editorial side, there were no women in positions of power except Betsy Wade, who was the chief copy editor of the foreign desk. This job was very prestigious. Betsy was a prime mover and founder of the Women's Caucus and was our spokesman during meetings with the *Times*. The letter mentioned a great many specifics about how we weren't in the pipeline to any kind of management power and our salaries were less than the men's.

That was the real bomb: that women with equal or better training and education and experience in the newspaper field were shuffled off to women's news. I came from seven years in Europe as a foreign correspondent and was immediately sent to the women's page to cover fashion. This is the way it was when I joined the *Times* in 1955, in January. Our first direct contact, person-to-person, with the management, occurred in July 1972. The book begins with a description of that meeting, which left us very optimistic, but not facing reality.

DG: Who were the major women's trailblazers of the *Times* from the time you arrived in 1955 until the Women's Caucus was formed in 1972?

NR: There was Edith Evans Asbury, who was one of the stars in the city

---

*Nan Robertson is a former reporter for the *New York Times* (1955–88) and author of *The Girls in the Balcony: Women, Men, and the* New York Times (Random House, 1992).

room. One of the things I go into in my book *The Girls in the Balcony* is that the two most powerful women at the *Times* never joined the caucus. Ada Louise Huxtable, the architecture critic, was one of the two, and she was not concerned about other women's careers. Charlotte Curtis was the style editor who introduced serious topics to the page. She thought, wrongly, that she could change management. About fifty women signed that letter out of the five hundred women in business and editorial at the *New York Times.*

DG: Who were some of the other leaders besides Betsy Wade?

NR: The most important founders (I was a cofounder) were Grace Glueck, who was an art critic, but not at that time, and Joan Cook, who has died. But Joan and Grace and Betsy were the triumvirate, the troika that pulled the Women's Caucus ahead, and Betsy was our spokesman at that meeting. The only people from the Washington bureau who came were Eileen Shanahan and me. We flew to New York for that meeting, and I describe in the beginning of the book how Punch Sulzberger, who was then publisher, was startled that two such successful women would be there with complaints about how women in general were treated.

DG: He probably thought, "What are you mad about? You're doing well."

NR: That was exactly his thought. Punch has a very expressive face, and when Eileen and I burst a little late into the meeting, he looked absolutely stunned at the fact that two successful women would find anything to complain about on the *Times* plantation. The meeting was very amiable. These are all nice guys. Abe Rosenthal, the executive editor, was not there, and, I think, deliberately so because of a very close friendship with my husband, Stan Levey, who had died the year before. The two men, Stan and Abe, were bosom friends, and because of that Abe did not treat me as cavalierly as he did other people, including Betsy, and Joan and Grace. He was all-powerful, and the dreadful thing was because of his affection for my husband, that he was not there and, really, was against the whole idea of the Women's Caucus. He hurt a lot of colleagues, people I loved, and this led to estrangement. The meeting was amiable; we were encouraged. We felt quite optimistic at the end of it. We felt, "Gee, they're really gonna do something," but instead they didn't do anything. So in 1974 we decided to file suit to bring them to court. In 1978 the suit was settled in our favor, like all the media suits [all of the similar related suits were settled in favor of the women plaintiffs]. But until the very end, the *Times* management did not admit that they had lost.

DG: It was six years from the time the letter was dropped on the management desk to the time when management and the women were preparing to go to court and the final settlement. Can you think of any of the major moments between 1972 and 1978 that were particularly difficult for any of the members of the caucus?

NR: We knew that we were putting our careers on the line, and as the years went on and the management did nothing, they kept promising, "Things will

be better." Also, Punch Sulzberger was not firm enough with middle management as his son later was. As assistant publisher, young Arthur Sulzberger really did talk to his middle management and said, " This is very important. One
of the most important things that you have to do is to pay women better, give
them better jobs." I mean we were ghettoized in the women's news department.
This was very typical of women in that era. You know, even with the modern
women's movement in full flood, it was just amazing how we were cut out. You
know, there were no women covering courts, no women covering sports, no
women vice presidents. This was in the 1970s and at this time we were fighting
for everything.

DG: It must've been very tense.

NR: It was, but I'll tell you that my feeling was one of exhilaration in this
bonding process of the women in the caucus. They realized that this was for real
and they wouldn't get anywhere if they didn't complain, in a group, and, finally,
if they did not sue. And to the bitter end, the only men in high positions who
gave a deposition in favor of the women were John Leonard, the Sunday book
editor, and the man who was his assistant editor.

DG: This is really an amazing case, and I was just thinking that when the case
was settled out of court, even your own lawyer recommended that you settle
out of court.

NR: Do you know why? She compared it to a divorce: both sides would get up
in court and vilify the other side. During the discovery process that preceded the
court hearing, we got many memos sent from one member of the management
to another, and they were devastating. The management, on its side, probably
had a lot of dangerous material about the women. For instance, I went to an
alcoholism rehabilitation center in 1975 and I was an alcoholic. And in that year
I went to a Manhattan rehab, a very well known one, called Smithers, and spent
four weeks there, in the fall of 1975, and became sober. I have been in Alcoholics
Anonymous—and I'm still active. I have celebrated thirty-one years since my
last drink. Now, they could have mentioned that, or they could have mentioned
people who were not all that competent in their jobs. It would have been like a
divorce in court, with all of this revealed, all the dirty linen revealed, and then
we had to go back and work side by side with the same people. We thought that
such discoveries would be so disastrous, so negative to both sides that it would
be far better to settle.

DG: Even so, the settlement was only $350,000, not much money.

NR: No, it was divided among five hundred women, the number of women
who worked at the *Times,* in both business and editorial sections at that time.

DG: There were women all over America with these types of grievances.
What made the women at the *New York Times* so special?

NR: Because, I think, of the reputation of the paper. I think—and many other
people feel the same—that the *New York Times* was and is the best newspaper

in America, the most respected. It is because of the towering reputation of the *Times,* though it was perhaps not more important, because the lot of women at that time was bad throughout journalism. It was interesting that immediately after the meeting in 1972, all of a sudden all kinds of women were hired, particularly for the editorial side, because their bylines would be visible on the front and inside pages of the paper. Anna Quindlen is one of the examples. Slowly, they stepped up their pace of hiring women. Most of them still ended up on the women's news page, called "Style" pages, under Charlotte Curtis. Charlotte, particularly, thought she could work from inside, which was a terrible mistake, which she realized in time. But she broadened the coverage of the important issues in society affecting women. Before, the subtitle for the women's page was "Food, Fashion, Family, Furnishing." That is what most women covered then. Charlotte was an imaginative, inventive, very talented writer and editor. But she didn't change the employment picture for women. She changed the subjects of the women's page. She had been a brilliant society reporter when she first came to the *Times,* and she had a sardonic view of the very rich people she was covering. Charlotte's fate was not a good one. She eventually was "promoted" to the news pages, to writing not a column exactly, but doing articles for the news pages. But she was marginalized and placed inside, in one-column articles, instead of better display. And she was sort of heartbroken. The person who suffered the most was Betsy Wade, because she was taken off the foreign desk and she wrote a sort of cozy travel column for the Sunday travel section, which is what she did to the end of her career. She really, really suffered. I did not suffer for [my role as cofounder of the caucus]. Indeed, I was sent to Paris five months after the meeting with the management in 1972 to a plum assignment. But Abe Rosenthal told me years later that there had been a terrific fight in the management over sending one woman to join another. Flora Lewis was the first woman chief of a bureau, any bureau, foreign or domestic. They said, "Oh, it's gonna be a catfight. Get two women together," you know. It was ridiculous! When I was sent there, the same kind of reaction. They used to call us the "Dolly Sisters," because we were two women working in the Paris bureau, and we became as close as sisters.

DG: As highly respected as Flora Lewis was, it was very telling, as you detailed in your book, that she was also paid less. It was almost an organic reaction—if it's a woman, you get the responsibilities and the trust of the institution, but not the rewards. There were many good writers at the *New York Times,* but you took on the task of writing *The Girls in the Balcony.* What motivated you to write that, and did you experience any particular difficulty? By writing the book, you made public what might have been obscure because there wasn't a trial.

NR: There were several things motivating my wanting to do this. I was looking to, and did, return to Washington, where I had a house on Capitol Hill. I retired from the *Times* in the end of July 1988 and came back here to watch my step-grandchildren grow up and to be back in my house, which I loved. I love the neighborhood. And so I retired early, at the age of sixty-two, and took a lesser pension. I wanted to study music and I wanted to write books. And I was casting about for a subject and was thinking I wanted to do a biography of a woman that might have been neglected before. But every time I started my research, I discovered that somebody was already ahead of me. That was the time, the beginning of many biographies of women. One after another, I must have tried six or eight different subjects to find out that somebody was there ahead of me in research and writing and so on. But then I started thinking, "What about the newspaper I know the best of all?" I really know the *Times;* I've been there for many years. I joined in January 1955 and stayed till the end of the eighties. I knew so many people at the *Times,* in management, in my peers, in the secretarial network—my friends, the secretaries, who knew really what was happening. They are like nurses in a hospital. The doctors sort of come in and out, but the nurses are there twenty-four hours a day and they really know the gossip. So I knew both management and the employees very well, plus the fact that I had been a union shop steward in the Washington bureau for ten years, and before that I was the person who organized the women's news department. In addition, as I think I mention in the book, my mentors were all men, because there weren't any women who could help me get ahead. They weren't in a position to do so. I thought, "Why haven't I thought of the *New York Times?* I know it deeply. I have hundreds, literally, hundreds of friends there. I've worked in the city room, in the women's department." But at the time of the actual settlement of the suit, I was abroad and foreign correspondents were exempted, by contract, from belonging to the Newspaper Guild. But I did organize the women's news department, and thirty of thirty-three members of the department joined the union. I also was on the negotiating committee of the union with the management, so I had a quite broad knowledge of the issues on all levels.

But when I began my interviews in 1989, I came up to New York dozens and dozens of times to the newspaper. I had retired, and so guys that I knew, my friends on the staff, all were asking how was retirement, and I would say, "It's fine, I'm really enjoying myself. There is life after the *New York Times.*" They said, "What are you doing?" And I said, "I'm writing a book." And they asked, "So what's it about?" And I would say, "It's about the women at the *Times.*" And this look would come over their faces—"Oooooh!" They all knew that I was a feminist. I had been so active in various ways at the newspaper.

DG: And those looks probably masked horror.

NR: They all knew the book would have to do with how things had gone not altogether right with women at the *New York Times.* However, I got total cooperation not only from everybody on the editorial and business sides, but also from the management. Punch Sulzberger later said—this was years later—

after everything had been settled, things were getting better for women; you know, their salaries were better; gradually, under the pushing of young Arthur, everything was getting better for women. There were women on the sports pages, for example. Things were better on the business side, too. Before, there was the "Gestapo kindergarten," where women were ghettoized in the classified ads department, taking ads, but men would very quickly move outside that area and be on commission, as well as salary, to go out into the world, and the women were never allowed to do that. Even my publisher, Punch Sulzberger, measured the length of the boardroom conference table for me. It was twenty-five feet long—two feet, six inches longer than the table in the White House cabinet room. Punch told me that if it hadn't been for the suit, the *Times* would have "never moved off the dime." That was an exact quote from Punch.

DG: Did the new women hires and later generations understand the role of the caucus?

NR: A lot of younger women at the *Times* had indicated to me that they knew what this book did, and the pressure from the suit. Another one of the things that made it so important that I write this book was the sort of, well, of silence that existed in New York City, because there was a newspaper strike going on at the time of the settlement. We were locked out and it was a long strike. Three months, the second-longest newspaper blackout that we had had since 1963. It was like a tree falling in the forest. Who was there to hear it? So it was important that this be put on the record. Let me tell you one more thing: when I told Joan Cook, one of the movers and shakers of the Women's Caucus, that I was gonna do this, she said, "All this will be written in sand," and I said, "No, it won't, because there will be this book." That was the exchange with her. Abe Rosenthal's comment was sometime later. He was at the next table in a restaurant, near a very close friend of mine, and he never talked to me about it, ever. But he went over to our mutual friend, and said, "What did you think of Nan's book?" She said she liked it, and Abe said, "How could she do this to me after all I've done for her?" That was his reaction. The rest of the people, really, the employees, were very positive, men and women.

DG: I guess I'm not surprised at Abe, because you say in your book that when he gave his deposition in the suit, you could see that he took it quite personally.

NR: Absolutely. He was enraged that somebody dared, somebody he had helped like this; he was my rabbi, my protector. And he suggested that I go to Paris in 1972, several months after the first caucus-management meeting.

DG: And that's why I think it took courage on your part to do it. Looking back, it may not seem that to you.

NR: It doesn't. I knew full well that it could be the end of a bright career. What can I say? My reaction was that I would have liked to punch Abe in the jaw. I was really angry with him. One of the heartbreaking things for me was that Abe was a genuine friend not only to my husband, but also, in a lesser sense, to me. He is the perfect personal example of absolute power corrupting absolutely, because he was at the top of the heap. He hurt so many people, and hurt their careers. And I knew the friendship was over. That was difficult for me, to know it was over, and that he was using the *Times* to punish his enemies and reward his friends outside the newspaper. He was not straight about it. He kept repeating that he kept the newspaper straight. Well, quite the contrary.

DG: What about Eileen Shanahan?

NR: I miss her to this day. She was such a wonderful person. Eileen's career was blighted at the *Times* by her outspoken explanation of the women's case and the fact that the *Times,* which prides itself in its editorials about being so liberal, was not fair—and not just to the women. Eileen did not speak out while she was still at the *Times,* but it [the suit] caused her to resign. She knew she'd never get anywhere. So the two people most affected were Betsy Wade, who was the leader of the troika and was the spokesperson, and Eileen—and Eileen quit because of that. And she loved the *Times,* and she was a marvelous, brilliant reporter as well as a wonderful friend. She was my closest friend in the Washington bureau. I came there right after she did, and I really miss her every day. I sort of want to pick up the phone and call her and tell her something. Her career was definitely affected by her activity and her public statements about the *New York Times* and women.

DG: There was only one woman of color as part of the suit. Tell me about her.

NR: The one woman of color was Andrea Skinner—she was terrific. She told me that she felt more discriminated against as a woman than as a black. It's in the book. I was interested by that. Of course, she was discriminated against in both ways, but that was her perception. I was very admiring of her and of the other plaintiffs, the seven signatories.

DG: What happened with the minority suit?

NR: It was settled much more to their advantage than to ours. Huge settlement. It wasn't that long after the women's suit.

DG: In our decades-old struggle for equality in the media industry, women and minorities have commonalities and differences. While each group may have won occasional advantages, we shouldn't miss the point of our common goal.

5

Learning about Discrimination

PEGGY SIMPSON

I began covering the women's political movement in late 1971 with a handful of other reporters, including Kay Mills, then of Newhouse News Service, and Eileen Shanahan, then of the *New York Times*. We educated ourselves as we told readers about actions aimed at expanding "women's place." My stories got wide use, which meant editors wanted more. The Associated Press bosses didn't always see it that way. In the mid-1970s I got contributions from AP state bureaus to write a roundup on the big increase in women seeking national office. A top male political editor spiked the story, however, with the caustic jibe of "Sell it to *Ms.*"

In 1975 I went to Mexico City to spearhead coverage of the first UN women's conference and was appalled to find that AP local stringers who were Mexican nationals had grilled arriving VIP dignitaries about whether they were feminists. My opening-day story was changed to lead with a description of how the Russian cosmonaut was dressed instead of a focus on the broadening roles for women in society by the president of Mexico. And the foreign editor in New York ordered me to leave the UN meeting to find Burt Reynolds at a movie-promotion gig across town and ask him about these feminists who might not lean on men as women had done in the past. (His costar, Liza Minnelli, was offended by the foreign editor's request of me; Reynolds said something about liking women who were independent.)

The final insult came from a photo. Near the end of the two-week conference, the New York foreign editor ordered up a story to go with a dramatic photo they had sent around the world, showing eight women struggling over a microphone. Trouble was, there was no story. As three thousand delegates quietly left a plenary session, these eight women had argued about who got to speak next. The photo, captioned by the AP as something akin to "Women

Fight at UN Conference," was the most widely used shot of the meeting. And of course it reinforced the stereotype that women couldn't get together without a catfight. That was sobering. So were congressional hearings I covered about gender inequities in salaries, credit, sports, pensions, and medical coverage. It was a time of enormous energy among the fledgling feminists, both Republicans and Democrats, nationally and at the grass roots.

In 1973 I found out from a Wire Service Guild newspaper about a discrimination complaint against the AP. UN reporter Shirley Christian wanted to be a foreign correspondent; the AP told her she had to know languages, so she learned several but still got nowhere. AP State Department correspondent Kenneth Freed, who headed the AP Wire Service Guild, suspected that something else was the problem and got a discrimination lawyer for Christian. She filed a complaint with the Equal Employment Opportunity Commission in 1973, and after the EEOC found "probable cause" of discrimination, the guild filed what became a class-action lawsuit against the AP in federal court, representing all women and minority employees. I was one of six new AP women who joined Christian as named plaintiffs. The EEOC also filed suit.

In 1983 the guild won a two-million-dollar out-of-court settlement from the AP, with half of the money going in back pay to every women employed since 1973, other money going to every black, and nearly five hundred thousand dollars earmarked for an affirmative action plan. It ranks as a major door-opening class-action media lawsuit, along with those against the *New York Times,* NBC, *Reader's Digest,* and *Newsweek.*

When the lawsuit was filed, I was on a Nieman Fellowship at Harvard. I joined the suit partly because of specific discrimination problems—those limitations enunciated in Dallas—but also because my AP reporting had shown that limitations on women's "place" were endemic across society. I felt strongly that this was unfair and needed to be fixed.

It is obvious that women have since moved ahead at the AP and many other news organizations, but much more progress is needed. The challenge ahead is to find ways to keep the pressure on for hiring and promotion both of blacks and of women, when unions have been defanged, when the EEOC is a shadow of its former self—and when the media world itself is in turmoil. It's not clear how this will be accomplished. Virtually no one can tolerate the idea of regressing to any semblance of the news media's sex and race segregation of the past. But preserving past gains and making more, when sea changes are under way in the news media, will take new visions and new organizing techniques.

6

Moving from Women's Pages
to the Editor's Office

SANDRA MIMS ROWE

To write about women and leadership and journalism I have to cast back—way back. I was in the sheltering environment of a college campus during the late 1960s, the last half of the assassination decade. I emerged from the college cocoon and made it through the interview for an editorial assistant's position at the afternoon newspaper in Norfolk by admitting that my job as a radio news reporter was to rewrite newspaper stories for the drive-time newscast. I neglected to mention I couldn't touch-type, even though the job was mostly typing the television listings. (In high school I was under the misapprehension that girls who wanted to be secretaries took typing, and I wanted to avoid that pigeonhole—evidently even at the cost of learning a skill I could actually use.) Before long the paper needed a reporter in the family living department. (Job qualifications: Female. Young. Willing to work on the cheap.) Trained to pitch in, I raised my hand.

During the early 1970s women's departments crawled inch by inch out of the journalistic ghetto, first dressed up as "family living," then as lifestyle sections including entertainment and a wider range of "nonnews" news. Those that were any good demonstrated that the world of family, love, work, health, schools, women's rights, and local arts went as much to the heart of what mattered in a community as the average city council meeting—or more so. Whatever the section name, "first women" stories were a staple of the era: first woman telephone lineman, first woman attorney general, first woman on death row. As a genre it devolved from mildly interesting to tiresome over the span of a couple of years, though it was clearly an improvement over the previous feature section staple, "woman behind the man."

In 1980, when I was named managing editor of the one-hundred-thousand-circulation *Norfolk Ledger-Star* (since absorbed into the *Virginian-Pilot*), a

Richmond Times-Dispatch reporter called to interview me for a profile on "the first woman editor of a large paper in Virginia." I politely declined to participate, explaining that having railed against the "first woman" genre in my own newsroom, I could hardly take the stage in that approach. Later that day I got another call from the reporter. His editor had sent him back, insisting, "no girl in Norfolk would tell him what was a story and what wasn't."

Looking back, I'm amazed we reacted to the absurdities of the time with more acceptance—even amusement—than anger. Today, enough women occupy high-visibility leadership roles that their gender isn't pointed out as if it were part of their name every time they are introduced. Just being the "editor" or "publisher," rather than "first woman editor," feels like success after so many decades. Women are CEOs of two large newspaper companies: Janet Robinson of the New York Times Company and Mary Junck of Lee Enterprises. Roughly 18 percent of executive-level jobs as CEO's, publishers, or presidents at daily newspapers are held by women.[1]

In the early 1980s there were about a half dozen of us representing our papers at American Society of News Editors' meetings. At my first such convention, we spontaneously gathered in the bar after a day of meetings to get to know one another and commiserate. That was the very first time I had related to other women as editors, and twenty-five years later it is the only thing I remember, the only thing important enough to leave a mark from the convention. That budding network of support and friendship was crucial to my path, although I didn't necessarily realize my hunger for it at the time.

Now you could fill a ballroom (not a large ballroom, but a ballroom nonetheless) with women managing editors, editors, and publishers of newspapers. Gender horror stories are mostly relics as attitudes have moved closer to reality. It's impossible not to celebrate the opening of opportunity in just one generation of women. As a case in point, when I went to college in 1966, I could not apply to the University of Virginia, the prestigious publicly funded university in my home state, because it did not admit women in the undergraduate school, a fact I accepted then but that horrifies me now. Less than fifteen years later, I was the editor of the largest newspaper in the state, an indication both of quickly changing attitudes and of a company that was ahead of many others in wanting to increase and enrich its talent pool. And celebrate progress, I do. But scratch below the surface and the progress is not the natural arc you might expect to see for half the population.

You can look to the statistics for encouragement, but don't expect clarity. The by-the-numbers status of women in journalism is more likely to leave you with statistical whiplash than enlightened conclusions. Women have been the majority of college journalism majors since 1977. But although more women are graduating from journalism school, fewer of them actually end up in newsrooms. Instead they are now more likely than ever to head in the direction of advertising or public relations. Despite the fact that women have been hired in increasingly greater numbers over the last five years, women still have not achieved equal gender representation in the newsroom. Women still make up about one-third of all full-time journalists, a percentage unchanged since 1982.[2] Another indication of the uneven progress and how it narrows at the top: 40 percent of managing editors are women, but only about one-fifth of the top editors in newsrooms are women.[3]

Ambiguity and contradictions lace the essential truth of the progress of women in journalism for the last thirty-five years. Transformational opportunity for women is a defining social change of the last fifty years, but many of the same questions and issues I faced twenty-five years ago continue to derail career advancement. Women with children still feel great pressure to accommodate and juggle (I long ago stopped calling it balance) home and family demands. Consequently, flexibility or lack thereof in a particular boss or workplace or day-care arrangement often can be more career-defining in crucial years than any other factor. That, along with whether there is positive encouragement in the workplace and the presence of successful role models, markedly affects the number of women who stay in the pipeline for promotion.

Twenty-five years ago, when asked about the dearth of women in executive ranks, I routinely answered and naively believed that because women were entering the pipeline in increasing numbers every year, roughly the same number would emerge as freshly minted, fully qualified top editors. It didn't work that way, and during the 1980s progress was marginal. Women, some discouraged, were leaving—and still are—in greater numbers than men. Even that bad news may indicate a freedom that has not always existed. Women have much more choice of what will be rewarding and challenging at different times in their lives, of what compromises are acceptable to them. And they have the confidence to make those choices, with the help of some pioneers who led the way.

The happy result of women in decision-making positions has been the diversification of news content. *USA Today* was the first of large newsrooms in which women were well represented at the news meetings. Even at its beginnings in 1982, about half the editors were women, according to Julia Wallace, now editor of the *Atlanta Journal-Constitution,* who went to *USA Today* as a reporter right after the launch and left ten years later as one of the top editors. In her ten years with *USA Today* as a reporter and an editor, Julia always had a female boss. Most visible among women at *USA Today* was the late (and great) Nancy Woodhull, news editor. Julia recalls newsroom lore of a news meeting when some editors wanted to lead the paper with the assassination of the president-elect of Lebanon. But Nancy argued for leading with the death of Grace Kelly—and won.

From the beginning, *USA Today* editors had a broad definition of page-one news that included developments or trends in health, travel, and entertainment. Of course, also consider how many years *USA Today* wasn't taken seriously by journalists because of the story-as-brief format and the proliferation of topics on life at home, at work, and at play (those are the things most of us actually do with our lives, aren't they?).

I used to deny any gender differences in news judgment, insisting news was and would always be gender-neutral. I assume now that my dismissal of a female perspective as a value in news judgment was unconsciously defensive. Already I was sensitive to the assumed question of whether women were serious enough to handle the big-deal news. Absurd when you consider just how formulaic many front pages of the day were. There were days I thought a trained monkey could have picked the top six stories. But in the 1970s, to acknowledge a gender component would have added weight to the mostly unspoken but ever-present gravitas question. Without knowing it, I was modeling myself as one of the guys, conforming to the only picture of "editor" I knew, most decidedly not wanting to be viewed as leaning toward "soft" news.

The influence of women and women's interests on the front pages of many papers, including my own, became more visible in the 1980s. This was reinforced in subjects as wide ranging as the celebrity marriage of Prince Charles and Lady Diana Spencer in 1981 and the constitutionally significant Supreme Court confirmation hearings for Clarence Thomas. For the wedding I suggested a morning special single-copy edition after the 5:00 A.M. (EST) event. The idea was greeted with eye-rolling derision on the all-male news desk. I went ahead with it, with shaky confidence that it would have huge appeal for thousands of women, especially since we could get it off the presses just a couple of hours after the wedding took place. The press run sold out.

More substantively, a decade later, on the first day of Anita Hill's testimony before the twelve-member all-male, all-white Senate Judiciary Committee in Clarence Thomas's confirmation hearing, editors grappled with what she had said. The question of whether she would derail the nomination dominated news, spotlighting the politics and the process much more than the underlying implications of her transforming testimony and the discomfort generated as a young black woman was questioned intently and publicly by the all-male, all-white power structure.

That first day of testimony I clamored to get women's voices loud and clear in the initial reaction story. And as we interviewed women and the testimony ground on for three days, their own stories came spilling out. Women of any age who had been in a workplace knew that the behavior patterns Anita Hill cited—and worse—were not unusual. Each person's individual reaction quickly dominated cocktail and dinner table conversations. Arguments between the sexes ensued. Men I knew thought she was making a big deal out of not much. A political agenda was assumed, and it probably existed to a certain extent, but the sociological implications of her testimony were profound, whatever your politics. Where others in the newsroom saw a political story, I hungered for the cultural gender story. Both were "real" news.

Anita Hill's testimony had a galvanizing effect, and the definition of appropriate workplace conversation and behavior changed. In the five years following the hearings, sexual harassment cases more than doubled, from 6,127 in 1991 to 15,342 in 1996, and awards to victims under federal laws nearly quadrupled, from $7.7 million to $27.8 million, according to records from the Equal Employment Opportunity Commission.

Amanda Bennett, former editor of the *Philadelphia Inquirer*, sees two gender-related forces at work in news judgment. Editors naturally bring their life experiences to story ideas and news judgments. Certainly, every reporter has experienced "news" as defined by what happens in an editor's life. So when private-preschool admission competition consumes high-income Manhattan or sports injuries plague middle-aged editors, they become cultural phenomena worthy of the front page. It's no different in Duluth or the District of Columbia. We all bring our life experiences, including our gender-based lens, to our view of the relative importance or interest of certain news.

Also, the way women look at a story or construct it, the approach they hook into, may be different. Is the linear aspect of what happened or the subjective experience of it of greatest interest? Bennett thinks having more women in newsrooms has encouraged a view that more easily disengages from the linear, basic facts of what happened and tilts toward experiential questions of how life is lived in relation to the event or issue. The "why" and "how" tap a richer vein for making connections and for intersecting ideas than the "what." Amanda believes women reporters and editors are more naturally skilled, at least at seeing those opportunities. "Right now we have enough of a critical mass we can assert it as a question of journalism, not as a question of gender journalism," she said. Whether causal or coincidental, the assertion of the value of nonlinear journalism didn't happen as often before women gained critical mass in newsrooms.

Today, smart journalism reveals and explains the intersections between the world of power, influence and politics, and real life. The most interesting stories are rarely about a single thing and rarely report simply what happened today. They reveal choices, conflicts, and consequences—life as it is lived, authentic and endlessly interesting. This journalism need not be lifestyle-heavy or "soft." What distinguishes the best from the rest is the quality and the range of the enterprise. Does the paper go get news or wait until it comes to it? Does it investigate and explain? Do the stories provide insight into matters of consequence in our lives? Do they reveal how power and influence play out in local institutions and decisions? Do they introduce you to people you don't know and the culture and diversity of the community in a way that makes you smarter about attitudes, social trends, and values?

Women also bring gender-based skills—and the accompanying stereotyping—to their leadership roles. Jill Geisler, who heads the leadership faculty at the Poynter Institute for Media Studies, a school for journalists in St. Petersburg, Florida, used to cringe when people asked her "how women lead." She wasn't convinced there were differences between men and women and didn't want to further stereotypes. But through years of study and experience teaching leaders, she concluded that women have been acculturated to become more collaborative, to cope, to see things from the other's point of view, traits now more often encouraged in the workplace than when command and control was the preferred leadership style in organizations. Having traditionally been the person in the home who brings people together evidently has its rewards.

Sally Sterling, a consultant for Spencer Stuart, a global executive search firm, who has interviewed hundreds of executive candidates, sees the same pattern and stereotype in play as she recruits CEOs for nonprofits and foundations. In her world it is now the norm that women are considered among the top candidates for CEO positions. She notes, though, that boards will often push harder for a woman "if the organization is in trouble and needs healing." It's a double-edged sword. Although a 2005 survey of senior executives of both sexes found that women were perceived as stronger in the "caretaking" skills of nurturing and supporting, women were also perceived as weaker in "take charge" skills like influencing superiors and delegating responsibility.[4]

One of my favorite journalism moments didn't happen in the newsroom. It was in my kitchen. In 2003, after a board meeting of the ASNE in Portland, Amanda Bennett, Janet Weaver, and I returned to my house, where we were all staying. In bathrobes and fuzzy slippers we gathered around the kitchen island, wine glasses in hand, executive pretext shed at the door. We automatically and immediately shared our current challenges and freely offered one another advice and support. There was no pretense of perfection, no war stories, no posturing. Just women who care about one another and about journalism connecting personally and professionally.

That night in my kitchen, I realized the moment was a first. I had hired Janet (twice) when I was editor in Norfolk and Amanda after I moved to Portland. Both were now editors of newspapers. Julia Wallace, whom I had also worked with and promoted in Norfolk, was staying in a hotel a few miles away with her family. I thought about the late Kay Fanning, Katharine Graham, Janet Chusmir, and other leaders I had admired throughout my career. They no doubt had inspired and encouraged other women, but none was able to experience the intersection of shared professional history and therefore kinship with other women who made it to the top of their organizations. I felt like an aging mother hen in my fuzzy slippers and bathrobe, cherishing the moment and hoping those who follow have the reward of abiding friendship with women they have mentored and with whom they are able to share the joys and challenges of directing newsrooms. For me, the two generations of women editors in the kitchen that night represented critical mass—for the first time in my career.

In most of my thirty-five years in the business, Kay Graham's presence and achievement dominated the stage for me. For one thing, when others were trying to make a big deal out of first woman editor in Virginia, I was keenly aware of being less than two hundred miles from the District of Columbia, where Katharine Graham was publisher of the *Washington Post.* I didn't know at the time the metamorphosis she was undergoing regarding her views on women's abilities and roles.

She was, as we all are, a reflection of her time and her experience. Just a year before I started my career in 1969, six years after her husband's death catapulted her into leadership at the *Post,* Katharine Graham told a *Women's Wear Daily* interviewer that she couldn't "see a woman as managing editor of a newspaper." A friend and employee walked into her office the day the interview appeared and asked if she really believed what she had said. If so, the friend said, she was quitting. That moment helped change Graham's perspective. But she never quite shed the notion that since, in her words, the only reason she had her job "was the good luck of her birth and the bad luck" of her husband's death, somehow she was different from the rest of us who were "first" in our own far less significant or visible ways.[5] It's a feeling of unworthiness I've heard often from women colleagues, but rarely, if ever, from men. Others earn their place. Many of us in the previous generation of female leaders believed we were somehow leading only through good luck.

In interviews with hundreds of talented executives for top leadership positions, Sally Sterling notices several enduring gender differences that may have the effect of limiting opportunity. More women stay with a company out of loyalty than men. They will cite what the company has done for them and what they "owe" the company, she said, rather than wonder what the company may owe them. Also, women, unbidden, often bring up in a background interview with Sally what they haven't done, what they think may be a weakness or perceived hole in their qualifications. Men being considered for the same positions never do that, Sterling says. They assume they are the complete package—whether or not that is in fact true.

Even after Katharine Graham retired as the most successful publisher in America and wrote her Pulitzer Prize–winning memoir, she remained self-deprecating with regard to her career and achievements. I wrote her a note of congratulations after the Pulitzer, an honor, she said, that had never occurred to her even as a *possibility* (emphasis hers). She concluded her generous note back to me with, "Congratulations on working your way up. I got there via a very different route."

One of the things she unknowingly helped me realize is that all of us who were "first women" were accidents of history and timing to a greater or lesser extent. But the point—in Katharine Graham's history as well as in each of our own—is our measure of competence, character, and courage. She had a more than ample supply of all three. Katharine Graham's career also reminds me that the credibility problems that plague journalism are in large part questions of journalistic character. Character is not theoretical, philosophical, or remote from our daily work. It also is not gender-based. Journalistic character cannot be measured merely in rating points or newspapers sold. It is felt more than measured or charted and ties to the whole of our journalism and leadership decisions, not just to the quality of the craft. Journalistic character is how we make decisions and choose stories, how we perceive our readers' needs and interests, what we value and how we show it.

Leaders for the future must be far more flexible and skilled at innovating and adapting and yet still honor traditional news values. They must be able to deal with ambiguity in a highly skilled fashion and in an ever-changing environment. It's a trait that women executives must work harder to develop, according to executive recruiter Sterling.

Millions of words have been written about leadership, thousands of courses taught, and extensive research has enriched our knowledge of the principles and most effective practices of leadership. But the essentials remain: integrity, the ability to see beyond yourself and build a vision others want to achieve, and having something worthwhile to offer, to teach. That's really all there is and all there ever will be. The steady hand of clear leadership has never been more desperately needed because of uncertainty of times and changing of the fundamental economic underpinnings of our business.

Media are changing at warp speed in the twenty-first century. It is fashionable to say that news is a commodity, as disposable and ubiquitous as a plastic razor or a throwaway camera. But some things don't change. More than two centuries ago, the framers of the U.S. Constitution gave the press unique protections with the First Amendment. That privilege brings with it the responsibility to be the eyes and ears of the public on issues large and small that affect the lives of the people in our communities. That is the central purpose of journalism that we must preserve and the debt we owe to those who came before us.

At a time when editors across the country despair from the unrelenting emphasis on economic viability rather than journalism, when new competitors clamor for advertising and ever-precious public attention, when challenges multiply and public trust erodes, clear leadership is needed more than ever. Journalism can't afford to ignore or fail to develop what should be half the talent pool of future leaders. There is too much at stake as newspaper companies fight to remain the most essential community information resource. We need to develop the next generation of editors who clearly articulate and relentlessly apply the highest ethical and professional standards, who honor their hopes and ideals in everything they do, everything they publish. They are out there— pushing against what, despite all the progress, still looks very much to some like a glass ceiling.

Notes

1. Mary Arnold and Mary Nesbitt, "Women in Media, 2006: Finding a Leader in You," Media Management Center, Northwestern University, 2006, 26–27. Available at http://www.mediamanagementcenter.org/publications/data/wim2006.pdf (accessed January 21, 2009).

2. David Weaver, et al., *The American Journalist in the Twenty-First Century: U.S. News People at the Dawn of a New Millennium* (Mawhah, N.J.: Erlbaum, 2007).

3. Mary Arnold and Marlene L. Hendrickson, "Women in Newspapers, 2003: Challenging the Status Quo," ed. Cynthia C. Linton, Media Management Center, Northwestern University, 2003, 15. Available at http://www.mediamanagementcenter.org/publications/data/win2003.pdf (accessed January 21, 2009).

4. Jeanine Prime, "Women 'Take Care,' Men 'Take Charge': Stereotyping of U.S. Business Leaders Exposed," Catalyst, 2005. Available at http://www.rochester.edu/sba/100years/PDFs/Women%20Take%20Care%20Men%20Take%20Charge.pdf (accessed January 21, 2009).

5. Katharine Graham, *Personal History* (New York: Knopf, 1997), 417.

PART 2

How Women Are Shaping
Newsrooms and Companies

7

Facing Unexpected Challenges

JULIA WALLACE

There was a time when the editor of the newspaper could be content with the status quo. Newspapers had to please so many people, and when so much as a bridge column changed, someone complained. So the safest strategy was to keep doing what had been done and keep as many readers as possible happy.

Those days are over.

Technology has brought unprecedented change and will continue to do so. In the old days, if people wanted information with depth, they needed a newspaper. Now they can find depth even on their cell phones. The competition is intense and reader demands are increasing on everything from speed to clarity to fairness.

Editors today also face challenges in finding common themes and interests in increasingly diverse metropolitan areas. In Atlanta, a metro area that spans twenty-eight counties, this is particularly difficult. Residents find their communities defined by geography, race, politics, or special interests. The 4.2 million people in metro Atlanta include a large suburban black middle class in DeKalb County, conservative Republicans in Cobb County, the polyglot international Atlanta along Buford Highway, a gay mecca in Midtown. The list goes on. And it's not just about demographics. In a post-9/11 world, a willingness by some to sacrifice basic rights in the name of security reminds us that the First Amendment and free speech in our society can no longer be taken for granted.

As the first woman editor of the *Atlanta Journal-Constitution*, it would have been nice to focus just on the journalism—making our reporting, writing, photography, and design the best in the country. But these days that is just the beginning of the job. A woman editor of another paper one day joked, "How come when the guys were in charge, they could just put out a good newspaper? Now that we're in these jobs, we're supposed to save the newspaper." We both laughed, but in fact these are critical times for newspapers and journalism and what they mean to our democracy.

That challenge was hard to fathom when I first landed in Atlanta in 1977 as an intern for the *Atlanta Journal.* I never imagined then that a woman would be editor of such a large newspaper—that it would be me was even more far-fetched. But does it matter that the *Atlanta Journal-Constitution* has a woman editor? I'm not sure. I do know that editors these days need to be willing to take chances, to challenge convention. They must be persistent and can have no fear. They need to know how to listen to their readers as well as their staff. Here are some of the challenges and how we, with a diverse group of strong leaders—women and men—have confronted them.

Challenge of Community

Atlanta is a complicated place where people identify with groups and eagerly take their frustrations out on the mainstream media. Spin the morning-drive radio dial and get an earful of conservative talk, rap, country, salsa. When we wrote a series of tough stories about a local black politician, we had protesters outside our building complaining about our coverage. When we wrote a series of tough stories about a white conservative running for lieutenant governor, we were accused of pushing a liberal agenda. Finding the connective tissue can be difficult.

Challenge of Changing Technology

Some people lament the impending death of the newspaper. I just think of the record album. As a kid, I loved my album collection—I even liked the way the needle slid or scratched its way around the black disc. But it wasn't really about the black vinyl; it was about the music. Since the demise of albums, I've had eight-tracks, cassettes, CDs, and an iPod. But it's always been and always will be about the music.

The digital age is changing our world, just as the printing press did hundreds of years ago. Right now we sit in both worlds—trying to create the best print newspaper we can every day and also trying to create the best online site every minute. It's difficult, it's unpredictable, but it's exhilarating. In Atlanta we understood the power of changing technology early, and much of the newsroom has embraced it. At this point the exact path and velocity of change are unclear, but it is clear that reading habits are changing. My two daughters knew how to click and point before they knew their ABCs. When they do a school project, they spend hours at the computer. Periodical digest? They never heard of it.

If you think about what life will be like twenty years from now, it's hard to imagine newspapers in their current form. Technology is quickly changing almost every aspect of human interaction. Need a date? Go online. Want some good running music? Download it. Need new underwear or an airline ticket? Click and buy. Get in your car and crave the nearest Chinese restaurant? The GPS system will find it and give you directions. To think that newspapers will be immune to this tidal wave of change is myopic and arrogant.

In the mid-1970s one of my journalism classes had a guest speaker who talked about the death of American newspapers as we know them. This was before personal computers. He envisioned printers in every home that would print personalized newspapers for every subscriber. Back then it made sense as a much more efficient and intelligent way to deliver information, but technology wasn't ready.

In 1999 Andy Grove, then head of the computer behemoth Intel, spoke at the annual convention of the American Society of Newspaper Editors. Grove, a refugee who came here from Europe and through his brilliance built Intel, was on a giant screen in an interactive conversation. The screen was primitive, distorting his head, giving him a Wizard of Oz aura. He talked about Intel, but he also talked about his frustration with American newspapers. He was increasingly going online for information. He raised questions about quality and our relationship with consumers. And then he said this:

> You're where Intel was three years before the roof fell in on us. You're heading toward a strategic inflection point, and three years from now, maybe, it's going to be obvious. Things like newsprint giving you a little bit of a lift, a little bit of a hand, are going to run their course. You're going to be in a profit squeeze, and it's going to be a very, very difficult time, more difficult to adjust later. All of this sets up what to do. You have to ask what your microprocessor is in the Intel analogy. What is it that you can do for me as a reader that the Web pages or online coverage can't do? I indicated what my preference is. I'm looking for depth. I'm looking for interpretation, and please don't give me length instead of depth. . . .
>
> From a publisher's standpoint, there's going to be huge push and pull. This requires more money at a time when margins are going to be under attack. Interpretation requires time and requires research and requires feet on the street, people on the phones calling, studying, going to the library, probably at a time when you're financially being pulled in the other direction. And my history of the technology industry is you cannot save yourself out of a strategic inflection point. You can save yourself deeper into the morass that you're heading to, but you can only invest your way out of it, and I really wonder how many people who are in charge of the business processes of journalism understand that.[1]

Many at the time scoffed at Grove's comments. Newspapers, with the dot-com and employment boom, were seeing record profits. This is a business model about to unravel? Hard to imagine! Some, however, including the *Atlanta Journal-Constitution*, understood it was a changing landscape. We believed early that online was not another business—but our business. We needed to jump in, do it, and learn as much as we could. More than 25 percent of employees in our newsroom now work full time on ajc.com and other digital products, and that number continues to grow. We understand that some people read us in print only, some online only, and some bounce between the two.

As we've discussed what drives online usage, we have focused on a few key areas. They are

- *Urgency:* It is exhilarating to be back in the breaking news business. We can be faster than any other media in providing news. When a rape suspect broke away from a sheriff's deputy at an Atlanta courthouse and went on a rampage that led to four deaths, we were online with the news in minutes. Throughout the day, we were updating, asking readers what they saw, then confirming it and letting other readers know what we learned. Our readers now know they can count on ajc.com for breaking news and come to us as soon as news breaks. If we don't post a story online, they send us a message and ask why not.
- *Utility:* Early on, the Internet established itself as a place to find information. Need a restaurant recommendation, a job, a movie listing? These are all services long performed by newspapers that can be done efficiently on the Internet.
- *Visual energy:* As we monitor page views, it is clear that the Internet is as much about photos as words. Viewers click through one photo gallery after another. Some are serious, such as our photo galleries showing Georgia soldiers in Iraq. Some are less so—dress up your pet for Halloween and send us your photos. As broadband usage increases, the increase in video and interactive graphics has spiraled.
- *Interactivity:* One of the great opportunities for us is that the Web is a two-way street. We can talk to readers. We shouldn't fear this; we should embrace it.

But technology is still evolving. While these principles are good for the Internet, they may change as the ability to receive information on mobile devices expands. We must constantly pay attention to the changing technology. People will continue to want and need quality news and information. How they receive it may change. How they interact with it may change. What they expect from it may change. But if we remember that we are the music, we will persevere.

Challenge of Credibility and What That Means to Democracy

Many of us entered this business because we are committed to truth, so it hurts when our readers don't believe us. How did it come to this? I wish I could say it wasn't our fault, but we share much responsibility. Newspapers became arrogant.

We stopped listening to our readers. We know best, we said. We made deals and hobnobbed with the powerful. We didn't diversify our staffs; in race, gender, and political beliefs, newsrooms still do not reflect this country. And when some politicians and talk-show hosts figured out they could gain attention and support by bashing newspapers, we stood by quietly. For a long time it didn't matter much. Readers would complain about the newspaper, but they kept reading it. If you wanted to be informed about the world, you might hate us, but you read us. That is less and less true now. The Internet provides information from a myriad of sources (some of it truth, some not). Another major source of information, talk radio, spends much of its time maligning us with half-truths.

It makes for troubling times, not only for newspapers but also for our democracy. In recent history, a strong and economically sound and independent press has been an important flashlight on our government. Just as our Founding Fathers envisioned, the press has watched over government, pointing out what's working and not working to its citizens. We need to recommit to our role of shedding light in the darkest of places. We need to fight constantly for public access to information. Citizens in a democracy cannot make informed decisions unless they have complete information. Newspapers are one of the few institutions with the resources to dig it out. It's not always easy, but it is essential. When the *Atlanta Journal-Constitution* launched a white-hot campaign for open government in 2005, readers applauded our efforts. Much of the battle was on the obscure rules of economic development and what should be open. But our readers understood that they would be better served by openness.

We also must respond to what our readers want and need—and we have so many ways now to learn what that is. Every minute, we monitor what they're reading on ajc.com. That affects how we play stories online as well as how we play them in print. For example, one day we had a major international story about bombs exploding on the London subway system. Overnight, we also had a tornado rip through Atlanta, virtually destroying Atlanta Motor Speedway. Throughout the day, the tornado story and photos drew more page views than London. In print we still played London as the lead story in the paper but made sure we had a strong above-the-fold refer to the tornado, with extensive coverage in sports. In the past we might have decided the story was thirty hours old and played it less extensively. We also regularly use focus groups and scientific surveys to explore what interests readers. When we recently changed body type fonts, our readership editor ran readability tests with about one hundred people to determine which typeface was easiest to read.

We need to explain ourselves more regularly to readers. In 1999 Ron Martin, then editor of the *Atlanta Journal-Constitution,* created a public editor position, designed to listen to readers and respond to them. The public editor wrote a weekly column for readers and regularly wrote to the staff about what he was hearing. It's a tough—but increasingly important—job. We must listen and then respond to our readers. That communication is critical. Our editorial cartoonist showed the increasing power of connecting with readers. When the U.S. death count in Iraq reached two thousand, Mike Luckovich painstakingly created a cartoon with the names of all the dead formed in the shape of the word *WHY?* Hundreds of readers and online viewers responded on a blog, letting him know what they thought of it—strong views on both sides. At one suburban Atlanta home, a mother cut out the cartoon and posted it on the refrigerator, where it caught the eye of her seventeen-year-old daughter, who supported the war. The daughter sat down, used the same names, and put them in the shape of the word FREEDOM. We ran her cartoon in print and posted it on ajc.com. Again, hundreds responded. Said one reader: "Mike Luckovich's political cartoon 'WHY?' was a poignant statement, but 11th-grader Danielle Ansley's response had an even greater effect on me. She and her mother differed in their views but were able to express them not only at home, but also openly in the *Atlanta Journal-Constitution*. Now, that is FREEDOM."[2]

Challenge of Change in a Newsroom

Newsrooms are paradoxical places. On the one hand, journalists are constantly trying to create a better world, create change. But when they are the ones who need to change, it's not so easy. In recent years newsrooms have gotten a bum rap. Too often it is the leadership that is afraid to change, not the staff. For change to happen, it takes regular and clear communication.

Several years ago, Michele McLellan, director of Tomorrow's Workforce, worked with us to develop a more robust training program. She conducted a series of staff interviews and learned that people felt they were getting mixed messages. The top editors were confused by this. We believed we were in alignment. Michele then asked about a dozen of us to list on a whiteboard our dreams for a better newspaper. We listed about forty items. After duplicates were eliminated, we still had twenty on the board. "Is this what you want?" she asked. We all nodded in agreement. "Well, that's what your staff is hearing, all twenty of these items." We then dug in and talked about what was really important. We agreed on three "pillars" for newsroom goals. They are:

- *Watchdog reporting:* Some of the strongest reader response we receive is to our watchdog reporting. People want and expect aggressive reporting from their local paper. They understand that we are in a unique position to expose wrongs. Whether it's millions wasted in Atlanta public schools or the candidate for sheriff with financial problems, it's compelling to read and can make a difference.

- *Community connections:* One of our reporters has a wonderful line about Atlanta. He says he never had to move, because the place where he lives keeps changing. It is sprawling and complicated. To cover it well, the entire newsroom needs to know it much better. We offer regular bus tours for staffers to learn about specific geographic areas. Community leaders join us for brown-bag lunches to discuss key issues. And we go out into the community, talking about journalism and why it matters.
- *Alternative story forms:* In focus group after focus group, we hear readers complain about long, boring, and repetitive stories. We also receive some of our strongest positive reaction from readers on some of our longest stories. For example, a two-part series on a mail-order bride stalked by the husband who brought her to this country filled five inside pages. Readers loved it. So what makes the difference? Not all stories are told best as a "stick of type." Before saying it's time to write a story, we need to think about the best way to tell it. Is it a grid? Is it a Q-and-A? Is it a photo essay? A graphic? We need much more variety and pacing in newspapers.

We talked about those goals all year. We rewarded good work in these areas in our best-of-quarter awards. We discussed them at news meetings. We pointed to them in kudo notes. Our training sessions were built around these pillars. And we saw real movement—more than eighty watchdog stories in 2005, everything from a weeklong series on the lack of consumer protection in Georgia to the revelation of a gambling trip made by county officials and developers. Alternative story forms appeared in every section, and some brand research showed we made real inroads with suburban readers, who now see us as writing about the entire metro area, not just the city of Atlanta. But the pillars are pliable. In 2006 we added online convergence as a pillar.

The newsroom has responded positively to the changes. Almost ten thousand training hours were logged in the newsroom in 2005. Most staffers are not afraid to change once they understand the goals.

What It Means

So in a book about women in the media, what does all this add up to? Our newsroom is filled with many strong women. Would we be a different newsroom if there were less diversity? Would we think differently about the future if we were all men? Would work take place in a different way? I asked the men. According to Hyde Post, vice president of Internet operations, vision and leadership skills trump gender by a wide margin, but clearly the latter has some impact.

Women in leadership roles introduce a dynamic to the workplace that is different from men. A heavily male-centric workplace can be either a very competitive place or a lazy place (we are born slackers). Men naturally compete with other men. In a workplace led by a woman, well, it's different. Men don't so much compete with women; rather, they want to impress them. Usually more than they want to impress men.

I think the work environment as a whole tends to be more collaborative with a woman in the key leadership role.

Bert Roughton, metro editor, added: "Women tend to focus more on the quality of the work and its importance to people and less on obtaining the kind of personal gratification and vindication you get from exerting the power of the newspaper and gaining personal glory. They are less clannish and less likely to prefer the company of cronies and sycophants. I have found women generally more collaborative and tolerant of opposing views."

A group of women editors gathered for lunch one day to ponder the same question. Clearly there are differences, and those differences continue to evolve. Our lunchtime theory was that the first generation of women in newsrooms had to be tough—fighting every stereotype and barrier along the way. For those of us in the next generation of female leaders, we have more freedom to be ourselves.

I am still inspired by a 1979 *New York Times Magazine* article by Italian journalist Oriana Fallaci. She was interviewing the Ayatollah Khomeini right after he had come to power. They were discussing the required head covering for women in Iran—something Fallaci was asked to don for the interview. "If you do not like Islamic dress, you are not obliged to wear it," Khomeini said, "because Islamic dress is for good and proper young women." Fallaci responded: "That's very kind of you, Imam. And since you said so, I'm going to take off this stupid, medieval rag right now. There. Done."[3] That struck me as an important lesson in the importance of being bold, a lesson that stays close to my heart and my head.

Here in Atlanta that boldness sweeps through much of what we do. We are willing to take risks. And that, along with an eagerness to collaborate and focus on the work, is a quality that will take us into the next era of news and information—wherever that is.

Notes

1. Andrew S. Grove, "A Conversation with Andy Grove," April 13, 1999, American Society of Newspaper Editors annual convention. Available at http://www.asne.org/kiosk/archive/convention/conv99/Grove.htm (accessed January 21, 2009).

2. Nancy Ortner, "Spells Out What Freedom Means," *Atlanta Journal-Constitution,* January 7, 2006.

3. Oriana Fallaci, "An Interview with Khomeini," *New York Times Magazine,* October 7, 1979.

8

Using New Media to Inform

CAROLINE LITTLE

You don't have to be that old, or wise, to see that the world is changing right before our eyes, and more rapidly than at perhaps any other time in history. Even if you are only ten years old, you've already seen things that have dramatically changed our outlook on the world. Technology in many forms—the Web in particular—is changing (and has already changed) the way we live, behave, interact, seek knowledge, find romance, and communicate.

When you live through times of intense change, the changes don't always seem so dramatic. For perspective, I enjoy looking again at classic films like *The Apartment, The Front Page, Man in the Gray Flannel Suit, All the President's Men, Working Girl*—any of the great films from the 1940s through the late '80s that center on office environments. If you go beyond the story and look at the scenery, the environment, the way people work and interact, you find a visual history of the transformation of the modern American workplace. That change demands that media companies continue to innovate, and to attract talented people with vision, creativity, and collaborative skills who embrace change. Gone are the days of a reporter doing only one thing. Understanding multimedia and its role is critical. So is knowing to tell a story most effectively with the best tools possible, whether text, photography, video or audio, mapping or databasing. Two major forces of change can be seen throughout that visual history: the growing empowerment of women, and the technology of processing, gathering, and transmitting information.

Differences on the Web are just as dramatic. Look at the Internet Archive (www.archive.org), also known as the Wayback Machine, and compare the Web sites that were considered cutting edge in 1996 and the best sites today. At work and at home, we send e-mail to people who are down the hall, we send instant messages (IMs) to roommates two feet away in the dorm room, and we watch commercials on screens in elevators and at the checkout counter. New industries are springing up to generate and carry content on cell phones and game platforms. Bloggers in their pajamas have just as much power to set the day's news agenda as a major news organization.

But is all this change a good thing? That depends. I think we can safely assume that the hundreds of people who have been caught in criminal activity through their e-mails and IMs no longer think those technologies are such a good thing. But I am certain that people in law enforcement think differently. I imagine that all the kids who posted pictures of themselves drinking a bottle of tequila on their MySpace pages thought it was a great idea. That is, until the HR department at the new job searched MySpace. So it's not about the technology itself, but how you use it. And this new media landscape is as wildly exhilarating as it is daunting.

What does this all mean for the young people who are entering the business today? By way of example, here's my story: What's a nice girl like you doing being a CEO? Sounds funny. But I do get asked that question sometimes. Let me start with online. I got into the online business in a circuitous way. I have always loved publishing—I worked for the Wesleyan University Press in college and then for Random House and Alfred A. Knopf. But I knew that a career in trade publishing at that time—the early 1980s—involved staying in New York City, and I wanted to make sure I could be financially independent, which was tough on my salary, and also have a portable career, but New York City at the time was *the* place to be. I thought about journalism school, but decided I probably wasn't aggressive enough and went to NYU's law school instead. (Go figure.) I practiced transactional law for nearly six years at Arnold & Porter, a large law firm in Washington, and then moved to *U.S. News & World Report* as deputy general counsel.

At *U.S. News* I was able to understand the business from both the editorial side and the business side. And I found the practice of law much more satisfying because one could apply the law to problems and create solutions more easily. Interesting intellectual property issues abounded, from insurance issues to copyright, with the digitization of content, the Internet coming into being, and the issues arising from that. We felt we were on the frontier of something transformative.

After I was at *U.S. News* for four years, the company moved its business offices to New York. Rather than move, I decided to look for another job and fell into one at Washingtonpost.Newsweek Interactive (WPNI), then called Digital Ink. I was its first general counsel. I was surprised by the scope of the differences between the online world and the print world. It was all so new—software development, understanding how users navigate the Web, trying all sorts of business models. I took on more business responsibilities over time and after three years became chief operating officer and three years later, chief executive officer and publisher.

But back to being a woman executive, a CEO. I have been extraordinarily blessed by supportive bosses and colleagues, both at the Washington Post Company and at Guardian News & Media. Also, media companies generally tend to have more top-level female executives than is the case in law. When I entered the work world after law school, the fashion was for women to dress like men (remember the bow ties on the women's Brooks Brothers oxford shirts?) and the Medical Leave Act had not been passed. The subterranean—or maybe not so subterranean—message was clear: If you want to succeed in corporate America, dress and act like a man. Don't talk about your kids or anything else personal, because it shows a lack of commitment to the job. I can't tell you how many times during interviews with law firms in 1985 a partner (always male) asked me what my husband did. I actually started carrying his resume with me and handing it to the interviewer!

But things have changed. People are recognizing the *value* of women in the workplace. More voices and perspectives—whether they are from the viewpoint of gender, race, sexual orientation, or nationality—add richness to a workplace and make a news organization more reflective of our readers. As for me, I never felt that I had to be someone I am not. I refuse to hide who I am. What kind of message would that send to our daughters? I get frustrated sometimes because the range of acceptable behavior for a woman in corporate America—or any woman in the public eye, for that matter—is narrower than for a man. A man, for example, may be praised for being tough, while the same behavior by a woman will likely bring forth unpleasant adjectives!

I have often been asked how a lawyer becomes a CEO. When I came to WPNI, there was a real need for some structure and processes. We were a young company, running fast. The company needed business expertise and adult supervision, and from the very beginning I bore a lot of responsibility. Over time, I negotiated some large deals. When the CEO of WPNI who hired me departed, I became chief operating officer under the new CEO. Having practiced law in two media companies, I understood how both "church and state" worked—separately and apart—so I understood the parts of the organization. Additionally, because of practicing law in-house, I had acquired the problem-solving skills critical for a COO. It was fun.

When I became CEO and publisher in 2004, my biggest challenge was finding my voice. I didn't have a lot of role models to follow. Sure, there were people I admired greatly, strong women like my mother and my former boss, Gail Lione, at *U.S. News,* the general counsel, who was a mother and a successful career person. I often thought of Katharine Graham, who took over the Washington Post Company after her husband's death, and how she chronicled her fear and aloneness during that time. She had immense courage, to state the obvious.

This raises another question I often am asked: How do you manage? Which can mean one or all of the following: as a mother of two, as a wife, as a woman in corporate America, which continues to be pretty much a man's world. There are so many answers. I love what I do. I am passionate about it. I have been extraordinarily lucky working for the *Post* company, and now the *Guardian,* where I have been supported every step of the way. I come from a line of strong and independent women, who in turn have given me strength, especially my mother. (And by the way, my mother did not work outside the home, although she was a successful investor. She taught us to question authority, stand up for ourselves, and open our hearts to others.) My husband is a true partner and takes genuine pleasure in my accomplishments. I have a lot of energy. And my father, with whom I have shared my work accomplishments and aches and pains, and who has been a steadfast supporter and mentor, has given me great advice over the years. He has always told me to be myself and do what I think is right. The rest, he always told me, will follow. And he has always been right. I like to think that I am setting an example for my daughters and their peers so that they will have more choices.

The basic communication model is transforming, with an incredibly fast change of media and technology, and with the audience members increasing their online readership. That change brings incredible opportunity. Because online communication is more experimental than other media, I believe there will be more opportunities for women to excel. But the skills necessary, for men and women, will remain the same: flexibility and the abilities to take risks, to embrace change, and to work in different media.

For my daughters I see a very different world from the one in which I grew up. Just in the last ten years, the Internet has fundamentally changed the way we live—from the way we shop and educate ourselves to communicate with one another, and of course, get news and information. Washingtonpost.com came into being more than ten years ago, online, because of the prescience of Bob Kaiser, the managing editor of the *Washington Post,* and a handful of others who sensed what the future would bring. It was also a defensive move to give an online presence to the very vibrant print classifieds business, which would be vulnerable to online competitors. In its early incarnation, washingtonpost.com was clumsy, and nearly all of its content was from the print newspaper. Over time, that has changed.

I have always been a firm believer in leveraging the power of the medium. If not, we should simply take text content from the print publication and put it up online. Cheaper, yes, but it would hardly leverage the medium. Online lets us show a story, as opposed to telling it. We can add interactive maps, video interviews, databases, and links to other relevant information. And the reader consumes it when he or she wants it. The Web is very much about utility, particularly in the local market. I want to find out where shoes are on sale in my neighborhood. I want to see what movies are playing. I want to look up the treatment for poison ivy. I want to see what the weather is in the city I will visit tomorrow. I want to see if my plane is on time. So in addition to providing content—movie listings, weather information, and local stories—we need to provide tools that allow our viewers to access essential life information as quickly and effectively as possible.

The *Washington Post* has an internationally recognized news brand, but the print version is local. The Web version, on the other hand, has an audience that is more than 80 percent national and international. Our consistent challenge nationally is battling the perception that the site also has limited, only local, reach. For both audiences on washingtonpost.com, our major focus has been unique differentiation of the Web product in comparison to the print product. For us, the best way to do that was to emphasize the strength of the Web as its own medium with a unique approach to telling stories. That is why we have focused on editorial innovation as strategic initiative. While a lot of newspaper companies take a very cautious approach to offering new things to readers—and we certainly have arguments about when and how to launch new things—we believe that Web users who are accustomed to rapid change all around sometimes appreciate our taking a risk. Unlike readers of the print version of a newspaper, who may generate a firestorm of protest because of a simple font change, Web users expect and in fact demand change when it is appropriate.

Here are some initiatives we launched in just the last couple of years: ad-supported video podcasts; dual local and national home pages; comments on articles; more than thirty staff blogs; Sphere (an Internet search engine for searching blogs), which links to blogs off the site that blog about washingtonpost.com stories; tags on articles; PostGlobal, an international group blog featuring dissident journalists from around the world; embedded links in articles to build depth; and pioneering database journalism, including a comprehensive congressional votes database. And we expect to add a social networking platform that I think may make a lot of people reconsider the role of a newspaper on the Web.

Those innovations are not just for innovation's sake. Each fits within the context of first exploring new ideas that further our ability to engage audiences and earn money from our content. But they are also about embracing the Web function as a two-way conversation. Innovation is also about connection. Fully 30 percent, and maybe even more, of our large online newspapers' traffic now comes from bloggers, Yahoo, Google, or routes other than directly to our home page. We expect that to increase. Thus each page must be considered a home page from a navigational and design sense, and each page is key to getting more eyes to a site and keeping them there longer.

Perhaps the main innovation for both washingtonpost.com and guardian .co.uk is the investment in developing a full-fledged multimedia operation. These sites have made real strides toward developing new methods of video journalism that are specific to the Web. They have been able to give focus to the use of a cinema verité short-form documentary style that has greatly expanded our ability to tell stories in different ways. Many correspondents at the newspapers now have video cameras so that they can choose the best platform for the news they are covering when it is appropriate. At washingtonpost.com in the last several years, the multimedia team won a local Emmy, a national Emmy, an audience award at the SilverDocs Film Festival, and more awards for video journalism from the White House News Photographers Association than any national TV news outlet. It's one more sign that platform-agnostic journalism allows journalists to select the medium or media that best convey the story rather than being limited to one method of storytelling. Video is the hottest thing today, but what video use means to one brand can and should be very different from what it means for another brand.

Web sites serve different purposes for audiences. Most people are probably used to having a favorite newspaper and sticking with that for basic information. But we've found that people come to each site or all of them for separate reasons. On washingtonpost.com they want hard news and analysis. With Slate they want an idea of how they should think about the hard news they've gotten somewhere else. And they come to newsweek.com for an authoritative and decisive perspective. With Slate in particular, its reputation for cutting-edge wit opened an opportunity to approach advertisers who were seeking to define their brand with an edge, generally by breaking new ground in digital media. That has been largely successful. In contrast, newsweek.com's differentiation was a matter of positioning content. The challenge was how to convince both readers and advertisers that a weekly print magazine had relevance within the context of the daily Web environment. And at the *Guardian,* the newspaper and its Web site aim to be the world's leading liberal voice. UK viewers come to the Web site for national and world news, politics, culture, and opinion. And U.S. viewers come to the site for a *Guardian* view of how the world sees the United States, and for a *Guardian* view of the rest of the world. The differing approaches simply point out that the Web is an environment of highly segmented audiences and interests, and no single approach or combination of interactive tools is appropriate for all brands.

Who knows what will be hot tomorrow? And more importantly, what is sustainable? I have no doubt that quality content matters, and that people recognize the difference between reportage by skilled journalists on the ground covering stories, on the one hand, and a blogger writing his or her opinion, on the other. Sure, news outlets don't always get it right, and the blogosphere has provided a welcome layer of quality assurance. Journalism, as Bill Moyers once said, is truth-telling. And it's that truth-telling that is the cornerstone of a democracy.

But the Internet, and Internet news in particular, will continue to play a critical role in showing news stories.

I am asked whether newspapers will disappear and how quickly that might happen. I view the newspaper as a distribution mechanism: At its core is content gathered by independent reporters and editors. The Web, too, is a distribution platform. We enhance that content from the print, give it context, and add tools and multimedia. We, too, sell advertising to clients who are interested in reaching our audience. I don't believe news on paper will go away, but the economics have changed dramatically, with considerably more choices available to consumers. Washingtonpost.com has increased its overall audience tenfold through the Web—the *Post* is distributed locally, by and large—and its Web audience is worldwide. The same is the case with guardian.co.uk.

So that leads me back to where we started. Life is changing rapidly. The method, reach, and scope of how we communicate have changed how we understand the world forever. In my opinion it is a *very* good thing. Why? Because no matter what the method of delivering news and information, the more people who can obtain that information, the better for us all. At least one of the millions of readers who come to our four sites each day will make a critical decision about her life based on the power and reliability of the information that we are providing.

That is an awesome obligation, and new media allow those people to be full participants in carrying that information forward or, indeed, challenging that information. And they can do it from Iowa or China or Turkey. New media are balancing the power that lies in the creation and distribution of information. People's voices are being heard from around the globe, and their spheres of influence are growing wider. That's the true definition of democracy. Whether it remains a good thing is really up to you.

9

Credibility

Are Readers Still Buying Ours?

We say we are in the newspaper business. It's more like the credibility business. Plunk down those quarters on the store counter or artfully push them into a newspaper rack, and you will be informed and entertained. In return for their quarters, we promise readers the whole truth and nothing but the truth. Truth is, a lot of people don't trust us.

A *Wall Street Journal* letter writer in February 2006 mused that traditional media are not dying because technology is rapidly altering news delivery systems but struggling to survive its own credibility issues.[1] Ouch. You can understand his point. We've experienced very public self-inflicted black eyes ranging from journalists plagiarizing others to passing off fiction as fact. Folks are checking up on us as fast as they can type the word *Google*.

The 2005 Annual Report on American Journalism by the Project for Excellence in Journalism (PEJ) aptly put it this way: the "era of trust-me journalism has passed, and the era of show-me journalism has begun."[2] The PEJ reports over the past several years show that since 1985 the public's attitudes toward the press have essentially tanked. In 2007 fewer than one-fifth of readers believed all or most of what they read in newspapers.[3] Americans think less of our professionalism and are more convinced than ever that we try to cover up our mistakes. Their perception of our organizational morality is spiraling downward. The public doesn't think we can even get the facts right.

Back in 1999 the American Society of News Editors released its groundbreaking "Examining Our Credibility" report that clearly called for newsrooms to take a serious look at how we explain ourselves to the public.[4] Readers told us then to be more serious watchdogs of our biases and our fact checking. Could we and not the Internet be responsible for our demise? That's about all the self-pity I can stand. The fact of the matter is that newsrooms are full of very smart people who are figuring out ways to reconnect with their communities and, in doing so, to build trust in their reporting. It's ironic that the buzz today is about reader-contributed content while we still struggle with reader-contributed suggestions or criticism. Thank goodness blogs are around to help us "talk" to readers or listen in to what our readers are talking about among themselves.

Carol Nunnelley got into the credibility business full-time as projects director for the Associated Press Managing Editors (APME) in 2001. Eight years later, with help from others, Nunnelley has turned up the volume on newspaper credibility issues by organizing hundreds of "credibility roundtables" in newsrooms across the country. She has a mile-high perspective on credibility conversations. A former managing editor of the *Birmingham (Ala.) News,* Nunnelley said the primary benefit of a credibility roundtable is bringing journalists face to face with readers. However, the substance of those meetings has changed dramatically over the past five years. "We are asking ourselves more questions about civility and language. The number of newsrooms that have said it is our mission to address credibility is truly incredible," she said.[5]

The *Lincoln Journal Star* in Nebraska is on a credibility mission. Theirs started at the heart of the matter with the simple question: What happens when someone tries to contact the newsroom? Let that one roll around in your head while you think about a typical newsroom. It goes something like this: "Newsroom," the reporter shouts as he or she picks up the receiver while simultaneously gulping coffee, booting up the computer, pushing aside notebooks, mouthing a message to a colleague, checking caller ID, and searching for change in the drawer. "Don't know what you are talking about, I don't cover that. I'll transfer you to sports." And so on.

Kathleen Rutledge, a former editor of the *Lincoln Journal Star,* says the mission began in 2004 when the newspaper, with assistance from APME's credibility project, asked two "very tightly buttoned-down" business students from the graduate program at the University of Nebraska–Lincoln to study how the newsroom interacted with the public—everything from answering telephones to responding to e-mails. As good researchers do, the graduate students charted every transaction and interviewed a lot of people. The diagnosis: When people called the newsroom, they were passed from person to person to person.[6]

Thanks to a core of very committed people, Rutledge said, the newsroom began searching for reasonable ways to change things. First they reorganized the front desk and created a position for "someone well-suited to helping people find their way." Luckily they hired the perfect person who loves to solve problems and talk to people. Beyond that, the newsroom defined what reader responsiveness meant, made expectations clear about promptly opening mail or e-mail and responding to voice mail and messages, and brushed up on telephone manners. They created a newsroom message form that asked for details and got serious about holding reporters and editors accountable for reading the newspaper *before* they arrived at work. It sounds so simple. But we know it's not.

"We often reiterated that all of this has a purpose. We will have a better newspaper if we listen to readers," Rutledge said. Anecdotally, there are signs that journalists get the connection between opening up to the public and building credibility. A young, hard-charging reporter admitted to Rutledge that he had responded to a venomous e-mail with newfound diplomacy, thanks to the emphasis on customer service. Another reporter turned a frustrated caller's question about cable television changes into a breaking news item online and a next-day newspaper story. A perturbed e-mailer who had not heard back from the newsroom expressed her gratitude when Rutledge simply explained a newspaper decision on story coverage. The key message from Lincoln is "we are now in conversation with our readers, and it has the potential to make us a better newspaper," Rutledge said.

Bobbie Jo Buel, executive editor of the *Arizona Daily Star* in Tucson, is a believer in opening the newsroom to regular visitors as the most direct way to gain the public's trust. She hosted one of the first National Credibility Roundtables in 2001. Since then the newspaper has hosted dozens of community roundtables on all sorts of topics, from headline writing to editorial pages. "We learned at the first roundtable that in our daily rush when we make a mistake, to us it's just a mistake, but readers think every single thing we do is deliberate. Readers are thinking we deliberately did not tell them the other point of view," Buel said. "The roundtable made us sensitive to fairness. Fairness is a big subject because it goes beyond getting it right. We are so worried about facts. Now we talk about the whole package. We've become acutely aware of *you don't know what you don't know*," she said.[7]

For example, the newspaper brought in both sides of the gun control issue for a roundtable discussion. Instead of a debate on gun control, both sides said, "We didn't know anything about guns. We were just putting in the papers details from what we thought were credible sources and we were getting it wrong." Buel said, "It's made us be more careful about our gaps in knowledge. We are trying to be more precise and questioning the people we thought were good sources."

Buel took it a step further. She bought gun handbooks for every copy editor and set up voluntary firearms training for the newsroom. The Saturday morning spent at the shooting range was "big learning" for everyone. "We've become a big believer you have to bring in readers even in an area where you are doing a good job. It changes the conversation [with reporters and editors] for a long while. Every time we've listened, we've learned something," Buel said.

According to Nunnelley, one thing stands out:

> The public seems to put high value on contextual as much as factual accuracy. You may get the facts right, but if you don't get the whole picture right, it raises the

question of whether we can get any of it right. The culture of newsrooms is still defensive, so responding to the public is still very hard. Newsrooms are changing. There is a big shift philosophically to making it a core value to involve and be involved with the public. I hear women say they've experienced what it's like not to be heard [in newsrooms], so they relate to what the public is saying.

Nunnelley says that a major conclusion from five years of credibility roundtables is that when readers don't see people like themselves in their newspapers, they conclude that newsrooms don't understand what's important to them or their community. Unfortunately, there's evidence that the push for more production with lower staffing levels has forced newsrooms to "hunker down or turn in," so they see even less of what's happening outside the newsroom, she concluded.

One National Credibility Roundtable report cited how the *Orange County (Calif.) Register* stepped up to the oft-heard complaint of media bias by inviting fifteen critics of the newspaper to meet with the staff and to send comments about fairness for ten weeks. Would the constant criticism help journalists address perceptions of bias? Understandably, there was trepidation on both sides, Nunnelley writes in her report. But *Register* editors insisted it was best to face the newspaper's critics despite the human tendency to spend time with sources we perceive as champions of the newspaper. The critics followed an agreed-upon scorecard for the ten-week period.

Did it make a difference? Nunnelley reports the exercise helped *Register* editors push more facts into the news reporting and to make those facts prominent. They also reviewed the scorecards as a whole before writing a credibility checklist that is applied daily to reporting and editing processes. The checklist asks simple questions such as: Is the story fair? Is the story forthright? Is the story accessible? Do we have the right sources? Do we avoid loaded language?

Conversations with women news leaders reveal a true urgency about credibility issues. No one claims to have the ultimate answer, but their perspectives on the challenge follow four primary themes:

- the need to be in constant conversation with our communities;
- the need to follow our instincts about what content is relevant to readers' lives to demonstrate our understanding of what's truly important;
- the need to put practical tools for building credibility into play;
- the need to articulate the business reason for changing the culture of newsrooms so that all voices are heard.

Carole Leigh Hutton, the former vice president of news for Knight Ridder and current president and CEO of United Way Silicon Valley, says newspapers need to be "very aggressive in engaging in conversation with our communities."

We listen to readers more, but I don't think we've perfected the art of having that conversation. We don't do so much of the routine transparency. How it is we make the decisions. Why we cover something. Why we don't cover something. As former publisher and editor of the *Detroit Free Press,* I would invite people to come to our news meetings. They'd be fascinated there was so much argument. People would come away so surprised. They tend to think someone is pulling all the strings. Yet we tend to be the antithesis of that.[8]

Credibility is not about just telling the truth. It's also about telling the "whole" truth. As we become more transparent in our decision making, we risk revealing how shallow we are when it comes to taking action. We say we want to be open so that people accept our sources and believe our reporting. Yet that requires time and listening skills we must be willing to develop. Rosemary Goudreau, a former editorial page editor of the *Tampa Tribune,* observed that "much richer conversations [with sources and readers] would happen if we put away our notebooks and just listened. We have to be there for more than a quote. I don't know that we give reporters permission often enough to just go talk to people—not because they are chasing a story. We should create an expectation that reporters out there really understand an issue from being in the belly of the beast."[9]

Now there's a thought: Assess the quality of the story by how well the reporter grasps the context of it. But don't assume reporters are good listeners just because their notebooks are full of quotes. Because context is directly connected to our credibility, consider training reporters and editors in the art of listening and conversation.

It starts with asking ourselves if we really understand the people we write about. Do we give reporters the time to be fully immersed in the context of a story or to understand the stakeholders before they pull out their notebooks and start scribbling notes? Do we want quotes more than true understanding? Guilty. We are the ones who allow "dial-a-quote" names to appear repeatedly on our news pages as if they are anointed representatives for whole sectors of the community. We know better. The show-me approach means allowing reporters to listen to people on their beats without being in the hunt for a story. It means teaching reporters how to develop sources and beats before they strip-mine them for a quick story that lacks meaning or relevance. It means finding new voices every day. It means rejecting our favorite "dial-a-quote" sources.

The expectation of readers is that we have a higher level of involvement with them. The world of instant messaging and blogs forever changed that equation. "It's one of the challenges," Hutton said. "The new expectation requires being more transparent and explaining a controversial decision. We used to deal with the reaction rather than dealing with it up front. We can have more regular conversations about how decisions are made. . . . We have a chance to turn things around with readers every twenty-four hours." Hutton continued:

> We have this immense flexibility to experiment because we publish every day. But we don't take a lot of risks even though we have the ability to re-do it every

day. I think that's a great orientation for newsrooms. We have this opportunity to change things and to change them again. We can be much more nimble than we allow ourselves to be. . . . When you extend that orientation to the community, they are more likely to be invested in you. There are so many ways to be informed, I think it erodes the connectedness we had when we were the dominant medium.

One way to reconnect is to pay more attention to our own instincts, not just as journalists but also as siblings, children, parents, homeowners, apartment dwellers, and grocery shoppers. We're people, too. For years we've professed total neutrality about life in order to appear to be perfectly objective observers. Baloney. In the process of sticking to the strict separation of community and newspaper, we've abandoned important connections. We've lost touch with what people really want newspapers to help them sort out. Our elitism is apparent to readers who have responded by leaving us.

The PEJ statistic cited earlier that reflects the decline in press credibility means we're not "real" to people. The stories on our front pages aren't about them or their lives. We're irrelevant more days than we're relevant.

The New Readers study of 2004, published by the Readership Institute at Northwestern University, reminds us that readers' "experiences" with newspapers determine whether they buy us or not.[10] The positive experiences that motivate people to read newspapers are about connecting with them. If we look out for their personal or civic interests or if we make them smarter, they will come back for more. But if we make readers plow through too many long stories or if our news pages are all about stereotypes, they won't come back. Hutton agrees: "People create time to spend with things that matter to them. I think some of the decisions about what is important are based on what we feel connected to. We could be much more selective and careful about those relationships through our columnists. . . . Columnists can have conversations with readers. We have to be thinking about how we use that connection. . . . I'm a firm believer in putting a column on page one when it resonates and draws a reaction from readers."

Now a vice president for Wrightway Consulting Inc., a leadership development company, Cynthia G. Miller conducted Women and the Newsroom workshops throughout the country for years.

> The credibility issue is about protecting the interests of readers. We told women in our workshops to bring their life into the newsroom. It's really that simple. Women readers are key. . . . They have the buying power so there's an economic reason to have women on all levels of the newspaper, so we are putting out a newspaper other women want to read. . . . [The news industry] is still putting out newspapers people don't want to read. . . . They [editors] don't even realize they are producing newspapers without women on the front page. . . . We forget what readers really want. We have to ask, "Why are we doing these stories?"[11]

Goudreau said, "I think credibility also speaks to the range of stories you have on your front page. Part of it is about who you quote. We still have a lot of excuses about that, but we have a responsibility not only to listen to readers but also to follow through. We often don't sustain the learning we take from listening and we go right back to our old habits." Goudreau demonstrated a commitment to the "show-me" kind of journalism when she was managing editor of the *Cincinnati Enquirer.* After police killed a young African American man, Goudreau orchestrated more than 140 neighborhood conversations in homes, churches, and schools to engage all segments of the community in resolving the residual racial tension. In Tampa, she embraced the community in a different way by inviting readers to regularly write for the opinion pages. The writers include a group of adult community columnists and a teen board of columnists.

Dozens of good ideas exist on how to engage the community and hit head-on the perceptions of media disconnect. We don't have to start from scratch in making a credibility action list. But we do have to act on the "action" part. Nunnelley's work with the National Credibility Roundtables puts her on the front lines as newsrooms take steps to restore the public's trust. "We are opening our eyes to the credibility problem, and a lot of processes that would have seemed radical in newsrooms are now more mainstream, such as tracking errors or being easy to reach. We are listening and acting in a way we have not before. . . . The roundtables have always been about spreading their findings and getting newspapers to do anything to improve their credibility. There's a willingness to change," Nunnelley said.

A lot of good advice can be gleaned from newsrooms and professional organizations about explaining ourselves and genuinely connecting with our communities if you look. It lives on Web sites and in archives. Among the most recent resources is a booklet titled "Building Trust in the News: 101+ Good Ideas for Editors from Editors," which is a compilation of the findings of the National Credibility Roundtables and a survey of newsrooms conducted in the summer of 2006 by Nunnelley and Kuhr.[12] The booklet, released in the fall of 2006, outlines 191 ways journalists have figured out how to talk to readers, improve accuracy, and analyze newsroom habits. "Some of us are doing it by man-on-the-street or online polls, and a lot of us have reader advisory panels. There's not one thing to do. It will be a menu of those kinds of things that will ultimately be the answer," Hutton said.

Newspaper content audits work, too. They provide a reality check on what we are publishing versus what we think we're doing. And they speak to how well we are connecting to the four corners of our communities. Not surprisingly, national newspaper audits confirm that men appear more frequently on page 1A than women. Women are quoted less often than men in main news stories and on sports pages. And let's put technology to work for us. The power of multimedia is just that, in its reach and in its immediacy. Many newspapers, including those in my company, Media General, ask readers to react to stories posted on our Web sites. The simple act of asking readers to respond draws them into community-wide conversations. The reactions, in turn, expand the reach of the reporting and widen the source base. Asking readers what they think, in real time, provides an instant pulse on community opinion.

Yet a list of good ideas won't do a thing unless it's accompanied by fundamental change in our newsrooms. Lou Anne Nabhan, vice president of corporate communications for Media General, explained how she sees credibility issues and the future of the business intersecting:

> To really understand the future, you have to develop a deep external perspective about where the competition is cropping up. You have to inspire employees to embrace change, not fear change, and to be eager to participate in it. The challenge is being able to spot and identify emerging competition before they start eating our lunch. Change can happen rapidly. The capacity for producing high-quality local content that people need to run their lives is what we do best. That's a cultural advantage we have—in creating an environment where quality counts. It seems there is a new division emerging for companies that operate in markets that are truly local. In the long term, companies like ours should be able to continue to grow and communicate that to Wall Street.[13]

Miller said, "My hope is that women will manage like women and key in on the culture in newsrooms and help change it. We have to figure out how to change the culture, because that's how we are going to keep and bring back women to the newsroom who will help us improve the product." Part of that culture shift means creating "on- and off-ramps" for women who need to leave the business to raise families but want to return. We're not very good at that in today's news organizations. In contrast, Wall Street firms in late 2005 launched a campaign to ensure that talented women have suitable opportunities when they are ready to rejoin the workforce. These companies see it as good business strategy that ensures a diversity of thought within their leadership ranks. "Editing a great newspaper starts with good ideas," Goudreau said. "We have to be deliberate about stopping meetings and listening to our introverts. We should listen to readers, but there are a lot of smart women and men in our newsrooms we should bring into our news decisions."

How much more evidence do we need? We have pounds of reports on the defensive newsroom culture, declining circulation, and credibility gaps. There are no quick fixes. We can be more deliberate and consistent in taking action. It starts with listening to our own instincts. It starts with honestly listening to readers. It starts with listening to people who don't trust us, yet. It starts with writing stories people want to read. It starts with critically examining how we sound when we answer the telephone. It starts with teaching journalists how to listen. It starts with taking personal responsibility for ensuring all of the voices are heard at news meetings. It's not going to be easy, trust me.

Notes

1. Andy Wood, *Wall Street Journal,* letter to the editor, February 15, 2006.

2. Project for Excellence in Journalism, "The State of the News Media, 2005: An Annual Report on American Journalism," Public Attitudes section. Available at http://www.stateofthemedia.org/2005/narrative_overview_publicattitudes.asp?cat=7&media=1 (accessed January 21, 2009).

3. Project for Excellence in Journalism, "The State of the News Media, 2007: An Annual Report on American Journalism," News Source Believability section. Available at http://www.stateofthemedia.org/2007/narrative_newspapers_publicattitudes.asp?cat=7&media=3 (accessed January 21, 2009).

4. American Society of News Editors, "Examining Our Credibility: Perspectives of the Public and the Press," August 4, 1999. Available at http://www.asne.org/kiosk/reports/99reports/1999examiningourcredibility/index.htm (accessed January 21, 2009).

5. Carol Nunnelley, interviews with Donna Reed, February 10 and January 4, 2007.

6. Kathleen Rutledge, interview with Donna Reed, January 12, 2007.

7. Bobbie Jo Buel, interview with Donna Reed, January 11, 2007.

8. Carole Leigh Hutton, interview with Donna Reed, February 7, 2007.

9. Rosemary Goudreau, interview with Donna Reed, February 12, 2006.

10. Mary Nesbitt, "The New Readers Study," press release from the Readership Institute, July 4, 2004, 1–3. Entire study available at http://www.readership.org/new_readers/newreaders.asp (accessed January 21, 2009).

11. Cynthia Miller, interview with Donna Reed, February 16, 2006.

12. Carol Nunnelley and Peggy Kuhr, "Building Trust in the News: 101+ Good Ideas for Editors from Editors," Associated Press Managing Editors National Credibility Roundtables Project, 2006. Available at http://www.apme-credibility.org/buildingtrust2006/building_trust_2006.pdf (accessed January 21, 2009).

13. Lou Anne Nabhan, interview with Donna Reed, February 8, 2006.

10

Interview with Diane McFarlin

DONNA M. REED

Donna Reed: How can we prepare to lead the necessary change in the news industry?

Diane McFarlin*: We can't simply lead change. We have to seek it out, with the kind of unabashed enthusiasm that will encourage everyone around us to want to be a part of it. Innovation and diversification are essential to our prosperity. The real key is knowing how to balance a respect for the past with an openness to the possibilities.

DR: How should women in the business today prepare to move into top leadership positions? Is your advice the same for men and women?

DM: Part of my advice is for both men and women: Understand that the formula for successful leadership continually evolves, because those who are being led are evolving. The authoritative, top-down style of leadership was beginning to lose its effectiveness when I got into management. As a woman, I had a more nurturing style of leadership, and that seemed to work well with the boomers who were reporters and copy editors back then. Now Gen X and Y employees expect a greater role in decision making, so a more consultative style of leadership is required.

The next part is just for women: Consider your leadership aspirations in any planning you do in your personal life. A study done a few years ago determined that women remove themselves from consideration for top leadership roles because of either a lack of confidence or the demands of family life. That demonstrates how important it is, if you want to be a top leader, to find a life partner who buys into your plan and will be supportive. If you want a family,

---

*Diane McFarlin is the publisher of the *Sarasota Herald-Tribune* and former president of the American Society of News Editors.

figure out how you can make that happen and still achieve your career aspirations. Lots of women have done it, but there's no one formula. It depends on your personal circumstances and the priorities you've set for yourself.

DR: What were the defining moments in your career—so far?

DM: There have been several. Two on opposite ends of my career stand out. The first was the summer after I graduated from high school. I was working at my hometown paper, the *Lake Wales [Fla.] Daily Highlander,* and had been left in charge of the newsroom when our sports editor was charged with abusing Little Leaguers. I conferred with the publisher by phone, wrote the story, put it on page one, and fielded the angry calls afterward. I loved the adrenaline rush of doing it responsibly. That's when I decided that I wanted to be a top editor.

The second was when the former publisher of the *Sarasota Herald-Tribune* picked me to succeed him. I'd never aspired to be the publisher, nor had I envisioned myself on the business side of our industry, but it's been the most challenging—and certainly the most rewarding—phase of my career. So far!

DR: What are the obstacles—real or perceived—to reaching the top ranks of the newspaper industry?

DM: Some of the greatest obstacles can be self-inflicted. Women especially can suffer from a tendency to think they're not good enough, or to defer to men at meetings or in decision-making situations. Women who feel inferior because of their gender may have a greater tendency to perceive that they are being slighted because they are female. I've always thought that one of the keys to my success coming up the ranks was that I was completely tone-deaf to discrimination. As a result, I wasn't handicapped by it.

DR: What do women need to know to make it to the top?

DM: Two things, courtesy of Sunday school and my parents: one, the Golden Rule, and two, you can do anything you set your mind to do.

DR: Is leadership about gender at all?

DM: No. Leadership is about character, integrity, energy, resilience, perseverance, and passion.

DR: Envision a room of young, female J-school graduates in front of you. What is your advice to them?

DM: Specialize and generalize. Specialize in a particular topic or discipline— say, health reporting or videography or Web programming—so that you can excel at it and so that your talents will carry a high premium. Be agnostic, though, about how your particular capabilities are utilized—whether it's in print, online, on the air, or all of the above. Learn to be fluent in all media so that you can contribute your special talents to whatever platforms or devices the public favors.

DR: What is your vision for the future of our business?

DM: Newspapers, and the institutions that produce them, will always be around, but their scale will change and their family of related products will proliferate.

DR: From a personal perspective, what defines a leader?

DM: See above: character, integrity, energy, resilience, perseverance, and passion.

DR: What are the steps the industry needs to take to recapture the public's trust in us? To be transparent in our decision making?

DM: I can't think of anything I could say here that wouldn't sound like it came out of one of the many reports done on this subject!

DR: What woman or women contributed significantly to your career success?

DM: All of my mentors were men, but women that I mentored have contributed to my success by: (a) making me look like a very astute judge of talent, and (b) supporting my career. When Janet Weaver [vice president and executive editor of the *Tampa Tribune*] worked for me at the *Herald-Tribune,* for example, she was as interested in my success as I was in hers. It's amazing what a partnership like that can accomplish.

11

Women in Sports as the Final Frontier

CATHY HENKEL

Ah, sports, the final frontier. Women have inched their way to the far corner of the newsroom, where sports departments traditionally settle, and they've moved into the locker room to gain equal footing with their male colleagues. But their numbers never take off.

When I became the sports editor of the *Seattle Times* in 1990, I knew of no other woman in a similar position at a major metro. And over the next eighteen years, the number was never more than a half-dozen at a time, less than 3 percent. It was a threshold that couldn't be crossed. It was the same for all jobs in sports departments. A 2006 diversity report card by the Institute for Diversity and Ethics in Sport, drawn from 304 newspapers on the gender makeup in the sports department, found this: 12 percent of assistant editors are women, 10 percent of reporters, and about 13 percent of copy editors. They repeated the study in 2008, but the numbers did not improve.

Our overall gender grade? An F, in all areas. "We wag our fingers about the importance of diversity, but this shows how bad we really are in our business at attaining it," concluded John Cherwa of Tribune Media, who led the gender study. "There is really no good reason for it, because women have been forces in sports departments long enough to where those numbers should have turned around."

Even though the first wave of women came into sports journalism in the 1970s, the situation hadn't progressed much beyond tokenism three decades later. "The numbers are disappointing," said Christine Brennan, a published author, longtime *USA Today* columnist, and one of the pioneers in the business. "The question is about a backlash. There is almost a retrenching where newspapers are going backward. You'd think that because of Title IX and all the incredible growth there, there'd be a trickle-up effect." But that hasn't happened, other than the trickling part. "It definitely hasn't gone the way I thought it would," said *Miami Herald* columnist Linda Robertson. "We made a whole lot of progress for a while, then it just fell off. And I don't think it will change until more women are in positions of authority, both as sports editors and managing editors."

But here's the rub: Women aren't clamoring to become sports editors, and just a few stay in the job over the length of their career, citing lifestyle issues, glass ceilings, or being in urgent need of a fresh breath in another environment. "Well," ventured a former male sports editor, "you could say it's guaranteed proof that women are smarter than men. It's a pretty sucky job." Following a nontraditional career path most always means giving up or postponing a traditional lifestyle. Something's gotta give.

"Newspaper jobs are tough; working in sports is even tougher," said Holly Lawton, the sports editor at the *Kansas City (Mo.) Star* and married to a former journalist who understands the lifestyle. "It is hard on home life and family life. I worked nights, weekends, and holidays year after year after year, and six days a week during the fall." Said one longtime female sports editor, who chose not to have children: "I don't think I could be both a good mother—meaning one who spends a significant amount of time with her children—and a good journalist able to respond to news at a moment's notice."

I remember a few years back when the light went off in my own head that a nontraditional career path meant that a husband and children weren't going to be part of the equation. It sends many of us to the exit. Tired of neglecting a personal life and from fighting isolation in the workplace, I finally left the business after thirty-one years in sports journalism, choosing early retirement to regain my foothold. It wasn't a move a man would have made.

As difficult as it is for the editors to balance personal and professional goals, female reporters have even more to juggle because of the travel. Among many others, it led Annette John-Hall, a sports reporter for some ten years, to flee sports for the features section of the *Philadelphia Inquirer.* "The trajectory of your career collides with the trajectory of your family life," John-Hall told Leah Etling and the Women's Sports Foundation. "I was never focused on my family, even when I was home. I was worried about when my next trip was going to be, when my expense reports needed to be filed, what my advance was going to be about, and how I was going to get the superstar I needed to interview." All of which leads to the theory that the average career of a female sportswriter who wants a family life is about ten years. At the very least, it takes an understanding partner who's willing to share the load.

"We can't keep up the pace and also have a personal life," said Miami's globetrotting Robertson, who along with her news-reporter husband is raising three children. "You make a lot of compromises, and look back and see all that you had to let go. It's really hard, harried. Sometimes you think you're doing everything halfway. There is a lot of guilt, relationships suffer, and in the end what you give up is yourself. There is no time for personal enrichment." As a result, Robertson took a year's leave from newspaper life for a Knight-Wallace Fellowship at the University of Michigan. She needed a change of pace to catch up with herself and her family.

Another woman, who works in a small town in the South, quit her job as sports editor so that she could date a man in the community's sports scene who had shown interest. But—stop me if you've heard this before—as soon as she became available, he moved on as well. "I think as an industry we make it too difficult for women, and not just about their social life, either," said the woman, forty-four and still single. "I think the industry holds women to a higher standard than men, but if you are serious, you play by the rules. And I understood the rules before I joined the game."

Brennan, who wrote a touching book about her life, *Best Seat in the House*, has accepted her solo journey, overflowing with experiences that very few share. In her book, she writes about the epiphany she had after telling her mother that she was once again disappointed that a relationship hadn't worked out. This is what her mother told her: "You know, if your life were a movie and after covering the Redskins and Super Bowls and traveling around the world to cover the Olympics, if the movie ended with your deciding to get married to some nice man and have two children and a nice house with a picket fence and a dog, do you know what the audience would do?"

"No," Brennan replied.

"They would cry," her mother continued, "and it wouldn't be tears of joy. It would be tears of sadness. The people in the theater would be sad that you gave up all that excitement in your life to do what people are supposed to do and get married."

Brennan was surprised that her mother wasn't pressuring her to marry as other mothers were with her friends. "You don't choose to be single," Brennan wrote. "At least I didn't. It just slowly starts happening to you over time. A woman who leads this kind of life is a curiosity to many people. If you're the one living it, you not only have to understand that, but you also have to be able to laugh at it."

Sports is a career choice for women that also comes with a responsibility to pay it forward. In 1987, when about forty of us gathered at a seedy hotel in Oakland, California, to form the Association for Women in Sports Media—shortened to AWSM and pronounced "awesome"—we were full of first-generation pride and energy to push the door open so that others could follow. We knew it was pretty raw inside, but nonetheless women were everywhere in those times, breaking barriers and becoming the first this or the first that. It was fifteen years after Title IX was passed into law and fourteen years since Billie Jean King had bumped off Bobby Riggs in "the battle of the sexes"—long enough for some of us to play sports and want to weave a career around them. But that wasn't my path. I graduated from college before Title IX, from an era when girls were taught half-court basketball—only three dribbles and pass—and field hockey in gym class. There were no leagues and no potential to turn a physical gift into a college scholarship or a profession.

I was nearly thirty when I joined the sports section, already having served nearly a decade as a news reporter. I hadn't played sports, outside of gym class, but the world of athletics was near and dear. My father was a high school coach and athletic director for forty years; my brother pushed all the way from pee-wee sports to a college football scholarship; and my mother, who taught dance before I was born, always sat on the sideline and kept statistics at their games. And you know what? She still does, even after my father passed away. Even into her eighties, she still sits in front of a TV and keeps score.

Most of the women at that first AWSM convention migrated to sports because of the men in our lives—brothers, fathers, friends, mentors, boyfriends, husbands. I'll always remember cheering my high school boyfriend as he ran sixty yards for his first touchdown, and the comforting warmth of his letter jacket. Or when I was a kid, dressing as a pint-sized cheerleader or hawking popcorn at my father's games. Sports was palpable to me then, but always as a spectator.

Christine Brennan is ten years younger than I am, but her father was her ticket into sports as well. She asked him for a baseball mitt when she was eight, which soon escalated to getting a bat, taking trips to cheer on their local college team, and, finally, to playing high school basketball, earning her own Ottawa Hills Green Bears letter jacket as the team's captain. But even then, sports may have stymied a personal life. She never had a date in high school and watched *All the President's Men* with her friends on prom night. While other girls might have fantasized of dancing and flowers in the dark movie theater that night, Brennan began a wakeful dream about working for the *Washington Post*, which she eventually did for a dozen years.

For Brennan, AWSM's first president, and other of us founding mothers, the responsibility that came with breaking new ground also meant speaking up as a voice of diversity, for women's sports and women's issues. But it was anything but a universally held truth even among the few of us pounding out our bylaws at that first convention.

Many theorize that progress in women's sports coverage will be slow until females occupy more seats of power and opinion. But in reality it takes female sports editors awhile in the chair to assert themselves, most women columnists want to be where the brightest lights are, and others remain uncomfortable ever pushing a gender agenda.

How many times have we said it? We are journalists first, women second. "I don't feel a special responsibility because of my gender to get more women's sports coverage in the paper," said Sherry Johnson, who served as the sports editor at the *Raleigh News and Observer* and before that at the *Wichita Eagle.* "The section I lead should accurately reflect the interests of the region covered." Or from Holly Lawton, when I asked about this in her first month as sports editor at the *Kansas City Star:* "There is not a whole lot more women's coverage in the paper just because I'm a woman sports editor. To do that would assume that women are interested in women's sports, and I'm just not sure that's the case." And the thought is echoed by Rachel Wilner, whom I also asked soon after she became the sports editor at the *San Jose (Calif.) Mercury News,* a position that eventually had to be given up for motherhood: "I do feel an obligation to ensure fairness, but not necessarily to promote women's sports beyond a certain level of reader interest. I am more concerned about attracting women readers to the section, which doesn't always correlate with covering women's sports."

All of us hear from women's sports fans, who give us little credit for raising girls' high school sports coverage to the level of the boys, something that has happened at all-female-led sports sections. And from the other side, too—readers who can't understand why we would spend our precious resources covering women's sports. "I do get feedback from both sides of the gender issue," Raleigh's Johnson said. "Women readers who think we should do far more with women's sports because I am a woman sports editor; men readers who profess no interest in women's sports and think we are providing heavy coverage of that because I am a woman."

I can almost hear Brennan pound her fist on the steering wheel as we chat about the issue via cell phone. She's on the road again. "I know I once felt that way, that you'd be labeled if you covered women's sports," she said. "Some of our colleagues shy away from it; they don't want to be typecast. But I'll tell you, it can be one of the reasons we are hired. We need to open our mouths, add to the discussion; it is the point to having diversity. We should be chiming in; we should be telling our bosses about stories about women that ought to be in our newspapers. Frankly, I think women are shirking their duty if they are not opening their mouths on this."

It doesn't mean we have to publish only mainstream or feel-good stories. Plenty of women's sports stories in the news are anything but that—think Marion Jones and her steroid scandal, or Northwestern's soccer team being accused of destructive hazing. At the *Seattle Times,* we published a book excerpt from *Game On* by our WNBA reporter Jayda Evans that delved into the league's difficulty in acknowledging its lesbian fans and players. "Now that was something I read all the way through," one male sports reader told me afterward.

"I think this is a burden for every woman in our business," said Pam Clark, who became the sports editor at the *Springfield (Ill.) News Leader* after twenty-five years as a sports reporter. "We run into it at every stop—women coaches/

athletes/fans who think female reporters and editors should carry the banner and provide more coverage of women's sports. Probably, as I have gotten older, I've felt a bigger responsibility to push coverage where I think it's merited."

It took me years before I felt comfortable boosting women's sports coverage. How many times have I heard and said and quoted studies that say women readers pretty much want the same things as men do—the men's pro and college sports—except when it comes to figure skating and Olympic sports. But I believe that is a conditioned response, and perhaps a case of if-you-build-it-they-will-come. The lack of good, readable stories about women in sports sections does not encourage interest. Many of our women readers don't know what they're missing and rely on the men in their lives to set the dial when it comes to sports. That is expected to change over time as more and more women set their own agendas.

After a couple of years in the editor's chair in Seattle, I looked for a women's team to cover with more force and found an exciting University of Washington women's basketball team with gobs of personality and ready to make an imprint. We began following them on the road in the 1980s, the only newspaper to do so. Their crowds built; their fans became rabid. The more we did, the more they wanted and the more they felt entitled. But push ahead twenty years and we were the only newspaper in the nation consistently traveling with the WNBA. At age ten, the women's pro basketball league was doing as well as or better than the NBA did at the end of its first decade, but newspapers are still slow to recognize the appeal, or if they do, are reluctant to spend precious resources on it.

The proof that new readership exists for us comes every two years during the Olympics. Women flock to sports sections each Olympiad to find as many female as male faces, as many important headlines about women, and many female writers telling their stories. "The Olympics are the equivalent to the female Super Bowl," said Brennan, who covered more than a dozen Olympics and wrote two books on figure skating. "It's where women are the superstars. I have always loved the Olympics as we all did growing up. It was our only chance to see women being glorified as the men were."

One of the real trailblazers in encouraging women's sports coverage was a man, however. James "Jay" Shelledy, then the editor of the *Salt Lake Tribune*, sent an edict to his sports department in 1994 that they cover every girls' high school sport in the state, and two years later mandated that there be a women's story on the sports cover every day. "When we started out, compliance in sports was at the end of a gun barrel," Shelledy said. "But generally they came around. For one thing, circulation went up, and we saw the spike. We found many more women were reading our sports section, too—as high as 38 percent of our readers were women. And we also heard from men, from fathers who couldn't thank us enough, that it was important to do for the sake of their daughters."

I introduced a sliver of that at the *Seattle Times,* but it came nearly fifteen years after I became the section's editor. I asked our sports desk to get a woman's face *somewhere* in the section every day. Small steps. "We strive to put women on our sports cover, period," said Mary Ullmer, sports editor of the *Grand Rapids (Mich.) Press,* her third paper in the top spot. "Our goal is to get more women readers. One way to do that is to have stories about women, stories women can relate to."

A 2005 study by the Center for Sports Journalism at Penn State surveyed 285 sports editors—97.5 percent of whom were male—about their beliefs about women and sports. About one-quarter to one-third said women are less interested in sports and naturally less athletic than men. Half of the respondents said Title IX has been unfair to men's sports. More than 40 percent of these sports editors formed their opinions without any formal research.

Another study, conducted by the Project for Excellence in Journalism and Princeton Survey Research Associates, looked at about a month's worth of sports section covers of sixteen papers in 2004. They showed that sports sections are passive and reactive, focusing on familiar territory. The big three men's sports— football, basketball, and baseball—occupied 65 percent of the space, and females were the main character in stories 5 percent of the time regardless of circulation size. This comes after one of the most notable trends in sports over the past thirty years: the increasing number of girls and women playing sports. The number of women competing in college, for example, went from 2 to 43 percent of students participating in sports in that same period.

The conclusion is that our sports sections are like that comfortable corner bar or café where everyone knows your name and the food is always the same. Where you can order "the usual." In the end, it's a small risk to add a new dish to the menu, to tell good stories about women along with the men. And to know that even when it's obvious that a women's sports piece should take front and center, there will always be detractors. Take this recent e-mail I got from an angry reader as an example: "You know, even before I saw your name, I could tell that ovaries were behind the sports section today. Either get with it, or get out of the business, lady." Oh, how sweet that was. I was on vacation when that day's section was put together, and men were behind the decision to make a WNBA feature the cover centerpiece. That made me feel like I had accomplished something. That after I leave the sports department, after I become one of the statistics, a sensibility of the importance of stories about women will remain.

As for the rest of the country? I am not optimistic, and neither are my colleagues. "I'm sorry to say that I think the percentages of women sports editors likely will be the same in ten years," Ullmer said. Cindy Fairfield, who followed Ullmer as sports editor at the *Muskegon (Mich.) Chronicle,* agreed: "I don't see a big change. It takes a special person, male or female, to do what we do. The hours are grueling and the responsibility is overwhelming. I write a column once or twice a week, handle some game and feature coverage, work the desk, including the slot three or four times a week, and plan a major sports project once a year. I work in the office most every Friday night during football and basketball season and about 50 percent of the Saturday night desk shifts. Not to mention general assigning and planning." Sounds great, eh? Where do I apply? Oh wait, I already did.

And what's ahead? Add a big helping of the 24-7 Internet, podcasts, Web blogs, online chats, and multiplatform challenges to the plate. And sadly, the concurrent decline of print. "I think people are seeing the business for what it is—really tough, high pressure, bad hours, mediocre pay, not family-friendly," said Springfield's Pam Clark. "Does it still get in their blood like it has ours?" But even she ranks her job satisfaction at seven on a scale of one to ten, as do most of the female editors I surveyed. Nobody rated it below a seven.

And then there is this: "Several weeks ago, I received a letter and a hand-knitted scarf from the grandmother of Missouri State basketball players," Clark recalled. "One paragraph was unlike anything I'd ever seen in my twenty-six years in the business and it will stick with me forever: 'When we learned that our new sports editor was a woman, some of the men in the family held their breath, but I have never heard anything but praise from them as well as other sports fans. Way to go! I think you're terrific and you make me so proud of my womanhood.'"

Until we see bigger change, it is the little things that keep us going.

Sources

Personal interviews (in person, by phone, or by e-mail) in 2006:
Christine Brennan, author and sports columnist, *USA Today*
John Cherwa, sports coordinator, Tribune Media
Pam Clark, sports editor, *Springfield (Ill.) News Leader*
Shannon Conner, sports editor, *Arizona Republic*
Jayda Evans, sports reporter, *Seattle Times*
Cindy Fairfield, sports editor, *Muskegon (Mich.) Chronicle*
Emilio Garcia-Ruiz, AME-sports, *Washington Post*
Melissa Geisler, sports editor, *San Luis Obisbo (Calif.) Tribune*
Tracy Greer, sports editor, *Los Alamos (N.M.) Monitor*
Judy Hildner, sports editor, *Pueblo (Colo.) Chieftain*
Sherry Johnson, sports editor, *Raleigh News and Observer*
Kim Kaufman, sports designer, *Dallas Morning News;* former sports editor, *Battle Creek (Mich.) Enquirer*
Holly Lawton, sports editor, *Kansas City (Mo.) Star*
Kate Magandy, city editor; former sports editor, *Biloxi (Miss.) Sun Herald*
Holly Mullen, city columnist; former sports editor, *Salt Lake Tribune*

Linda Robertson, sports columnist, *Miami Herald*
James "Jay" Shelledy, professor, Louisiana State University School of Communications; former editor, *Salt Lake Tribune*
Susan Shemanske, sports editor, *Racine (Wisc.) Journal Times*
Sandy Smith, sports editor, *Concord (N.H.) Monitor*
Betty Szudio, sports editor, *Medina (Ohio) Gazette*
Terry Taylor, sports editor, Associated Press
Mary Ullmer, sports editor, *Grand Rapids (Mich.) Press*
Celeste Williams, sports editor, *Fort Worth Star-Telegram*
Rachel Wilner, sports editor, *San Jose (Calif.) Mercury News*
Lynn Zinser, sports reporter, *New York Times*

Articles

"Box Scores and Bylines," from "The State of the News Media, 2006: An Annual Report on American Journalism," Project for Excellence in Journalism, August 22, 2005. Available at http://www.journalism.org/files/sports.pdf (accessed January 21, 2009).

"Editors Fail to Gauge Interest in Women's Sports," Center for Sports Journalism, College of Communication, Penn State, May 27, 2005.

Etling, Leah, "Missing in Management," Women Sports Foundation, 2001. Available at http://www.womenssportsfoundation.org/Content/Articles/Careers/M/Missing%20 in%20Management.aspx (accessed January 21, 2009).

Examination of membership of the Associated Press Sports Editors, 1996 and 2006, by Cathy Henkel.

"The Explosion of Women in Sports," panel discussion, American Society of News Editors, April 13, 2000. Available at http://www.asne.org/kiosk/archive/convention/2000/ womeninsports.htm (accessed January 21, 2009).

Flores, Jose Alfredo, "Women's Sports Coverage Still Lacking," American Society of News Editors, April 14, 2000. Available at http://www.asne.org/reporter/2000reporter/ friday/s/wosports.html (accessed January 21, 2009).

Gibbons, Sheila, "Women at Newspaper Helms Face Risky Business," WeNews, May 10, 2006, http://www.womensenews.org/article.cfm/dyn/aid/2735/context/archive (accessed January 21, 2009).

Ricchiardi, Sherry, "Offensive Interference," *American Journalism Review,* January 2005. Available at http://www.ajr.org/Article.asp?id=3788 (accessed January 21, 2009).

"Sport Careers for Women," Women's Sports Foundation, http://www.womenssports foundation.org/Content/Articles/Careers/S/Sport-Careers-for-Women.aspx (accessed January 21, 2009).

"Study on Women/Minorities in Sports Departments," postings on www.sportsjournalists .com, November 2005.

"Women in Sports Media Remain Committed to Jobs Despite Abuse, Harassment," Center of Sports Journalism, College of Communication, Penn State, May 16, 2006.

"Women in Sports: Observations," American Society of News Editors, January 1, 2000. Available at http://www.asne.org/kiosk/editor/00.jan-feb/hertz3.html (accessed January 21, 2009).

Books

Brennan, Christine, *Best Seat in the House* (New York: Scribner, 2006).

Creedon, Pamela J., ed., *Women, Media, and Sport: Challenging Gender Values* (Thousand Oaks, Calif.: Sage, 1994).

12

"Gender Genie"

CATHY HENKEL

Remember the "Gender Genie"?[1] A computer program that used algorithms developed by Israeli researchers, the Gender Genie maintained it could correctly guess the sex of any writer with 80 percent accuracy. Met with hoots and hollers after a quick test was placed online, the Gender Genie took a drubbing. A passage from Shakespeare was deemed "female." The author of Charlotte Bronte's *Jane Eyre* was "male." The same could be shown in much of sports writing. Without the byline, could the reader tell if it were by a woman or a man?

Mary Garber, who became the first woman sports editor when she moved over to fill the gap during World War II at the *Winston-Salem Journal*, once showed several newspaper articles sans bylines to editors and asked if they could identify the writers' gender. They could not do it with any degree of accuracy, no more than the Gender Genie could. Celeste Williams, sports editor of the *Fort Worth Star-Telegram*, has many women on her staff, including the rarity of a female as the lead beat reporter for the Dallas Cowboys. The NFL has had fewer women covering it than any other league in pro sports. "I got into a fight with a reader who told me he couldn't read my section because there were too many women writing it," she said. "I asked him to black out the bylines and try again. He got mad and called my editor to complain. He was told that we sure hated to see him cancel his subscription but that women will continue to write about sports."[2]

So do men and women write about sports differently? They do and they don't. "They didn't start with all the clichés," said John Cherwa, sports coordinator for the Tribune Company. "Women grow up differently, so they bring that variety of experience to the sports section. The most significant and terrific thing in our business is because of that. We're not reading the same old stuff all the time."[3]

In a landmark book in 1994, sports columnist Ron Rapoport published an anthology of sports writing by women, *A Kind of Grace*. In collecting the articles, he concluded that the kinds of stories women write are different from those written by men. "The changes they have brought to the sports pages often reflect experiences and perceptions men cannot share," Rapoport wrote.[4] "When Betty Cuniberti wrote about the late Heather Farr's harrowing battle with breast cancer for *Golf Digest*, she brought to her assignment the passion of a survivor of that disease. Beyond this, it is clear that athletes tend to react differently to being questioned by women than by men. Often they seem to view female reporters as sisters in whom they can easily confide. And in the case of women athletes, there can be a frankness, a sense of camaraderie that is absent when they speak to men."

I don't think there's any doubt that the tenor of sports writing began to change when women entered the field in countable numbers back in the 1970s. We didn't spend as much time on play-by-play and statistics, but instead were looking more for the humanity in our stories. What was the athlete like off the court, off the field? One study published by the *American Sociologist* in 1992 found that letters of recommendation for a higher-education teaching position varied depending on the gender of the author. Women were much more likely than men to describe how the applicant worked in a group, as opposed to their intellect. In other words, it wasn't all about the batting average. Sometimes it took some teamwork.

In a book published in 2006, *The Female Brain*, neuropsychiatrist Louann Brizendine asserted that women have 11 percent more neurons devoted to emotions and memory. Because of this, she said, they are better at observing emotions in others. "Picture, for a moment, a map showing the areas for emotion in the brain of the two sexes," Dr. Brizendine wrote. "In the man's brain, the connecting routes between areas would be country roads; in the woman's brain, they'd be superhighways."[5]

Perhaps the biggest change with women sports writers came with the culture of the press box and in the sports department itself. The men were finding that their pinup posters were no longer welcome, and that other parts of their language and behavior had to evolve. And women found they had to toughen up, to desensitize a bit. "Just by being there, by being present, women had a significant impact," said Christine Brennan, an author and columnist for *USA Today*. "The old yuck-it-up-boys-will-be-boys club was broken up a little. After all, our readers are not all boys, and we have to serve them all."[6]

Notes

1. "The Gender Genie," www.bookblog.net/gender/genie.html (accessed January 21, 2009).

2. Celeste Williams, interview with Cathy Henkel, summer 2006.

3. John Cherway, interview with Cathy Henkel, summer 2006.

4. Ron Rapoport, ed., *A Kind of Grace: A Treasury of Sportswriting by Women* (Berkeley, Calif.: Zenobia, 1994).

5. Dr. Louann Brizendine, *The Female Brain* (New York: Morgan Road Books, 2006).

6. Christine Brennan, interview with Cathy Henkel, summer 2006.

PART 3

Women as Op-Ed Columnists and Editors of Editorial Pages

13

Women Op-Ed Columnists

Why Aren't More of Them Published?

KEVEN ANN WILLEY

I'd read op-ed pages off and on for years, but it wasn't until I became an editorial page editor that I fully appreciated the dearth of female op-ed writers. The year was 1998 and the only nationally syndicated women writers my newspaper subscribed to at the time were Mary McGrory and Ellen Goodman. *Why only two?* I wondered. *And why only liberals?* This was my introduction to the women-on-op-ed-pages debate, a debate that began long before I became an editor and one that, sadly, swirls around us still.

A recent mega-incarnation of this debate featured a vicious and much-publicized exchange of e-mails in early 2005 between commentator Susan Estrich and Michael Kinsley, then running the opinion pages of the *Los Angeles Times,* about the *Times*'s rather pitiful representation of women on its op-ed pages. The vitriol of the increasingly personal feud cast neither Estrich nor Kinsley in their best light, but it did serve to raise some legitimate questions, among them:

- Why are there so few women on America's op-ed pages?
- Is this something we should be concerned about?
- Is this going to change?

The answers, in short, are:

- The reasons are different today from what they were yesterday.
- Yes, but for reasons other than you might suspect.
- I believe so, but it depends on how quickly newspapers rethink their "gatekeeping" responsibilities.

Let's take them one at a time.

Why are there so few American women op-ed writers?

It used to be for the same reason there were so few women in the international columns: There just weren't many of them writing. In biographer Caroline Moorehead's 2003 book about one of my favorite journalists, the late Martha Gellhorn, who covered every major international conflict from the Spanish Civil War to the Cold War, she vividly describes how rare it was to be a female war correspondent in the early and mid-1900s.[1] The situation wasn't much different for female op-ed columnists. Op-ed pages began to gain popularity in the 1920s and 1930s, but they rarely featured women writers, even fifty years later. That's one reason why my newspaper was still subscribing to only two women op-ed columnists in 1998. And with so few women op-ed columnists out there, why bother trying to strike an ideological balance? (Never mind that Georgie Anne Geyer, Suzanne Fields, and Debra Saunders were among conservative women writers syndicated at the time.)

Times have changed. There are more women war correspondents now, just as there are more women op-ed writers. There's still a gap between the number of men and women columnists, but it's narrowing. It's not nearly as wide as even some of the most prominent women in journalism today would have you believe.

The hooey about women tending to shy away from having strong opinions or being hesitant to opine quickly about breaking news is just that—hooey. Is Maureen Dowd a shrinking violet? Does Michelle Malkin wait until a second news cycle to fire her rhetorical guns?

Editor and Publisher published a story in early 2006 quoting a Women's eNews commentator who suggested that one reason there aren't more female op-ed columnists is that they tend to get more vicious e-mail than their male counterparts, and this makes them reluctant to go public with their opinions.[2] As a former political columnist at the *Arizona Republic,* I can attest to the ugliness of such reader feedback. Sexism, anatomically graphic put-downs, and threats of rape—even death—aren't unusual. Columnists of color suffer similarly. I've hired two and worked with several, and the mail they receive is unbelievable. Hate mail is hate mail, but the vulgarities many women and minority columnists are subjected to are simply on a different plane than what most male columnists encounter.

I've yet to see any evidence, however, that this is a statistically significant deterrent to women publicly expressing their opinions. Thanks to the increase in women in professional fields in general and to the Internet specifically, more women opinion writers are available for publication in newspapers now than ever before. Michelle Cottle, Amy Sullivan, and many other sharp, talented women write from the left. Charlotte Allen, Heather Mac Donald, and many others are very much their equal from the right.

Here's an example: At the *Dallas Morning News,* where I've worked since late 2002, about 40 percent of what we review for our daily op-ed pages comes from "traditional" sources—chiefly the syndicates; other regular columnists on the wire; and "specials" on the wire from experts, think tanks, academia, advocacy groups, big political names, and so forth. We estimate this group being about 60 percent male. Another estimated 40 percent of what we review are the unsolicited "spontaneous" pieces that come in by e-mail directly from freelance writers, experts, think tanks, academia, advocacy groups, big names, and so forth. This group is probably closer to 70 percent male. It's clearly the most voluminous group, but it's also easiest to click through fairly quickly to separate the gems from the rocks. About 20 percent of what we review comes from specific outreach. Our targets, again, are often freelancers, experts, think tanks, academia, advocacy groups, big names, and so forth. Our emphasis here is often on more localized issues. We initiate the contact and invite the submissions. This group is closer to fifty-fifty on the gender scale, or may tip slightly female. So what do all these numbers mean? That men opinion writers still outnumber women, but by not nearly as large a margin as just a few years ago.

But let's move past the measuring-the-gap component of this discussion. More important is that in some ways the gap doesn't matter. The overall pool of cogent analysts among whom editors can select has exploded with the advent of the Internet. So what if men writers still outnumber women writers 60 percent to 40 percent? That's 40 percent of an overall pool as large as the Pacific, as opposed to what used to be, say, 10 percent of a pool the size of the Mediterranean. Yet just 19.5 percent of the op-ed voices published by the *L.A. Times* in early 2005 were female, according to a column written by *Washington Post* media critic Howard Kurtz during the Estrich-Kinsley rhetorical warfare.[3] The *New York Times* published women on its op-ed pages 16.9 percent during the same time period, and the *Washington Post* barely made it to double digits, checking in at just 10.4 percent. And what about the *Dallas Morning News?* Thanks to the vision and energy of deputy editorial page editor Sharon Grigsby, 40 percent of the daily op-ed columns we've published in recent years have been by women. We don't publish them because they're women; we publish them because the writers have something important to say and they happen to be women. (See Grigsby, "Finding Great Women Op-Ed Columnists," pp. 137–39 of the present text. Grigsby oversees the *Dallas Morning News*'s daily op-ed page.)

So even though I recoiled at Susan Estrich's over-the-top attack on Michael Kinsley in those awful e-mails, she made one fundamentally sound point: Saying that there aren't enough good female opinion writers these days is "a self-fulfilling prophecy." Women aren't getting on op-ed pages because they don't exist. They're not getting on op-ed pages because editors aren't publishing them. Stated more simply: There are plenty of women columnists with important things to say; they're simply not being selected for publication by the gatekeepers of America's newspapers.

Is this something we should be concerned about?

Yes, but for reasons other than you might suspect. "Whether women are better than men I cannot say," opined a wry Golda Meir not so terribly long ago. "But I can say they certainly are no worse."[4]

Let me be clear that nobody's advocating publishing women columnists just because they're women. (Well, maybe some people are, but I'm not.) I'm not a fan of quotas. If we're publishing a woman just to meet some sort of arbitrary number, and in so doing we're denying a platform to a more cogent, timely, provocative writer who happens to be male, what exactly have we accomplished? Nothing.

The fact is that it's easiest to publish columnists who are easiest to find. Editors work on deadlines. Pages come and go, every day, 365 days a year. Who's got the time to dig a little deeper, to read a little more broadly, to consult a little more comprehensively? Nationally syndicated columnists and writers for some of the best-known national publications, ranging from the *New Republic* to the *Weekly Standard,* are easiest to find. These writers require the least editing, the least fact checking—they're a known quantity. Most of these writers are men. But to troll the syndicates and a few other traditional publications and call it a day is unfair to readers. Particularly readers who have less and less need for newspapers to act as gatekeepers. Readers today have unfettered access to millions of blogs and Web sites, thanks to the Internet. The smartest op-ed editors aggressively explore the blogosphere and check in regularly with a wide variety of Web sites. As a result, they find many great op-ed writers who are women.

Here are a few examples of women we've published on our daily op-ed pages:

- *Xenia Dormandy* of the Belfer Center for Science and International Affairs at Harvard's Kennedy School of Government and former director for South Asia at the National Security Council. Her column, "India's Breaking Point: The Nuclear Power Can Take Only So Many Attacks before It Lashes Back," appeared on our pages within forty-eight hours of the train bombings in India and helped our readers understand the fuller context of this terrorist attack.
- *Tamar Jacoby,* senior fellow at the Manhattan Institute, who has led efforts among conservatives for comprehensive immigration reform, a position that found her swimming upstream against more vocal fellow conservatives who favor simply building a wall at the border and criminalizing the estimated eleven million illegal immigrants in the United States.
- *Alison Acosta Fraser,* director of the Roe Institute for Economic Policy Studies at the Heritage Foundation, on why Congress should fix the budget process and outlaw earmarks.

- Dallas United Methodist pastor *Sheron Patterson,* who has written many columns for us, including one affirming Bill Cosby's message in his 2006 commencement speech at Atlanta's Spelman College that graduating women should go it alone because the unfortunate truth is that more black men are in prison than in college and thus make unsuitable marriage partners.
- *Salma Ghanem,* associate professor and chair of the communications department at the University of Texas–Pan American, who writes on a number of topics from the perspective of an Arab American woman who grew up in a Muslim culture.

These writers aren't necessarily recognized names. Their work may not be a known quantity, at least not at first, so you have to mine deeper into the wires, and in some cases they'll take more time to contact and edit. But they'll be more reflective of the ocean of opinion that is out there. In 2005 we published 244 new voices on our daily op-ed page, columnists who had never before appeared in the *Dallas Morning News.* This was by design. We made a conscious effort to constantly update and expand our bank of commentators to better serve readers.

There's a greater diversity of opinion journalists out there today than ever before, but providing a rich sampling to readers requires newspaper editors to dig deeper and think differently than ever before. Why bother? Because if we don't, we're just hastening the demise of newspapers. The role of gatekeeping has changed dramatically in recent years, and providing a richer diversity of opinion—ideological, gender, ethnic, age, and so forth—in our newspapers is more important than ever before.

Is this about to change?

I believe so, but it depends on how quickly newspapers rethink their "gatekeeping" responsibilities.

For years it's been generally assumed that as more and more women became editors, they'd publish more and more women writers. Perhaps that's true; I don't know. When Gail Collins ran the *New York Times*'s editorial pages, barely a sixth of the op-ed columns her newspaper published were written by women, a percentage that distinguishes her leadership not at all from her male counterparts.

Even if it were true that women editors published more women writers, I'm not sure much change is in the offing. According to the National Conference of Editorial Writers, fewer than a third of its 542 members in 2006 were women and fewer than a quarter of the 129 editorial page editors who were members were women. This is the twenty-first century and we're still such a minority of the decision makers? I'm not sure we have enough time to wait for more women to become editorial page editors before we start running more women on the op-ed pages. We don't have to. You don't have to be a woman editor to find and publish outstanding woman writers. You just have to be an editor who is willing to do things differently.

Newspaper editors used to have a near-monopoly on gatekeeping. Readers had few other sources for information; they relied almost entirely on newspapers, radio, and television—and the editors in charge at each medium—to provide them with the most important news and analysis of the day. So pulling mostly from the syndicates and few big-name think tanks worked well. No more. Readers today have an unlimited supply of Web sites, blogs, and Wikipedia entries to surf. If they don't like what they see on TV or read in the newspaper, or don't think they're getting the broadest picture available, they can seek out other sources of news and analysis themselves with just a click of a mouse.

Frankly, I believe there will always be a market for trusted gatekeepers. In some ways, the explosion of information available on the Web makes the role of an aggregator or gatekeeper all the *more* important. But newspapers no longer have a corner on that gatekeeping market. If they don't "diversify" what they provide to readers—if they don't rethink their own habits and biases as they're keeping that gate—readers will simply look to other gatekeepers. Many already are. If newspapers don't want to be shut out of the action, we simply must do a better job of providing readers with varied and reasoned opinion journalists. Those voices should be from the left and the right, male and female, white and of color, young and old.

One added benefit of robust op-ed pages: The more diversity of opinion we provide there, the more credibility our institutional editorials have with readers who can trust us not to hide the opposing arguments. Newspaper editors need to be sure we're providing our readers the very best of everything that's out there.

There's a lot more out there than ever before.

Notes

1. Carolyn Moorehead, *Gellhorn: A Twentieth-Century Life* (New York: Henry Holt, 2003).

2. "Columnist Discusses Hate Mail Aimed at Women Writers," *Editor and Publisher,* May 24, 2006. Available at http://www.allbusiness.com/services/business-services -miscellaneous-business/4696159-1.html (accessed January 21, 2009).

3. Howard Kurtz, "For One Ed, Strong Op: Susan Estrich Addresses the Male," *Washington Post,* March 7, 2005. Available at http://www.washingtonpost.com/wp -dyn/articles/A12722-2005Mar6.html (accessed January 21, 2009).

4. Golda Meir, *Great Quotations* (Lombard, Ill.: Great Quotations, 1984).

14

Finding Great Women Op-Ed Columnists

SHARON GRIGSBY

Let's start by busting a lazy myth. It's just flat wrong to say a shortage of women's voices prevents editors from publishing as many female columnists as male. It's just a matter of hunting them down. And in some cases, a lot of other folks—whether at the syndicate services or in the blogosphere—are doing much of the work for you.

Be deliberate. Maintaining gender diversity—along with ideological, racial, and topic diversity—is as easy as counting to three (or four, depending on how many columnists you run each day on op-ed). You set the goal of seeking diversity among those three or four every day, not just "when it works out that way."

Reintroduce yourself. The list of "top" syndicated columnists varies, depending on whom you ask, but a good third to a half of those on most lists are women. Even better, the women mentioned—for instance, Trudy Rubin, Kathleen Parker, Froma Harrop—are among the quickest to anticipate the buzz issue of the week or to turn on a dime when news breaks. It's worthwhile to visit the sites of syndicates with which you do business every now and then just to see who's there. Once a columnist is "launched," it's easy to lose sight of that person in the crush of the day. The syndicate tour also allows you to discover someone you never knew was writing.

Go deep. Pay attention to what the major wire operations provide beyond the syndicated columnists. The *Washington Post/L.A. Times,* the *New York Times,* and McClatchy (formerly Knight Ridder) each offer regular columnists, generally editorial board members or editorial page editors, who do strong work but who are not syndicated. And beyond those offerings, the same wire operations offer five to seven pieces daily (a quarter to a third of which are written by women) from one-time contributors. Some of your best finds will turn up here. It's all a matter of looking past the recognizable names in the wire slugs. Take the time to read the entire piece, even if you just skim it. If that topic doesn't work for you, save the person's name for another time.

Don't be shy. When you solicit individual opinion pieces—from think tanks, experts, or local community groups—speak up and specifically ask about female writers on staff. That way you overcome the (perhaps unconscious) bias within these groups that prompts them to think first about their male voices. You not only score a woman for your page, but you also build up the voice of women in each of those organizations in the process.

Be an eagle-eye, 24-7. It might be a bright perspective you hear in a local public radio commentary. Or the one-shot analyst who shows up on a cable news show. Or a professor whose long piece you read in a scholarly magazine. Jot the name down. Our Internet world generally makes it easy to locate the person's e-mail address. With that in hand, it's a matter of sending a quick query inviting the person to write for you. Hand out your card to smart women you meet outside the office; follow up each one of those meetings with a quick e-mail. It's more important that they have something to say than that they have hefty writing credentials. After all, limiting our columns to just professional writers is a self-selecting approach.

Explore the blogosphere. Aggregates (or "portals" or "communities") are popping up all the time to help identify popular, quality blogs. A new one that I expect will be especially helpful in identifying women's voices is WIMN'S (Women in Media and News) Voices at www.wimnonline.org. It positions itself as "a diverse online community of approximately 50 women writers monitoring media coverage of current social, cultural and political issues from a progressive perspective." This operation has been created specifically to "answer the marginalization of women's voices on the nation's op-ed pages and in other print and broadcast news areas by positioning a diverse group of feminist intellectuals as opinion-leaders, sources and pundits for mainstream and alternative media."

WIMN'S Voices is just one of many. I have bookmarked a dozen or so of these aggregates and troll through them several times a week. Sometimes I am not interested in the topic the women are writing about, but I can tell how they think and write. If the writer has potential, I file her name away for when I do need a voice on her field of expertise.

Explore free-form opinion. Thinking of ways to write and present commentary in addition to the standard format column opens up lots of possibilities for getting more women on your pages: Q-and-As, blog roundups, a digest of syndicated columnists, such as the "Balance of Opinion" column Nancy Kruh and I created. Those devices certainly have helped the *Dallas Morning News* get more women's voices on the page.

Think big. Every editorial page in the country needs gender diversity within its own staff. That's the first step to thinking more expansively and meeting the fifty-fifty or so goal. The best investment you can make, based on readership surveys, is to give people plenty of commentary, particularly staff-produced columns. Hire your own female columnist or solicit occasional columns for the women on your editorial board. That regularly appearing column, clearly grounded in local commentary, will create a sense of your city on the page and provide a bond with readers.

PART 4

Women in International Journalism

15

Covering War through a Woman's Eyes

KIRSTEN SCHARNBERG HAMPTON

I have seen the gray streets of Baghdad as a journalist. I have feared them as a woman. I have trained to mitigate the risks of getting killed covering war as a journalist. I have been haunted by the prospect of being captured covering war as a woman. I have relished the assignment of covering front-line troops as a journalist. I have struggled with the realities of living in austere, close-quarter conditions with all-male infantry battalions as a woman.

On the January morning that correspondent Jill Carroll, a longtime freelancer for the *Christian Science Monitor,* was abducted in Baghdad, I found myself reacting to the news both as a woman and as a journalist. I'm not sure which part of me reacted first, nor am I entirely sure when those previously inexorably linked pieces of who I am became their own separate entities. But much has changed in the world in the twenty-first century, and therefore much has changed in the way that we as journalists—and as women—cover this increasingly dangerous world. One-third of the news media today is female.[1] We cover politics and coups d'etat. We cover famines and natural disasters. We are just as likely—more so, if one judges the press corps ranks in Baghdad throughout this war—to cover conflicts and wars as our male counterparts.

Yet there are harsh—and often little realized—realities that come with our increased presence in the realm of international news reporting: Women correspondents face physical dangers that men do not in the world's most dangerous places. Women correspondents struggle with unique challenges when it comes to interacting with the militaries found in conflict zones as well as the local staffs they must hire wherever they work. And women—unlike men—often tend to view international reporting as a zero-sum career, one that can be successful only if they give up any hope of family or personal life.

There are also distinct advantages that are afforded to those of us who pursue this nomadic reporting life. Women are able to blend into the backgrounds of some of the most hostile regions of the world in ways that male reporters never could. Women often see stories in ways quite different from how men see them, and often these are ways that deeply resonate with readers. And in some of the world's most closed societies, particularly in the Middle East, female reporters usually are able to interview other women, a seemingly simple act forbidden to male correspondents.

In order to explore all of these issues, I draw from my own experience during three tours covering the conflict in Iraq and time on assignment in Africa. In addition, I closely study the experiences of three female correspondents at my newspaper, the *Chicago Tribune*. There is Liz Sly, the *Tribune*'s Rome bureau chief, who has predominantly been stationed in Baghdad for the past several years. There is Kim Barker, the paper's New Delhi correspondent, who not only travels extensively throughout India but who also spends considerable time in Afghanistan and throughout the Asian villages that were so devastated by the 2004 tsunami. And there is our South Africa correspondent, Laurie Goering, who essentially is responsible for covering that entire continent in all its rich, fascinating, and often unstable detail. The four of us are, certainly, a microcosm of a much larger group of international female correspondents. But our stories—personal and professional—well illustrate just what being a female foreign correspondent at the beginning of the twenty-first century is all about: the sacrifice and the satisfaction; the risk and the reward.

Danger and Disguise versus Opportunities and Open Doors

All journalists are operating in an increasingly dangerous world; that is especially so in Iraq. According to numbers released by Reporters without Borders, the international group that advocates for freedom of the press, by 2008, 207 journalists and other media workers had been killed in Iraq since 2003. Another 25 journalists were kidnapped in 2007 alone.[2]

It has become apparent that journalists are most vulnerable in parts of the world where Islamic fundamentalism—and the kidnappings, beheadings, and suicide bombings that so often accompany it—is on the rise. Yet longtime correspondents, like Sly, remember when in virtually any war zone it was assumed that although male expatriates and journalists might be snatched or harmed, taking a woman was deeply taboo. "For a long time, in many places women had a certain immunity," Sly said.[3]

Iraq has changed all that. I was in Baghdad in the summer of 2005 when our security company alerted us that new intelligence pointed to one terrifying conclusion: insurgents desperately wanted to kidnap female Western journalists. For a while the insurgents had wanted Westerners in general, usually poorly guarded civilian contractors. Then they had wanted Western journalists. Then, having already snatched contractors and male journalists, insurgents had begun hoping for a new kind of victim to generate a fresh wave of public terror and shock: a Western woman journalist, or what we female journalists in Iraq dubbed the "war zone trifecta." "I think kidnappers have seen that they get lots of mileage out of taking a woman, and that's their real interest now. We all recognize that," Sly said.

It is not something frequently spoken of by correspondents in international danger zones, but there is an added fear for women journalists: rape. No statistics exist that track how often female correspondents are the victims of sexual assault as they travel the world, often alone, on assignment. But, again, the nation of Iraq has given correspondents a statistic to fear: of the two American female service members who were captured by Iraqis during the 1991 Gulf War, both have been reported to have been sexually assaulted.

Ironically, though, in the most fundamentalist societies, where women are allowed the fewest freedoms, female correspondents today enjoy advantages their male counterparts do not. When she is on assignment in increasingly unstable Iraq, Sly routinely leaves the newspaper's hotel-based bureau to do in-person reporting, a rarity these days. Sly does so by wearing a veil in an effort to blend into the chaos of Baghdad's streets. British by birth, Sly has been told by a number of people that they took her to be Kurdish because of her manner of dress and skin coloring. "It is an enormous advantage," Sly explained. "Men are not able to disguise themselves in this way. In many places in the Middle East, if you are wearing a veil, you are largely just overlooked." Female journalists can use—and frequently have—the art of disguise even more to their advantage in virtually off-limit places like Afghanistan in the days of the Taliban's regime. By wearing the burka, a dark shroud that covers a woman from head to toe, a foreign female journalist could blend in as no man could.

Even more, in these societies where women are prohibited—often by law—from speaking to men who are not their husbands or close family members, male correspondents are literally cut off from half the population. How can one tell the story of the Taliban—which oppressed women by outlawing their education and virtually every other freedom—without getting the input of Afghani women? "Even with a female interpreter, almost none of these women will speak with a male reporter," said Barker, who covered the 2001 war in Afghanistan and has been covering the region ever since. "Men are literally unable to unlock the stories of 50 percent of the people in these entire countries and regions."[4]

Barker, on the other hand, has had unfettered access. Even the most devout of Muslim women will often invite her to see and experience parts of daily life that she could never fully understand or report otherwise. She has been invited to Muslim weddings, where she goes behind closed doors with the women while they ready the bride for the ceremony. She has been in the kitchens where women gossip and talk freely about their lives, attitudes, dreams, and aspirations. And when Barker is finished talking with the women, she has usually found herself welcomed into the rooms where the men are gathered as well. "Essentially what I've found is that I'm like some third sex to them," she observed. "I'm not a man. But I'm not a Muslim woman. So, as a Western woman, I am something entirely different that they are curious to speak with—a freak of nature to some degree. But they understand and respect that I must be smart and very good at what I do in order to have the job that I have. So they will either talk to me because of that or because they feel obligated to impart their wisdom on me."

A Woman among Men

The *Washington Post*'s Molly Moore was one of the few women to cover the Gulf War in 1991. She was on the front lines with U.S. Marines and later wrote a book whose title broadly hinted at what a novelty she was at that time: *A Woman at War: Storming Kuwait with the U.S. Marines* (Scribner, 1993). Moore later went on to cover Somalia, Kosovo, the rise of the Taliban in Afghanistan, the war in Afghanistan after 9/11, and the Israeli-Palestinian intifada. Her book has served as something of a how-to manual for young women preparing for a career in international coverage—a path that inevitably will require living with and interacting with predominantly male military divisions in combat zones.

I read Moore's book in a sandstorm-battered tent just south of the Iraqi border in the weeks leading up to the U.S. invasion in 2003. What I gleaned from those pages shaped the way I operated for three months in the field with all-male infantry battalions of the 101st Airborne Division. I humped my own gear. I didn't demand special accommodations. I ate the same bad food; I slept in the same crowded tent; I followed their rules; I tried never to be a burden, but I would not be pushed around either. I earned respect by being respectful, hardworking, and dedicated to learning everything I could about their equipment, their orders, their structure, and their way of operating. I took things seriously, practicing again and again until I could get my chemical mask on in the Army-regulation nine seconds, and participating in their training exercises in combat first aid. (Several weeks into the war, a soldier shot a photo of me holding IV bags for a medic who was treating someone for a grave gunshot wound to the stomach.) The soldiers I traveled with trusted me and another woman, the Associated Press's Kim Hefling. They certainly never forgot that we were women or that we were reporters, but we were given high levels of access to information and commanding officers. Another female correspondent—one who had not thought to bring a sleeping bag for an assignment that would require months of sleeping in the desert, who routinely pulled out a compact to put on makeup during briefings with high-ranking commanders, who made no attempt to carry her own oversized bags—was treated very differently. I'm not sure if she ever realized why.

Still, the truth is that when women live for months with men in the field, under adverse and often terrifying conditions, the practical complications of being female are inevitable. Privacy is not a characteristic of the Army, and tree and shrub cover are not characteristics of the desert. Because we were living in tight perimeters, I could never go to the bathroom in anything but direct sight of the very soldiers and commanders I would have to interview later. When the sirens that were to detect chemical weapons went off—mandating that we strip instantly and don the protective chemical suit—I had to do so in front of the Humvee full of soldiers with whom I had been riding. When the soldiers set up makeshift, fully exposed field showers, I had little choice but to use them if I wanted to get some of the grime of two weeks' worth of sandstorms off me.

And these are the small—indeed, cosmetic in the larger scheme of things— concerns of being a woman among male troops in a foreign conflict. Soldiers worry—and rightly so—that standing next to a woman increases their likelihood of getting shot, because military studies show that snipers take aim at something that looks out of the norm, as it helps them zone in and aim more accurately. Even more, it is a rare woman who is physically capable of all the things that nineteen-year-old infantrymen are. At the age of twenty-nine when the 2003 Iraq war started, I was sure I could keep up with anything the Army threw my way. I had just run the Chicago Marathon and was in top-notch shape. Yet just a week or so into the conflict, while walking at night through uneven terrain, I found myself struggling. We had several more kilometers to go, and I was carrying a seventy-pound rucksack, a computer case, a satellite phone, a supply of food and water, and a car battery that I needed to use as a power source in order to file my story that night. I had long ago made the vow to hump all my own stuff, but I could go no farther carrying the load I was carrying. I finally let a young private carry the battery, a decision that haunts me still when I let myself wonder what would have happened had we come under attack and that young man could not have defended himself and his comrades quickly enough because he had my battery in his arms instead of his weapon at the ready.

Not Tonight, Dear, I've Got a Deadline

About a decade ago, several editors at the *Chicago Tribune* asked Sly, one of the paper's most intrepid foreign correspondents, to travel to Chicago and talk with staffers about her job. The goal was to get the paper's young, talented reporters interested in international reporting and to encourage them to make getting a foreign posting one of their career goals. A group of nearly a dozen reporters crammed around Sly at a table at the Billy Goat Tavern, the bar of choice for Chicago journalists since the days when Mike Royko's editors knew to call him there if they needed him for edits on his legendary newspaper column. The *Tribune* reporters peppered Sly with questions: How are living conditions in many of the places where you are expected to be based? What about security in war zone regions? How do you navigate your way through so many foreign languages and cultures? How much do you make? Do you miss living in the United States?

At long last, Sly remembers, a young woman at the table asked about balancing a personal life—as a potential wife or mother—around a job that requires hopping on airplanes at a moment's notice to cover stories such as tsunamis and earthquakes and coups, the kind of unpredictable news events that are the bread and butter of a foreign correspondent's repertoire. "A personal life?" Sly laughed as she looked at the woman. "Forget it. If you have a boyfriend, you will lose him. If you don't have one, you won't find one."

Sly is far from being alone in her assessment of the difficulties of melding a personal life around the demands of international reporting. A 2000 study by the International Women's Media Foundation found that a full 64 percent of female correspondents said that creating some kind of balance between work and life was the biggest challenge they faced.[5] Sly is candid about the toll her lifestyle has taken on her social life. "I went into [journalism] to cover the biggest stories of our time," said Sly, who was in Beirut for the civil war, China for Tiananmen Square, South Africa for the fall of apartheid, Iraq and the Middle East for the Gulf War, Afghanistan and Pakistan for the war after September 11, 2001, and Iraq for the latest war. "I've done that, and I've personally never regretted the effect that has had on my personal life."

Sly, who has traveled throughout the world and who knows a good portion of the Western foreign correspondents, said she knows hardly any female correspondents who are married with families. The exceptions are female correspondents who are married to another reporter—and these couples rarely have children while they are still working abroad.

Sly speaks not only about the press corps she knows from various news organizations but also about the trend at her own paper. Of the *Tribune*'s four female foreign correspondents in 2006, three of them were unmarried. That was the mirror opposite of the *Tribune*'s male foreign correspondents; out of eight, six of were married, most with children as well. "The guys can do it," Barker said of her male counterparts.

> They have a wife who stays home and keeps the house together and the family stable while they are running off to war zones or natural disasters. They have the

perfect setup: they can have this amazing career and still have a life at home. But there are very few men who are willing not only to do all the home-front stuff but also to follow a woman around the world and pack up and move every few years when she takes a new posting somewhere else. And, honestly, the kind of guys who would are probably not the kind of guys that your average strong-willed, intelligent, independent woman foreign correspondent would be interested in.

In looking at one of today's biggest stories, it is clear that, at least in a professional sense, many women foreign correspondents' choices—conscious or not—to stay single and childless have resulted in their willingness and availability to cover Iraq. Virtually every news organization in the country is struggling to find staffers willing to take on Iraq assignments. Reporters with children cite the perfectly valid fear that something could happen to them, leaving their children without one parent. Married reporters say their spouses won't agree to such perilous duty. "People just don't want to go, and I can't blame them," the *Chicago Tribune*'s managing editor at the time, Jim O'Shea, told me over lunch.

The demographic of reporters who are still agreeing to Iraq assignments increasingly tends to be reduced two characteristics: young reporters looking to make a name for themselves, and single female foreign correspondents. Certainly there are the veteran male foreign correspondents who are exceptions to this trend, but to illustrate the point, Sly tells of being at a dinner party at one news organization's Baghdad bureau. "I started looking around the table and it was all women," she said. "I said to the two or three men who were there, 'Hey, what are you doing here? This is a girl's job.'"

The woman who bucks the trend within the *Tribune*'s ranks is Laurie Goering, the paper's South Africa correspondent until 2007. The paper's South America correspondent before that, Goering was asked to open and manage the *Tribune*'s Kuwait City bureau in the months leading up to the 2003 invasion of Iraq. There, as the lead-up to war lagged on for so long that the press assembled in Kuwait began joking that they were the victims of "pre-traumatic stress disorder," Goering met and fell in love with Simon Robinson, then the South Africa correspondent for *Time* magazine. Goering was pregnant as she rolled north into Iraq in the early hours of the war. The couple was married right after the war. And Grace was born and quickly became the youngest foreign correspondent to traverse Africa.

Goering had known that it was virtually unheard of for a woman to have her kind of job and a family, but she had decided she would do them both. Her solution: she took Grace on assignments with her, to cover the election in Senegal, the genocide in Sudan. The baby went everywhere Goering did. "In Grace's first year, I think I only spent one night away from her," Goering said. "That's a pretty incredible statistic for any new parent, I think—and particularly for one who travels as much as I do."[6] It wasn't easy—or cheap. Goering hired a full-time nanny ("a young woman with a passport and a desire to see the world") and paid for her to fly everywhere she and Grace went. Where Goering had once traveled only with what she could put inside a small carry-on bag, she now lugged diapers and a breast pump, a suitcase for Grace and the nanny, baby toys, and baby medicine. "It's like the most complex military operation," she jokes.

In the summer of 2005, Goering and Robinson had their second child, Noah. He now travels with her, too. The costs can be staggering. On a recent trip to Zambia, Goering's ticket, which the paper paid for, cost four hundred dollars. Two more tickets for Grace and the nanny (at six months, Noah still sat on Goering's lap) came to eight hundred dollars, which Goering paid out of pocket.

Goering's editors supported her decision to blend career and personal life. They made a conscious decision—with her—to focus the paper's Africa coverage on longer-term projects, textured narratives, major stories with worldwide consequences. "If I had to run off to cover every coup or famine, I couldn't do this anymore," she said. "I wouldn't have the energy for it, and I couldn't afford it." Indeed, energy is at a premium for someone on this kind of schedule. Where Goering used to get up, read the papers, and have a long breakfast, she later breast-fed Noah, got the children ready, and prepared for her interviews for the day. She might have rushed off to interview the president of whatever African nation she was in, then darted back to the hotel to play with the children for an hour. "The days of leisurely dinners with sources were gone," she said.

But having the children with her has often opened doors and cleared reporting hurdles. She remembers arriving at an African ministry of information one day to apply for press credentials. The press office "was somewhere around the seventeenth floor" and the elevator was broken. Goering climbed the stairs and staggered into the office, lugging Grace and a bag filled with baby supplies and reporter's notebooks. "They gave me my credentials with less trouble than I've ever had," she said. "I think the people working there could relate to me as a person and a mother. People often see reporters as these difficult, rude people, but I think my kids make me more human to the people I meet as I work."

Goering got a call once from a female correspondent who is based in South America for a major American newspaper. The correspondent was pregnant and considering following Goering's lead and attempting the same kind of juggling between reporting and motherhood. "I told her what I knew, how I was doing it. Maybe she'll become the second person to try something this crazy," Goering said with a laugh. "All I know is that so far it's working for me. Everyone's situation is different, and this job is difficult, which clearly accounts for the fact that so few women have attempted to do both things at once."

Women Running the Show

In an age of smaller news bureaus—both nationally and internationally, as a result of financial cutbacks at most news organizations—foreign correspondents often are stationed alone in a foreign land. With varying degrees of language and cultural training, they arrive in their new locale to set up a news bureau, including hiring and managing a staff of local office managers, interpreters, drivers, and potentially a security detail should the situation on the ground require it. In many places of the world, this is no small task. A correspondent in Cairo remembers waiting for more than three months to get a local phone set up in his office. Several days after it was finally installed, the line went dead. It took another five weeks or so before someone arrived to fix it.

For many female correspondents, being a one-person foreign bureau means taking on roles that normally would be relegated only to men in the country and culture in which they are living. They are the bosses to male staff members; they control the bureau's budget, finances, and banking; they meet routinely with male politicians and businessmen. Because her daily responsibilities and roles in the New Delhi bureau are so different from the responsibilities and roles traditionally filled by Indian women, Barker is routinely called "sir" by the Indians—both male and female—whom she encounters. "They mean it as a title of respect, I think," Barker said. "But it's clear that when they talk to me and observe me, I am not the kind of person they would think of as a 'madam.'"

Barker employs both males and females on her permanent staff in New Delhi, as well as the staff she regularly uses during frequent trips to Afghanistan and Pakistan. There are situations where Barker's male staff members are required to gain her entrée to a person or location she might otherwise be unable to get as a woman. But the realities of being a female boss to male employees is apparent. Barker says that her male translators are much more inclined to interpret the meaning behind her interview subject's words rather than to simply translate them verbatim. "It's the male-female thing. They see it as their obligation to explain things to me that I couldn't possibly understand on my own," she said sarcastically. "The women that I work with almost never do that. They simply translate directly and leave the interpretation out."

Male translators and fixers—the term used for an employee who is sort of an all-purpose helpmate in aiding the correspondent as she tries to report a story—often tend to try to switch roles, becoming the boss of the very correspondent who pays their wage, Barker says. They will tell her that a story she plans to work on is not a good one and that she should scrap it. They will tell her that something she wants to track down is impossible to find rather than attempt to locate the information. "What really drives me crazy is when you go into an interview and discover the person speaks perfect English," she said. "I've had male translators who still try to take charge, despite the fact I don't need their help to do the interview."

Sly, who oversees an all-male staff in the paper's Baghdad bureau, has had decades of practice when it comes to being a female manager in a part of the world where women manage little outside the home. She finds that as a Western woman in a position of authority, most men automatically give her what she calls "the honorary status of a man." But, she says, that status can be lost quickly. "You have to behave in a way that doesn't conflict with their culture too much," she said. "I don't wear clothing that shows my arms or legs. I never let them see me drinking alcohol. I do not swim in the hotel pool if they are around to see me. If I swim, I do it late at night, when no one is around. The essential rule is that you can't get the honorary status of being a man if you throw it in their face that you are, indeed, a woman."

But Barker has discovered that even the most businesslike approach will garner a female correspondent the kind of unwanted advances her male counterparts do not have to face. Barker remembers calling one of her translators one night to ask for a phone number. He gave it to her but then made it clear he thought the reason for her call was a ruse for something less platonic. "I will come to you at midnight," he said suggestively.

Through a Woman's Eyes

A 2001 study by the International Women's Media Foundation came up with a startling statistic, if for no other reason that it was nearly unanimous. Ninety-two percent of the women who responded to the group's study said they believed that women journalists bring a more human perspective to stories.[7] Goering doesn't know if she would have believed that three years ago, in the days before she was both a mother and a journalist. But she sees that theory borne out in her work now.

In her first year of motherhood, when she traveled extensively with baby Grace, Goering found herself in all the usual kind of situations one might expect to see in Africa: famines, coups and the wars that result, genocides, refugee camps. She had seen poverty, death, and horror before in her first foreign correspondent assignment in South America and during her coverage of the war in Iraq. But she found herself looking at the sadness before her differently than she ever had before. "I see the world in a whole new way," she said, "and that is compounded even more when my children are with me on these stories. I find myself seeing things through the eyes of mothers and children and families. You never get numb—at least I didn't—to the terrible things I see, but these days I feel it all even more. My children have made me a better journalist."

In Love in War Zones

On my third reporting tour in Iraq, every plan I'd ever made for my future—a future that always had included goals of being a foreign correspondent—was forever changed. On a reporting trip to Kirkuk, I learned of a U.S. Army unit that was living in a house right in the center of the war-torn city (as opposed to living on a heavily fortified military base on the outskirts of town, the way most American troops in Iraq were). I was granted military permission to spend some time with them to observe how patrolling a city might change when soldiers lived inside it. When I arrived at the house—a mansion complex that had once belonged to a high-ranking Baath party official—I met Army captain Bill Hampton. He was as impressive a military officer as I had encountered in months of travel throughout Iraq. We talked late into the night about the war, about his soldiers, and eventually about our lives—mine of constant travel to stories throughout the country and the world, his as a soldier and widowed father of a five-year-old daughter.

After I left the house—bound for a couple weeks of reporting in Abu Ghraib and Baghdad—I wrote a story about the situation in Kirkuk. Captain Hampton liked the piece and e-mailed to say so. We kept in touch after that, during what were the final weeks of his yearlong tour. He called me the day he arrived safely back in the United States. Within months, we had fallen in love and were traveling to see each other every few weeks—him to New York (where I was based for the *Tribune*), me to Hawaii (the home base of the 25th Infantry Division), or both of us, along with his daughter, Savannah, to random meeting spots on the West Coast.

After a year of this, when the paper asked me to return for a stint in Iraq and another in Africa, I found myself confronting all the scenarios I had been researching for this chapter: Can a woman be a wife, mother, and intrepid national and foreign correspondent? Do female correspondents have to compromise their work—perhaps take a metro job or an editing slot—in order to have personal lives? Should we continue to accept the same dangerous assignments we did when we were single? Can we really have it all? There are no easy answers. Many female journalists say that striking the balance between the personal and the professional is their greatest struggle.

I went to both Africa and Iraq after meeting Bill and Savannah, but when the vehicle in which I was traveling in northern Iraq came under heavy fire, I suddenly understood why so many friends with children had turned down their opportunity to cover one of the biggest stories of our time, why Sly had found herself sitting around that dinner table with so many single women. Even the most dedicated of us find our willingness to dive into deadly situations changing once we feel a sense of responsibility for a partner and children.

A few months after my Africa trip—to cover the famine in Niger—I prepared to leave the *Tribune* to move to Hawaii to be with Bill and Savannah full-time. I did not want to leave my job, the paper I loved, the bosses I admired, but I had come to the conclusion that I could, indeed, not have it all. The newspaper, however, shocked me when my editors came up with a plan that would allow me to temporarily base in Hawaii for the eighteen months that Bill had left in his tour there. I would cover the West Coast and the Pacific Rim, help as needed in Asia, and work on a special project in Korea.

As I write this, I have been here only two months and am still finding my way as I juggle the demands of being a national and foreign correspondent as well as a partner and mother. I am no longer doing routine stints to Iraq. It is hard to leave that story behind, but I know I am no longer the best person for the job; I worry more about coming home than about covering the story while there. I spoke with Goering about our situations the other day. She was on assignment in Zambia with the kids and trying to transcribe notes, order room service, and feed baby Noah; I was rushing out the door to get Savannah to school and be back in time for a telephone interview that I had scheduled days before. We should start a support group, I told her. "We wouldn't have time to have meetings," she laughed. "And there wouldn't be many women to attend anyway." [Kirsten Scharnberg married Major Bill Hampton, left the *Tribune* in 2008, and they now live in Europe with their two children.]

Notes

1. David Weaver, et al., *The American Journalist in the Twenty-First Century: U.S. News People at the Dawn of a New Millennium* (Mahwah, N.J.: Erlbaum, 2007), 6.

2. Hajar Smouni, "Between Repression and Servility," Reporters without Borders, http://www.rsf.org/rubrique.php3?id_rubrique=741 (accessed January 21, 2009).

3. All quotes from Liz Sly are from an interview by Kirsten Scharnberg Hampton, January 25, 2006.

4. All quotes from Kim Barker are from an interview by Kirsten Scharnberg Hampton, December 25, 2005.

5. "Leading in a Different Language: Will Women Change the News Media?" International Women's Media Foundation, August 1, 2001.

6. All quotes from Laurie Goering are from an interview by Kirsten Scharnberg Hampton, January 24, 2006.

7. "Leading in a Different Language."

Buried Alive. Omayra Sanchez looks up from her watery grave. The thirteen-year-old girl was trapped in the mudslide that covered her town of Armero, Columbia, which killed more than twenty-five thousand people. Although rescuers tried to free her, they were unsuccessful. After fifty-nine hours she died, becoming a sad symbol of the devastating tragedy. Photo by Carol Guzy (*Miami Herald*), 1985. Photo courtesy of the *Miami Herald*.

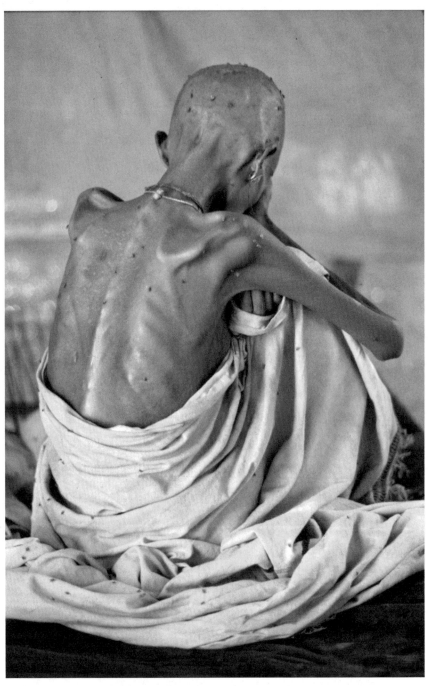

Famine. A pitifully frail, emaciated woman rests at a refugee camp in Ethiopia during a devastating famine. Photo by Carol Guzy (*Miami Herald*), 1985. Photo courtesy of the *Miami Herald*.

Final Look. A dying woman gazes into the eyes of her husband before collapsing in his arms at a refugee camp during an African famine of biblical proportions. She had just left a clinic at the camp, but there was no more they could do for her. She later died from tuberculosis and complications of starvation that had weakened her frail body. Photo by Carol Guzy, (*Miami Herald*), Sudan, 1985. Photo courtesy of the *Miami Herald*.

Freedom. In November 1989, East German leaders opened the Berlin Wall, which marked the end of the Cold War. The first part of the wall removed was at Potsdamer Platz. The crowd bears witness to one of the most important historical events of modern times. Photo by Carol Guzy (*Washington Post*), 1989. Photo courtesy of the *Washington Post*.

Out of the Darkness, a Whisper of Hope. Shortly after the military intervention in Haiti, a U.S. soldier steps in to protect a man suspected of throwing a grenade into a joyous democracy march, killing and injuring numerous pro-Aristide demonstrators. The soldiers arrested him, saving his life from an angry crowd. Photo by Carol Guzy (*Washington Post*), Port-au-Prince, Haiti, 1994. Photo courtesy of the *Washington Post*.

Street Justice. In Haiti, faith has long been lost in a corrupt and inept judicial system. A person's trial and sentencing is often carried out by an angry mob, swift and brutal. After the funeral for a beloved community leader who was killed by a band of thieves, a mourner identified this man as one of them. The crowd grabbed him and began beating him. At one point an off-duty policeman with a gun tried to save him. But the mob, thirsty for revenge, beat him with rocks, clubs, and bare fists. The neighborhood vigilante group eventually ended his life with a knife. Photo by Carol Guzy, Port-au-Prince, Haiti, 1996. Photo courtesy of Carol Guzy.

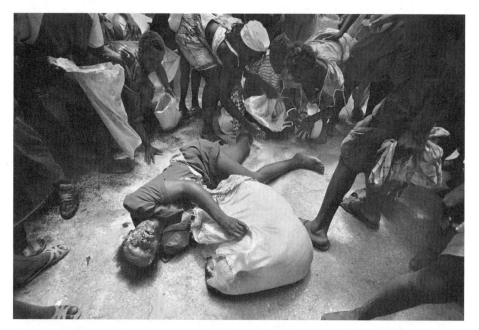

Limits of Civilization. Haitians scramble to steal rice from a woman who was knocked unconscious when a mob tried to grab her sack of rice during the looting of a food warehouse. The crippling economic embargo against the impoverished nation caused an increase in hunger and malnutrition, and the power of that hunger erupted in chaos and looting during the U.S. military intervention in the troubled country. Photo by Carol Guzy (*Washington Post*), Port-au-Prince, Haiti, 1994. Photo courtesy of the *Washington Post.*

A World of Violence. A group of children wait for their school bus as yet another body lies in the streets of Port-au-Prince. The man had been bound and the flesh torn from his head in an apparent statement of terror and political violence during the armed rebellion that forced president Jean-Bertrand Aristide from power. Death and atrocities are common sights in the world of Haiti's daily struggles. Photo by Carol Guzy, Port-au-Prince, Haiti, 2004. Photo courtesy of Carol Guzy.

Tender Mercy. Sisters from Missionaries of Charity comfort a woman at a home for the destitute and dying in Calcutta, India, after Mother Teresa's death. Photo by Carol Guzy, Calcutta, India, 1997. Photo courtesy of Carol Guzy.

Kosovo's Sorrow. Two-year-old Agim Shala is passed through a barbed-wire fence into the hands of grandparents at the camp run by the United Arab Emirates in Kukes, Albania. The members of the Shala family were reunited here after fleeing Kosovo. Serb aggression was unleashed on ethnic Albanians in a massive ethnic cleansing. Refugees fled to neighboring Albania and Macedonia. Photo by Carol Guzy (*Washington Post*), May 3, 1999. Photo courtesy of the *Washington Post*.

War and Innocence. A young Albanian schoolboy watches as war comes to his backyard. Albanian tanks rush to reinforce the border with Kosovo at Morini crossing. The fighting was raging between Kosovo Liberation Army forces and Serb troops as NATO forces dropped bombs on Kosovo just before the peace treaty was signed. This battle led to the Serb pullout being ordered, paving the way for the return of the refugees. Photo by Carol Guzy (*Washington Post*), Kukes, Albania, May 1999. Photo courtesy of the *Washington Post.*

Flood of Humanity. Kosovar refugees weep as they cross the border by foot at Morini into Albania, fleeing their troubled homeland and Serb ethnic cleansing. The group of mostly women and children and elderly men showed great distress. They were transported to camps in Kukes, Albania, to wait with uncertainty during the conflict. Photo by Carol Guzy (*Washington Post*), April 1999. Photo courtesy of the *Washington Post.*

Wounded Messengers. Children were among the most victimized in Sierra Leone's war. Rebels in Sierra Leone ordered children to put an arm on the roots of a cottonwood tree and watch as the arm was cut off with a crude machete. Some fainted with the first cut; others bled to death. The rebels in Sierra Leone used this particular form of brutality as a means to intimidate the civilian population. Dr. Matthew Mirones, a New York prosthetic manufacturer, read about their plight and started a program to donate artificial limbs to the victims. The first group of eight arrived in Washington, D.C., in September 2000, including Damba Koroma and Memunatu ("Memuna") Mansaray. Photo by Carol Guzy (*Washington Post*), 2000. Photo courtesy of the *Washington Post*.

Wounded Messengers, Old Soul. With the tiny face of an old soul, four-year-old Memunatu Mansaray bears witness to the atrocities inflicted on society's most innocent at a House Subcommittee on Africa hearing on Capitol Hill in Washington, D.C., where the group of amputees from Sierra Leone's civil war gave testimony about their ordeals. People broke down in tears at the sight of such brutality. Photo by Carol Guzy (*Washington Post*), 2000. Photo courtesy of the *Washington Post*.

16

Photography in Distant Lands

CAROL GUZY

It has been said that when you make a photo, you take a piece of the soul. As well, you give a part of yours. There are pieces of my soul scattered all over the earth. Indeed it's what makes me whole.

Photojournalism has taken me to distant lands where I've experienced other cultures and documented a vast range of the human condition. Sometimes the world has spun out of control amid conflict and chaos. I've looked up close at the anguish of war, the thrill of revolution, the rapture of liberation. I've seen famines of biblical proportions, watched communism crumble, trekked with Hutu refugees, and covered ethnic cleansing in Kosovo that left a flood of refugees and an abandoned psychiatric hospital with patients to fend for themselves. I've seen wretched poverty, men beaten to death by mobs, and refugee children watching their parents die on the side of a road, their whispers giving way to eternal silence. I've seen the eyes of evil, the hands of injustice, and the face of repression. I've been to Magunga, Zaire, and Kukes, Albania. I've met Mother Teresa and documented acts of dictators and champions.

I have seen the reality of Memuna, a tiny girl with one arm and the eyes of an old soul. She, along with other war victims from Sierra Leone, endured a particular brand of brutality. Rebels there had a nasty habit of cutting off the arms and legs of civilians to intimidate the population. Imagine a child trembling in terror as her parents are savagely killed before her eyes. That same child is then ordered to put her arm on the roots of a cottonwood tree and watch as it is cut off with a crude machete. Some mercifully faint with the first cut, others bleed to death, and those who survive are haunted the rest of their lives by the memories. The youngest of victims suffered atrocities in a conflict they did not yet even comprehend. These things rip your heart out and tear at the very fiber of civilization.

I've walked with mountain gorillas in Rwanda and have felt the deep bonds we have with nature and been deeply saddened by the disregard and destruction our species has wrought. I've walked over bodies piled deep under the muck of a devastating mudslide in Colombia and climbed to a mountaintop with Haitians who believe if they just get a little closer to their god, he may finally hear them. I've photographed the first breath of a baby and the unmistakable expression of death as the light leaves someone's eyes.

I have stood on the steps of the Supreme Court in Washington, D.C., as the world's greatest democracy struggled with its very meaning in a hotly contested election year. But struggled peacefully—no riots, no tanks, no coups d'etat. Recently, I viewed history through a long lens as Barack Obama became a powerful symbol for a new day in America. I rode in a boat past homes and street signs in the surreal city that was once New Orleans. Inside those homes were mementos of shattered lives, family photos thick with mold, many including a beloved pet. Animals—the most silent of victims apparent again in the wrenching images of Hurricane Katrina's lost pets. And the smell—one thing you can never photograph.

September 11 is etched eternally in our collective consciousness with a profound sorrow that cut deep into the heart of this nation. Many Americans seem to be reevaluating priorities, seeking deeper meaning and a sense of purpose. At ground zero, I wept.

Out of the catastrophe of war or the ashes of the World Trade Center or the toxic floodwaters of New Orleans comes a strength and resilience. There are everyday folks who have shown us the meaning of grace. Our definition of hero has been revised. Firefighters and rescue workers are my heroes. Teachers, who shape our destiny, are my heroes. Journalists who persevere in the pursuit of truth are my heroes.

Sometimes photographers are the only ones to hear the silent screams of the suffering. Trying to translate what we experience is a formidable task. Photojournalists are chameleons by nature. We inhabit someone's skin intimately enough to tell their story yet remain an impartial spectator of their world. We keep a delicate balance in which the lens is a shield from personal feelings, but only a temporary respite.

Photojournalists bear witness to history, to the major news events as well as the small moments that provide a record of our time. But there's an emotional toll from witnessing man's inhumanity. I have learned that it is damaging to repress feelings, because the emotions *do* come back to haunt me. When the whispers in your mind become inconsolable screams. You crash and burn, then learn how to look again. I am enraged when I see the price paid by those most fragile in a society for a war they didn't wage. When I move the camera away, the sense of hopelessness can be overwhelming. The stories of conflict pose a dilemma, as many deem these stories a cliché. But it's hard to tell a desperate woman holding her wounded child that she's merely a cliché. These people can't turn the page or change channels when they don't like the story. They're stuck in reality long after the headlines are gone. You wonder how many pictures you can take until someone really sees.

The dignity with which people deal with adversity is moving and revealing, and to tell their stories is an honor. When I glimpse the profound splendor of the human spirit, even in the most desolate of circumstances, it becomes imperative to record their plight. I also have been struck by the poetry in everyday lives. I'm humbled by acts of genuine courage and gestures of kindness by those whom some would unwisely think the least among us. People living in abject poverty have offered me, a stranger, their last piece of bread and shelter from harm. They are not famous or world leaders. Their success is not measured by wealth or even literacy but by character and virtue.

I've found that it's important to have a balance between one's personal and professional life. Photographers today also face physical dangers, both obvious and hidden. At times I have been screamed at, knocked down, had cameras ripped off my neck, been trampled by mobs, trampled by mobs of fellow photographers, arrested, shot at, and deemed obsessive by my editors too many times to count. I do prefer the word *dedicated*.

Some advice for international coverage: I try to pack light but not to find myself in the middle of nowhere without medicine or other items that would be difficult to find. I am reminded of the time in Haiti when all hell was breaking loose, airports and shops were closed, and everyone ran out of film. Running out of clean clothes is one thing—film is another. Trying to anticipate the conditions under which I will be working saves time and discomfort. You can't run in high heels.

I've learned the importance of listening to your own instincts. It's easy for a spark to ignite into a raging flame in volatile situations. There is no need to speak the language, to feel when emotions are escalating to fever pitch. There's a phrase that if your pictures aren't good enough, you're not close enough. But sometimes too close can kill you. Certain risks are necessary, but foolish bravado is not worth your life. There are times when photographers need to decide if and when to intervene. It seems obvious that if you can save someone from death, you should put the camera down. But sometimes professionals go on autopilot when working and are used to letting things happen without intrusion. In Haiti there were times when journalists saved people from machete-wielding crowds, but on one occasion it wasn't possible. Watching someone being ripped apart in front of me was beyond words.

A mob killed a man while other journalists and I were covering a funeral. People were screaming, knives flailing. The story was more complicated than it appears on the surface; street justice is a fact of life in that country, and killers and victims become interchangeable. The incident was over in minutes, but I have wondered since then if there was something I should have done to try to stop it even though I know the crowd was past the line of reason. Still, there is a guilt that lingers.

One of my "wow" moments was watching the fall of the Berlin Wall in 1989. The morning that officials were about to take out the first chunk, I found myself in a crushing crowd unable to see anything. One annoying detail with photography is the need to *see* your subject. I surveyed the scene and noticed a very large, sturdy German male "tripod" smiling at me. He graciously put me on his shoulders and spent one of the most memorable moments of his life with my cameras clanging off his forehead. Another unforgettable time was being unceremoniously arrested during an International Monetary Fund protest in front of a gaggle of my peers with loaded cameras. I later identified with my vegetarian peacenik cellmates, who were dismayed that the only cuisine offered at the D.C. jail was bologna sandwiches.

I have found that flexibility, patience, and tenacity are important character traits. Those are not nearly as much of a challenge, however, as conquering the disadvantage of being short.

In news photography, the ever-changing technology is fascinating but sometimes frustrating. I've developed film in toilets and blown up scanners, satellite phones, and cameras along the way. Technical is not my middle name. But whatever the latest gadgets, it's important to remember they are merely tools to learn well enough to forget. Eyes and minds and hearts make the most compelling images. There is anxiety about the state of newspapers and the world of Web multimedia, but it can be an exciting evolution and provide a vehicle for photojournalism with unlimited space and a worldwide audience. However, it will be impossible for me to replace that tactile pleasure of holding a paper in my hands.

Although sometimes conditions are miserable, the rewards of photojournalism are immeasurable. Photographs can be important tools to build a bridge of empathy in times of divisiveness. They reveal not only our differences but also the qualities that make us all part of a world family. Empathy—a small word with mammoth meaning. Someone once told me that empathy is not imagining how you would feel in a given situation but rather the ability to break through your own veil of life experiences and truly see how someone else *is* feeling.

I can't quite pinpoint when the media became the enemy, however. A "shoot the messenger" mentality seems to be escalating. Seeing too much violence in the newspaper over morning cereal can generate a helplessness that numbs or infuriates readers. Then the fingers start pointing at the press for running those disturbing images. Certainly there is a need for sensitivity in news coverage, but there is also danger in censoring reality. Yes, those photographs are uncomfortable to view, but for many in this world there is no breakfast cereal or freedom from fear. Perhaps that's what society should find most intolerable, not the pictures that remind us of it.

As long as injustice remains, it's our responsibility as journalists to have a social conscience and bring these issues to light. Photographers may not change the world, but sometimes one defining moment can change a life or an attitude. And there is satisfaction in hearing your work has made someone disturbed. Then made them think. And then made them act. Or simply made them smile.

A photograph can make a difference—perhaps a small difference to one person on one day but meaningful nonetheless. Photographers endlessly pass through people's lives. Each story is a like a doomed romance. The passion and mystery are intoxicating but destined for bittersweet farewells. Some photographs have become a lasting and tangible memorial for loved ones lost or an irreplaceable keepsake. Pictures I've taken of many a kindergarten class are proudly displayed on folks' refrigerators.

I have learned about the poignancy of small acts, such as treating the janitor with the same dignity and deference as the chief. Or looking past the disfigured face of a leprosy victim and seeing beauty—the real kind. Our timeless task is to photograph that inner essence—the camera is our pen, light is our ink. I have found that greatness is not in a title or awards, but in the graciousness with which people accept both glory and defeat. And knowing that risk at times means the potential for failure, but never risking what you believe in may be life's greatest regret.

Times have changed since my career began. Female faces were few on photography staffs of newspapers and even more uncommon on international stories. Today, however, more and more women are covering the most important stories of our times as photojournalists. It's encouraging when young students view past generations as role models and firmly realize gender or race can no longer deter them from their dreams. Change occurs slowly in any society or culture. But journalism in this new twenty-first century is now embracing the importance of diversity in newsrooms.

A photograph can be a powerful witness and an eloquent voice for those who have none. Pictures inform, educate, enlighten, captivate, and spur governments into action. They are historical documents and poignant reminders of our human frailties. They're our life's work, our legacy. Each of us leaves behind what we've done and who we've been. As photographers, we should follow our hearts, trust our guts, and keep the inquisitive eyes of a child. We change our world not only by words or pictures but also by example. We must tread lightly and with purpose. Cherish our loved ones more than our photographs. Embrace hope.

There is an old proverb that has helped me gain perspective on this odd and magnificent journey: "Tell me, I'll forget. Show me, I may remember. Involve me, I'll understand." If one picture reaches one person on one day, we've done our job.

17

Women in News Photography

CAROL GUZY

I hosted an event for Women Photojournalists of Washington several years ago and marveled at the fact that so many female professionals were packing my home. Many people recognize names like Dorothea Lange, who was perhaps the best-known documentary photographer in American history, and Margaret Bourke-White, a pioneering female photojournalist who worked for both *Time* magazine and *Life* in the early years of those publications. But there also were courageous women like Catherine Leroy, veiled by anonymity even among many of her peers today. During a discussion event in New York, none of the panelists of female war photographers had heard of Leroy. Her gritty photographs from Vietnam had earned her the distinction of being the first female recipient of the Robert Capa Gold Medal, for coverage of the civil war in Lebanon in the mid-1970s. The award was created in 1955 by the Overseas Press Club and *Life* magazine to honor a man whose photos showed war in a way that war had never before been photographed.

The Vietnam era was a time when women covering conflict with a camera were certainly the minority. Leroy passed away in 2006, in virtual obscurity, frustrated by a lack of work and the inability to publish her later projects, including a book on the environment and an exhibit at the Vietnam Veterans Memorial Wall. At great personal risk, Leroy documented important pieces of history and in doing so broke new ground for women photojournalists. We didn't know her name. A thankless business this can be.

Women trailblazers in news photography have been few in what has historically been a predominantly male profession. No news industry organization keeps precise records, though certainly the numbers of female photographers have grown in recent years. About a quarter of the membership of the National Newspaper Photographers Association is now female. Only a few women photojournalists have won Pulitzer Prizes in news photography. I am fortunate to be among them as a recipient in 1986 as a photographer for the *Miami Herald,* and in 1995 and 2000 as a photographer for the *Washington Post.* Like many female news photographers, I would not trade my job for the world. But it comes with a cost.

While the physical dangers of covering certain stories are evident, the most insidious risk may be the future effects of the toxins our bodies are exposed to. I spent a great deal of time near ground zero after 9/11 covering the New York firefighters, their grief and grace during their final salute to so many fallen brothers. Since then I have been plagued with the same respiratory symptoms that have surfaced for many of the rescue workers and volunteers. The health issues intensified after covering Hurricane Katrina, wading through toxic sludge and breathing in nasty mold growing on the walls of submerged homes. After six months, like most folks who were there any length of time, I battled "Katrina cough." Photojournalists tend to spend time in countries with lax pollution controls. It is becoming more evident how destructive the human species has been to the environment. As news photographers, we many times have a front-row seat to contamination. Our lungs may one day be a science project. Over the years, many women who work with chemicals in photography labs have taken the same risks. No one knows the impact of the buildup of these toxic chemicals, for women or men.

Stress is another factor that significantly affects the well-being of photographers—and not only stress from the physical demands of the job but also the constant need to be "on" and aware. So many factors can foil a photo—turning left instead of right, the planets not being aligned, forgetting to put that roll of film in the camera. Yes, we've all done it back in the day before digital. Or you blink. And the moment is gone forever. Photographers have only one chance. There is no opportunity to interview someone after the fact and still accurately write about it.

My love is long-term projects. I have never been good at capturing that one defining instant in news photography, but prefer to spend the time and delve below the surface, like peeling away the layers of an onion. In fact, quality journalism requires an immense investment of time to make those compelling images. With in-depth visual reporting, it's crucial to gain the trust of subjects and tell their stories with truth and fairness. Total objectivity is a myth, of course. We are subjective beings with individual thoughts and opinions. But the best reporters and photographers can put those aside and see through others' eyes.

In the process of gaining trust, we often also gain friends. I wonder if the extreme attempts in news to maintain the perception of objectivity in fact perpetuates the view that we are uninvolved in the community and unconcerned as journalists. But "distance" has not been my experience, nor has that been the case with many other news photographers I have worked with around the world.

I'm still in contact with many people I have covered, and the greatest reward is when your subjects later become friends. After a four-year journalistic endeavor about a Sierra Leone amputee, one of my proudest moments was when her new family adopted me and made me her godmother. There are kids in Haiti who are extended family. They call me Mother. I found that one person can make a small difference. During the period when Haiti continually spiraled out of control, I despaired when pictures of the destruction did not bring change. As human to human, the only solace came in helping individual families to provide school and food and shelter. These families could not scrape together enough for rice for dinner.

Like many other news photographers in history, I have walked the path alongside those who were suffering. And today I count as my friends an eclectic motley crew of folks from vastly different walks of life. They are genuine; some are quite eccentric. These people humble me with their passion and convictions. This journey with a camera has taken me through some monumental milestones of history as well as through instances of devastating despair or heartbreakingly beautiful humanity. Photographs can document events, but it is the small moments that give life to your memories.

I have watched evening light touch the face of a Haitian girl whose smile literally glowed with expectation, even amid strife in her country. I have walked through a morgue in Port-au-Prince and seen unclaimed bodies of babies thrown onto a towering pile and realized people had no money to bury their dead. I have longed for a seatbelt on a harrowing Humvee ride with U.S. soldiers who were policing a foreign land.

I have witnessed a child bringing flowers to an East German border guard as the wall that separated their lives crumbled away. I have witnessed a Czech resident shaping a piece of the dreaded iron curtain into a heart. When a Kosovar refugee child was passed through a barbed-wire camp fence to relatives fleeing ethnic cleansing, I was overwhelmed by the symbolism of war and innocence that the scene reflected. When I walked through an abandoned psychiatric hospital in Kosovo, I felt I was in a Hitchcock film—the difference being, I could walk out the gates while the other actors were still locked in hell.

I met Sierra Leone amputees who could speak only Creole when they arrived in the United States. They decided to call this odd photographer who would not leave "Yema," because "Carol" was too hard to remember. Those same children gained political asylum. One enchanting girl named Memuna sent me a card four years later. The card was of an angel with one wing. An African child who had so little, living at this end of the earth in the sub-Saharan desert, gave me his necklace as a parting gift to remember him. A taxi driver in Ghana was buried in a Mercedes-like coffin as family members sang joyfully and toasted his passage to a better life. Rwandan refugees and I trekked through scenery that took our breath away. It is difficult to process the savagery that occurred there, or to completely process gunfire or understand the coldness in a tyrant's eyes that spoke of atrocities to come.

Protesters caught up in the moment of revolution have knocked me down and then politely picked me up. I have been a bystander to the most private moment of farewell as a dying victim of the Ethiopian famine looked at her husband's face for the final time. Sometimes life pauses and we must put the camera down and let our feelings in.

In our own country, my work as a news photographer has taken on yet another dimension of covering war. The "mask" of distance we photojournalists often wear was torn asunder for me during the aftermath of 9/11. It's impossible not to remember the wind kicking up just as the names of 9/11 victims were read and the dust of ground zero making a swirling circle as if the spirits of those victims were still there. The dust was in my hair. It felt as if I carried the memory of them away with me. When the ethereal blue World Trade Center memorial lights first shined toward the heavens, it seemed as if eternity was at the end of my lens. One FDNY firefighter in his dress uniform at a memorial service reached up with a spotless white glove to graciously assist my clumsy descent from a ladder. A different firefighter at another of the seemingly endless torrent of funerals stepped out of formation to hug a photographer who broke down in unprofessional tears.

I have heard the children's letters to their fallen dads blare from loudspeakers at the church and watched them stand bravely as the bagpipes played that mournful song. My father died when I was six years old, and now so many of these kids will grow up never knowing theirs. The kind of war fought by terrorists is hard to comprehend. Hate is a terrible thing.

The war in Iraq is also a war on the home front. Through a two-hundred-millimeter lens, I have seen the intensely intimate look of a new bride bidding her soldier good-bye as he leaves for Iraq and an uncertain fate. I was fortunate to also photograph that same couple's reunion and delight in the much-too-infrequent pictures of a happy ending. In fact, it all takes part of our hearts—and gives back immeasurable riches. The valuable kind.

18

International Journalism in a New Era

KATHLEEN CARROLL

Foreign: external to
one's own country or nation

International: extending across
or transcending national boundaries

Once upon a time, news organizations with overseas operations usually had a foreign editor to supervise their foreign correspondents. Today, John Daniszewski, who is responsible for the Associated Press's ninety-plus bureaus outside the United States, is quite properly called the international editor. It's an important distinction, one that recognizes that reader interests—like news itself—transcend national borders. One of the reasons is money.

When an oil pipeline explodes in Nigeria, the effects are felt at Chevron's headquarters in California, at ExxonMobil outside Dallas, at Royal Dutch Shell PLC in Amsterdam, at Total SA in Paris, and at Eni SpA in Rome. All have significant business in Africa's largest oil country, where violence halts production of millions of barrels a year. And that keeps oil prices high everywhere.

General Electric Company has done business around the world for many years. But in 2007, for the first time in its history, more than half of GE's revenue came from its overseas operations. That means GE employees and GE shareholders all have pretty tangible reasons to be interested in what's happening in GE markets such as India, China, Thailand, and Portugal.

You don't have to be a conglomerate to be global. West Virginia says investments from overseas companies created more than thirty thousand jobs in the state. That's why West Virginia's development office has an international division and offices in Germany and Japan. And how about the tortilla effect? As gasoline prices hit the roof in 2006, U.S. companies began buying more corn to make ethanol. Then the price of corn shot up. And the next thing you know, corn tortillas had gotten too expensive for many of Mexico's poor. So Mexico's government moved to invoke price controls and competitive penalties to help bring tortilla prices back down. So there are dozens of reasons for readers to care about news from elsewhere. But they won't care if journalists simply tell them what happened.

International journalists need to speak the language and understand the culture and connections (economic, political, and just plain human) of the places they cover. And they must be able to explain those places. A piece about the French tolerance for dogs in restaurants can sparkle with cultural insight. But there's more to France than pampered pooches. Readers need to understand the crippling legacy of French colonial rule in North Africa: Generations of North African immigrants in France who feel marginalized. The image of Paris's splendor isn't complete if you don't also show the impoverished suburbs ringing the city, their concrete high-rises filled with families from Algeria, Morocco, and Tunisia and their French-born children who can't find work and who feel the sting of discrimination because they are Muslim or black. When those angry young Frenchmen begin rioting night after night, readers will better understand why.

More than twelve hundred journalists—reporters, photographers, editors, television camera operators—work for the Associated Press outside the United States. They are based in one of more than ninety countries where the AP has a bureau. It might be high atop a high-tech office building in Tokyo or in a converted house in Kabul. Many of these journalists' surroundings crackle with technology that delivers news at the speed of light. Others' reflect the state of things in their host country. Until just recently, for example, the correspondent in one remote former Soviet-bloc country had to chop wood for the stove that was the only source of office heat. Many of those journalists are covering their home countries for a global audience, and readers benefit from their insight.

A few cannot cover their own countries. They've been chased from their homelands, often for their aggressive journalism—the kind of reporting that journalists in the United States may take for granted. Salah Nasrawi left Iraq more than fifteen years ago after being threatened for years by officials who didn't like what he wrote. Saddam Hussein's information minister once publicly told him he was going to hang Salah from a bridge next to the ministry building if he didn't stop writing "unauthorized" stories. Salah's credentials were finally yanked shortly after the 1991 Gulf War when he refused to fake a story about the Shiite uprising. Convinced he would join the list of Iraqi journalists who disappeared without a trace, he left. Since then, Salah has worked for the AP in Cairo.

Scheherezade Faramarzi's reporting from Beirut on the Iran-Iraq war irritated authorities in her native Iran. They were particularly unhappy with her story on the execution of children who distributed dissident newspapers. At one point, her brother saw an ominous sign at the Ministry of Foreign Affairs:

"Scheherezade Faramarzi: Who is this counter-revolutionary?"—a label applied to people who often ended up being shot themselves. Scheherezade stayed away from Iran for fifteen years and still cannot get permission to report there.

More recently, correspondent Bagila Bukharbayeva left her native Uzbekistan after authorities withdrew the credentials that allowed her to legally report. Why? Because she gave an eyewitness account of a peaceful protest in the eastern town of Andijan—a protest that ended when government troops opened fire on the civilian crowd.

And Michelle Faul, who has written and spoken publicly about her colleagues who can't go home again, has a story of her own. In 2005 she returned to southern Africa for the AP, though not to her native Zimbabwe. She left there long ago after years of harassment from authorities who were unhappy with her coverage. The final straw: a summons from an Information Ministry official who warned he would throw her into an infamous prison the next time she wrote something he didn't like.

The work can be dangerous. And far too often, deadly. Since the AP was founded in 1846, thirty-one journalists have been killed on assignment—twenty-nine of them overseas and almost all covering a conflict. The global battle-grounds of World War II were especially dangerous. In the last fifty years, AP blood has been spilled in Vietnam, Afghanistan, the Balkans, the West Bank, several places formerly under Soviet control, and in the madness of Somalia and Sierra Leone. The war in Iraq has taken a very bitter toll. Between 2004 and mid-2007, six AP employees were shot to death, three while working to cover this historic period in their native land.

AP's editors at headquarters and in the field take very seriously the responsibilities of keeping staffers safe. Enormous time and resources are spent on training and safety equipment. There are many conversations about how to cover a dangerous place, about how to measure the risks. And sometimes we decide not to go. The risks are particularly high for visual journalists—the photographers and television crews who need to be at the scene to capture the images that tell the story. Their equipment can make them a target. There's no blending in when you have a camera on your shoulder or a long photo lens in front of your face. The risks can be from any side in the fighting—government troops or rebel forces. Anyone who doesn't want the world to see the images those journalists are there to record.

In 2005, while covering a devastating earthquake in a remote part of Pakistan, photographer David Guttenfelder captured a harrowing image: a shirtless young boy howling in pain and reaching for his father as a doctor treated the stump where the boy's left arm had been. You just couldn't stop looking at the picture of the anguished father trying to comfort his child in pain. The boy was

Zeeshan Shah, just nine years old. That photo ran in newspapers and on Web sites the world over.

Sylvia Eibl, a German philanthropist who runs the Children First charity, saw that picture and wanted to help Zeeshan. But no one could find him. He had long ago left the field hospital where Guttenfelder met him. So Eibl took one hundred color copies of that picture and carried them up and down Pakistan's Neelum Valley until she found Zeeshan and his family, living in a tent on the ruins of their home. Children First flew Zeeshan and his father to Italy, where doctors gave the boy a brand-new artificial arm. And when the boy and his father went back home to Pakistan, David was there to photograph his joyous return, new arm and all. A single image that changed a boy's life.

Those images—and stories and sounds—can be a powerful force because they touch so many: AP news reaches one billion people around the world every single day. Sometimes it only needs to reach one.

PART 5

Women Leaders in an
Era of Corporate, Legal,
and Commercial Pressures

19

The Imperiled Media

At Long Last, Promise?

GENEVA OVERHOLSER

December 12, 2005, dawned icy gray through most of the country—just the right weather for Black Ink Monday. This was the day when cartoonists throughout the United States would call attention to the imperilment of the American press, as exemplified by the quickly dwindling numbers of political cartoonists. Across the land appeared drawings of watchdogs chained to their houses, journalists skewered by their own pens, cartoons outsourced to foreign nations, newspapers with gaping holes cut out. "The pen is mightier than the sword," read one caption, but a bean counter held his sword victoriously aloft as a hapless cartoonist's pen sank into the muck. "Lost my job at GM," says a sign held by one fellow. "Lost my job drawing cartoons about you losing your job at GM," says the sign held by the fellow in the companion panel. "So you want a job ridiculing the running dog corporate capitalists," an employment counselor says to an out-of-work cartoonist. "Who would be paying you?"[1]

In the waning days of 2005, as all manner of media bedevilments came to seem the norm, this was the question: Who will pay for the journalism? While the cartoonists portrayed themselves as the spotted owls of journalism, nearing extinction, there was a broader truth: The mainstream media as a whole—at least the familiar format and business model—increasingly felt doomed to extinction. "The End of News?" read a headline on a *New York Review of Books* article.[2] "A moment of silence, please, for the imminent death of the old Mainstream Mass Culture," read the lead of a *Los Angeles Times* story.[3]

"There has been nothing in our times like this," longtime television newsman Bill Moyers told a gathering commemorating the twentieth anniversary of the National Security Archive in Washington three days before Black Ink Monday. He cited the Bush administration's practiced secrecy, its censorship of scientific research, the faking of news reports, the weakening of the Freedom of Information Act. "They couldn't get away with all this if the press was at the top of its game. Never has the need for an independent press been greater."[4]

Few indeed thought the press had been at the top of its game in recent years, and the *lack* of independence Moyers implied was a common complaint. The week of his speech, national-security reporters gathered at the Aspen Institute's Washington offices for a postmortem on American journalism during the lead-up to the war in Iraq. "I think the U.S. news media failed in covering this story as miserably as the intelligence community did in its . . . assessments," said then Knight Ridder's Jonathan Landay. His company's Washington bureau chief, John Walcott, said, "Without transparency and accountability, I don't know how you get to self-governance."[5] Many in the public apparently shared that concern. Some began to act. The progressive citizens' organization MoveOn.org, for example, protested job cuts at the Tribune Company, whose elimination of cartoonist positions at the *Los Angeles Times* and *Chicago Tribune* had triggered Black Ink Monday. "The key for us is to get people to recognize that the *Tribune*'s business model is at fundamental odds with a good journalism model," said a MoveOn .org spokesperson. "We want to bring more public attention on these cuts and slow the trend, to bring them more in line with a good journalism model."[6]

The underlying issues were several: Years of quarter-to-quarter profit pressures had steadily eroded the quality of journalism in newspaper and broadcast newsrooms across the nation. Some observers lamented in particular the decline of international news, running directly counter to the needs of citizens of the leading nation in an increasingly interdependent world. Others deplored the way the relentless repetition of scandal and gossip was displacing the much more expensive undertaking of enterprise, investigative, and other original reporting. Meanwhile, revenues from advertising, particularly classified, were migrating to the Web, increasing the pressures on news executives to cut costs.

Deep ideological divisions, forcefully voiced, also pressed on journalists, some of whom acknowledged occasionally pulling their journalistic punches. A survey in 2000 by the Pew Research Center cited some 30 percent of local reporters saying they had "softened the tone of a news story on behalf of the interests of their news organization."[7] Dan Rather told a Fordham University audience in September 2005, "Fear runs stronger in every American newsroom—and I mean every American newsroom—now than any time that I'm aware of in my career."[8] And ethical scandals rocked the big media institutions one after another, from Jayson Blair to Judith Miller at the *New York Times,* Jack Kelley at *USA Today,* and Dan Rather and his producers at CBS News.

The engaging new landscape of the Web offered the promise of revitalization and democratization. But whether it could fill the public's need for a sustained, comprehensive, and fair report was very much an open question. The hash that Wikipedia—the Web's answer to Encyclopedia Britannica—made of newspaperman John Seigenthaler's life in its howlingly error-ridden posting provided a powerful example of why this was so.[9] Add the nation's post-9/11 insecurities, the courts' threats to press freedom, and the polls showing a continuing slide in journalism's credibility, and the state of the press was looking parlous indeed.

Of course, fearful times in the media world are nothing new. Lamentation over the end of serious news attended the birth of the telegraph, the radio, and television. Accusations that the press is awash in scurrilous gossipmongering and scandalous sensationalism ring throughout the nation's history. Nonetheless, the events of 2005 were remarkable. The economic model of mainstream journalism seemed—after a long period of rumored endangerment—to be collapsing. Knight Ridder, the nation's second-largest newspaper company, was pushed onto the market by its top institutional shareholders, citing its (comparatively) low profit margins in the high-margin newspaper industry.[10]

With the public less inclined to view "mainstream media" as an essential part of life, the question of who would buy Knight Ridder was hotly debated: Would it be another media company, an investment group, a technology company? Would it be split up, with local investors "rescuing" some of the less profitable companies? Would Google, Yahoo, or other search-engine companies want to own a news-gathering (or "content-producing") organization? When the McClatchy Company bought Knight Ridder in March 2006, CEO Gary Pruitt called the purchase "a vote of confidence in the newspaper industry."[11] Yet before the year was over, Pruitt was compelled to announce the sale of the *Minneapolis Star Tribune,* McClatchy's largest newspaper, to a private equity group—to pay down debt from the earlier acquisition.[12]

For all the gloom, there were some bright spots. Newspapers were losing subscribers, but they were gaining readers online. Online revenues, although far more modest than the traditional ones, were growing quickly. And several other sectors of the media world were thriving, including ethnic media, weeklies, and alternative publications. Also, it seemed that an industry that had been virtually paralyzed by its embattlement might at last be goaded into action. There had been years of little or no research and development, of declining training budgets (being a cash cow is a strategy, one wag had noted), and of newsrooms clinging to the past as though they were hanging on to a cliff by their fingernails. Now the media world was so rocked by change that torpor seemed no longer an option. So how might a more hopeful media landscape look? Many began to ponder that question.

The wide-open, near-anarchic world of the Web tends to dominate visions of the future. As a *Washington Post* piece of November 13, 2005, put it, "The soul of the Google machine is a passion for disruptive innovation." With its "healthy disregard for the impossible," Google and other online innovators were injecting energy into the long-dispirited media world.[13] Not that the old mainstream media were not performing well on the Web themselves. According to *Editor and Publisher* magazine, "While the Audit Bureau of Circulations' latest [numbers] showed a 2.6 percent decline in daily paid circulation for U.S. newspapers, Nielsen/NetRatings reports that newspaper Web sites grew 11 percent year-over-year to 39.3 million unique visitors in October 2005, comprising 26 percent of the active U.S. Internet population. The 11 percent increase exceeds the growth of the active Internet universe as a whole, which rose 3 percent year-over-year."[14] By September 2006, the number of visitors to newspaper Web sites had risen to 58 million.[15]

Though revenues were growing, they were nowhere near matching the kinds of profits that Wall Street had come to expect. Nor were newsroom cultures finding the fast-paced shift toward online delivery easy, what with its 24-7 pace, its nontraditional voice and attitude, and its presumption of interactivity. Political editors within the *Washington Post* newsroom were so eager to make clear the difference between their work and that of washingtonpost.com's "White House Briefing" that they fairly bristled at the confusion.[16] Online readers, meanwhile, scorned what seemed to them a misguided old-line sputtering over a far richer and more compelling form of journalism. But the old-liners had one very important point: They were doing original reporting while the online version gathered their work and that of other White House reporters. The aggregators—the "screen scrapers"—rely on having someone out there getting the goods. As the advertising revenues flowed onto the Web—still not approximating the customary profits—the question of who would pay for the journalism loomed large.

One piece of the answer, increasingly, seemed to be the citizen journalist, brought to public attention in Dan Gillmor's book *We the Media: Grassroots Journalism by the People, for the People.*[17] Meanwhile, in symposia and journalism reviews and discussions throughout the industry, there were questions galore: Would "bloggers" develop ethics codes about such matters as using anonymous sources? Would advertising on the Web be clearly labeled? For all the doubts, the allure of this wide-open world was unmistakable.

Nonprofit media constituted another hopeful arena. National Public Radio, for one, had been seeing its audience grow by leaps and bounds. "Today more than 30 million people listen to public radio stations every week, up from about 2 million in the early 1980s," said the NPR Web site.[18] Though the growth had slowed by 2005, NPR's model of substantial journalism, rich with national and international news, was an established and welcome success. And investigative work such as that done by the Center for Public Integrity, funded by foundations and private donors, was greatly enriching the ever more constrained supply emanating from corporate media.

Still, the work done by those traditional companies was understood by most to be essential, so conversations about how to strengthen and nurture newsrooms were also a common occurrence. Responsible investment groups, such as Trillium, explored working with shareholders to effect the kind of change that similar efforts have brought to environmental policies in the corporate world. Others discussed a greater role for retired journalists on media boards of directors, longer terms for board members, and other measures to counter the addictive short-term profit pressures that have so reduced American journalism.[19]

Journalists themselves have undertaken powerful moves toward more accountability and transparency. The *New York Times* and the *Washington Post* strengthened their anonymous-source policies. The *Times* appointed a reader representative, and the *San Antonio Express-News* and PBS created new public editor, or ombudsman, positions. Within newsrooms, journalists were grappling with the meaning of *objectivity* as citizens complained about the tyranny of evenhandedness and the undermining effect of artificial balance, in coverage such as that of global warming or the teaching of evolution. Star reporters like Judith Miller and Bob Woodward were derided as too-credulous carriers of official information, on the one hand, while those of another ideological bent kept the "liberal media" charge in the forefront of the debate. *Transparency* and *accountability* were the new journalistic watchwords—in many ways the sunny side of what otherwise seemed to be an endless self-examination of one journalistic scandal after another.

People in the media world began talking, too, of the need to speak out on behalf of a beleaguered journalism—when reporters are jailed, for example, or when journalism is misrepresented. Thus, John Carroll, then editor of the *Los Angeles Times,* regretted publicly the presence of "pseudo-journalism." "Today, the credibility painstakingly earned by past journalists lends an unearned legitimacy to the new generation of talk-show hosts. Cloaked deceptively in the mantle of journalism, today's opinion-brokers are playing a nasty Halloween prank on the public, and indeed on journalism itself.[20]

That the time-honored and essential craft of journalism needs such vocal support was repeatedly made clear. A John S. and James L. Knight Foundation survey showed woeful ignorance of the First Amendment among high school students.[21] Nor were adult responses about press freedom likely to give comfort. The Freedom Forum First Amendment Center has asked in public surveys since 1997: "Overall, do you think the press in America has too much freedom to do what it wants, too little freedom to do what it wants, or is the amount of freedom the press has about right?" From 1997 to 2003 the average response came close to a majority saying the press has too much freedom.[22] An Annenberg Public Policy Center survey revealed a similarly worrisome truth, a substantial divide between the public and the press when it comes to views about partisan bias, accuracy, and press freedom, with the press seeing itself in a vastly more favorable light.[23]

A bright spot in the bleak landscape of journalism came, ironically, with the tragedy that Hurricane Katrina wrought on the Gulf Coast. "Essential Again," said a 2005 *American Journalism Review* story about the coverage that had compelled the nation's attention and won many a plaudit.[24] But the coverage raised as many questions as it brought praise. While journalists made plain to the public eye the incompetence of federal disaster officials during the tragedy, it was clear, too, upon reflection, that the press's failure to do the routine government reporting of appointments had allowed the incompetents into office. As *Washington Post* media writer Howard Kurtz asked in a September 19, 2005, story, "But why did journalists never get around to pointing this out in the past? Why are agencies such as FEMA never covered until disaster strikes? A database search found only one story and an editorial about [Michael] Brown's 2003 nomination as FEMA chief. Both were in the *Denver Post*—Brown is from Colorado—and both described him as experienced because of his tenure as the agency's No. 2 official."[25] Similarly, what appeared to be a sudden realization of the presence of wrenching poverty in New Orleans only made more apparent the lack of consistent coverage of the poor in cities across the land. Meanwhile, the sometimes overly avid reporting of unsubstantiated reports of violence may have slowed the arrival of assistance, as an October 5, 2005, *Washington Post* story noted.[26]

If the big guns of the mainstream media were truly on the road to eclipse, however, they certainly had their moments of blissful unawareness. The 2005 White House Correspondents Dinner, as always, had them dining with the powerful from the world of government. Jon Stewart of the *Daily Show* deliciously summarized what was really going on when the two groups entered the room: "Deep down, we're both entrenched oligarchies with a stake in maintaining the status quo—enjoy your scrod."[27] But the status quo did not seem destined to remain in place much longer. As the tumultuous year drew to a close, many felt that the old media world was fast becoming unrecognizable, and the future looked—at best—frighteningly unknown.

But unknown isn't the worst thing imaginable. The media had been battered for years, their work steadily undermined by the corporate dictates that increasingly trumped the public's needs. If that era was coming to a close, a new era was opening. It was a time of enormous change and instability—that was for sure—and therein lay the peril and the promise. Ah, at long last, promise.

Notes

1. Association of American Editorial Cartoonists, "Black Ink Monday," Association of American Editorial Cartoonists, http://editorialcartoonists.com/blackinkmonday .cfm (accessed January 21, 2009).

2. Michael Massing, "The End of News?" *New York Review of Books* 52, no. 19 (2005), http://www.nybooks.com/articles/18516 (accessed January 21, 2009).

3. Reed Johnson, "2005 Shaken & Stirred: Mass Media's Last Blast," *Los Angeles Times,* December 18, 2005. Available at http://www.boycott-riaa.com/article/print/19027 (accessed January 21, 2009).

4. Bill Moyers, "In the Kingdom of the Half-Blind," address at National Security Archive, December 9, 2005, http://www.gwu.edu/~nsarchiv/anniversary/moyers.htm (accessed January 22, 2009).

5. Aspen Institute, *Homeland Security Initiative Roundtable,* December 7, 2005.

6. James Rainey, "MoveOn Protests Cuts in Tribune Co. Newsrooms," *Los Angeles Times,* December 3, 2005. Available at http://articles.latimes.com/2005/dec/03/nation/na-moveon3 (accessed January 22, 2009).

7. Andrew Kohut, "Self-Censorship: Counting the Ways," *Columbia Journalism Review* May/June (2000): par. 8. Available at http://archives.cjr.org/year/00/2/censorship.asp (accessed January 22, 2009).

8. Matea Gold, "PBS News Programs Awarded Six Emmy's," *Los Angeles Times,* September 21, 2005. Available at http://pqasb.pqarchiver.com/latimes/access/899208361.html?dids=899208361:899208361&FMT=ABS&FMTS=ABS:FT&date=Sep+21%2C+2005&author=Matea+Gold&pub=Los+Angeles+Times&edition=&startpage=E.4&desc=PBS+news+programs+awarded+six+Emmys (accessed January 22, 2009).

9. Project for Excellence in Journalism, "Seigenthaler and Wikipedia: A Case Study on the Veracity of the 'Wiki' Concept," Journalism.org, October 1, 2005. Available at http://www.journalism.org/node/1672 (accessed January 22, 2009).

10. Matt Marshall, "Pressure Is Applied for KR Sale," *San Jose Mercury News,* November 3, 2005, http://www.mercurynews.com/mld/mercurynews/business/13069223.htm.

11. Pete Carey, "Knight Ridder Sold to McClatchy," *San Jose Mercury News,* March 13, 2006, http://www.mercurynews.com/mld/mercurynews/14084153.htm.

12. Dale Kasler, "McClatchy Is Selling Minnesota Newspaper," *Sacramento Bee,* December 27, 2006, http://www.sacbee.com/103/story/98981.html.

13. David A. Vise, "What Lurks in Its Soul?" *Washington Post,* November 13, 2005. Available at http://www.washingtonpost.com/wp-dyn/content/article/2005/11/11/AR2005111101644.html (accessed January 22, 2009).

14. Editor and Publisher Staff, "Report: Online Newspaper Readership Up 11% in Oct.," *Editor and Publisher,* November 15, 2005, http://www.editorandpublisher.com/eandp/news/article_display.jsp?vnu_content_id=1001480273.

15. Jeff Sigmund, "Online Newspaper Audience Experiences Record Month in Third Quarter," Newspaper Association of America, October 26, 2006, http://www.naa.org/PressCenter/SearchPressReleases/2006/ONLINE-NEWSPAPER-AUDIENCE-EXPERIENCES-RECORD-MONTH-IN-THIRD-QUARTER.aspx (accessed January 22, 2009).

16. Jay Rosen, "John Harris and Jim Brady Get Into It about 'White House Briefing.' Dan Froomkin Replies," Pressthink, December 13, 2005, http://journalism.nyu.edu/pubzone/weblogs/pressthink/2005/12/13/frm_qa.html (accessed January 22, 2009).

17. Dan Gillmor, *We the Media: Grassroots Journalism by the People, for the People* (Beijing: O'Reilly, 2004).

18. National Public Radio, "The Expansion of NPR News," NPR.org, http://www.npr.org/about/news.html (accessed January 22, 2009).

19. Steve Lippman, Trillium executive, telephone conversation, December 6, 2005.

20. John Carroll, "The Wolf in Reporter's Clothing: The Rise of Pseudo-Journalism in America," Ruhl Lecture, May 6, 2004, http://jcomm.uoregon.edu/awards/ruhl/2004.php (accessed January 22, 2009).

21. John S. and James L. Knight Foundation, "Survey Finds First Amendment Is Being Left Behind in U.S. High Schools," John S. and James L. Knight Foundation, January 31, 2005, http://firstamendment.jideas.org/professionals/news_release.php (accessed January 22, 2009).

22. *State of the First Amendment 2003* (Nashville: First Amendment Center, 2003), 2.

23. Tommy Acchione, "Study: Public, Press Often at Odds," *Daily Pennsylvanian,* June 2, 2005. Available at http://media.www.dailypennsylvanian.com/media/storage/paper882/news/2005/06/02/News/Study.Public.Press.Often.At.Odds-2147875.shtml (accessed January 22, 2009).

24. Marc Fisher, "Essential Again," *American Journalism Review,* October/November (2005), http://www.ajr.org/Article.asp?id=3962 (accessed January 22, 2009).

25. Howard Kurtz, "The Media Discover the Poor," *Washington Post,* September 19, 2005. Available at http://www.washingtonpost.com/wp-dyn/content/blog/2005/09/19/BL2005091900424.html (accessed January 22, 2009).

26. Robert E. Pierre and Ann Gerhart, "News of Pandemonium May Have Slowed Aid," *Washington Post,* October 5, 2005. Available at http://www.washingtonpost.com/wp-dyn/content/article/2005/10/04/AR2005100401525.html (accessed January 22, 2009).

27. Michael Massing, "The Press: The Enemy Within," *New York Review of Books,* December 15, 2005. Available at http://www.nybooks.com/articles/18555 (accessed January 22, 2009).

20

The Challenges for a Free Press
in the Twenty-First Century

JANE KIRTLEY

> Congress shall make no law respecting an establishment
> of religion, or prohibiting the free exercise thereof; or
> abridging the freedom of speech, or of the press; or the
> right of the people peaceably to assemble, and to petition
> the government for a redress of grievances.
>
> —First Amendment to the U.S. Constitution

The forty-five words that protect expressive activity, including freedom of the press, look absolute. They seem to prohibit any interference in the editorial process by Congress. That was more or less the reality during most of the latter half of the twentieth century, when many journalists argued, or assumed, that their news gathering and publishing activities were immune from any government scrutiny or control.

They had good reason. The Constitution depends on an independent judiciary to interpret and apply it. From approximately 1930 to 2001, the American judiciary, particularly the Supreme Court, kept expanding the legal recognition that broad protection for the press was essential to a free society and to democracy itself. It was an exciting time to be a journalist, or to be a lawyer representing the news media, as the highest court in the land handed down landmark decision after landmark decision.

Then came the terrorist attacks of September 11, 2001, and the resulting drive to expand government investigative powers to try to keep anything like it from happening again. Although journalists seem to have fairly easy access to front-line troops in Iraq and Afghanistan, many other types of government information have disappeared from public view or are much more difficult to access. Administrative procedures such as deportation hearings sometimes go on behind closed doors. In this restrictive atmosphere, more and more government sources refuse to speak on the record. Courts do not seem generally inclined to let journalists claim the First Amendment as a shield, and some press critics even talk of applying laws against spying to them.

But to fully understand the attitude changes since 2001, we need to review the seven-decade expansion of First Amendment freedoms. For example, since 1964 the Supreme Court has recognized that the Constitution protects the "right to be wrong"—that is, the right of a news organization to make a factual error when reporting on the conduct of a public official without having to fear being sued for libel.[1] Acknowledging that some mistakes are inevitable in political debate, the opinion by Justice William Brennan said that the official could prevail only if the official was able to prove "actual malice"; that meant proving that the news organization knew or should have known that what it published was false. The Supreme Court extended the "actual malice" rule to include public figures as well as public officials and decreed that even in cases involving private individuals, a suit could be successful only if some fault on the part of the speaker or publisher could be demonstrated.

Expressions of opinion, as distinguished from statements that can be proven to be false or true, enjoy even greater protection under the First Amendment. In *Gertz v. Robert Welch Inc.,* Justice Lewis F. Powell Jr. declared that "there is no such thing as a false idea."[2] The absolute protection for pure opinion was further refined in *Hustler Magazine v. Falwell.*[3] The unanimous decision, written by Chief Justice William Rehnquist, rejected a lawsuit seeking damages for emotional distress brought by the Rev. Jerry Falwell after *Hustler* published a cartoon parody that portrayed him as a drunk and a hypocrite whose first sexual encounter occurred with his mother in an outhouse. In many countries, insult laws permit journalists to be sued or criminally prosecuted for offending the "honor and dignity" of an individual.[4] However, the U.S. Supreme Court declined to adopt the "outrageousness" standard urged by Falwell's lawyers. Rehnquist dryly observed that *Hustler's* satire "is at best a distant cousin . . . and a rather poor relation at that" to more sophisticated political commentary. But he concluded that there was no principled way to distinguish between the two.

Another essential concept in American law is the idea that the government cannot stop the press from publishing what it chooses, even if those choices might seem to be harmful to the public interest. That protection is clearly spelled out in the seminal 1931 decision in *Near v. Minnesota,* the first case to strike down a state law regulating the press on First Amendment grounds.[5] The justices ruled that any government attempt to impose a "previous restraint" on publication would be presumed to violate the Constitution. "The fact that the liberty of the press may be abused by miscreant purveyors of scandal does not make any the less necessary the immunity of the press from previous restraint in dealing with official misconduct," Chief Justice Charles Evans Hughes wrote for the majority.

Hughes cautioned, however, that the prohibition on prior restraints was not absolute. He listed several possible exceptions—obstructing recruiting of soldiers or publishing details about troop movements in wartime; obscenity; incitement to violence—though none of these exceptions applied in the *Near* case.

Forty years later, in "The Pentagon Papers" case (*New York Times Co. v. United States)*, the high court further crystallized this principle.[6] This was during the Vietnam War, after the *New York Times* and the *Washington Post* had obtained copies of a classified government report and had begun publishing excerpts. The Justice Department immediately sought to halt publication, arguing in federal district courts in New York and the District of Columbia that continued publication would damage national security. The cases moved quickly in the courts. After two federal appeals courts issued conflicting rulings, the Supreme Court took the case on an unusual expedited basis. A little more than two weeks after the *Times* printed the original story, the justices ruled in a terse, unsigned opinion that the government had failed to meet its burden to justify the prior restraint. Each of the nine justices wrote separately, with those in the majority ruling that, at least in the absence of a statute, the executive branch has no inherent authority to stop the press from publishing simply by invoking a claim of threats to national security. However, several justices did not rule out the possibility that the press could be punished after the fact for violation of federal espionage laws.

All of these decisions are based on a common principle: The government has virtually no authority to restrict or to provide mechanisms to punish the press for reporting that criticizes public officials, public figures, or governmental activities. The few exceptions, in addition to Chief Justice Hughes's list in *Near,* primarily involve intellectual property interests such as alleged violation of copyright. Broadcast news, though, faces some restrictions that print media do not. Broadcasters are exempt from most government content regulation but still are subject to possible penalty for airing material deemed to violate federal laws prohibiting the transmission of indecent material, at least during certain hours of the day. However, "indecency," unlike obscenity, is protected by the First Amendment in other contexts.[7]

Even so, when U.S. laws are contrasted with the laws of other countries— even other mature democracies—where restraints on speech and the press are routinely allowed based on such vague pretexts as "maintaining public order" or "protecting public morals," the American press enjoys virtually unsurpassed freedom to publish what it chooses. Furthermore, freedom of the press, as defined in the twentieth century, encompassed more than simply the right to publish what one wishes without fear of restraint or reprisal. It also included the right to gain access to information, particularly information about government and its actions. The Supreme Court embraced this concept in a series of decisions beginning with *Richmond Newspapers, Inc. v. Virginia* in 1980.[8] In order to promote accountability, the justices ruled, the press and the public enjoy a First Amendment right to attend criminal court proceedings.[9] "People in an open society do not demand infallibility from their institutions, but it is difficult for them to accept what they are prohibited from observing," Chief Justice Warren Burger wrote.

After the Watergate scandal engulfed the Nixon administration in the 1970s, openness in democratic institutions was viewed as the antithesis of the secrecy most often associated with autocratic regimes. "Transparency" became a watchword during the final decades of the twentieth century as new democracies emerged from the remains of the Soviet Union in Eastern and Central Europe. Yet in the United States, "the right to know" has never been considered to be a central tenet of the First Amendment. As Justice Potter Stewart observed in a speech at Yale Law School, "the Constitution itself is neither a Freedom of Information Act nor an Official Secrets Act."[10] Thus, it has fallen to the legislative branch to craft laws like the federal Freedom of Information Act, which guarantees the presumption of a right of public access to the records created and maintained by executive branch agencies, subject only to nine narrow exemptions.[11]

At the beginning of the twenty-first century, the state of press law can be summarized in this way: Journalists were protected from most libel suits by public officials or public figures. Editorial cartoonists and satirists could lampoon and criticize to their hearts' content. It was impossible for the government to stop the press from publishing whatever it chose. Journalists, as well as the public, could gain access to government proceedings and documents in most instances. In almost every case, the party trying to restrain or punish the press would bear the burden of justifying it—and rarely succeeded in doing so. And then the bubble burst.

In the aftermath of the terrorist attacks of September 11, 2001, the administration of president George W. Bush adopted policies of unprecedented secrecy in the name of protecting national security. A memorandum issued to federal department and agency heads in October 2001 reversed the pro-disclosure policy of the Clinton administration.[12] In the memo, attorney general John Ashcroft assured agencies that the Justice Department would defend their decisions to deny access to records provided they could articulate "a sound legal basis" to justify the denials.[13] Shortly thereafter, the 6th and 3rd Circuit Courts split on the question of whether the right of access to criminal trials extends to deportation proceedings, which take place in federal courtrooms and bear many similarities to trials. Judge Damon Keith of the 6th Circuit defended the right of access and declared that "democracies die behind closed doors."[14] His counterpart in the 3rd Circuit, Judge Edward Becker, dismissed this concern, predicting instead a "perverse result" if the right of access were deemed to encompass administrative proceedings. He contended that the Founding Fathers never "contemplated a perfectly transparent government."[15]

Another access issue arose as the military launched invasions of Afghanistan and Iraq: Does the press enjoy a special First Amendment right of access to military bases, or to the battlefield?[16] Despite a long tradition of journalists accompanying the troops and reporting on military operations, as federal circuit judge David Sentelle wrote in *Flynt v. Rumsfeld,* "neither this Court nor the Supreme Court has ever applied *Richmond Newspapers* outside the context of criminal proceedings, and we will not do so today."

When this development is coupled with a growing trend of increased secrecy based on the appealing but dubious ground of protecting national security, the practical consequence for the working journalist has been less effective access to government actions and records, and accordingly, less information for the public.[17] It is not surprising, then, that in the post-9/11 world many journalists began to rely more heavily on unofficial or anonymous sources of government information. Depending on your point of view, these sources might be considered to be "leakers" or "whistle blowers," "traitors" or "heroes." Regardless of how they are characterized, most have one trait in common: They demand that their identities be kept confidential.

Reliance on anonymous sources raises ethical questions. The motives of sources who insist that their identities not be revealed are suspect. Do they hide behind a cloak of secrecy in order to manipulate the journalist and to promote a hidden agenda? Is their information inherently less credible because they are unwilling to put their names on it? Are the interests of readers and viewers served when they are unable to assess for themselves the source of information reported in the news? On the other hand, journalists argue, without the freedom to make some promises of confidentiality they have few or no sources, leaving the public less informed. Journalists point particularly to the revelations of Mark Felt, the former FBI official finally unmasked in May 2005 as "Deep Throat," the confidential source who was instrumental to the Watergate investigation conducted by *Washington Post* reporters Bob Woodward and Carl Bernstein.

The debate over the use of confidential sources was forced out of the newsroom and into the courtroom because of two women, Valerie Plame and Judith Miller. In July 2003 Robert Novak published a column in which he identified Plame as a CIA operative.[18] The revelation prompted calls for an investigation to determine who had leaked the information. A series of high-profile confrontations culminated in the jailing of *New York Times* reporter Judith Miller for contempt of court after she refused to testify before a grand jury. The Supreme Court had set the stage for this confrontation between the press and the government nearly thirty years earlier, when it decided *Branzburg v. Hayes* in 1972.[19]

Branzburg involved four cases of journalists who had witnessed illegal activity while gathering news. They resisted government attempts to force them to testify about their sources and observations before grand juries. In all four cases the journalists insisted that they had been able to gain access to their subjects only because they had promised to keep their identities confidential, and that therefore the First Amendment should grant the journalists a testimonial privilege to resist involuntary disclosure of the information to the government. In a fractured and controversial ruling, four justices wrote that the Constitution afforded journalists no such privilege. This plurality opinion, by Justice Byron White, rejected the assertion that the public interest in the free flow of information outweighed the public interest in bringing criminals to justice. He wrote, "We cannot seriously entertain the notion that the First Amendment protects a newsman's agreement to conceal the criminal conduct of his source, or evidence thereof, on the theory that it is better to write about crime than to do something about it."

The court was skeptical of the argument that sources would dry up if they could not be guaranteed confidentiality. White worried that recognition of a constitutionally based privilege inevitably would require courts to define which journalists would be qualified to invoke it, "a questionable procedure in light of the traditional doctrine that liberty of the press is the right of the lonely pamphleteer . . . as much as of the large metropolitan publisher." The problem was better left to Congress, or the legislatures, to resolve, the justices concluded. A concurring opinion by Powell emphasized that the ruling was a narrow one and that in other circumstances a balancing test should be applied to weigh the competing interests presented case by case. In any event, he said, subpoenas issued purely to harass journalists would not be countenanced. The four dissenting justices argued for either an absolute privilege or, in the alternative, a qualified privilege that would place the burden on the government to demonstrate a compelling need for the information sought: It must be both clearly relevant to the investigation and could not be obtained from some other source.

In the years that followed, many, although not all, federal circuits and the majority of state courts adopted some version of the qualified privilege. Thirty-one states and the District of Columbia enacted shield laws providing varying degrees of protection. But in August 2003, in a case seeking disclosure of tape recordings of journalists' interviews with an FBI informant who was not a confidential source, the influential judge Richard A. Posner of the 7th Circuit wrote that no federal testimonial privilege for journalists exists. Although he conceded that any subpoena to the press must be "reasonable in the circumstances," he also said, "We do not see why there need to be special criteria merely because the possessor of the documents or other evidence sought is a journalist."[20]

Just weeks before Posner's opinion was released, Novak "outed" Valerie Plame, triggering a federal investigation by special prosecutor Patrick Fitzgerald into the possible violation of the Intelligence Identities Protection Act of 1982.[21] Inevitably, a number of journalists who had covered the story, including Miller, Matthew Cooper of *Time* magazine, Walter Pincus and Glenn Kessler of the *Washington Post*, and Tim Russert of NBC, were subpoenaed to testify before the grand jury. Pincus and Kessler agreed to testify after their source, Lewis "Scooter" Libby, released them from their promises of confidentiality, but Russert, Miller, and Cooper continued to resist.

After a federal district judge refused to recognize any privilege under the First Amendment or federal common law, Russert agreed to testify, contending that he had not received an unauthorized leak and would not be breaking a confidence. Miller and Cooper, however, were found in civil contempt of court. A three-judge panel of the federal Circuit Court for the District of Columbia upheld the finding, rejecting any First Amendment privilege in this instance and suggesting that Congress, not the courts, was best equipped to resolve the question.[22]

The Supreme Court declined to review the case, but on the day Cooper was to appear again before the district judge to complete the contempt proceedings, he announced that his source had waived confidentiality and so he agreed to testify. Miller, however, spent eighty-five days in prison when she continued to defy the court order. She was released only after she, too, said that she had received an express waiver from Libby, and agreed to testify. But the threat to Miller and her counterparts may not end there. Special Counsel Fitzgerald announced the indictment of Libby,[23] and then, almost exactly six years after Novak's original column appeared, Plame and her husband filed a lawsuit against Vice President Dick Cheney and others in the Bush administration, contending that they conspired to violate their constitutional rights.[24] More subpoenas of journalists, and thus more constitutional confrontations, seem inevitable.

Miller's imprisonment prompted renewed calls for a federal shield law to provide some form of protection. Identical legislation introduced in both houses of Congress by Indiana senator Richard G. Lugar and congressman Mike Pence garnered only lukewarm support from legislators and a mixed reaction from journalists. Shield laws had been attempted several times on the federal level but were always controversial and unsuccessful. Some journalists opposed the idea of the news media seeking special privileges from the legislature in principle, contending that the First Amendment provided all the privilege necessary. Others argued, as had Justice White in *Branzburg*, that any shield law would necessarily require Congress to define who a journalist is, a prospect regarded by some as tantamount to licensing. That would raise significant constitutional issues, especially at a time when bloggers and other unconventional content providers have begun to clamor for parity with their mainstream media colleagues by seeking—and in some cases, receiving—equivalent rights of access and First Amendment protection for their speech.[25]

But even more chilling than jailing journalists for refusing to disclose their sources is the prospect of prosecuting them for violation of federal laws designed to keep classified information secret. In late April 2006 the Central Intelligence Agency fired Mary McCarthy, an analyst accused of having provided classified information to *Washington Post* reporters about secret prisons in Europe where terrorism suspects are detained.[26] The *Post*'s stories by Dana Priest won the Pulitzer Prize, but some commentators accused McCarthy of being a traitor and suggested that the reporters and news organizations who published the classified information were no better than traitors themselves.[27]

Attorney General Alberto Gonzales refused to rule out the possibility that journalists could be prosecuted under the 1917 Espionage Act[28] for publishing classified information about the National Security Agency's monitoring of telephone calls between the United States and other countries.[29] Although espionage laws historically have been used primarily against those who commit classic espionage,[30] some commentators argue that nothing in the law would preclude prosecution of journalists, too.[31] Whether that would be constitutional remains an open question.

Thus in 2009 we find ourselves back where we began: with the judiciary. Although the language of the First Amendment is unchanged after more than two hundred years, the courts have interpreted those forty-five words to give them life and meaning. The prohibition on prior restraints, the extension of constitutional protection to libelous speech, the recognition of a presumed right of access to government activities—all of these are products of judge-made law. As Justice Potter Stewart once reminded a gathering of lawyers, judges, and journalists, "Where do you think these rights came from? The stork didn't bring them! The judges did."[32] If the judiciary fails to appreciate and value the role of the press in a free society, there is no guarantee that these hard-won rights will remain intact in the twenty-first century.

Notes

1. *New York Times Co. v. Sullivan,* 376 U.S. 254 (1964).

2. 418 U.S. 323 (1974).

3. 485 U.S. 46 (1988).

4. See, for example, Ruth Walden, *Insult Laws: An Insult to Press Freedom* (Reston, Va.: World Press Freedom Committee, 2000).

5. 283 U.S. 697 (1931).

6. 403 U.S. 713 (1971)

7. 18 U.S.C. § 1464; 47 C.F.R. § 73.3999.

8. 448 U.S. 555 (1980).

9. See also *Press-Enterprise Co. v. Superior Court,* 464 U.S. 501 (1984); *Press-Enterprise Co. v. Superior Court,* 478 U.S. 1 (1986).

10. Potter Stewart, "Or of the Press," *Hastings Law Journal* 26 (1975): 636.

11. 5 U.S.C. § 552 (2005).

12. See Janet Reno, memorandum to Heads of Departments and Agencies re: The Freedom of Information Act (October 4, 1993), *FOIA Update* 14, no. 3. Available at http://www.usdoj.gov/oip/foia_updates/Vol_XIV_3/page3.htm (accessed January 22, 2009).

13. John Ashcroft, memorandum to Heads of All Federal Departments and Agencies, October 12, 2001, at http://www.usdoj.gov/04foia/011012.htm (accessed January 22, 2009).

14. *Detroit Free Press v. Ashcroft*, 303 F.3d 681, 683 (6th Cir. 2002).

15. *North Jersey Media Group v. Ashcroft*, 308 F.3d 198, 215 (3d. Cir. 2002), cert. denied, 538 U.S. 1056 (2003).

16. See, for example, *Flynt v. Weinberger*, 762 F.2d 12 (D.C. Cir. 1985); *Nation Magazine v. Dep't of Defense*, 762 F.Supp. 1558 (S.D.N.Y. 1991); *JB Pictures Inc. v. Dep't of Defense* (D.C. Cir. 1996); *Flynt v. Rumsfeld*, 355 F.3d 697 (D.C. Cir. 2004).

17. On December 14, 2005, President George W. Bush issued an executive order directing agencies to establish FOIA operations that would be both "citizen-centered and results-oriented." Among other things, agencies would be required to establish a chief FOIA officer and to develop a plan for improvement. Executive Order 13392 of December 14, 2005, "Improving Agency Disclosure of Information." *Federal Register* 70 (December 19, 2005): 75373–75277.

18. Robert Novak, "The Mission to Niger," *Chicago Sun-Times*, July 14, 2003.

19. 408 U.S. 655 (1972).

20. *McKevitt v. Pallasch*, 339 F.3d 530 (7th Cir. 2003).

21. 50 U.S.C. <§§> 421 et seq.

22. *In re: Grand Jury Subpoena, Judith Miller*, 397 F.3d 964 (D.C. Cir. 2005).

23. Jim VanderHei and Carol D. Leonnig, "Cheney Aide Libby Is Indicted; Rove Spared but Remains under Scrutiny," *Washington Post*, October 29, 2005.

24. Eric M. Weiss and Charles Lane, "Vice President Sued by Plame and Husband; Ex-CIA Officer Alleges Leak of Her Name Was Retaliatory," *Washington Post*, July 14 2006.

25. See, for example, Communications Decency Act of 1996 (CDA), 47 U.S.C. § 230 (protecting those operating interactive Web sites from liability for content provided by others); *John Doe No. 1 v. Cahill*, 884 A.2d 451 (Del. 2005) (shielding the identity of anonymous posters on the Internet from compelled revelation to libel litigants unless a prima facie case is pleaded).

26. Dafna Linzer, "CIA Officer Is Fired for Media Leaks; The Post Was among Outlets That Gained Classified Data," *Washington Post*, April 22, 2006.

27. See Cal Thomas, "A Traitor in Our Midst," *Baltimore Sun*, April 26, 2006.

28. 18 U.S.C. § 793 (2005).

29. Walter Pincus, "Prosecution of Journalists Is Possible in NSA Leaks," *Washington Post*, May 22, 2006.

30. An important exception was the prosecution of Navy analyst Samuel Loring Morison, who provided classified photographs to the British publication *Jane's Defence Weekly*. *United States v. Morison*, 844 F.2d 1057 (4th Cir. 1988).

31. See, for example, Gabriel Schoenfeld, "Has the *New York Times* Violated the Espionage Act?" *Commentary*, March 2006. Available at http://www.commentarymagazine .com/viewarticle.cfm/has-the—new-york-times—violated-the-espionage-act—10036 (accessed January 22, 2009).

32. Anthony Lewis, "Why the Courts," *Cardozo Law Review* 22 (2000): 145.

PART 6

Women Making Choices

21

The Choice to Stay

MARGARET SULLIVAN

Mom forgot to tell me *how*. She wanted me to have a great career. And she wanted me to have a marvelous traditional family. But if she knew how to blend those elements together smoothly, she never passed that wisdom along before she died, when I was only thirty, still childless and still a reporter. Most of my choices were still ahead.

So, like thousands of other baby-boomer females—but one more driven than most—I did the best I could, stumbling along in the post-feminist universe, blazing a trail here, falling on my face there. I felt triumphant at times and like a failure at others. My choice of career was easy: By high school I knew I wanted to be a journalist, and I never looked back. I wanted the thrills that I knew came with the job. Over three decades I've had them: I interviewed Mother Teresa at her Calcutta orphanage at dawn. I enraged President Clinton with a nervy question in front of a national audience. As a newly minted chief editor, I stretched the production deadlines to the limit on the surreal night of the 2000 presidential election and managed not to declare the wrong man president. I directed coverage of 9/11, helped redesign the whole paper, and fostered a tricky agreement with the newsroom's union to allow our reporters to write for the Web.

I never "opted out" of journalism and never thought seriously about it. I married in my late twenties, had two children—they are now teenagers—and after six months off each time, came back to work. I had a solid stint as a hard-news reporter, followed by several years as a metro columnist, while also stringing for the *New York Times,* and then felt compelled to start climbing the management ladder. Nineteen years after I was a summer intern at my hometown paper, the *Buffalo (N.Y.) News,* I became its top editor and, just into my forties, the youngest female editor of a metro paper in the United States. "I hear the sound of shattering glass," read the card on a bouquet of flowers I received the day I got the big job.

The highs and lows have been dramatic, and the balancing act, at times, precarious. I've fallen off the high wire and gotten back up there to try again. Stress? I'm an expert. I've had reason to question my choices, but they *are* mine. As editors like to say about stories that are under fire, I stand by them.

- I stand by the day that I visited the *Washington Post* style section, in preparation for becoming features editor at the *Buffalo News*. I had had my first baby only a couple of months before, and as a nursing mother, I simply had to pump during the course of a long day. So I excused myself from meetings with *Post* editors and went off to the ladies room to use a breast pump I'd stuffed into my briefcase. It didn't go too smoothly.

- I stand by the time a close family member died—the day after 9/11. As editor of the newspaper, I couldn't even think of taking a few days off after the biggest news event of my lifetime. Nor could I think of missing my mother-in-law's wake and funeral, taking place about an hour from the newsroom. Somehow I managed to do both.

- I stand by the days I left work in the middle of the day, when I really shouldn't have, to get to a pediatrician's appointment or a grade-school basketball game, and then rushed back afterward, knowing I hadn't been fully present in either of those places—wishing I could somehow clone myself into a full-time mom and a full-time editor.

- I stand by the magical moments in which it all seemed to work perfectly: the lunchtime, for example, when I dashed from work to my daughter's grade-school Halloween parade, taking photos of my grinning fourth-grader in an elaborate costume we had made together the previous weekend. Her head poked out of the top of a red-and-white-striped box of movie theater popcorn, liberally dotted with cotton balls that we had individually dipped in butter-yellow paint.

Now, with those craziest of times largely in the past, I pause and take stock. I have, after all, just turned fifty, so what better time?

First off, I didn't really "have it all," although it might have looked that way for a while. (And, frankly, I liked giving that impression. My bio, for years, listed my professional accomplishments and ended with a sentence about my long-term marriage and two young children.) I believe I am what British psychoanalyst D. W. Winnicott called a "good-enough mother." I've certainly wondered, in weaker moments, if my two older brothers and I—directed full-time by a mother who, in keeping with the mores of the 1950s, gave up a promising retail career to raise a family—were better off than my kids. I was in a stable marriage for more than twenty years, but, now separated with a divorce pending, I can acknowledge that the strains of my job had at least some role in its outcome, although that's a complicated subject. (A voice from the sensible feminist in my head demands to be heard now, so let's allow her to speak to these points: *Why apply the standards of the sexist 1950s to the twenty-first century? It's a different world, a better one for women, so let's not wax nostalgic for the bad old days. As for your marriage and your career, what successful man has ever blamed his job promotion for his marital problems?*)

From a strictly journalism or career perspective, I would give myself good grades. I broke the glass ceiling at my hometown newspaper, becoming the first female editor in its 120-year history. I chaired the Pulitzer Prize commentary jury in 2006 and served as a Pulitzer juror three other times. I've written for national magazines and been named one of the ten most powerful women in western New York state. The investigative team I set up, the paper's first, has done admirable work, benefiting the community I live in, and has won lots of awards. Enterprise reporting is still a top priority at my newspaper. I'm proud of the dozens of young journalists I've hired: a standout political cartoonist, a top-flight crime reporter, a fledgling editor talented enough to move into my office someday. Perhaps most important to me, some commentary pieces I've written over the years have really resonated, generating a big response among readers. Although I've never worked on the staff of an elite paper, served as a foreign correspondent, written a book, or won a Pulitzer, I keep in mind that life is long, and I haven't ruled anything out. I also realize that I probably could have achieved those goals had I been more single-minded about my career instead of trying for a workable career/family balance.

As for my children, I have reason to feel proud. My son, an easygoing and universally well-liked young man, gets top grades at Yale and is devoted to child-literacy projects. My daughter's sparkling wit keeps her friends in stitches. What's more, she has a talent with words that could lead her right into journalism if she's not careful. In casual conversation, for instance, she recently described some suburban mansions as having "a faux individuality." And as a coxswain for her high school rowing team, she clearly has a flair for leadership. Watching her direct her crew at a regatta, another "rowing parent" turned to me and said with a knowing smile, "I wonder where she gets the air of command."

This may be the acid test: Would I recommend this demanding life course to my own daughter or to any of the dozen or so female interns now working in my newsroom? The answer is a cautious "yes," with a sizable asterisk attached.

"Follow your bliss," I like to tell young journalists. Keep doing what you find meaningful, what you love, what you're good at, and your career will go just fine. But I would add: Take care of yourself. Some of that is attitude, a gentleness toward the self that recognizes accomplishments and realizes that trade-offs come with every life choice. And I would tell young women, too, that it's not necessary to try to do everything at the same time. There *is* such a thing as burnout, and it's no great surprise to me that so many women journalists—especially those with heavy family responsibilities—are looking for something slower-paced and saner to do with their lives. A talented reporter in my own newsroom once gave me a start by sitting in my office and telling me that someday she wanted to be in my chair. But when an opportunity arrived for a promotion that would have started her on the editing/management track, she turned it down. She had a good reason: She was pregnant, and while she had every intention of returning to work full time, she didn't want to return to a high-pressure job with less flexibility than she'd have as a reporter. I have no doubt that she, and others like her, will be successful in both journalistic and maternal pursuits, perhaps without putting the pressure on herself that I have.

Even so, I don't regret my decisions. They are mine, and I own them. Given my strong drive and my belief in the journalistic mission, along with a desire to be deeply involved in my children's lives, I did the best I could, absorbing the stress that came with the satisfaction. And so, getting back to my mother, I'd sum it up like this for her: "Mom, I've tried to figure out the balance. I made some mistakes, and I'm not sure I'd do everything exactly the same way again. But I sure have enjoyed being a journalist—and there's still nothing I'd rather be doing. It's a noble calling, and one where I've been able to make a difference. I may not have the white-picket-fence family life, but I do have great kids. I think, overall, it's gone pretty well and I hope you'd be proud of me."

And if my fourteen-year-old daughter wants to be a journalist someday? I wouldn't dream of discouraging her. I might just tell her to be gentle with herself and, yes, to follow her bliss.

22

Balancing News and Family

JAN LEACH

It was the 1970s, and we had lots of new options. The women's movement opened career doors for us, and Watergate showed us that journalism was important and necessary for the good of the democracy. I liked writing, talking to people, and storytelling, and when it was time for college, I found I could combine those strengths toward a journalism degree. At Ohio's Bowling Green State University, news was my addiction. I walked in to the *BG News* as a freshman and practically lived in that dingy office for the next four years. Journalism seemed busy, fun, powerful.

I didn't know when I went to college how much I'd love news. I didn't know where journalism would take me, about the people I'd meet, and the responsibility that would come. I didn't know that more than twenty-five years later, leaving the newspaper business would be gut-wrenching. Today I wonder if I would have made the same life choices and career decisions if I'd known the excitement and the anguish that would result. But I am not alone.

Keeping women in newspapers, and specifically in management, has been the focus of many studies and wide-ranging debate. Women report numerous barriers to their career advancement. Women journalists grapple with the balance between work and family and decry the dearth of mentors and role models. Only one in five of the nation's top female editors said they wanted to move up in the newspaper industry, and one in two expected to leave their company or leave the news profession entirely, according to a 2002 study.[1] For women, success in newsrooms seems to hinge on choices—those they make for themselves and those that others make for them.

A Closer Look at the Choices

Journalism is about making choices—what to cover, whom to talk to, what to photograph, when to follow up. But it is the choices that must be made, although they seem outside of "journalism," that have affected the careers of many women in journalism. This essay examines the choices I made through my career, along with the career choices of three other women in journalism. Kay Tucker Addis is the retired editor and vice president of the *Virginian-Pilot* in Norfolk, Virginia. Pam Luecke is the Donald W. Reynolds Professor of Business Journalism at Washington and Lee University in Lexington, Virginia, and the former editor of the *Lexington (Ky.) Herald-Leader*. Debra Adams Simmons is managing editor at the *Plain Dealer* in Cleveland and former editor and vice president of the *Akron (Ohio) Beacon Journal*.

Addis helped break barriers for the rest of us. When she started her career as a reporter for the *Richmond News-Leader* in 1970, she began in the women's department typing wedding and engagement announcements. Later she wrote features. But when she asked about transferring to the city room, where there were just a handful of women reporters, she was told, "If we let those of you in the women's department transfer out, we'll never have staffers for the women's department."[2] She decided to leave.

It was the first in one of a series of important choices Addis made in journalism. She moved from Richmond to Charlotte, North Carolina, where she was quickly hired in 1972 as a copy editor. She later was a reporter and then became the first woman sportswriter at the *Charlotte News*. "Now I remember with embarrassment and some horror that I was even photographed with the subjects of some of my stories—Kay in her seventies miniskirt interviewing a seven-foot-two University of South Carolina basketball player, for instance," she recalled.

In 1974 Addis moved back to Norfolk, taking a reporting job with the *Ledger-Star* as one of two women reporters in the newsroom. "On my first day, a male editor assumed that I had been hired as a secretary and asked me to retype some copy . . . Being new, naive, eager to please, and not sure what was and wasn't expected of reporters, I retyped the copy," she said. "That male editor later ended up working for me, and I told this story at his retirement party." For the next fourteen years, Addis took various supervisory positions with the *Ledger-Star* and the *Virginian-Pilot* until she made what some might call an unusual decision to become director of human resources at the Norfolk paper. Addis held that position for five years until she was named editor of the *Virginian-Pilot* in 1996. All of these choices for Addis represented challenges. "No matter how tough things got—whether, early in my career, it might have been mediocre editors or dull assignments or, later, complement [staffing] and budget control—I always remembered two things: One, as my mother always said, 'This, too, shall pass,' and two, I could never see myself doing anything in the world except newspapering," she said. "I loved the fact that every day was different, that we were at the center of whatever was happening and that it was a creative process. And that what we did mattered. We weren't selling insurance; we weren't making cars; we weren't doing taxes."

After thirty-five years in journalism, Addis is proudest of putting high value on good writing and strong editing, of creating a family-friendly newsroom, and of strengthening the diversity of the newsroom. "It took me far too long to realize that some things were more important than 'face time' at the office. My daughter was playing number one on her high school tennis team, and I missed far too many of her matches because I felt I needed to stay at the office. Looking back, I have no recollection at all of what I thought was so important at work, but I still regret missing all those field hockey games and tennis matches. Once your child is grown, you realize how quickly those years have gone by."

Family Choices and Newspaper Management

Addis's comment strikes a chord with me. I had gone to the *Akron Beacon Journal* as editor when my oldest daughter was six and my twin girls were three. I had worked during both pregnancies and returned to work quickly after they all were born. I admit that the baby stage is not my favorite, so it was easy to go back to work (as city editor in Phoenix with my oldest child and as managing editor in Cincinnati with the twins). By the time I got to Akron as editor, working was just the way it was; the way it had always been for our family. But as the girls got older and involved in more activities, I started to realize what I was missing as a mom.

I was completely comfortable as managing editor at the *Cincinnati Enquirer* when Akron's publisher, John L. Dotson Jr., called in 1998. Another move and another newsroom were not in our plans. But Dotson is persistent and persuasive, and the job as editor of the *Akron Beacon Journal* was tempting. I had grown up in Cleveland, so Akron would bring us near my home and family. I was familiar with the paper's rich journalism tradition. I wanted to be an editor. Dotson was a strong and well-respected publisher, and the newsroom was flush with people, resources, and gumption. I was the paper's first woman editor.

The idea of being editor was challenging, fulfilling, empowering, inspiring. I quickly learned it was not going to be easy. "John S. Knight is rolling in his grave because a *woman* is editing *his* newspaper," one caller barked over the phone. "Today's front page is another example of how you've turned our paper into the 'Ladies Beacon Journal,'" another was fond of telling me when he didn't like the stories we had emphasized that day. Thirty years after the women's movement had supposedly opened doors for women, I was still facing, or at least often hearing, silly stereotypes.

Sometimes that criticism was funny. Sometimes it was painful. I wondered whether being editor was worth it. Who wants to be a "pioneer" so late in the game? I knew I had Dotson's confidence and that of his successor, Jim Crutchfield. Dotson and Crutchfield are well-respected African American journalists who overcame discrimination in their own careers. I also had the support of the mostly male news executives at Knight Ridder. I had twenty years' experience at many larger newspapers; I had the journalism degree, the management training, and the supportive spouse. Still, the disparagement was distracting.

I dispute those who say they can tell by a newspaper's front page whether the editor is a man or a woman. But the job satisfaction I thought I'd found in Akron proved illusory. It was 1999 and the newspaper business was under a constant mandate to cut costs and improve profit margins. In 2001 the *Beacon Journal* was forced to lay off employees for the first time in its history. That meant ten people would lose their jobs in my newsroom. My role was no longer about journalism, but about managing crisis. I handled it badly because I took it personally. By then my choices were complicated. We had barely come through layoffs and buyouts and a dramatically reduced budget when the 9/11 attacks occurred. In what will remain one of my proudest moments as a journalist and editor, the *Beacon Journal* put out an "extra" edition on the day of the attacks, published large special editions for weeks thereafter, and raised money that eventually bought a fire truck for New York City.

Still, outstanding journalism and community service weren't enough to sustain the paper. Cost cutting continued in 2002. By that time family issues also surfaced. My husband was working thirty-five miles away in Cleveland. Our girls, then ten and seven, were heavily involved in school, sports, and scouts, but my time with them was erratic. I could not help with homework on a regular basis. I did not volunteer in their classrooms or with their activities. Once I actually forgot to pick up my daughter from soccer practice. I was ashamed and embarrassed when I learned later that night that another mother had dropped her off safely at home. I was frayed. When I was at home, I thought about what was happening at the office. When I was at work, I worried about what was, or wasn't, happening at home.

Among the recommendations in the "Women in Newspapers, 2003" study, published by the Media Management Center at Northwestern University, was that "newspapers must address the work/family balance issue because it is a significant problem for many women managers."[3] According to the study's authors, Mary Arnold and Marlene L. Hendrickson, work/family balance "is the area where women exhibit the most uncertainty and conflict between the demands of an executive career and societal expectations for women." That was true for me. I felt growing dissatisfaction at work. I was not content with what I could accomplish in journalism or for my staff. I was at odds with my role as mother and parent. After six months of personal and professional turmoil, I resigned as editor in 2003. It was agonizing and painful because of all I had hoped to accomplish at the *Beacon Journal,* and it was unfathomable because I had never seen myself as anything other than a newspaper journalist.

Choosing to Leave Journalism

Pam Luecke made a similar decision. She had gone to graduate school at Northwestern University and was job hunting in 1975, just after Watergate, when everyone wanted to be a reporter. Luecke says she leaped at the chance to write wedding and engagement announcements at the *Hartford (Conn.) Courant.* When she finished her announcements, she was allowed to write feature stories. After a while she started working on an MBA at night, and she became interested in reporting on business, which was just emerging as a journalistic niche.

When she saw an opening for a business reporter at the *Courier-Journal* in Louisville, Kentucky, she applied and got the job. "It was scary," she remembered. "I'm pretty sure I was the first female business reporter in Louisville."[4] Because she "sort of detected that some managers were not well-prepared for news management," she started thinking about newspaper management.

After a year and a half, Luecke applied for the job of business editor at the *Louisville Times.* She got it, stayed in Louisville ten years, married a journalist, had various jobs at the two papers, and eventually became regional editor, supervising all reporters outside the city of Louisville. In 1989 both Luecke and her husband were offered jobs back in Hartford, she as assistant managing editor and he as assistant business editor.

At that point Luecke's future seemed full of bright opportunities. Then she was diagnosed with cancer at the age of thirty-seven. "It was the last thing I ever expected," she said. "It just sort of blew me away. Somebody told me I had cancer, that I would have surgery, that I would go into treatment. I just made getting better my main job." During Luecke's cancer treatment, she directed the *Courant* staff that worked on a series about the Hubble space telescope. She missed several days because of treatments and their effects, but says others picked up things that fell through the cracks and helped her and the staff. The Hubble series won the Pulitzer Prize in 1992, the first for the *Courant.*

Luecke wanted to be managing editor or editor, but when the managing editor job opened up at the *Courant* in late 1994, she didn't get it. She was devastated, she says. Soon thereafter the newspaper offered buyouts and Luecke and her husband took that option. Tim Kelly, then editor of the *Lexington Herald-Leader,* talked to her about becoming the editorial page editor. Luecke balked at leaving news, but Kelly told her that being editorial page editor would make Luecke a stronger candidate for editor one day. She took the job in Lexington, even though it meant her husband would have to leave journalism. "We figured if I was going to be an editor, he couldn't work for that paper and he couldn't work for a competing paper," she explained. (The *Herald-Leader* was then owned by Knight Ridder and is now owned by McClatchy.)

When Kelly became publisher, he promoted Luecke to editor and she finally realized her dream. "I was just thrilled," she said. "I thought it was such a privilege and such a responsibility. . . . I remember the first time I drove to the *Herald-Leader* parking lot after being named editor, thinking, 'This is my paper.'"

Her first years as editor were "great," according to Luecke. She says she made changes, put an imprint on the paper, and made mistakes but made good decisions, too. She started to enjoy her public role in Lexington. But the excitement faded by 2000, Luecke says, when budgets kept getting squeezed and she found herself spending more and more time in meetings trying to figure out how to cut more and achieve a higher profit. She says she was frustrated with what she considered unreasonable corporate goals. "I was surprised when I was editor how little autonomy and power I really had. I felt like I knew how to put out a wonderful paper in Lexington."

While she was struggling with mandates for the paper, she learned about a faculty position at Washington and Lee University. She had always hoped to teach, and the idea of building a new program in business journalism was more appealing than undoing improvement she'd made at the paper. Luecke left the newsroom in 2001 and she and her husband moved from Lexington, Kentucky, to Lexington, Virginia. "Having cancer made me realize life really is short, so I've tried to become more deliberate about how I spend my time. You must always remember that your career path is for you to set. It's not something that happens to you; it's not something that others draw for you. When you encounter a brick wall, rather than stand there and curse at it, make a right turn and explore some other avenues."

Management Takes Its Toll on Women in Newsrooms

"I see my career decisions as a game of chess," said Debra Adams Simmons. "I ask myself whether each move is a strategic move; whether each move is going to be good for the step I might want to take after that move."[5] Adams Simmons has taken many of those kinds of steps since age eleven, when she first thought she would be a television reporter. She considered many options when her job as editor of the *Akron Beacon Journal* (she followed me in the job) was eliminated in the fall of 2006 after the paper was sold and resold in the Knight Ridder demise. Hers has been a career based in reporting, editing, and management. In September 2007 she became managing editor at the *Plain Dealer*.

Adams Simmons went to Syracuse, New York, to pursue her idea of being on TV, but, she says, she "hated being in front of the camera." In her junior year, a professor recognized her abilities and suggested she try print instead. She never looked back.

An internship at the *Syracuse Herald-Journal* led to a full-time position and a first-place award from the New York AP for in-depth reporting on abuses in the local foster care system. She moved from Syracuse to the *Hartford Courant*, where she covered education, and from Hartford to the *Detroit Free Press*, also covering education but in a much more competitive environment. "It was a grind," she recalled. "There was lots of competition from the *Detroit News*. The reporter [at the *News*] was a veteran who was very well connected." She says her own expertise in the subject made her think she could compete.

She covered a teachers' strike and a U.S. Senate race, did some regional reporting, and then was assigned to cover the local connections to the Oklahoma City bombings. (Timothy McVeigh and Terry Nichols were from Michigan.) While she was on vacation in 1995, reporters, editors, printers, and drivers at both Detroit papers went on strike. Adams Simmons was out of work for three months and took part-time jobs to pay the bills until she took a new position as education editor at the *Virginian-Pilot*. "It was a smooth transition to editing because I had covered education for eight or nine years by that time," she said. In a few years, Adams Simmons was named metro editor.

Marriage in 1998 took her back to Detroit, but in 2000 Kay Addis called her with an exciting idea. Adams Simmons, her husband, and their toddler son returned to Norfolk, where she became deputy managing editor for local news. She had a second child and settled into the job in Norfolk. That's where she was when as editor of the *Beacon Journal* I called to recruit her to Akron.

Adams Simmons was to be the managing editor of the paper but became editor within six months after I resigned. In Akron she managed not just the news, but also the sale and resale of the paper from Knight Ridder to the McClatchy Company to private owner Black Press Ltd. Jim Crutchfield, the publisher who had hired and promoted her, was replaced. She also managed the dramatic restructuring of the newsroom involving layoffs or buyouts of more than forty people in late 2006. In further "restructuring," Adams Simmons's job was eliminated shortly after the rest of the downsizing was accomplished at the *Beacon Journal*. In Akron, she said that when people were deciding whether to resign voluntarily, many more women than men raised their hands. "The impact is that this opens the door for many women to leave the business . . . and certainly there are a number of managers and writers whose perspective will not form the decisions of what the coverage will be."

Adams Simmons remains optimistic about the future for women in journalism. She doesn't think women are any more vulnerable to the current gyrations in the news business than men, though she does note that to the extent that seniority may be a variable in employment and job security, younger women could be adversely affected by cutbacks. Still, she says there are lots of choices in the newspaper industry for both women and men. Women can lead departments and be managing editors and editors, but they have to understand the risks associated with an industry that is fighting for its survival. All of this will likely have an impact on the choices women make. "The retraction that's going on in the industry really trumps women's issues right now," Adams Simmons said.

Marriage, family, and journalism careers involve some tough choices, as our stories show. Addis, Luecke, Adams Simmons, and I spent decades in journalism. Today Addis is retired, Luecke and I are teaching, and Adams Simmons is committed to the newspaper industry. We are not the only examples of women making choices in journalism. Women in leadership positions have made newsrooms different, more inclusive, while these women have remained strong and aggressive managers. Our career choices are some of those that young women also face today—in turbulent times for the news industry. The choices they make will help determine the future of the industry and women in the news profession.

Notes

1. American Press Institute and Pew Center for Civic Journalism, "The Great Divide: Female Leadership in U.S. Newsrooms," September 2002, 3. Available at http://www.pewcenter.org/doingcj/research/r_apipewstudy.pdf (accessed January 22, 2009).

2. Kay Tucker Addis, e-mail and phone interviews with Jan Leach, February 20, 22, 27, 2006.

3. Mary Arnold, Marlene L. Hendrickson, and Cynthia C. Linton, "Women in Newspapers, 2003: Challenging the Status Quo," ed. Cynthia C. Linton, Media Management Center, Northwestern University, 2003, 57. Available at http://www.mediamanagementcenter.org/publications/data/win2003.pdf (accessed January 22, 2009).

4. Pam Luecke, e-mail interviews with Jan Leach, February 18, 19, 2006, and phone interview February 21, 2006.

5. Debra Adams Simmons, interviews with Jan Leach, March 2, 2006, and January 18, 2007.

23

Young Women Making Career Choices

JAN LEACH

While professionals lament dying newspapers and industry experts debate the media of the future, three smart young women are happy with their choice of journalism careers. Ebony Reed, Leila Atassi, and Rachel Dissell, all in their mid-twenties, chose journalism majors, excelled in demanding internships, and are fulfilling their dreams to write, report, and edit. Reed, twenty-seven, is deputy metro editor for suburbs/online at the *Detroit News*. Atassi and Dissell are on the metro staff at the *Plain Dealer* in Cleveland. They came to newspapers from different backgrounds. They worked hard to prove themselves. All three have decided that journalism, in some form or format, is their future.

Ebony Reed

Ebony Reed always liked to write. "My parents say I've been nosy from day one," she says. "I was always asking 'Why?'" She was editor of her high school paper in Michigan and wrote freelance articles on teen issues for the *Detroit Free Press*. She had her own *Teen Talk with Ebony* television show on a local cable access channel. Still, Reed says, she was surprised in 1996 when the Journalism Education Association named her high school journalist of the year. But the award's scholarship money and guarantee of an internship helped focus her future.[1]

Reed went to the University of Missouri and had internships at the *Birmingham (Ala.) News* and the *Plain Dealer*. She saw herself as a feature writer until she was assigned to the city desk her first summer in Cleveland. During that first Cleveland internship she wrote several stories about a woman who had acid thrown in her face. "I was so grateful to the *PD* that they let me stay on [the story] as an intern and didn't say it belonged to a more seasoned reporter. That one story made me stand out. I left the *PD* that summer with twenty-five clips, but that one story convinced me to stay in news," she recalls.

After graduation, Reed returned to the *Plain Dealer* as a night general assignment reporter. She moved on to covering the beleaguered Cleveland public schools, started work toward her master's degree online, and then expressed an interest in editing. She knew it wouldn't be easy. "I wanted to impact stories that got into the paper; maybe even keep some out," she says. But she was young, female, and African American, and says she was "terrified" of supervising former colleagues.

She got her graduate degree from Missouri's online program, became a night assistant metro editor at the *Plain Dealer,* and taught newswriting at Cuyahoga Community College before moving back to Detroit. Reed says her decision to move into editing had advantages and disadvantages. She says she misses reporting, but she enjoys coordinating coverage and finding stories that others might not have considered. She also recognizes her important responsibilities as a journalist, such as offering a different perspective on news and sources.

Reed's long-term goal is to become a managing editor. For her, it's a dream and very doable. She thinks there will always be a newspaper for her. "I'll need to make department head and maybe have the experience of running more than one department. I'm mindful of that," she said. She also wants to expand her "life outside the newspaper so that when things happen, you don't feel like your whole world crumbled."

For now, Reed is comfortable with the choices she's made and the future she sees for herself. "Change takes time; accomplishment takes time. Everything cannot happen overnight. I think my choices have been okay, but I have to remember that everything happens when it's supposed to."

Leila Atassi

Leila Atassi was Reed's colleague at the *Plain Dealer.* Atassi's parents are Arab American and Polish Catholic, a doctor and a nurse. She was influenced by their medical careers and originally chose a premed major at the College of Wooster. But she had always been interested in writing, she says, and had to change majors because she spent all of her time in the school newspaper office.[2]

One summer during college, she worked at a Boston publication, *Teen Voices,* written entirely by at-risk teenage girls. She got an internship as the writing coach for the teenagers even though all positions were to go to ethnic or racial minorities. "When I applied, I told them what it's like to be a blonde Muslim in the Muslim community. They were surprised by what it's like to be discriminated against in your own community. We talked about racial stereotypes. The result was that I was the only white person there" that summer.

The experience at *Teen Voices* sealed Atassi's fate. "It was the best summer of my whole life," she said. When she returned to Wooster, she knew she had to write, so she did a class project publishing a magazine for women called *Siren*. "There was one issue of *Siren,* one printing, within my budget," she recalled. "It was so great. I wrote all the stories, took almost all the pictures . . . did all the layout and design; sold ads." At that point, Atassi says, her heart was set on a magazine career. After getting her degree, she decided on graduate school at Missouri, though unlike Reed (who did her master's work online), Atassi studied on campus.

Atassi interned at the *Plain Dealer* after her first year at Missouri, then freelanced for the paper from school until she returned to Cleveland for a second internship after graduation. She had another job offer after the second internship ended, but she took a full-time job at the *Plain Dealer* in one of its outer-county bureaus. From there Atassi asked to move into a downtown beat. "I guess I just have a decent instinct for what is the best thing to do," she said. Her most powerful decisions were going to graduate school and taking the full-time job at the *PD*. She says she made a choice to step into her career "at the highest possible level" so that she could move up. Moving up may or may not mean newspaper journalism, but it will involve reporting and writing, Atassi says.

In her mid-twenties, she says, she is coming up on the next stage of adulthood, and it's both exciting and frightening. "When my mom was my age, she had three kids. I'm now in this serious relationship that might become a marriage in the next couple of years. What is the feasibility of having this career and raising a family? What should I do? My mom gave up her career of nursing to raise three kids."

Atassi appreciates the changes occurring in the newspaper industry and says she knows she will have to make sacrifices in the future. "I'm excited about the future," she said. "I wouldn't be completely unhappy as long as I'm able to write and report while raising children. Or write a book while raising children." This much she knows for certain: There are stories she must tell. "I have a feeling of an intense sense of purpose. I feel like there's something big that I'm supposed to get done."

Rachel Dissell

Rachel Dissell says she was "kind of a screw-up" in high school. Her high school newspaper adviser threatened her into coming to a newspaper meeting, enticed her with what she calls the "mysticism" of journalism, and made her fill out her college application for journalism school at Kent State University. Since then, she says, journalism "is exactly what I was going to do. It made sense."[3]

It might have made sense, but it wasn't easy for Dissell. She worked because her family could not afford college. As an undergraduate, she interned at a small weekly newspaper in Nigeria. She was naive about the Africa experience but says it was important to live somewhere else and be cut off from what was comfortable. Then she interned at the *Plain Dealer,* where she covered a five-city beat.

Despite her experience, there weren't many jobs available when she graduated from Kent State, so Dissell took a general-assignment reporting job at a small paper in Harrisonburg, Virginia. She worked hard, "tried to cover things that others didn't cover," and learned on the job. After about a year in Virginia, the *Plain Dealer* asked her to come back to Cleveland to cover police, courts, and crime. By then she realized the responsibilities that come with asking people questions, she says. Now she covers justice and children and family issues. She is content to be a reporter. "I feel like everyone wants you to say you want to be an editor. I'm not sure I have the right skills. I would be a really mean editor, very demanding."

The future is clear to Dissell. "I like writing. I like reporting and writing stories. I still have a lot of stories I want to write, and I should keep writing them." She says she is not worried about newspapers vanishing, because she doesn't care about the format for presenting her work. Whether she writes for print, online, or "there's some hologram of me standing on your doorstep," Dissell wants to be able to tell stories well and she is willing to do the work.

Dissell says her choices haven't always been clear, but she is happy with them and her prospects. She adds that nothing short of a personal crisis will pull her out of the newsroom. "I see myself writing, because I always have to write. It doesn't matter to me what the format is. When it comes down to it, my job of reporting is going to stay the same—getting people information that they can rely on."

Notes

1. All Ebony Reed material from interview with Jan Leach, February 28, 2006.
2. All Leila Atassi material from interview with Jan Leach, February 28, 2006.
3. All Rachel Dissell material from interview with Jan Leach, February 21, 2006.

24

Women in Community Journalism

JAN LEACH

Journalists are nomads, traveling on assignments, moving for different jobs with various organizations. It's part of the career landscape. Claire Regan chose a different landscape. Although she travels often for professional development or industry conferences, Regan has spent her entire career at one newspaper. It just happens to be the newspaper in her hometown.[1] Regan grew up in Staten Island, graduated from Wagner College there, and now is associate managing editor of the *Staten Island (N.Y.) Advance*. She has worked at the *Advance* for more than twenty-seven years.

After leaving Wagner in 1980 with a teaching degree, Regan started substitute teaching in New York City schools. But she needed more money than the per diem she made as a substitute teacher, so she applied for a part-time job as wedding writer at the *Advance*. It was the first of many important career decisions.

The editor who interviewed Regan liked that she was from Staten Island and asked if she knew how to type. She said no. Regan believes the editor appreciated her honesty and that's why he gave her the job anyway. She fell in love with the newsroom. She soon realized that she couldn't wait to go to work every weekday morning, so she started showing up whenever she wasn't teaching, even at night and on weekends. She became "obsessed with getting every single wedding perfect. . . . I knew how important they were to the readers. I'd be there late on Friday night triple-checking the grids . . . I did not want to be responsible for any mistakes." Eventually, Regan became so good at weddings that she was allowed to do engagements and birth announcements. Sometimes she would write up the weddings of people for whom she had written their engagement stories. Later she wrote anniversary announcements. She calls it the "hometown advantage," because she knew people in town who would call her to get their news in the paper. "I had a role that I loved and I had a crash course in journalism at the same time," she said.

Regan soon realized that journalism was her calling. She was still teaching and she had the twenty-hour-a-week job at the paper, but she spent almost all of her free time at the paper. She resolved to get a full-time reporting spot by demonstrating her feature writing. Her first story was published on the cover of the features section. "I wrote these stories to prove myself. I also offered to cut and paste and design my own pages," she explained. "I loved the design part." Still, it took two years of writing features before Regan was hired full-time as a feature writer in the lifestyle department at the *Advance*. "There might have been a little chauvinism going on," she conceded. "There was an older male editor; I was a young woman. The ladies' room had one commode; the men's room had four. The newsroom was built for men. Women were not given the chance then that they have today."

Regan was excited about all the stories she could do, plus she was still designing pages and writing headlines. Eventually, she moved to the night news desk as a reporter and filled in on the night city desk. She also designed the business section pages and remembers "feeling very inadequate about it." But she embraced both assignments as learning opportunities, even though her male colleagues made her "uncomfortable a little bit and intimidated a lot."

From the night city desk, Regan moved to the dayside copy desk, then became entertainment editor before being named lifestyle editor. "I enjoyed it, but I had the same editor. Even though I don't think he gave young people, especially young women like me, the chances they deserved, I still appreciate the fact that I worked for an old-fashioned newspaperman, because that's what he was. I appreciate the fact that he hired me as the wedding writer, but I think I would have climbed the ladder faster elsewhere."

When a new editor assumed the top spot at the *Advance* in 1992, Regan said, "He appreciated my talents; he knew me and had been my advocate during the difficult times . . . so the choice I made to stick through it paid off very well. I have always been loyal to my hometown paper. It was my choice."

Eventually, Regan was named page-one designer and assistant news editor. She also started teaching journalism at her alma mater, Wagner College. She worked nights on design, wrote headlines, and studied deadline production. During the day she taught what she was learning at night.

Always curious and willing to take on new projects, Regan was named project editor for the paper's complete redesign, which was to coincide with installation of a new press. The redesign, with all its creativity, technology, equipment, and endless meetings and decisions, took ten months, but she finished it on time. "That was definitely a milestone for my career. It really secured my place in the newspaper." Immediately after the redesign, she was promoted to associate managing editor, a new position. "I don't know whether it's because I'm a woman or because I've been here a long time and I grew up here. You have to sort of struggle for impact when you've been in a place a long time."

Regan says she knows her community and she knows her newspaper, but she often feels restless. "I know I'm supposed to be a journalist. I'm a good journalist. I'm restless about the fact that I've stayed in the same place. I wonder about the opportunities I missed. . . . But it's the perfect size paper for me to have impact. . . . My choice was to stay here, and I've been here so long the paper lets me do things, so I've made a disadvantage into an advantage."

Regan has had job offers from papers in Wisconsin, Virginia, New York, and Pennsylvania, especially since the redesign, but she has turned them down. She says she recognizes her career would be different if she had moved around or taken other offers. "Lots of people raise eyebrows and become suspicious, asking, 'Why would you stay so long in one place?' But I've made the most of my own situation. I teach at Wagner, I participate at Poynter [she was an Ethics Fellow at the Poynter Institute in St. Petersburg, Florida, in the class of 2004], and I'm a teacher in my own newsroom now."

Teaching seems to have threaded its way into most of Regan's career tapestry. Now the tapestry is bright and varied with interesting options ahead. Regan says she would like to be the editor of a paper someday. She also says she enjoys development and networking opportunities and women's issues. "I always tell my students that sometimes the way you get into a job can be nontraditional, like the way I started. Don't ever think a job is not good enough for you, because you never know what doors it can open. Be persistent and confident."

Regan made unusual choices but now has respect and tenure. "There's a lot to be said for a smaller paper," she said. "It built my confidence as a journalist. I have a role at the newspaper and it's clear, and I have a role in the community and it's clear."

Notes

1. All Claire Regan material from interviews with Jan Leach, January 4, 2006, and March 13, 2006.

PART 7

Beyond Gender Diversity

25

Civil Rights and Searching for Community Values

WANDA S. LLOYD

When Rosa Parks refused to give up her seat to a white passenger on a Montgomery, Alabama, city bus on December 1, 1955, her defiant act set off a storm of protest that led to the nation's first modern-day boycott for civil rights. The Montgomery bus boycott was led by Martin Luther King Jr., a young Baptist pastor who was drafted and elected president of the newly formed Montgomery Improvement Association because he was new in town and because he and his family were not beholden to the local white establishment. And, of course, because he was so dynamic.

Boycott leaders had a communications strategy that included fliers run off on a mimeograph machine and delivered to black neighborhoods and black-owned businesses. This strategy, repeated in local civil rights boycotts across the South, including my own hometown of Savannah, Georgia, was a way to avoid sending messages through the white-owned media. The fliers invited black citizens to attend weekly mass meetings at churches, where stirring speeches and soulful spirituals would rally them to walk several miles to work for 381 days.

The arrest of Parks was not front-page news in 1955. A short story on the bottom of page 9A of the *Montgomery Advertiser* was headlined "Negro Jailed Here for 'Overlooking' Bus Segregation":

> A Montgomery Negro woman was arrested by city police last night for ignoring a bus driver who directed her to sit in the rear of the bus.
>
> The woman, Rosa Parks, 634 Cleveland Ave., was later released under $100 bond.
>
> Bus operator J. F. Blake, 27 N. Lewis St., in notifying police, said a Negro woman sitting in the section reserved for whites refused to move to the Negro section.

> When Officers F. B. Day and D. W. Mixon arrived where the bus was halted on Montgomery Street, they confirmed the driver's report.
>
> Blake signed the warrant for her arrest under a section of the City Code that gives police powers to bus drivers in the enforcement of segregation aboard buses.

Evidently, because of the length and placement of the story, there was no inkling that this event would change the course of history.

Fifty years later, as Montgomery was gearing up to celebrate the fiftieth anniversary of Parks's arrest and the bus boycott, the *Montgomery Advertiser*, now Gannett-owned, was led by a black female executive editor. The planned celebratory coverage would be widespread, with a series of news projects that included a forty-four-page special section called "Voices of the Boycott," a book, a Web site with historic stories and video oral histories of boycott participants, and educational tools for schoolchildren to learn about the boycott history.

Sadly, Parks did not live to see the boycott's fiftieth anniversary. A few weeks before that milestone, she died, on Monday, October 24, 2005. The anniversary celebration would be eclipsed—and elevated—by news of her death. The *Advertiser*, already in high gear for the boycott anniversary, published an eight-page special section the following day. Then came the announcement of the celebration of Parks's life. Her body was flown to Montgomery for a memorial service, then to Washington, D.C., the first time a woman or an African American would lie in repose in the U.S. Capitol, and then back to Detroit, her adopted home, for a seven-hour funeral and burial.

For ten days the *Advertiser* carried front-page stories of this celebration, with photos and references to extensive coverage online. The new Web site, montgomeryboycott.com, which was being developed for the boycott anniversary, was launched a few weeks early and drew worldwide attention from people who were hungry for information about Parks's and Montgomery's roles in history. Many local readers in Montgomery lauded the newspaper for the blanket coverage of Parks's death, but not everyone appreciated its coverage. Many white readers called or wrote letters to the editor, complaining that the newspaper (and local television stations) went overboard by elevating Parks to international stature. "This isn't news," one reader said in a voice message. Yet many others—especially blacks—said they were buying multiple copies of the newspaper to send to friends and family members out of town, or saving copies for their grandchildren, born and unborn. They saw the historical significance.

Fortunately, Montgomery's newspapers did cover civil rights as the movement occurred. As documented in the *Advertiser*'s book "They Walked to Freedom: The Story of the Montgomery Bus Boycott" (2005), by Kenneth M. Hare, the *Advertiser*'s former city editor, the late Joe Azbell, wrote many of the stories about the boycott, including reports on the bombings of homes of King and other boycott leaders. But in several other cities, newspapers ignored civil rights turmoil and changes in the 1950s and '60s. Forty or more years later, some newspapers were compelled to own up to the misplaced judgment of omission of coverage by publishing series of stories about their failures.

In a 2006 article in the *American Editor,* the magazine of the American Society of News Editors, ASNE diversity director Bobbi Bowman captured some of the missing links. "For the past six years a group of editors from around the country have given their readers a series of riveting, painful stories revealing the dark and sometimes murderous chapters in the history of their communities."[1] Bowman recounts the confessions of these newspapers:

- In North Carolina, the *News and Observer* in Raleigh and the *Charlotte Observer* "told their readers of the nearly forgotten events of Nov. 10, 1898, in Wilmington, N.C., where an unknown number of blacks and whites were killed or driven from town and the elected city government was literally overthrown. The two papers also reported that their former owners were part of the white elite conspiracy that fomented the insurrection."
- In Jackson, Mississippi, the *Clarion-Ledger*'s Jerry Mitchell spent sixteen years "uncovering the perpetrators of that state's murderous civil rights past and bringing them to justice with the help of Mississippi prosecutors."
- In Jackson, Tennessee, the *Jackson Sun* "told readers how that paper failed to cover that city's civil rights movement because former owners [of the newspaper] wanted to keep the peace." Later, the *Lexington Herald* in Kentucky "told virtually the same story."

"Why is it important for newspapers to shine a light on the dark disturbing chapters of a community's past?" Bowman asked in the article. "Why do heartbreaking stories long buried in the past make good journalism today? . . . The thread lacing together all the stories: This dark past shadows the present affecting and infecting how black folks and white folks relate to each other, deal with each other and even how government works."

Bowman quotes Marilyn Thompson, who as editor led the Lexington newspaper's coverage of the failed local civil rights movement: "Sometimes journalists need to resurrect the past to understand the present." Part of the reason the past wasn't being told is because mainstream daily newspaper newsrooms were mostly male and lily white in the decades leading up to the 1970s.

I recall the day I told my family I wanted to become a journalist. I was a high school student in Savannah, Georgia, a city not necessarily known for outstanding accomplishments in journalism at the time—in the mid-1960s. As an African American growing up in the segregated South, I don't recall the name of a single woman who worked for our local newspaper or television station.

One may assume women were working behind the scenes, but none, as I recall, had bylines or on-air television news presence in my hometown. I'm sure there were no African Americans.

So there I was, standing in the family kitchen announcing to my grandmother and anybody else who would listen that I wanted to work for a daily newspaper. My grandmother, a professional woman who ran her own business, asked me how I thought I would accomplish this goal, because "Negro girls don't work for newspapers." Good point, but I was either too obstinate or too naive to think I could not overcome those odds. My grandmother's advice was this: "Just take some education classes so you will have something to fall back on. Then you can always get a job as a teacher," like other women in our family.

After high school I left for Atlanta's Spelman College, a school for African American women. Spelman did not offer journalism courses, and I never took an education class. Fortunately, a teacher, Alan Bussell, at Spelman's neighboring school called Clark College (now Clark-Atlanta University), guided me to the Dow Jones Newspaper Fund. In 1970 I found myself working as a Dow Jones intern on the copy desk of the *Providence (R.I.) Evening Bulletin,* a generation away from the teachers in my family and a world away from my southern roots. I fully expected to be a reporter someday, but somewhere along the way someone told me that copy editors make more money (in those days we got a whopping five dollars a week in differential pay!) and could get to management faster. My goal was to be a top newspaper editor, and copy editing would lead my path.

At the end of the summer internship, *Bulletin* managing editor Joseph Ungaro invited me to return to Providence after graduation for a full-time job. I didn't have the good sense to know how lucky I was at the time. No one had told me how unusual it was for a woman—a black woman—to walk from graduation to a metropolitan daily newspaper. Some of my African American peers (and there were not many in the early 1970s) got their start on black weekly newspapers, mostly in the South, where they were lauded for coverage of segregation and the civil rights movement. Some worked in radio.

Even though I had a solid job offer, toward the end of my senior year at Spelman I wanted to explore other options. Growing up in Savannah, I looked to the *Atlanta Constitution* and the *Atlanta Journal* as our big-city newspapers. When I was a teenager, my family purchased the Sunday Atlanta newspaper from a street hawker every week. I devoured that newspaper. Years later I was awarded a scholarship in honor of longtime *Journal-Constitution* editor Ralph McGill, a scholarship set up to encourage young people from the South to go into journalism and, presumably, stay in the South to work. I was audacious enough to think that scholarship help would also help me land a job at the newspaper where McGill became famous for his progressive editorial stand on civil rights.

So one day, with the Providence job offer still on the table, I went into downtown Atlanta and met with Bill Fields, who, as part of his job as a manager at the Cox newspaper in Atlanta, had some oversight of the McGill scholarship program. I told Fields I wanted to stay in Atlanta and work for his newspaper. He seemed pleased. After all, this was a few years after African Americans started to demand the presence of more black professionals in daily newspaper newsrooms across the country. I told Fields about the great experience I'd had the previous summer in Providence. I wanted to continue my work on the copy desk. His eyes went dark.

"I can't do that," Fields told me.

"Why not?" I asked.

"Because people in this community are demanding that we hire more Negro reporters," he replied, "and if you work on the copy desk, no one will know you are here." I returned to Spelman and called Ungaro to accept the offer to return to Providence, a city with relatively few black residents at the time. It didn't matter. I wanted to be a copy editor, and the *Evening Bulletin* was ready to embrace my ambitions.

Fields wasn't totally off base with his refusal to support my application in Atlanta. Newspapers across the country—mostly newspapers in big metropolitan areas—suddenly and desperately were reaching out to hire African Americans as reporters and photographers. Fields's response to my interest in working at his newspaper came on the heels of the 1968 report by the Kerner Commission, formally known as the National Advisory Commission on Civil Disorders. After a seven-month study the commission reported that before the urban riots in the mid-1960s "the media report and write from the standpoint of a white man's world."[2] The report came to the conclusion that the "white press" at the time "repeatedly, if unconsciously, reflects the biases, the paternalism, the indifference of white America."

Newspapers, it seemed, were clueless about the abject frustration in the nation's ghettos and slum areas and even—in some cases—among young professional blacks who were college educated or in school at the time. The urban riots of the 1960s brought to light the frustration of generations of people who had been disenfranchised. Yet local newspapers had no interest in and no means of covering these groups.

The same surprises came to light more recently, in 2005, after damage from Hurricane Katrina in New Orleans. Local and state leaders ordered everyone out of the city before the storm because of the threat of flooding if the levees didn't hold. The levees broke and that's when the world discovered that so many African Americans had no means, no money, no transportation to get out of harm's way. These were the untold stories of modern times. After the tragedy, the national media—many of them broadcast reporters—swooped into New Orleans to tell the emotional stories. From most perspectives, the stories came too late.

The same may be said in coming years of the stories of illegal immigration of Latinos, mostly from Mexico. But there is a big difference between newspapers' ability to tell these stories in the twenty-first century and the untold stories of blacks in the twentieth century. There are more Spanish-speaking and Latino journalists working in mainstream media. There are more ethnic newspapers all across the country to help keep Latinos abreast of news from home nations and to give needed advice on how to cope in their new homeland.

In its list of recommendations, the Kerner Commission proposed a privately organized, privately funded Institute of Urban Communications, an idea that eventually manifested itself in many small and large programs to train journalists of color and encourage racial diversity in newsrooms. These organizations included the Maynard Institute for Journalism Education, the American Society of News Editors, and the Freedom Forum (founded as the Gannett Foundation). They helped increase attention to developing credible journalism programs at historically black colleges and universities. Some of the better-known journalism programs of these colleges include Howard, Florida A & M, and Hampton universities. The commission also found that media organizations were "shockingly backward in seeking out, hiring, training and promoting Negroes." Over the years since Kerner, there has been increasingly more outreach by mainstream universities to recruit students of color and to hire faculty members who are from minority groups. Still, with the increased emphasis in these recruiting areas, the nation's newspaper newsrooms remain largely white.

Almost a decade after the Kerner report, in 1978, ASNE president Eugene Patterson of the *St. Petersburg (Fla.) Times* appointed ASNE's first Minorities Committee (later called the Diversity Committee). Chaired by Richard Smyser of the *Oak Ridger* in Oak Ridge, Tennessee, that committee made five recommendations to the ASNE board of directors a year later:

- The commitment to recruit, train, and hire minorities needs urgently to be rekindled. This is simply the right thing to do and is also in the newspaper industry's economic self-interest.
- There should be at least an annual accounting by ASNE of minority employment, including not just total jobs but types of positions held.
- There should be special emphasis on increasing the number of minority newsroom executives.
- Small newspapers should especially be encouraged to add minority members to their staffs.
- Leaders among minority journalists urged the industry to set a goal of minority employment by 2000 equivalent to the percentage of minority persons within the national population. The committee believes this is a fair and attainable goal.[3]

That final goal was the one that gave the industry hope, when ASNE director John Quinn suggested strengthening the committee's recommendations by having ASNE pledge to have newspapers achieve the minority percentage in newsrooms equal to the minority proportion of the total population before the year 2000 suggested in the committee report. (ASNE defines "minority" along the lines of the U.S. Census definition: African American, Native American, Asian American, and Hispanic or Latino.) The ASNE board adopted the committee report.

Still, almost two decades later, as the benchmark year 2000 closed in, contentious discussions sparked the realization that the industry would fall far short of parity at the end of the twentieth century. In 1978, when the so-called Year 2000 goal was set, the nation's minority population was about 11 percent, mostly made up of African Americans. ASNE launched an annual census of newsroom staffs by asking daily newspapers to voluntarily submit the percentage of people of color working in their newsrooms. The first ASNE census showed that newsrooms were made up of just under 4 percent people of color, a mere seven percentage points from the goal. Over the next two decades, people of color in newsrooms inched up about one-half a percentage point per year, on average.

But the nation's population of people of color rose drastically. Largely because of immigration, the minority base was no longer almost all African American. Along with Native Americans, a larger national pool of Latinos and Asian Americans changed the face of the nation, and newsrooms were nowhere close to keeping up. The 2000 U.S. Census predicted that people of color would make up about 50 percent of the population by the year 2050, and newsrooms were only 12.7 percent minority at the time of that projection. Also, while a number of training and development programs attracted a relative few minorities to newsrooms, as the industry barreled along toward 2000 there were no benchmarks for meeting the goals.

In October 1998, with the realization that the Year 2000 goal was little more than a pipe dream, the ASNE board, on which I served at the time, adopted a new goal of seeking parity by 2025 or sooner. This time the goal called for creating a series of three-year benchmarks to help the industry better track its progress. Later, after a meta-analysis conducted by Princeton University professor Lawrence McGill, now director of research and planning for the Cultural Policy and the Arts National Data Archive, the ASNE board also recognized that retention is a major factor in increasing the number of minority journalists. The ASNE board voted to include retention figures for minorities and nonminorities in the report of the annual newsroom census.

Still, in 2008, the thirtieth anniversary of the survey, the ASNE newsroom census report did not offer great hope that parity is near. Although the U.S. Census shows the national minority population at more than 30 percent (years ahead of the census's own projection), newspapers reported to ASNE that news-rooms are made up of slightly less than 14 percent people of color.

In a year of critical downturn in the nation's economy, ASNE president Gilbert Bailon said of the 2008 ASNE survey, "The numbers represent a dual reality: It's mildly encouraging that the minority percentage held steady despite difficult economic times that are causing many cutbacks."

ASNE diversity chair Caesar Andrews said, "Certainly the slight percentage increase is better than the alternative, especially during another tough year with overall staff reductions. But if we're not able to accelerate diversity inside newsrooms, and if we miss opportunities to produce more compelling news coverage, then the challenge of connecting with changing communities becomes that much more difficult."[4] (Indeed, Andrews himself became part of the chang-ing newsroom climate in 2008. As one of few African American top editors in the nation, he left daily newspaper work later the same year.)

Women working full-time in daily newspapers totaled 19,700 in the 2008 ASNE report and 17,300 in 2009. The percentage of women decreased slightly to 37 percent from the previous year. Minority women accounted for 16.6 percent of female newsroom staffers, a drop from 17.16 percent in 2008.[5]

Women of color have taken some leadership roles in this new diversity move-ment. The four main minority journalism associations have been led by women who raised their hands to run for office among their cultural groups. Among women leaders of the National Association of Black Journalists (NABJ) have been Sidmel Estes-Sumpter, Condace Pressley, Dorothy Butler Gilliam, and Vanessa Williams. Women presidents of the National Association of Hispanic Journalists have included Veronica Villafañe and Nancy Baca. The Native Ameri-can Journalists Association has been led by women presidents Kara Briggs and Mary Annette Pember. The Asian American Journalists Association presidents have included Evelyn Hsu, Dinah Eng, Catalina Camia, Mae Cheng, Esther Wu, and Jeanne Mariani-Belding. Several women leaders of these organizations have gone on to lead UNITY: Journalists of Color, the partnership of the four minority associations that held its first national conference in 1994 in Atlanta. One woman of color—Karla Garrett Harshaw, editor of the *Springfield News-Sun* in Ohio—has been president of ASNE.

Although women are proven leaders of journalism organizations for people of color, top newsroom leadership is a different story. A report on the NABJ Web site (www.nabj.org) compiled and updated in 2005 by Don Hudson, managing editor of the Jackson, Mississippi, *Clarion-Ledger,* counted seventeen African American top editors at mainstream daily newspapers. Of those seventeen, only five were women: Harshaw (a Cox Newspapers executive who was reassigned from her newsroom to a corporate job in 2006); Sherrie Marshall, executive editor, the *Macon (Ga.) Telegraph;* Debra Adams Simmons, editor and vice president, *Akron Beacon Journal;* Antionette Taylor-Thomas, managing editor, *Eagle-Gazette,* Lancaster, Ohio; and Wanda Lloyd, executive editor, *Montgomery Advertiser.* However, in 2006, because of changes both personal and professional, some of these women dropped off the list of top editors at daily newspapers. No African American women were added.

Meanwhile, among Latinas, top editors included Carolina Garcia, executive editor, the *Monterey (Calif.) Herald;* Rachel Benavidez, editor, the *Brownsville (Tex.) Herald;* and Diana Fuentes, editor, the *Laredo Morning Times,* also in Texas.

The Future

Just as the Kerner Commission report ushered in the first era for integration of newsrooms and the call for inclusion of people of color in news media reporting in 1968, another organization seems poised to pick up the mantle of the commission's work and see it through to the next generation. In December 2006 the Washington, D.C.–based Milton S. Eisenhower Foundation held a forum of high-profile journalists and public policy experts to help determine a framework for funding and programming the future of news. The foundation bills itself as the international nonprofit continuation of the National Advisory Commission on Civil Disorders (the Kerner Commission) and the National Commission on the Causes and Prevention of Violence (the National Violence Commission, formed after the assassinations of the Rev. Martin Luther King Jr. and senator Robert Kennedy). The foundation identifies, funds, evaluates, and builds capacities for multiple-solution ventures for poor urban children and families.

The December 12, 2006, National Media Forum on Poverty, Inequality, and Race included commentary and analysis from notable journalists like DeWayne Wickham, columnist for *USA Today* and Gannett News Service; Kevin Merida, Eugene Robinson, and Colbert King, all of the *Washington Post;* Barbara Reynolds, formerly of the *Chicago Tribune* and *USA Today;* Ray Suarez of "The News-Hour with Jim Lehrer"; freelance journalist Rochelle Stanfield, formerly with the *National Journal; Newsweek's* Ellis Cose; Felix Gutierrez of the University of Southern California Annenberg School for Communication; and Gregory Kane of the *Sun* in Baltimore. Eisenhower Foundation communications director Leila McDowell said the organization's leaders would synthesize the discussions and come up with a framework to help fund and direct a national dialogue to help improve media diversity coverage.

That dialogue may be a path to the future, but other organizations are seeking solutions for the slow but steady road to media diversity. For example, the American Society of News Editors, through its annual newsroom census, has determined that retention of people of color is one of the industry's biggest hurdles to achieving parity. People of color have been leaving newsrooms faster than their white counterparts. There is no question that parity in staffing has a direct relationship with the inclusion of topics related to people of color in content. Yet University of Georgia professor Lee Becker has published research that debunks the myth that there are not enough minority students available to fill the pipeline, or that they are turning down media jobs. "The point is a simple one," Becker wrote in an analysis on FreedomForum.org in 2002.[6] "The problem isn't supply, at least in gross terms. The problem is that there is not a suitable link between supply and demand." Becker said, "The problem is that many minority graduates do not get job offers, and many of those who do get offers decide not to take them. For whatever reasons—and there probably are many—the job market is not functioning efficiently enough to produce the kind of diversity industry leaders say they want and many—including us—feel is crucial if the media in this country are to serve their communities and the larger society."

So what steps are being taken to close the gap? The Freedom Forum has years of experience in developing talent. Since 1991, that organization's Chips Quinn Scholars program has placed 1,140 college students in internships in small, medium, and large newspaper newsrooms. The Freedom Forum Diversity Institute, founded in 2002 and based on the campus of Vanderbilt University, recognized the need to help newspapers develop homegrown talent among mid-career professionals of color. The institute contacted newspaper editors across the country and asked them to identify local people with the talent and passion for writing, as well as knowledge of their local area. In twelve weeks these newspapers got back well-trained entry-level journalists who were ready to hit the ground running as reporters, copy editors, and photographers.

The journalism academic world also recognizes that diversity is an important issue and holds accredited university programs accountable. The Accrediting Council on Education in Journalism and Mass Communication's diversity standard requires that any unit seeking accreditation must have "a diverse and inclusive program that serves and reflects society."[7] That means any school seeking first-time or renewed accreditation must have a written plan for achieving an inclusive curriculum; must foster understanding of issues and perspectives that are inclusive in gender, race, and ethnicity; and must demonstrate effective efforts to recruit women and minority faculty. Furthermore, the unit must support the retention of these diverse groups.

Many mainstream news organizations are serving diverse readers by fragmenting coverage—in print and online. Multimedia microsites are cropping up on companion Web sites as a way to address the diverse needs of customers. In print, several metropolitan newspapers see the wisdom of developing separate ethnic products to address the needs of Spanish-speaking readers. Among them, the *Miami Herald* was one of the first when it launched *Nuevo Herald* in the 1980s. Perhaps ahead of its time, the product didn't sit well with Cuban immigrants and the *Herald* pulled it. It was revamped and relaunched several years later as *El Nuevo Herald.* In more recent years, other newspapers followed with their own Spanish-language products. For example, the *Dallas Morning News* launched *Al Dia;* the Tribune Company's *Newsday* in New York, the *Los Angeles Times,* and the *Chicago Tribune* publish *Hoy* in those communities; the *Washington Post* publishes *El Tiempo Latino;* the *Arizona Republic* publishes *La Voz.* Newspapers in some smaller cities also developed Spanish-language pages, special features, or Web products in locations where the Hispanic population is growing.

Moving forward in the twenty-first century, most news organizations are building a strong component of multimedia journalism. Skills and climates must be nimble and react quickly to this change, which many see as a survival tactic for traditional media companies. Whether diversity becomes top of mind during these waves of change remains to be seen. So far diversity has not been articulated as part of the strategy for survival.

Notes

1. Bobbi Bowman, "Exhuming the Long-Buried Past," *American Editor* (November-December 2006), American Society of News Editors.

2. National Advisory Commission on Civil Disorders, *Report of the National Advisory Commission on Civil Disorders,* Kerner Commission Report (Washington, D.C.: U.S. Government Printing Office, 1968), 203.

3. American Society of News Editors, "A Brief History of ASNE Diversity Efforts," ASNE, April 16, 2003, http://www.asne.org/index.cfm?ID=4571 (accessed January 22, 2009).

4. American Society of News Editors, "U.S. Newsroom Employment Declines," 2009 Newsroom Employment Census, ASNE, April 16, 2009, http://www.asne.org/index.cfm?id=7372 (accessed May 3, 2009).

5. Ibid.

6. Lee Becker, "Diversity in Hiring: Supply Is There. Is Demand?" Freedom Forum, September 12, 2002, http://www.freedomforum.org/templates/document.asp?documentID=16949&printerfriendly=1 (accessed January 22, 2009).

7. Accrediting Council on Education in Journalism and Mass Communication, Standard 3 (ACEMC accrediting standards). See http://www2.ku.edu/~acejmc/PROGRAM/STANDARDS.SHTML#std3 (accessed January 22, 2009).

26

Finding Voice

ARLENE NOTORO MORGAN

Since the days of Ida B. Wells, women journalists have championed the causes of the poor, the disenfranchised, the underrepresented, the immigrant, and the exploited. It is clear that women have established themselves as major role models in hiring and reporting across differences since Columbia University's "Let's Do It Better!" Workshop on Journalism, Race, and Ethnicity started collecting data in 1999. To be sure, there are a countless number of male reporters—Steve Magagnini of the *Sacramento Bee;* Leonard Pitts of Knight Ridder; Ted Koppel, John Donovan of ABC News; Jonathan Tilove of the Newhouse Washington bureau; and Keith Woods, dean of the Poynter Institute, come to mind—who have devoted their careers to giving voice to the voiceless. But if the workshop's statistics tell us anything, it's that women have assumed a major leadership role to foster inclusiveness in our newsrooms, news pages, and television screens. Their stories and the work they have done personify diversity and all that the word means across gender, sex, generations, class, age, race, and ethnicity.

The women cited in this chapter have participated, as either award winners or advisers, in the workshop I directed at the Columbia University Graduate School of Journalism through 2008. Sponsored by a Ford Foundation grant, the program honored topics that spanned everything from white flight to interracial romance. Honorees Mirta Ojito, Anne Hull, Anh Do, and Allie Shah; editors Sandy Close and Sharon Rosenhause; and work by television newscasters Ann Curry and Lynn Sherr have been turned into workshop presentations to influence newsroom managers who ostensibly have the power to change the culture and the content of their newsrooms and the content they produce.

Until I directed this project, I never thought seriously about the specific contributions women journalists were making to better understand our diverse and changing communities. Granted, women generally are the majority of the

American Society of News Editors' diversity committees and, for the most part, make up the ranks of recruiters who attend the annual minority job fairs. But it still surprised me when I counted who had won a "Let's Do It Better!" award. Women, both individually or in teams, crafted almost 70 percent of the two hundred pieces honored and dominated eleven out of the thirteen pieces selected for *The Authentic Voice: The Best Reporting on Race and Ethnicity* (Columbia University Press, 2006) project that has grown out of the program.[1]

Could it be that reporting on racial and demographic changes has become a women's cause? Or are the statistics simply a reflection of who is now populating our newsrooms and classrooms? Whatever the answer, it is clear that more women are feeling empowered to push for an agenda of change on the type of stories they tell and who populates the newsroom.

For Walterene Swanston, the director for diversity at National Public Radio (NPR), who served two terms as executive director of the UNITY: Journalists of Color organization and convention, it's natural to see women leading the fight for inclusion. "So many of the race, family and social justice beats were viewed as 'the ghetto' back in the '70s and '80s, when women were starting to gain in the ranks of working journalists," Swanston said in an interview. "When women took on the role of fostering newsroom diversity—roles men shunned as inconsequential to their careers—women benefited as those jobs gained in influence and power," said Swanston, a longtime fixture in the fight to bring people of color into the news business.

Joining Swanston in the quest for diversity are editors like Sandy Close, head of the Pacific News Service and New America Media Association, and Sharon Rosenhause, the retired managing editor of the *South Florida Sun Sentinel,* who now volunteers her time for newsroom diversity causes. "When I think of a hero, I inevitably think of Sandy Close," said Jon Funabiki, former deputy director of Ford Foundation's media, arts, and culture division, who is now a professor of journalism at San Francisco State University.

Close did not earn her "hero" status easily; nor does she wear it lightly. A 1964 University of California–Berkeley graduate, Close took an unconventional approach to her career. After graduating she went off to Hong Kong, where she became the China editor for the *Far Eastern Economic Review.* She eventually returned to Oakland, California, and started the *Flatlands,* a newspaper that was designed specifically to give voice to Oakland's minority communities. By 1974 she was heading the Pacific News Service, a role that has given her an important vantage point from which to report and analyze the demographic and cultural changes of California. Never content with the status quo, Close started a youth newspaper called *YO!* in 1990, becoming a mentor to dozens of young people who wanted a critical sounding board to the multicultural and pop cultural mix in the Bay Area. "I never thought of myself as anything but a journalist until I began to work with kids," Close told a meeting of the Online News Association in October 2005. Emphasizing her belief in the "communal" function of news, Close consistently confronts the mainstream press about the challenges it faces to write about the "new" America and the work it needs to do "to give its audiences a sense of how they connect to one another."

As an outgrowth of her role as a change agent, Close founded the New California Media in 1996, shepherding it from seventy-five ethnic news organizations to the national New America Media organization, which now represents more than a thousand ethnic press outlets. The first national Ethnic News Media Expo at Columbia University, in June 2005, drew more than fifteen hundred participants, the majority of whom were under the age of thirty. A recipient of a 1995 MacArthur Foundation "genius" award, Close envisions creating partnerships between the ethnic and mainstream media on projects that bridge the stratification of society. "Ethnic media's limitations are also its power because more mainstream media is bringing ethnic media to the table," Close told the Online Association. "In this partnership, a new journalism will emerge and a sense of where we all fit in as a whole."[2]

In contrast to Close, Sharon Rosenhause used her considerable talents and abilities in the mainstream press, first as a reporter and then as an editor. As the managing editor of the now defunct Hearst-owned *San Francisco Examiner*, Rosenhause was one of the first award winners in the "Let's Do It Better!" competition with a series that examined the city's multicultural neighborhoods. "I have long believed that women journalists who grew up or came of age at a time when women faced discrimination issues in the world [and in the newsroom], when feminism was evolving, are simply disposed to understand, explore, and explain the story about how race is lived in America," Rosenhause said in an interview. Honored with the workshop's newspaper leadership award in 2005, Rosenhause has chaired the American Society of News Editors' diversity committee and its effort to provide culture competence training to the membership. The workshop statistics didn't surprise Rosenhause. "Women are better storytellers. They see and live the drama and they have an eye for detail that keeps the narrative going." Rosenhause also thinks women editors assumed leadership roles on diversity issues because of the history of their "second-class citizenship, a history of not being listened to and of being disrespected."

At the *South Florida Sun Sentinel*, where Rosenhause served as managing editor from 2001 to 2007, she instilled a definite commitment to diversity, forged in partnership with editor Earl Maucker. One of Rosenhause's jobs was to oversee the policy that required that every job opening be filled from a diverse pool of candidates. At the content level, the paper regularly covers Cuba, with one of the few U.S. bureaus in Havana, and has undertaken major series that have appeared in the paper on topics ranging from how AIDS/HIV has impacted the Caribbean and South Florida to the integration of racial and ethnic awareness throughout the paper. The *Sun Sentinel* started a four-reporter race-and-demographics reporting team and was a regular contender for "Let's Do It Better!" awards, which ended ten years of competition in 2008.

Rosenhause joined Funabiki in her admiration for Sandy Close, whom she met in San Francisco. "She was a big fan of the *Examiner*," Rosenhause said, "because we were the first newspaper to publish *YO!*—a column put together by disenfranchised young people in the Bay Area. Over time, we became friends and, as she likes to say, coconspirators. . . . Sandy is brilliant and a terrific newsperson, though she has always operated just outside the mainstream," Rosenhause continued. "Some people worry about her politics. I don't know anything about her politics, but her journalism is incredible. She sees stories that others will never see—or understand."

The two editors worked on a joint program between ASNE and the New America Media Association to develop several mainstream/ethnic press collaborations, including one at the *Sun Sentinel*. Close, who has pushed this idea, is convinced that the future belongs to news organizations that take advantage of the knowledge offered by the ethnic press in their communities and, in turn, the ethnic editors will benefit from working with experienced mainstream journalists.

Workshop Emphasis on Reporting

Ultimately the proof of the workshop's success rested in the stories. If they didn't reflect all of America, what's the point? To this end, the Columbia workshop served as a model for "diversity" training because of its emphasis on reporting as the best test of a news organization's inclusion. The workshop's winning stories displayed voice, provided historical context, tackled complex subjects, and, above all, reached an authenticity that moved the audience past an "us and them" paradigm that so often defines minorities and women as if they were in test tubes, to be examined as an alien species.

The women the workshop honors eagerly contributed their wisdom. "You're not going to get it [the story] by doing a man-on-the-street interview and saying, 'So how do you feel about African Americans?'" said Elizabeth Llorente during an interview for the *Authentic Voice* textbook. Llorente, the workshop's 2004 Career Achievement winner, has carved a reputation as a specialist in demographics reporting at the *Record* in Hackensack, New Jersey. "There's something to be said for spending time with someone, which we don't do often enough," she said. "We want explosive quotes; we want exciting quotes, by two o'clock today so we can have that story at five. That just doesn't happen with stories that are this sensitive."

Consider the time it took Llorente to learn the Korean immigrant culture to produce her 1999 "A Tale of Two Cultures," an insightful series about how the demographic changes, fueled by Korean and Guatemalan immigration, impacted longtime residents in Palisades Park, New Jersey. Llorente's story repeatedly allows whites to speak out about their fear of change. She quotes Roger Brauer, president of the Palisades Park Homeowners Association: "I work in Manhattan. I want to come home to a grassy town with families on the front porch. Now it's people who don't want to adjust to our culture."[3] But then she goes on to break down a barrier to understanding why the new Koreans isolate themselves from whites in the community. "Koreans who came as adults were reared in a culture of strict protocol. While small talk is valued as sociable in the United States, it is frowned upon as unpolished in Korea, Koreans say. The immigrants also were shaped in Korea at a time when people were suspicious of the government and there was little civilian access. Life in Korea was confined largely to the extended family and close neighbors."[4]

By the end of the story, readers are left with a sense of progress for the town's future rather than hopelessness when they read about Peter Suh, a real estate broker, who became the first Korean American candidate to seek a council seat in the Palasides borough, under the slogan "Harmony, Equality, Fellowship" to help resolve the ethnic conflicts.

Hull's Reporting about Ordinary Lives

Anne Hull is a Pulitzer Prize–winning reporter who is not afraid to take risks to ensure authenticity in her work. Hull crafted stories that display a level of trust and respect for her sources that can be honed only through painstaking patience and sensitivity. Hull grew up in Florida, where the daily experience of race was defined as black and white. Her "Rim of the New World" series, featured in *The Authentic Voice,* explored what she calls "immigration's epochal transformation of the American South." Hull uses the series to detail ordinary lives—from the multiracial and ethnic workers in the Dairy Queen to the African immigrant who works at Atlanta's airport.

The Atlanta Dairy Queen provided the major character for one story and the setting for a world of working-class white, black, and immigrant kids. "Being in this global audio stew was a good awakening for the reportorial senses and made me realize how bland most newspaper stories are when it comes to capturing authentic voices," Hull wrote in her textbook essay that deconstructs her series. "I think it takes a lot of time, to get to truth, and to have truthful words emerge," Hull said in an interview with Keith Woods, a coeditor of *The Authentic Voice.* "I think sometimes it is helpful if a reporter of the same color or ethnic background interviews someone. If a black reporter interviews a black family, there is a slight camaraderie there that just takes place, from having a similar experience, and it makes it tougher on an outsider to kind of break through to that. So for the daily story it's very hard to get to real truth-telling on race."

Hull gets to the truth-telling with a detailed narrative style that has made her one of the most admired newspaper writers in America. Here's an example from the first part of her Rim series, "Old South Goes with the Wind," from inside the Dairy Queen:

> "Do you have super-size drinks or is the large the biggest?" Cisco Montanez is 15 and working the window. His DQ hat is cocked on his head like a tilted ornament, his khakis circus-big. He is half Latino and half black, so he has plenty of reason to glare at the Confederate flag moving toward him on a GMC Suburban. At least one flag comes through a night.
>
> Cisco turns his back on the flag and reaches for a plastic banana split boat. As he fills it with three puffs of vanilla ice cream, he begins to rap.
>
> This life hurts
> No cushion for me, no carpet laid out
> either sell or we're getting sold."[5]

As a reader, you immediately connect with Cisco and his life. You see him taking orders, flinching at the Confederate flag, using rap to shield him from the world outside the Dairy Queen.

Later Hull brings context to the story with her "nut graph," a description of the story's relevance for readers who are seeking a greater understanding about the new America they are facing.

> Atlanta is at the front edge of this new pluralism. Some sociologists call it a mini–Los Angeles in the making. The metropolitan area, with 4.1 million people, is a mix of urbanism and suburbs that radiates out in a 20-county sprawl. The cradle of the civil rights movement, Atlanta represents the two-tone world of the past that is now giving way to a new society. Between 1990 and 2000, more than 256,000 foreign-born people arrived here.
>
> A Dairy Queen hardly seems like a staging ground for the future. The store in Stockbridge looks like any other. On sunny days, the red sign creaks in the wind. Car exhaust from the road blows up on the patio tables. At night, the white-lit building glows luminous and cold.
>
> Inside, there are wooden booths and chairs, and a freezer that holds cakes and Dilly Bars. A menu board with pictures hangs above the counter—"HOT EATS"—along with the ice cream concoctions. A silver counter and three cash registers separate the customers from the crew.
>
> Half the crew is Indian or Pakistani. In their blue polo shirts, they work as if each sale brings a handsome commission instead of low wages in the grubby trenches of the American economy.[6]

This is masterful writing. Everyone knows the Dairy Queen, but few understand its orbit. Hull brings us inside, connecting the reader through her strong observations that ultimately speak to generations of immigrants who came to America for a new life.

How Race Is Lived

Former *New York Times* reporter Mirta Ojito also uses a southern city to set the stage for her "Best of Friends, Worlds Apart" story, part of the Pulitzer Prize–winning *Times* series "How Race Is Lived in America." Ojito grew up not that far from Hull—a few hundred miles—across a stretch of water in Cuba, a place that would forever define her life. A refugee in the Mariel boatlift, Ojito wrote *Finding Manana: A Memoir of a Cuban Exodus* (Penguin, 2005) about her experience as a sixteen-year-old refugee. Now a professor of journalism at the Columbia University Graduate School of Journalism, Ojito credits the famous Barbara Walters interview with Fidel Castro for her interest in journalism.

In "Best of Friends, Worlds Apart," Ojito paints a rare portrait about how race defines the unequal opportunities Miami offers two Cuban immigrants, one black and one white, based on the color of their skin. The beginning of her story immediately signals how race trumps ethnicity:

> Havana, sometime before 1994: As dusk descends on the quaint seaside village of Guanabo, two young men kick a soccer ball back and forth and back and forth across the sand. The tall one, Joel Ruiz, is black. The short, wiry one, Achmed Valdés, is white.
>
> They are the best of friends.
>
> Miami, January 2000: Mr. Valdés is playing soccer, as he does every Saturday, with a group of light-skinned Latinos in a park near his apartment. Mr. Ruiz surprises him with a visit, and Mr. Valdés, flushed and sweating, runs to greet him. They shake hands warmly.
>
> But when Mr. Valdés darts back to the game, Mr. Ruiz stands off to the side, arms crossed, looking on as his childhood friend plays the game that was once their shared joy. Mr. Ruiz no longer plays soccer. He prefers basketball with black Latinos and African-Americans from his neighborhood.
>
> The two men live only four miles apart, not even 15 minutes by car. Yet they are separated by a far greater distance, one they say they never envisioned back in Cuba.
>
> In ways that are obvious to the black man but far less so to the white one, they have grown apart in the United States because of race. For the first time, they inhabit a place where the color of their skin defines the outlines of their lives—where they live, the friends they make, how they speak, what they wear, even what they eat.[7]

In doing the story, Ojito felt that her Cuban ethnicity and awareness helped her more than the color of her skin, which is white. "I frankly don't think that these two people would have opened up to the level they did with a reporter who did not speak Spanish, for example, or who was not Cuban," Ojito says in her interview for *The Authentic Voice*.

Hull, Ojito, and Llorente have devoted their careers to finding stories that go beyond the "saints and sinners" theme. All represent a commitment to community reporting that is detailed, energized, analytical, and poignant. They have gained a reputation for writing with authority, often taking risks by writing with brutal honesty about their characters.

In another Llorente series, "Diverse and Divided," she digs deeply into the tensions and political power struggle between Hispanics and African Americans living in Paterson, New Jersey, a city in North Jersey that has been battered by the loss of jobs in what was once a fertile industrial area. "One of the biggest challenges was getting people in both communities to speak candidly and comfortably," Llorente wrote in the textbook essay that deconstructs the elements that went into the series. "I wanted people to tell me what they truly felt, not what they thought they should say. I asked open-ended questions about the people and about the city's diversity."

At first the answers were predictable and safe, but Llorente stayed the course, sometimes for hours, even days, talking to people to expose what they really felt about one another. "I was surprised when some people condemned the racism within their own communities," Llorente writes. "Some leaders and ordinary residents spoke in strong terms about how the black community had to push itself forward and focus less on the problems that others create for them."

That kind of reporting takes self-confidence that can only be attained by taking to the streets to talk to countless people about the stereotypes they encounter or themselves generate. The stereotypes, Hull says, should not be ignored. They exist and should be confronted. "I think, you know, we have to be conscious of stereotypes," Hull noted in her interview. "Stereotypes used to hurt people are damaging. But if there is a baseline of truth that runs through something, I say explore it—and talk with the person about it. Never have a stereotype and just—as a journalist—put it out there. But talk about it, with the subject."

If anyone represents the new, more collaborative element that Sandy Close strongly espouses in the cause for authenticity, it is Anh Do, an "Asian Perspective" columnist for the *Orange County Register* in Southern California, who also edits *Nguoi Viet 2*, the weekly English section of *Nguoi Viet Daily News*, the largest Vietnamese-language newspaper in the United States, founded by her late father in 1978. Do, who gave up a job as a full-time reporter at the *Register* to run *Nguoi Viet*, represents the level of outreach and creative thinking that Close urges editors to consider as they try to gain new readers in ethnic communities. "Ethnic media's limitations are also its power, because more mainstream media are bringing ethnic media to the table," said Close, who has been working with

Rosenhause's ASNE diversity committee on a number of projects that emulate Do's path.

Do says that having a foot in both worlds enables her to take "the coolest best practices" of both newsrooms and blend them together. "The more you soak up in life, the more you know how to portray life," she said. "I like work that makes me think, and this balance, writing for readers in each community—and digging beneath the surface of observable events—help make my journalism more real. What we need is to connect. We never flourish alone."

Do points to her story "The Boy Monk," a 2004 "Let's Do It Better!" winner, which took her on a yearlong journey to record the transformation of an Orange County boy into a monk, as an example of how she used journalism to connect her two communities.[8] After the series appeared, Do and her fellow writer, Teri Sforza, and photographer Cindy Yamanaka presented a documentary on the story before a series of town hall meetings, bringing them face to face with diverse audiences on college campuses, in writing seminars, and in Little Saigon, California. "People shared their faith with us," Do recalled in an interview. "They asked about the consequences of a boy choosing his calling at so young an age, and they wanted to know how three women penetrated the closed world of monks. Luckily, we were able to do that by listening, and not just lending an ear, but offering empathy. I saw that this child, in his solitude, in essence found a kind of freedom."

Do agrees that women may be devoting more energy to the racial and ethnic story because they characteristically display more patience and "an innate ability to establish intimacy with sources that are not as visible in the light of day, sources that are rarely quoted or targeted." But she adamantly dismisses the idea that the race beat may be evolving into an exclusive territory for women. "Having it as the exclusive domain of women is like saying only women can edit race relations stories."

Still, there are some stories that because of culture may be "women only" productions. "Tug of War," a warm portrait of two Somali Muslim teenage girls and their struggle to assimilate to life in a Minneapolis high school, most likely would not have been published if it weren't for the woman's touch, in this case reporter Allie Shah and photographer Rita Reed. "I was considered a Muslim 'sister,' which helped me gain the confidence and trust of the people we met," said Shah, an American-born Muslim of Pakistani descent, in her *Authentic Voice* book essay. Shah, a reporter at the *Minneapolis Star Tribune,* still had a lot to learn about the Somali culture and was careful not to make assumptions just because she shared a religious belief with the girls. Her story carefully guided readers through the gender relationships faced by the teenagers, using a familiar event: the high school prom. Here is an excerpt from her story:

In the perfect Somali world, boys and girls don't date. They marry. At school, Somali girls may disappear for a few days and return married to men twice their age.

Dates and school dances are tricky in a culture that prohibits unmarried males and females from even touching one another. Some of the girls at Nimco's school have boyfriends who walk them to class and call them on the phone, but they do it on the sly. Some girls dance with partners, but only a few dare to tell their parents.

This year's prom proved to be more trouble than it was worth for Nimco. She'd planned to go with a friend, a Somali boy. It wasn't a date, she insists.

A week before the dance, her friends warned her that it might not look good to have her picture taken, all dressed up, with this Somali guy. She didn't want people talking about them like they were a serious couple, so she backed out.

On the day of the dance, Nimco stood barefoot with a curling iron in one hand and hair spray in the other, holding court before a small crowd of girls in the school locker room. Instead of going to the prom, she did hair for girls who were going.[9]

Shah hopes that any journalist could tackle this type of story, but it's obvious that being a woman enabled her and Reed to mix comfortably with the girls, both at their homes and in school. Considering what she writes about Nimco's dilemma over a relationship with a male, it's clear that a male reporter would never have the same access. "I'm a big believer in immersion, especially when it comes to reporting on race and ethnic matters," Shah wrote in her essay. "It's like learning a foreign language. The quickest way to become fluent is to live in the world and soak up as much as you can."

As one of the nation's young women reporters, Shah is confident about using her journalistic talents to explore just who is an American. Like the women who paved the way, she has uncovered characteristics that separate and bind. By putting the two Somali teenagers, Nimco and Fartun, on the front page of the *Star Tribune,* she fulfilled a key journalistic responsibility to help readers see themselves in "others." Shah represents the next generation of women who will use their formidable skills to tell America's untold stories. In doing those stories, she most certainly will influence hundreds of young women now populating journalism classrooms to continue the fight for equality.

The work cited here speaks with an authority and authenticity that I believe is unique to women journalists. They are not afraid to use their voice to write with affection and candor about the richness of life that diversity brings to the nation. We are a healthier people because of these women. And that's a worthy goal for any journalist.

Notes

1. The Authentic Voice Web site, http://www.theauthenticvoice.org.

2. Kara Andrade, "Close: Online Media Can Foster Community," Online News Association, October 29, 2005, http://conference.journalists.org/2005conference/archives/2005/10/close_online_me_1.php (accessed January 22, 2009).

3. Elizabeth Llorente, "A Tale of Two Cultures: Palisades Park Grapples with Change," *Hackensack (N.J.) Record,* August 23, 1998. See http://www.theauthenticvoice.org/Tale _Of_Two_Cultures_Intro.html.

4. Ibid.

5. Anne Hull: "Old South Goes with the Wind: Entrepreneur and His Workers Reflect Region's Racial Transformation," *Washington Post,* December 8, 2002.

6. Ibid.

7. Mirta Ojito, "Best of Friends, Worlds Apart," *New York Times,* June 5, 2000. Available at http://partners.nytimes.com/library/national/race/060500ojito-cuba.html (accessed January 22, 2009).

8. "The Boy Monk," *Orange County Register,* series began in January 2003, by Ahn Do and Teri Sforaz, with photography by Cindy Yamanaka. Available at http://www .ocregister.com/features/monk/index.shtml (accessed January 22, 2009).

9. Allie Shah, "Tug of War," *Minneapolis Star Tribune,* June 25, 2000. See http://www .theauthenticvoice.org/TeachersGuide_TugOfWar.html.

27

Coming Out

DEB PRICE

Lesbians in the newsroom must all cope with the challenges that go with being women in a predominantly male, still sexist profession. But while female journalists have no choice but to reveal their gender, most of us who are lesbian have some control—at least initially—over information about our sexual orientation. So we must try to find our way through a thicket where personal ambition can often seem at odds with personal or professional integrity.

Will we be out at work? If so, will we limit our self-disclosure to trusted peers, or will we be open with supervisors and subordinates as well? And what about sources and readers? Will we risk being branded "activists"—a career-killing label—by questioning the wording, approach, and play of gay stories? Will we risk pointing out inequities in employee compensation that favor married heterosexuals? Will we find our professionalism questioned, our assignments restricted and our prospects diminished if we opt not to hide our orientation? Will we suffer professionally if we try to protect our families by taking public steps, such as legally marrying, that society encourages heterosexuals to take?

The experiences of Sue Reisinger at the helm of the Associated Press Managing Editors, Pam Fine at the *Indianapolis Star,* Rachel Gordon and Liz Mangelsdorf at the *San Francisco Chronicle,* and Nancy Andrews at newspapers large and small illustrate various ways lesbians have hacked through a jungle of personal and professional issues, blazing trails that make it far easier for the lesbian journalists of today and tomorrow to thrive professionally, socialize unself-consciously, and begin to take for granted that they can put their partners on their company health plan or take time off to attend the funeral of a partner's parent without committing professional suicide. The saga of each of the women profiled in this chapter illustrates the personal and communal benefits of pushing heterosexual colleagues to better understand the gay people in their midst—in newsrooms and in the wider world. But some of their sagas also bear witness to the cost of choosing visibility.

Opening a Door for a Younger "Sister"

At the 1992 national convention of the Associated Press Managing Editors (APME), held amid the swaying palms of Honolulu, Sue Reisinger, the prestigious group's president, introduced the latest in diversity to her colleagues: the first openly gay columnist in mainstream journalism. After becoming the first female editor of Ohio State University's student newspaper, in 1968, Reisinger had climbed a tall professional ladder, reaching rung after rung never before grasped by a woman. Even though Reisinger was out to her *Miami Herald* bosses, she opted not to tell APME colleagues that she was their first lesbian president, not simply their first female one. But she used her hard-earned power to enable a younger lesbian—me—to deliver a keynote address explaining the importance of adding an openly gay voice to commentary pages.

"It was damn tough enough to be the first woman," Reisinger said, looking back. "When I started, it was an all-male world. It never occurred to me to fight the lesbian battle along the way. If anyone wants to fault me for not being more open and a standard-bearer for other lesbian journalists, that's a fair criticism, and I accept it."[1]

Beginning at the *Dayton (Ohio) Daily News* in the mid-1970s, Reisinger selectively came out to editors above her. "It could never be a team if I weren't completely open about one of the most important facets of my life," she explained. "I never flaunted it around the newsroom. I didn't bring my spouse to office parties and dance with her, but I just never wanted to lie about it." Now a senior reporter at *Corporate Counsel* magazine and thoroughly open, Reisinger recalls her fear that drawing attention to her sexual orientation would somehow diminish what she had achieved for women and undermine heterosexual women journalists by feeding the ancient stereotype that career women are lesbian. Instead of overtly enlisting in gay battles, lesbians of Reisinger's generation have tended to work to improve coverage of women and racial minorities. And they've opened doors for the more open lesbians who followed, a generational passing of a baton that has been critical to creating the dramatically improved professional environment that lesbian journalists work in today.

By, in effect, speaking through me to the APME, Reisinger sparked an overdue discussion among the movers and shakers of newspaper management about whether they, too, should have a gay voice at their publications, how well they were covering gay issues, and what messages they were sending to gay employees. Yet for Reisinger, sexism has continued to feel like the biggest personal obstacle.

"Through the years, I've talked to lots of black women journalists. And they've said, 'I always felt more discriminated about as a woman than as a black.' I've felt that way about being lesbian."

Everywhere but the Pinnacle

Beginning in the late 1980s, more journalists, including a few high-level editors, took the plunge and came out completely. While no less ambitious than Reisinger's generation, many of today's mid-career lesbians feel that having a fully integrated life twenty-four hours a day is as important as professional success. To them, one facet of integrity is refusing to pose as single if they are partnered.

Pam Fine came out at forty in 1997 while serving as the managing editor of the *Minneapolis Star Tribune*. She had fallen in love and didn't want to lie. "Judy wasn't somebody who was going to accept being a secret partner," Fine said. "It was in for a dime, in for a dollar. . . . I wanted to be able to bring her to company functions and other social events that would be natural for anyone married."[2] When Fine later interviewed to be managing editor of the *Indianapolis Star*, the hiring executives already knew of—and made clear they were comfortable with—her openness. "One of the things I like about being out, about having people know I have a relationship, is that it humanizes me to the staff," she said. "I used to feel as if I had to hide who I was. In some ways, keeping that secret distanced me from my colleagues, and I felt like I was being dishonest. I feel much more comfortable in my own skin. That makes me a better leader and colleague and editor, I hope."

Yet she says that abandoning the closet has caused her to be passed over for top editorships. In one case, she recalls, a newspaper executive told her "he didn't feel he could have a gay editor running his newspaper, because the town was conservative and he didn't want to deal with the potential backlash." Discrimination, particularly at the highest levels of the profession, continues in part because top executives defer to the presumed prejudices of their readers, she says. "While things are slowly changing, I think that in many companies and with many corporate leaders, it would still be uncomfortable to have an out gay editor or out publisher running their companies or newsrooms," Fine said. "Whether warranted or not, there is a perception that having a gay leader could be offensive to other community leaders, including religious leaders in the community. I think there is a preference for people's personal lives to be a nonissue, and in the case of a gay person, it can become a point of discussion. The best indication to me [of continued barriers] is that we can count on one hand the number of out senior editors at newspapers, and I'm not aware of any out top editors or publishers. That's the best evidence of where we are."

No More "Gay Wages," Please

A magician with a camera, Nancy Andrews has a way of attracting awards to whatever newspaper her work graces. As a result, she knows she is viewed as "a keeper," a status that has reinforced her natural instinct to expect to be treated respectfully. "I can't recall a single instance where it hurt me to be a lesbian in a newsroom," she said.[3] But from her earliest days at the *Free Lance-Star* in Fredericksburg, Virginia, she has butted up against "gay wages," the reduced benefits given anyone who isn't a married heterosexual. Trained to have a keen eye, Andrews noticed the disparity and repeatedly called bosses on it, fully expecting it to be eliminated.

In the first instance, in 1988, Andrews's photography had won the Virginia Press Association's prestigious "best in show" award, a coup for the forty-thousand-circulation *Free Lance-Star* in a state with many larger papers. The tiny paper had had a terrific year and had won other awards as well. A rule came down from on high that only winners and their spouses could attend the awards banquet. Andrews headed into a manager's office. "It was like saying, 'We are giving married spouses a fifty-dollar bonus,'" Andrews recalled. "I said, 'I'm not going if I can't bring my date.'" The editors, she says, said they hadn't intended anything anti-gay. Andrews received her award with her girlfriend in tow.

Her next "gay wages" stop was in the private office of one of the most powerful men in journalism, Donald Graham of the *Washington Post*. Her talent had landed her a job there. "'Don,'" she recalled saying in 1998 with tears in her eyes, "'you might not realize it, but you are discriminating against your gay and lesbian employees by not giving us domestic partnership benefits.' The personal contact mattered most. I think he valued my work. I don't think a group or petition would have had the same effect." Soon the *Post* joined the growing ranks of papers offering health benefits to their gay workers' partners.

Andrews's next career stop was as director of photography at the *Detroit Free Press*, a job she says she wouldn't have taken had the then–Knight Ridder paper not assured her it offered partner benefits. "Even though I knew they did, I asked so they would know it was important for me in considering the job," she said. But after the new employee chose a health plan for herself and her partner, a call from human resources informed her that she—unlike married heterosexuals—was limited to one option, because only one provider offered partner benefits. "I said, 'I'm sorry, but I was told Knight Ridder offers domestic partner benefits, and I have made my choice.'" She was determined not to quietly consent to "a two-tiered health insurance policy where gay employees get less." She alerted her editors, who backed her: Andrews was enrolled in the health plan she wanted.

"Most people might have just accepted it," said Andrews, a deputy managing editor of the *Free Press*. "There is a view in the newsroom that the status quo is neutral, but the status quo has a point of view as well. There's a different level of responsibility for me as a successful photographer," she said. "I believe that those of us in a position of strength—I had a book and had won awards—have a responsibility. If I can't be out and point out these kinds of [disparities], then who can?"

Newlywed, Newly Questioned

By 2000 a large portion of the nation's top newspapers offered partner health benefits.[4] To the best of any number of gay journalists' memories, no gay employee who signed up a partner or a partner's legal child has ever been told that as a result she or he couldn't handle stories about domestic partner benefits or gay parenting. Ironically, professional trouble came when a gay couple at the *San Francisco Chronicle* was finally able to do what heterosexual colleagues have always taken for granted: marry in the United States.

In February 2004 Gavin Newsom decided to use his power as mayor of San Francisco to start marrying gay couples. The decision became around-the-clock news for weeks, splashed across front pages and beamed around the world by CNN. *San Francisco Chronicle* city hall reporter Rachel Gordon and her partner, photographer Liz Mangelsdorf, broke the story after witnessing the first wedding. Their scoop—Mangelsdorf's photograph of Del Martin and Phyllis Lyon, married after fifty-one years together, was used literally worldwide—probably would have been missed had the journalists not been so out that the brides invited them into the room. The *Chronicle*, in other words, benefited tremendously from the fact that Gordon and Mangelsdorf are openly gay.

After weeks of writing about and photographing gay couples lined up to marry, the two *Chronicle* staffers realized that they, too, wanted to wed. Already registered with California as domestic partners, the forty-something couple wanted to legally protect their relationship in every available way, especially since they intended to adopt. They informed their editors of their plans. The couple received a warning that they'd be bumped from the marriage story if they followed through. They wed at their home in front of family and friends but far from TV cameras.

The private ceremony became very public news when *Chronicle* executive editor Phil Bronstein issued a memo saying the couple would no longer be allowed to cover gay marriage: "Are we willing to accept the public perception that results when two lesbian staffers get married? If the perception is that the *San Francisco Chronicle* is in favor of legal marriage for gays and lesbians, could we live with that?" Bronstein added, "Maintaining credibility with the public means journalists should avoid working on stories where their personal beliefs have led to a specific action."

He continued, "An editor might say, 'Participating in a public commemoration marking the anniversary of *Roe v. Wade* would disqualify a journalist from reporting or editing stories about abortion. By doing so, the journalist has entered the public debate.'" Returning to same-sex marriage, he suggested that appropriate yardsticks of ineligibility might be whether a staffer has attended a same-sex civil marriage ceremony or belongs to an organization that supports or opposes legalization of same-sex marriage.[5] Taken to their illogical conclusion, Bronstein's guidelines would mean that no journalist belonging to, say, the Catholic Church or registered as a Republican voter could cover same-sex marriage.

Bronstein's reaction to the Gordon-Mangelsdorf marriage casts the spotlight on the inherent heterosexual bias in the idea that rules based on society's status quo—what it deems noncontroversial—are neutral. Had a heterosexual couple on Bronstein's staff married shortly after covering the nation's first same-sex marriage, it's impossible to imagine that Bronstein would have responded by yanking husband and wife off their beats. Gay journalists long stayed closeted precisely because they feared being judged by the content of their private lives, not the quality of their work. Bronstein made their fear come true.

As the backlash to the gay civil rights movement continues to roil our country, newsroom managers need to make certain that they don't inadvertently establish ethics double standards that treat gay journalists' private behavior as suspect simply because they are gay. Can anyone imagine a divorced heterosexual being quizzed by his editor about whether he deducts alimony payments and thus should be disqualified from covering a debate over elimination of popular tax breaks? Hardly. If marrying renders a gay journalist too biased to cover gay marriage stories, what about a heterosexual who marries in a place gay people cannot, who leads a troop in the Boy Scouts, a group that persuaded the U.S. Supreme Court that being anti-gay is one of its core values, or who contributes to the Mormon Church, which pours money into trying to stop gay marriage?

"We wanted to do both—cover the story and marry," recalled Mangelsdorf, who questions the idea that gay journalists' marrying is somehow different from their being registered domestic partners and adopting a child together, other subjects of intense public debate, litigation, and newspaper coverage.

> We didn't personally feel it would change how we covered the story. Our feelings about gay rights and marriage were no different after we married. No one is truly objective. You can only try to be fair. And your life experiences make you a better journalist. As for the way they should have handled it: They should

have said they saw no bias in our work. And if someone approached them from outside and questioned our ability to be married while we were covering a story about gay marriage, the paper should have said, "Yes, we know they are married. And if we see bias, we will pull them from the story."[6]

Converging Forces Create Tidal Wave of Change

My generation entered the profession shortly before the grotesquely unprofessional coverage—or lack of coverage—of the AIDS crisis prompted many gay journalists to come out and speak out. I wasn't fully out until thirty-four, when I started my syndicated column at the *Detroit News*. I wouldn't have risked proposing the first weekly column in mainstream newspapers to be written from an openly gay perspective if two things had not happened. First, Gannett, which then owned the *News,* launched NEWS 2000, a chain-wide effort to be "on the cutting edge" and to represent a diversity of voices. I was hardly alone in being painfully aware that gay voices were not regularly heard in the mainstream press. Yet NEWS 2000 gave me hope that the idea of a gay column might be well received. But if not for the courage of reporter Michael Hodges, I would never have pitched it.

At the beginning of 1992, Hodges, then far more out than I was, asked publisher Bob Giles why the *Detroit News's* written antidiscrimination policy didn't include sexual orientation. Giles immediately added it. The revised policy was posted in the Washington bureau, where I worked. Suddenly I felt that I could safely propose the column that debuted on May 8, 1992, and was instantly recognized as a journalistic milestone.[7] My breakthrough spurred many journalists to come out as gay or gay-friendly, as they've told me over the years. In addition to breaking news—such as revealing that 1996 Republican presidential nominee Robert Dole accepted, then returned, a one-thousand-dollar check from the gay Log Cabin Republicans—my column has sparked countless newsroom discussions about gay coverage.

News and opinion pages aren't the only ones that shape and reflect how gay Americans are perceived. One of my proudest achievements is having broken onto the trendsetting *Washington Post's* engagements, weddings, and anniversaries page. The *Post* allows only lawful marriages to be honored on that well-read page. Everything else, from an eight-year-old's birthday to a gay couple's civil union, is relegated to a "Celebrations" section. In June 2003 journalist Joyce Murdoch and I legally wed in Canada after eighteen years together. We notified the *Post* that we had finally cleared its very high bar. Publication of our marriage announcement was a first, one cited on national news broadcasts and reported around the globe.[8] A year later Joyce and I became the first gay couple to announce a wedding anniversary in the *Post.*[9]

The newest generation of gay journalists enters newsrooms today that feel far safer than in the past, where partner benefits are likely available, and where their input on gay coverage probably will be respected. In addition to the efforts of earlier gay journalists, the tidal wave of change draws strength from five forces:

1. NEWS EVENTS FORCING COVERAGE

The gay legal breakthroughs of recent years have been too significant for even the most backward publications to ignore. At the start of 2007 more than eighty-seven hundred gay and lesbian couples had legally wed in Massachusetts, and by 2009 could wed in Connecticut, California, and Iowa. Meanwhile, anti-gay activism colors politics, from the Bush White House, which pushed to write anti-gay language into the U.S. Constitution, to school board races. The debate continues under President Barack Obama, who supports civil unions.

All of the attention—pro and con—on the progress of the gay civil rights movement has begun to normalize gay coverage. The first baby born in the Washington, D.C., area in 2003 happened to have lesbian moms, as the *Washington Post* matter-of-factly reported on its front page.[10] The article explained that the family would be moving from Virginia to Maryland so that both women could be recognized as their daughter's legal parents.

Feature sections now devote endless ink to the coming-out stories and love lives of gay stars. Who doesn't now know that singer Elton John got hitched or that comedian Ellen DeGeneres is lesbian and married in August of 2008?

2. WATCHDOG GROUPS STANDING GUARD

The National Lesbian and Gay Journalists Association (NLGJA) and the Gay and Lesbian Alliance Against Defamation (GLAAD) are vital resources, suggesting unbiased terminology, offering local gay sources, and proposing fairer benefit policies. But all the pressure for improvement isn't from outside. The *New York Times* has a task force that scrutinizes its gay coverage. "When I look back at how it was in the mid-eighties and the fight you had to fight versus now, it's so different," said Kim Severson, a food writer on the task force. "Now it is not unusual to find gay and straight allies all the way up the chain. I know there are editors above me taking this seriously, so I don't have to be the only one doing the worrying."[11]

3. A STAMP OF APPROVAL

In 2001 David Moats of Vermont's *Rutland Herald* won a coveted Pulitzer Prize for editorials advocating enactment of civil union legislation. Certainly, that was a powerful signal to the profession to take the gay civil rights movement seriously.

4. HARDER DATA, DEEPER STORIES

The "gay activist said/anti-gay minister said" quote war still dominates too many gay-related articles. But that unhelpful approach is slowly yielding ground to the citation of actual research findings such as gay parenting figures based on census numbers, for example, or the one-billion-dollar annual price tag that the investigative arm of Congress came up with when asked how much not recognizing gay marriages costs Uncle Sam.[12]

After former President George W. Bush claimed children are better off being raised by a mother and a father, a *New York Times* article pointed out that his view is contrary to what mental health experts have found.[13]

5. HUGE SHIFT IN PUBLIC ATTITUDES FELT IN NEWSROOMS

Polls showing that public attitudes toward gay people have dramatically shifted— with overwhelming majorities opposing job discrimination and favoring legal recognition of couples—have helped ease senior editors' fear of being accused of being too liberal if their papers treat the gay movement with respect.[14] Many editorial pages now provide a steady drumbeat of support for full legal equality for gay Americans.

Improving Newsroom Climates, News Coverage

Gay and lesbian journalists surveyed by NLGJA in 2000 rated gay coverage as weak, too conflict-driven, and too focused on white men. Some gay journalists reported job discrimination, including having their objectivity questioned or being passed over for promotion. Many more told of rarely being tapped as resources for gay stories.[15]

The following are ongoing problems and my proposed solutions:

Problem: Thin, spotty, conflict-driven coverage that fails to reflect gay diversity
Solution: Assign a reporter to keep abreast of local and national gay news. Senior editors should clearly signal the beat's importance and should follow the *New York Times's* example in mainstreaming local gay men and lesbians into all sorts of articles. On December 23, 2005, a *Times* article about couples with multiple homes featured a lesbian couple, a gay male couple, and an interracial heterosexual couple. The story focused on the couples simply as homeowners.[16]

Problem: Op-ed pages rarely feature gay perspectives
Solution: Add openly gay voices—a surefire way to also spice up letters to the editor and grab readers' attention.

Problem: Ethics double standards
Solution: Gay employees shouldn't have to fear retribution for securing legal protections for their families. Senior editors must defend the right of gay journalists to have private lives. There is a clear difference between marrying your partner and contributing to a political candidate you cover.

Problem: Lack of openly gay publishers, executive editors
Solution: No qualified person should be passed over because of some readers' presumed prejudices. Women and African Americans faced a similar problem; it is fading because of the refusal of newspaper owners to cater to prejudice.

Notes

1. Sue Reisinger, interviews with Deb Price, November 2005.

2. Pam Fine, interview with Deb Price, December 2005.

3. Nancy Andrews, interviews with Deb Price, December 2005.

4. The National Lesbian and Gay Journalists Association posts a list of news media outlets offering domestic partner benefits at its Web site: http://nlgja.org/workplace/ dp_newsmedia.html (accessed January 22, 2009).

5. Phil Bronstein sent his lengthy memo to the *San Francisco Chronicle* staff on March 12, 2004. See "Chronicle Bans Two Female Journalists from Same-Sex Marriage Story for Marrying Each Other" at Grade the News, http://www.gradethenews.org/pages2/ marriage.htm (accessed January 22, 2009).

6. Andrews interviews.

7. For more details about how the Deb Price column started and reactions to it, see Deb Price and Joyce Murdoch, *And Say Hi to Joyce: America's First Gay Column Comes Out* (New York: Doubleday, 1995).

8. "Price-Murdoch Celebrate Nuptials," *Washington Post,* July 23, 2003.

9. "Price-Murdoch 1st Anniversary," *Washington Post,* July 28, 2004.

10. Peter Whoriskey, "A New Year's Baby with an Additional Difference: 2 Moms," *Washington Post,* January 2, 2003.

11. Kim Severson, interview with Deb Price, December 2005.

12. "The Potential Budgetary Impact of Recognizing Same-Sex Marriages," attached in a letter from the Congressional Budget Office to Rep. Steve Chabot, June 21, 2004. Available at http://www.cbo.gov/showdoc.cfm?index=5559&sequence=0 (accessed January 22, 2009).

13. Benedict Carey, "Experts Dispute Bush on Gay-Adoption Issue," *New York Times,* January 29, 2005. Available at http://www.nytimes.com/2005/01/29/politics/29marry .html?oref=login&oref=login (accessed January 22, 2009).

14. Examples of recent polling showing dramatic shifts in Americans' attitudes include polling by the Pew Research Center. See its "Less Opposition to Gay Marriage, Adoption, and Military Service," released March 22, 2006. Available at http://people-press .org/reports/display.php3?ReportID=273 (accessed January 22, 2009).

15. Leroy Aarons and Sheila Murphy, "Lesbians and Gays in the Newsroom: 10 Years Later," National Lesbian and Gay Journalists Association, October 1, 2000. Available at http://www.nlgja.org/resources/NLGJA_2000_Survey.pdf (accessed January 22, 2009).

16. Melinda Blau, "The Third Home Comes within Reach," *New York Times,* December 23, 2005. Available at http://travel.nytimes.com/2005/12/23/realestate/23THREE.html (accessed January 22, 2009).

28

Covering Asian Americans

CATALINA CAMIA

The story of how Sandy Louey, a *Sacramento Bee* reporter with more than thirteen years of experience, became a journalist should sound familiar to many Asian Americans in the news media. Louey attended prestigious Lowell High School in San Francisco, a college preparatory school with a large Asian population. Most of her friends at the time were aiming for careers as engineers or doctors, but not Louey. After attending a summer journalism workshop for high school students at San Francisco State University in 1987, Louey knew she wanted to make a career of writing and telling other people's stories.

Louey's father, a restaurant dishwasher who emigrated from Hong Kong, spoke little English and relied on his eldest daughter, Sandy, to translate and navigate for her parents through American society. Jock Toon Louey had difficulty accepting journalism as Sandy's chosen profession. My father "felt I should use my brains to pursue a career that would pay well," Louey said, ticking off such careers as accounting or medicine.[1]

Louey's father eventually accepted his daughter's career choice when she won a scholarship from the Asian American Journalists Association (AAJA). Founded in 1981 by six Los Angeles–based journalists, the organization's goal is to promote better coverage of Asian Americans and their issues, foster partnership and camaraderie among Asian American journalists across the country, and grow a new generation of Asian American journalists. When Louey's father attended the AAJA–San Francisco Bay Area chapter reception for scholarship winners, he thanked the crowd in Mandarin for embracing his daughter and recognizing her potential. There wasn't a dry eye in the ballroom.

Sandy Louey's story highlights the cultural and parental pressures that young journalists of Asian descent often face. Those pressures feed into the stereotype that Asian Americans are the model minority. It is the one that says we all get good grades, obey our parents, and are geniuses when it comes to math, computers, science, and playing the piano or violin. Overlay that with common caricatures of Asian women—images of the subservient mail-order bride, the demure geisha, and the domineering dragon lady—and it's no wonder that Asian American women have had a hard time being accepted as journalists and, especially, newsroom managers.

In recent years, Asian American women journalists have shown that we can be creative, use words and images expressively, tell stories of the world around us, and give voice to those in society who need it the most. Just look at a recent list of Pulitzer Prize winners: Cheryl Diaz Meyer, a photographer born and raised in the Philippines, took home journalism's top prize in 2004 for her harrowing and poignant pictures of the Iraq war for the *Dallas Morning News.* Evelyn Iritani, a business reporter specializing in Pacific Rim issues, was part of a *Los Angeles Times* team that won a 2005 Pulitzer for its investigative series on Walmart.

Finding Roots in America

My story is a lot like Sandy Louey's. My parents came to San Francisco in the late 1940s–early 1950s from the Philippines, where both my grandfathers fought for the United States in World War II. My father, Ben, took courses at San Francisco City College even as he worked nights for the U.S. Postal Service. My mother, Marina, worked for the federal government in various agencies after graduating from high school, eventually making a career as a claims representative at the Social Security Administration. I was the first person in my family to graduate from college, and I attended the University of Southern California on a patchwork of scholarships from the state, college, and local organizations such as the Sonoma County (California) Press Club and the then-fledgling AAJA. My initial dream was to produce *ABC's Wide World of Sports,* but that gave way to print journalism and newspapers.

The morning after I graduated, my mother asked me why I wasn't going to law school like my best friend was about to do. Never mind that I was one of only a handful of people in my J-school class who already had a job in our chosen profession: an extended internship at the *Press-Enterprise* in Riverside, California, that paid $305 a week before taxes. Years into my newspaper career, my father begged me to take the management test at the post office, the institution that provided him, my uncle, and thousands of other Filipinos in the San Francisco Bay Area with steady incomes, generous benefits, and a union that protected their jobs from any downturn in the economy. Today I am one of the editors directing coverage of the White House and politics at *USA Today,* the nation's largest newspaper. Not many women who look like me are sitting in the daily news meetings, trying to decide what should be covered at *USA Today.* And, unfortunately, I have spent twenty years in this business trying not to be in such a minority.

For years, when I covered Congress for the *Dallas Morning News,* I was one of a small band of journalists of color in the nation's capital and among a small handful who were Asian American. Because we were few, I suppose it's understandable that people would sometimes mistake the two Asian American men covering Congress in the 1990s for each other. Once, as I stood in the venerable Speaker's Lobby of the U.S. Capitol, a House page handed me a note intended for Rep. Patsy Mink, D-Hawaii, the only Asian American female in Congress at the time. Mrs. Mink was about thirty years older than me and was of Japanese descent. I tried not to take offense—at least the page knew I was Asian!

I understand the doubt about journalism as a viable career path expressed by Asian American parents: It doesn't pay well compared with other professions, especially as someone is just starting out; it's not considered "honorable" like law or medicine; and the rise of the Internet as a news source clouds the future of print and broadcast media.

Esther Wu, a former columnist for the *Dallas Morning News,* remembers when she announced during her senior year in high school that she was going to be a reporter (influenced, in part, by coverage of the 1968 Democratic National Convention in Chicago). Wu overheard her mother tell her father in Chinese that after saving for so many years to send Esther to college, all the child wanted to do was become a paperboy and deliver newspapers on her bike.[2] Wu, who finished her term as AAJA national president in December 2006, says debunking stereotypes about women when she was growing up was a challenge. My mother "told me journalism was not a suitable job for a woman," she said. "Women needed to find jobs that would allow them to be home with their children when they came home from school—jobs like teaching."

A few years ago after her mother died, Wu and her sisters were cleaning the family home in San Antonio when she came across a box filled with stories she had written throughout her newspaper career. It was the tacit approval of her career choice that Wu had longed for.

A Young Asian American Finds Journalism in College

Mi-Ai Parrish, publisher of the *Idaho Statesman,* and her sister were raised by parents in suburban Washington, D.C., in what she described as a "socially progressive" environment that was shaped, in part, by what her mother did not have as a young girl in Korea. Parrish's mother grew up during the Japanese occupation of Korea, which ended in 1945. "She felt keenly the limitations on you in a place that is not free," Parrish said.[3] The Parrish family would read the

Washington Post and discuss stories about politics and current events. When Parrish got to the University of Maryland, she joined the student newspaper on a lark and caught the journalism bug. "My parents thought it was cool," said Parrish, now thirty-seven.

More Asian American parents appear to be embracing journalism as a career choice for their children. There are 1,768 journalists in the United States who are of Asian descent, representing 3.22 percent of those employed in daily newspapers, according to the 2006 newsroom employment survey by the American Society of News Editors (ASNE). Compared to our black counterparts, who have fought since the height of the civil rights movement in the 1960s to increase their newsroom ranks, the number of Asian American journalists continues to climb, according to the annual ASNE survey. Reporters make up the largest segment among Asian American journalists, or 47 percent. The smallest, representing 16 percent, are copy editors and newsroom supervisors like me. Within AAJA's membership rolls, 35 percent are in print journalism (mostly in newspapers), 23 percent in broadcasting (mostly in television), and 17 percent are working in online and ethnic media, according to the AAJA 2006 annual report. Part of the newsroom increase among Asian Americans is natural, given the demographic shift in the United States. There are more than 12 million people of Asian descent in the United States, or a little more than 5 percent of the total population, according to a 2005 census estimate.

Asian Americans, of course, are not monolithic. Our ancestors hail from dozens of countries within Asia: from China, Japan, India, and Korea, to the Philippines, Vietnam, and Cambodia. There is a common thread among those Asian countries: Strong women with leadership skills, who show grit, determination, and uncommon survival instincts, are often the backbone of their families—and even their countries. The United States has yet to elect a woman president, but that's not true across Asia. Among the Asian women leaders are Nobel Peace Prize winners Indira Gandhi in India and Aung San Suu Kyi, the democratic opposition leader in Burma. My parents' homeland, the Philippines, has elected not one but two women presidents, Corazon Aquino and Gloria Macapagal Arroyo, so far in my lifetime.

In journalism, Asian American women have not yet achieved that kind of widespread success. Today no Asian American woman leads a daily newspaper as the top editor. Catherine Shen, a trailblazer when she became publisher of the *Honolulu Star-Bulletin* in the mid-1980s, leads a chain of Pacific Northwest newsweeklies for Horvitz Newspapers. The highest newsroom rank attained by an Asian American woman at a daily newspaper is deputy managing editor (usually the third rung in the newsroom leadership ladder), a post now held by Katharine Fong of the *San Jose Mercury News*. Jeanne Mariani-Belding, editorial page editor of the *Honolulu Advertiser* in Hawaii, is believed to be the first Asian

American woman to lead the opinion section of a major metropolitan newspaper. Mariani-Belding also took the reins as national president of the AAJA in December 2006, the sixth woman to do so since the organization began in 1981.

Among popular mass-market magazines, Asian American women broke the glass ceiling a long time ago. Jeannie Park, former executive editor of *People,* and Janice Min, executive editor at *US Weekly,* are both of Korean descent. They follow in the footsteps of Helen Zia, a former top editor at *Ms.* magazine. Parrish, who was named publisher of the McClatchy Company newspaper in July 2006, said the lack of Asian American women—and other minorities—in the upper ranks of journalism may result from preconceived notions from some in the industry about what a leader should look and act like. "I've had people say, 'You're so nice,' or, 'I didn't know you could be so tough,'" Parrish said.

Retention and Promotion Still Obstacles

Ask anyone to name an Asian American woman journalist and the response is likely to be Connie Chung, Julie Chen, or someone else in television news. Chung made history in 1993 when she became coanchor of the *CBS Evening News with Dan Rather.* While Chung is now pursuing other media ventures, the networks still boast an array of Asian American female stars, from Ann Curry of NBC, to Julie Chen of CBS, to Juju Chang of ABC. None is behind the prime-time anchor desk full-time.

Although newspapers (and our broadcast counterparts) have been making strides recruiting Asian Americans and other minorities to the business, they have done a poor job in retaining and promoting them. A 2000 survey by the Freedom Forum for the American Society of Newspapers showed that minorities were more likely than their white counterparts to leave the profession. Among Asian American journalists, 53 percent were more likely to leave newspapers, and nearly three in four said they would flee because they were interested in another field of work. Sixty-three percent cited feelings of burnout.

There is no magic formula for keeping Asian American journalists, or other journalists of color, in the business. Kristen Go, who in 2005 was dubbed one of the top journalists under thirty-five by the *Boston Phoenix,* believes in the power of cultivating mentors and learning from role models. She remembers what it was like to walk into the *Denver Post* newsroom in the late 1990s. "I didn't see people who looked like me and no one near my age," said Go, now thirty-two, who is of Chinese descent. "My first day, none of the reporters talked to me. Next day, I heard them say, 'Oh, she's the diversity hire.'"[4]

Now an assistant metro editor at the *San Francisco Chronicle,* Go was rankled by the thought that her Denver colleagues believed it was the color of her skin that got her the job. She had already done several reporting internships at the

Tennessean and *Dallas Morning News* and earned a national award for high school journalists from the Journalism Educators Association in 1994. Go kept to herself in Denver and was doing poorly until she confided in two mentors, both journalists of color: one black, the other Asian. "It was absolutely devastating," Go said about the isolation and doubts about her abilities in Denver. "If I didn't have these people to go to, I don't know if I would have wanted to stay in this career."

Parrish said it's important for young journalists to find mentors who will be honest with them about their ambitions and their skills. And women, she said, especially have to learn how to help each other. "Women are not always good to each other," Parrish said. "This is not a competition."

Reaching Multicultural Communities

A driving force for many Asian American women in journalism is the chance to tell stories, especially from our own communities. Wu says she used to become upset when she read newspaper stories about Chinese dragon dancers and lunar New Year celebrations. She has learned to look for ways to weave ethnicity and race into stories without hammering it into the heads of newspaper readers. "People of color are also doctors, lawyers, teachers, and moms and dads, too," she said. "Why don't we see more of their faces in nonethnic stories?"

As a journalist who happens to be Asian American, I find it hard to separate my race and ethnicity from who I am, any more than you can separate that I am a married woman, with no children, and a huge baseball fan. Each perspective has played some role in my career.

In the midst of the 2004 presidential election, UNITY: Journalists of Color held its joint convention of Asian, black, Hispanic, and Native American journalists in Washington, D.C. I was asked to represent AAJA on a panel of reporters questioning Democratic candidate John Kerry. Knowing I'd only get to ask two or three questions, I decided I had to ask about an issue important to the Asian American community as a way to educate my black, Hispanic, and Native American colleagues in the audience. My query to Kerry on whether he supported full benefits for Filipino American veterans of World War II—many of whom retired from service without receiving recognition from the United States—and the senator's emphatic answer of "Yes, I do" reverberated in the Filipino community. It was written up in Asian American and Filipino American newspapers across the country. The day after I questioned Kerry, two elderly Filipino American World War II veterans came to the mammoth Washington Convention Center to say thank you. They had tears in their eyes when they did.[5]

Does race make a difference in what is covered and in the quality of the news report? The answer is yes. It was documented for the first time, perhaps, in 1968 when a special panel appointed by President Lyndon Johnson to study race relations issued a landmark report. The Kerner Commission said America was moving toward "two societies: one black, one white, separate and unequal." It blasted the media for inadequately covering the plight of African Americans or employing them in more than token numbers. There's no question that coverage of minorities, including Asian Americans, has gotten better since the Kerner Commission report. Many people would argue that there is still plenty of room for improvement. In 2005, AAJA's MediaWatch project cited culturally offensive coverage such as a *Wall Street Journal* headline referring to an "Asian invasion" of Far East design influences in furniture (February 2005) and a swipe at Koreans in a Rex Reed movie review (April 2005).[6]

The best coverage of Asian Americans, like reporting other minorities, is inclusive and presents a multidimensional, complete picture of where we fit in society. Among the best I've read in recent years: a look at Asian American immigration in the suburbs by the *Washington Post* a few years ago and an exhaustive look at the Hmong twenty-five years after they came from Cambodia to the United States by Gannett's Wisconsin newspapers. One of the best stories I read about rebuilding after Hurricane Katrina was the moving saga of a Vietnamese doctor's family in St. Bernard Parish, just outside of New Orleans. It was emotional and uplifting, written by the doctor's daughter, Ylan Q. Mui, a reporter for the *Washington Post*.[7] To me, it was not an "Asian" story, but a poignant tale about family, perseverance, and hope.

For the first time, a study commissioned by AAJA in 2005 found strong evidence that newsrooms with larger numbers of Asian American journalists have better and deeper coverage of Asian American communities. "It appears clear that the more Asian American staff members a paper has, the more stories about Asian Americans it is likely to report," said the study by then Ohio University School of Journalism professor Ralph Izard and Louisiana State University communications professor Denis Wu.[8] The authors surveyed stories in the *Baton Rouge Advocate, Boston Globe, Raleigh News and Observer, San Diego Union-Tribune, Seattle Times,* and *St. Louis Post-Dispatch.* The researchers found the most frequent topics about Asian Americans were culture and entertainment, features on people, and immigration and naturalization—or 71 percent of all stories found. Stories on business, education, and food rounded out the list of top Asian American subjects.

Sue Stock, a reporter at the *News and Observer* in Raleigh, North Carolina, says her ethnic heritage makes her more aware of stories about the Asian American community. Stock, who is of Korean descent but was raised by white parents, wrote a story once about a small shopping center in Cary, North Carolina, that has become a hub of Indian businesses, including a grocery and a clothing store. "The man who is largely responsible for the evolution of that shopping center felt comfortable talking with me because of my ethnicity," Stock said. "As a result, others in this community have since reached out to me with questions about how to send press releases and get items in the paper."[9]

The Future

Where do Asian American women in journalism go from here? Louey of the *Sacramento Bee* understands that race and ethnicity may have helped get her foot in the door but are not the only factors in her career. She understands, for instance, that she got an Associated Press internship because it was designed to encourage minorities to get into the business. "Newsrooms need diverse voices and faces, and that has helped me as I have moved throughout my career," Louey said. "But the reality is that it was my talent and dedication that I had to demonstrate on a daily basis."

Louey and Go are typical of those journalists who are driven to break down racial and cultural stereotypes in the profession. Louey volunteers for AAJA and was a mentor in UNITY's multicultural mentoring program, helping a Native American journalist who now works online for the *New York Times*. Go volunteers for AAJA and the Chips Quinn Scholars, an internship program run by the Freedom Forum, of which she is an alumna, and the Maynard Institute for Journalism Education, whose management program she attended. Asian American women in journalism "have to make a more concerted effort" to get more of their own in management. "Culturally, we're taught not to brownnose or network. We're taught if you don't rock the boat and you do well, you'll be recognized," Go said. "Yes, but you have to sing your own praises, too."

I believe in what Dinah Eng, a freelance journalist and one of my predecessors as AAJA national president, likes to call sustainable development in journalism: Give back and leave the industry a little better than you found it. In 1984 I won the first of two AAJA scholarships while attending USC. Fifteen years later I became the first former scholarship winner to lead the organization. For the past few years I have donated at least fifteen hundred dollars annually to AAJA, equal to what I was given in scholarship aid from AAJA. Although it's easier to write a check, I take the time to mentor, teach, and lend an ear when a young Asian American journalist—male or female—needs some encouragement.

Parrish said companies have to invest in developing talent. She credits the McClatchy Company for sending her to the newspaper management program at Northwestern University and to American Press Institute seminars and for putting her in charge of projects that allowed her to make the transition from the newsroom to the boardroom. Her advice to the industry: "Look for and value talent, and look down the road to cultivate people. Everybody is different and everybody brings something different to the table."

Notes

1. Sandy Louey, interview with Catalina Camia, December 12, 2005.

2. Esther Wu, interview with Catalina Camia, December 12, 2005.

3. Mi-Ai Parrish, interview with Catalina Camia, October 2, 2006.

4. Kristen Go, interview with Catalina Camia, March 3, 2006.

5. Lisa Chung, "Shining Light on Filipino Vets of W.W. II," *San Jose Mercury News,* August 10, 2004.

6. AAJA, "Annual Report, 2005," Asian American Journalists Association, 3. Available at http://www.aaja.org/resources/publications/AAJA_AR2005.pdf (accessed January 22, 2009).

7. Ylan Q. Mui, "Rebirth of the Phoenix," November 20, 2005, *Washington Post Magazine.*

8. Ralph Izard and Denis Wu, "Representing the Total Community: Relationships between Asian American Staff and Asian American Coverage in U.S. Newspapers," AAJA Focus Study Report, August 5, 2005, commissioned by the Asian American Journalists Association. Available at http://www.aaja.org/news/releases/2005_08_30_1/05Focus Project.pdf (accessed January 22, 2009).

9. Sue Stock, interview with Catalina Camia, December 2005.

PART 8

The Future:
Shifting Paradigms

29

Women in the Blogosphere

PAMELA J. CREEDON
AND JAN LEACH

In the late 1990s, the term *Web log,* describing personal opinion in the form of an online journal on the World Wide Web, was often shortened to the term *blog.* By 1994, *"bloggers"* were given credentials to cover the United States Democratic and Republican parties' conventions. Along with their popularity, blog search engines (blogdigger, Feedster, and Technorati) and even some on-line communities to connect bloggers to one another (e.g., MyBlogLog) began to develop.[1]

"Most loosely defined . . . blogs are simply Web logs produced by individuals/groups, the contents of which are available only online," according to Roberta de Boer, columnist/blogger for the *Toledo Blade,* in Ohio.[2]

Today most major news organizations also have some sort of interactive on-line presence loosely defined in one way or another as blogs. Reporters often start personal Web logs to invite interaction with readers, listeners, and viewers. Data from the "State of the News Media" study in 2005, showed that seven out of every ten Americans use the Internet to find information. Data from the Pew Internet and American Life Project in February 2006 showed that 39 percent of online users indicated they had read blogs, which is an increase of 12 percent from 2005. According to this study, this means at least 57 million Americans read blogs.[3]

In addition, some blog sites, such as the Huffington Post, have become major destinations for news and information consumers. Arianna Huffington, who founded the Huffington Post, said in November 2007 at a conference at the Shorenstein Center at Harvard University that the Huffington Post's bloggers "are not journalists in the sense of somebody who has a job with expectations, with deadlines. They basically are op-ed writers who can express themselves whenever they want." She said bloggers write "because they want their views out there."[4]

The *New York Times* and other news organizations are breaking news on blog sites, a relatively new trend that is bound to accelerate. The Huffington Post has hired top reporters from mainstream news organizations to break stories "both in a traditional way but also by using distributive journalism, wisdom of the crowd," Huffington said.[5]

Blogs as Citizen Voices

Most editors, as well as TV news directors, now accept the idea that eyewitness accounts, photos, or videos of local events—even disasters—can be valuable to the news process. But many debate preeminent media scholar Jim Carey's view of journalism as citizens conversing—and its extension that bloggers are citizen journalists.[6] Many in the news business argue that that citizen bloggers do not even attempt to use journalistic standards. "Blogs are NOT journalism. They don't even aspire to be. They don't always aspire to be factual. Their value is in reacting to, truthsquading or commenting on journalism," according to Jan Schaffer, head of the J-Lab at the University of Maryland.[7] Schaffer added, "For beat reporters . . . blogs about companies or products or subjects covered deliver an efficient way to stay abreast of immediate developments. For editors, blogs can be a way of opening up the news process and providing a high degree of transparency."

Denise Polverine, editor in chief of cleveland.com, views blogs as an interactive publishing tool. "When a user blogs onto cleveland.com, we view the tool as an interactive, topical diary," she said. "I feel comfortable with the term 'citizen content' or 'user content,' but I do believe true journalism is held to different standards."[8] Anne Saul, Gannett News Service editor, said postings on blogs add "new sources of information that might never have been known—especially if the blogs are written by knowledgeable people with a lot of expertise."[9] De Boer widened the question to consider if "journalism is still journalism" and if "a blogger would frame the question to ask if newspaper staffers can be considered 'real' bloggers."[10]

What do blogs add to journalism? "Blogs add a key element; others' voices," according to Polverine.[11] "News is no longer a one-way street where news is simply fed to people who accept it as-is. People consume their news differently now, interact with it, send it to friends and become part of the story. Blogs are a different perspective and traditional journalists are paying attention. Smart ones are reverse-publishing the content from the best blogs (photos and stories) in print, video, and online."

Saul added, "Newspaper blogs that allow the community to contribute also open up new sources of information, such as eyewitness accounts."[12] But she cautions that it is often difficult to correct misinformation given by bloggers and printed, because the news organization is often accused of hiding something.

Schaffer said that blogs can be news *if* "they are used by beat reporters to expand the real estate for news and information. They can be news if they are following up and expanding on journalism or countering inaccurate journalism. The *Dallas Morning News* has an editorial page blog, explaining editorials," she said. But they are an inefficient way to get the daily news, she points out, adding that GlobalVoicesOnline, a blog aggregator, is "a good way to find a quick synopsis of what's important."[13]

De Boer said, "On a very crass level, blogs for the newspaper industry are now marketing imperatives." She added, "If a newspaper has a Web site, but no blogs, it's already hopelessly 'waaay' behind industry practices." She said that the quality of information seems almost immaterial, "since what passes for public debate now seems to be all about noise level and less about what people are actually shouting." TV and online news producers know the marketing relevance of blogs as well. She said on "a much less crass level . . . without any evidence or data . . . many of us live in a society that leaves us disconnected and even lonely and blogs are one possible antidote."

Polverine said, "Each day these methods shape how traditional news organizations tell their stories. We can immediately see online how people are reacting to stories. We are empowered with new techniques, new mediums, new voices. Traditional media is waking up to the fact that interactive storytelling enriches the way stories can be told. We have the ability to engage people on the most granular levels," she said. "The only drawback is that there are users who spoil the party . . . and abuse forums . . . but we have an entire team of sweepers and moderators who do an incredible job of handling our forums and comments."

The Blogosphere: Where Gender Wasn't Supposed to Matter

Ellen Goodman, *Boston Globe* columnist, tracked the "maleness of this media" while she was a visiting fellow at Harvard's Shorenstein Center. In her research, she found that only 7 percent of the top ninety political blogs were authored solely by women.[14] She adds in fairness, half of the 96 million blogs her research uncovered were written by women. But these blogs are not a force in the political arena, which she touts as looking like a "new boy network."[15]

"For men, the act of blogging is feeding your social affinity group," according to Schaffer. "Bill links to Bob, who links back to Bill, etc., etc. It's a mutual admiration society. Blogs provide a lot of 'validation.' 'I blog, therefore, I have something to say' . . . and when your 20 pals link to you, you must be important. . . . However . . . blogging requires a great deal more effort for women," Schaffer says. In her experience, "women tend to make longer, more textured posts— ones that require more brainpower to read and to write." De Boer suggests that for women, blogs will likely simply add to a newsroom's status quo in terms of gender equity. But she admits she is waiting for the first "in utero blogger" to begin posting.

A formal study of the top thirty political blogs from June 2004 to May 2005 proved the existence of a digital gender gap of female voices in political coverage. Of the top thirty political blogs, only three (10 percent) were authored by women.[16] And one of these, Wonkette, "mixes political gossip and analysis with a great deal of sex talk." The *New York Times* has called her "gossipy," "raunchy," and "potty-mouthed."[17] But as de Boer pointed out, Ana Marie Cox, formerly Wonkette, who now writes for *Time,* is considered less influential now than when she mixed sex and politics online.

Sure, there are women's blogs (pages) on the Internet. Ellen Goodman sums it up well: "Are we going to do the same thing we have done all along, but with computers? Or will we create a new institution that allows for marginalized voices" to be heard in the blogosphere?[18]

A recent study of the top one hundred blogs in the United States shows that 34 percent cover technology, 26 percent explore culture, and 25 percent focus on politics.[19] And a prediction by the Project for Excellence in Journalism states: "Blogging is on the brink of a new phase that will probably include scandal, profitability for some, and a splintering into elites and non-elites over standards and ethics."[20]

Blogs are not much more than two decades old and have gained considerable visibility within the past decade or so. But blogs are an application—not journalism. Schaffer sees them as "a piece of software, just like Quicktime or Adobe Acrobat or Quark. The Internet is the medium." They are an inefficient way to get information, but they provide direct contact with readers and citizens.

Arianna Huffington said at the Shorenstein Conference in November 2007 that she does not see blogs and other forms of new media "as a replacement of the old media," but rather that old and new media will coexist in a "hybrid future."[21]

Three major questions remain: First, how can citizens distinguish blogs from journalism? Second, how will women's blogs be equally incorporated as citizen journalism? Third, and most important, how can the news industry ensure that female journalists will experience equality in this new interactive world?

Notes

1. "Blog," Wikipedia, http://en.wikipedia.org/wiki/Blogs#1983.E2.80.931990_.28Pre-HTTP.29 (accessed January 22, 2009).

2. Jan Leach, electronic question responses from Roberta de Boer, columnist/blogger, *Toledo Blade,* August 6, 2007.

3. Project for Excellence in Journalism, "State of the News Media, 2007," Citizen Media section, http://www.stateofthenewsmedia.org/2007/narrative_online_citizen_media.asp?cat=8&media-4; Deborah Fallows, "Internet Users in Search of a Home," Pew Internet and American Life Project, 2006, http://www.pewinternet.org/PPF/r/196/report_display.asp. Both Web sites accessed January 22, 2009.

4. Arianna Huffington, keynote speech, "Women and News: Expanding the News Audience, Increasing Political Participation, and Informing Citizens," transcript pg. 17 from Women and News conference, November 30, 2007, Joan Shorenstein Center on the Press, Politics, and Public Policy, Harvard University, 2008. Available at http://www.hks.harvard.edu/presspol/publications/reports/women_and_news_transcript_2008.pdf (accessed January 22, 2009).

5. Ibid., 29.

6. E. S. Munson and C. A. Warren, *James Carey: A Critical Reader* (Minneapolis: University of Minnesota Press, 1997).

7. Jan Schaffer, e-mail with Pam Creedon, August 16, 2007.

8. Denise Polverine, e-mail with Jan Leach, August 7, 2007.

9. Anne Saul, e-mail with Pam Creedon, August 16, 2007.

10. Roberta de Boer, e-mail with Jan Leach, August 6, 2007.

11. Polverine e-mail.

12. Saul e-mail.

13. Schaffer e-mail.

14. Ellen Goodman, e-mail through boston.com, August 10, 2007.

15. Ibid.

16. Dustin Harp and Mark Tremayne, "The Gendered Blogosphere: Examining Inequality Using Network and Feminist Theory," *Journalism and Mass Communication Quarterly* 83, no. 2 (2006): 247–64. In the study, the top women's blogs were: asmallvictory.net by Michele Catalano (13th); Michell Malkin's michellemalkin.com (23rd); and Ana Marie Cox's Wonkette.com (26th).

17. Ibid., 256.

18. Goodman e-mail.

19. Brian Morrissey, "Tech, Politics Dominate Blogosphere," Adweek.com, October 11, 1006, http://www.adweek.com/aw/esearch/article_display.jsp?vnu_content_id=1003224023 (accessed January 22, 2009).

20. Project for Excellence in Journalism, "State of the News Media 2007," Major Trends section, 7. Available at http://www.stateofthenewsmedia.org/2007/narrative_overview_eight.asp?cat=2&media=1 (accessed January 22, 2009).

21. Huffington, keynote speech, 28.

30

Interview with Denise Polverine

JAN LEACH

Jan Leach: How do you define "blogs"?

Denise Polverine*: I define blogs in two ways. When we (cleveland.com and our main content providers, the *Plain Dealer* and Sun Newspapers) use our blogs to break news, we view them as an interactive publishing tool. When a user blogs on cleveland.com, we view the tool as an interactive, topical diary.

JL: Do you consider blogs as journalism?

DP: I do consider the content of blogs as journalism, depending on the content and the author. Meaning, I used to use the buzz phrase "citizen journalism" quite often to describe content provided by our readers. I now feel most comfortable calling this "citizen content" or "user content." I do not think the term "content" diminishes user contributions, but I believe true "journalism" is held to different standards.

JL: Can anyone post anything on your blogs without anyone editing the posting?

DP: Users can post directly to our blogs without being edited, but if the post violates our online user agreement it can and will be deleted. I would say more than 95 to 98 percent of our posts are *not* deleted. Again, we do not edit posts. If it violates our policies, the post is deleted.

JL: Do you feel obligated to respond to any posting?

DP: We typically do not respond to posts. We view comments as a place for open discussion. If a post grabs our attention, we or the *Plain Dealer* may follow up with that individual. Some posts have led to stories (leads).

JL: How much extra time does it take to maintain a blog?

---

*Denise Polverine is the editor of cleveland.com.

DP: It takes time to care for a blog and feed it daily. But as things evolve in the online world, I wouldn't say this takes us more time. Priorities and duties have changed, so maybe we are spending a good deal of time with blog content, but most likely we are no longer spending time on another duty that was not paying off in traffic.

JL: In your opinion, what do blogs add to journalism?

DP: Blogs add a crucial element: others' voices. News is no longer a one-way street where news is simply fed to people who accept it as-is. People consume their news differently now, interact with it, send it to friends, and become part of the story. Blogs add a different perspective and traditional journalists are paying attention. Smart ones are reverse-publishing the content from the best blogs (photos and stories) in print and online.

JL: What are "Mojos" and how are they journalism?

DP: Mojos are mobile journalists who may report from their community, an event or wherever they feel news is happening. Mojos offer journalism in that they cover events accurately and descriptively and most often with interactive, multimedia elements.

JL: Are these new interactive methods of gathering information and talking directly to the reader (online readers) adding to our newsgathering process?

DP: Each day these methods shape how traditional news organizations tell their stories. We can immediately see online how people are reacting to stories. We are empowered by new techniques, new mediums, new voices. Traditional media is waking up to the fact that interactive storytelling enriches the way stories can be told. We have the ability to engage people on the most granular levels.

JL: Do you see any downside or problem with such interactivity with readers?

DP: No downsides at all. I have learned so much about social networking and how I define news in my life, not how news defines me. The only drawback at all is similar to anything in life. There are always a few who spoil the party, meaning there are users who abuse forums and comments on blogs. But we have an entire team of sweepers and moderators who do an incredible job of handling our forums and comments.

JL: How much time does it take to maintain a blog?

DP: Difficult to answer. Really depends on the topic, but it needs to be fed and cared for daily, and that can range from minutes to hours.

JL: Who are considered some of the top women bloggers?

DP: Depends what you like. I always check out USAToday.com's Pop Candy, authored by Whitney Matheson. Ariana Huffington is also a great blogger. There are so many. Anita Campbell is a great local blogger with a national following. [See Campbell's blog at http://www.smallbiztrends.com.]

JL: Will blogs create a new gender gap for women in the news business?

DP: I do not believe so. This creates a new opportunity.

JL: Where is blogging headed?

DP: Blogging and social networking sites like Facebook are helping to change the way people communicate and consume and customize their news. Blogs and these other ways for users to participate will not go away, but will continue to grow in strength and influence. This is such an exciting, empowering time.

31

Reaching the
Changing Audience

PAULA ELLIS

We are in the midst of a media revolution that has forced "old media" firms to hasten their previously tepid efforts to adapt. We hope there is still time to adapt, that self-renewal is possible. But we worry that the media platelets will shift and whole species will become extinct. "It took awhile to realize how fast readers' habits are shifting," said Jennifer Carroll, vice president of new media content for Gannett. "We need to move a lot faster."[1]

Speaking to investment analysts two years ago, *Washington Post* chairman Don Graham said the future of news is on the Internet: "The business is changing faster than I expected."[2]

Sally Squires, then health and nutrition columnist for the *Washington Post,* experimented her way and ours into the future. "I would love to have said we planned it from A to Z, but we stumbled into this," said the convener of a growing conversation about food and fitness.[3] The Lean Plate Club met through Squires's column in the daily newspaper, her Web chats, and her radio talks. Readers of the youthful free daily *Express,* a tabloid first printed in 2003 and handed out during rush hour at Metro stations, "get a bite." For the *Post*'s subscribers an e-mail newsletter landed every Tuesday. Podcasts, videos, and an interactive book also proclaim the mantra "Eat smart and move more." While holding tight to her core journalistic values, Squires moved enthusiastically to embrace these new distribution platforms so that she can touch the lives of more people. "We see it as solid journalism, public health and public service," she said.

Talk about having an impact. The column had about five million readers in sixteen newspapers, and about 250,000 people subscribed to the e-mail newsletter. Squires seems genuinely surprised by how rapidly the audience grew. "The multimedia approach enabled it to grow in ways that would not have been possible."

Launched as a column and Web chat in 2001, the Lean Plate Club grew by trial and error. Squires appeared open to trying almost anything. She produced a video in which she joined members at a grocery to talk about food choices. She considered a daily recipe podcast for busy moms like herself; in addition to reading her column aloud, she would provide a list of ingredients "so you can shop on the way home." Club members, outfitted with pedometers and with their children in tow, would be invited to walk neighborhood trails, to share their experience and advice. In 2007 the Lean Plate Club helped readers keep their weight and fitness resolutions by developing a three-by-five card they could carry to toughen their resolve.

This is exactly how species adapt to rapidly changing external environments. One experimental step at a time. Experiment. Reflect. Change. It is a fugue that requires listening empathetically to customer wants and needs, paying attention to ideas at the margins where innovation is harbored and then moved to the mainstream. It is a process of shared learning that recognizes readers and other customers have more choice and thus more power. In newspapers across the country, women, grounded in the power of core values and guiding principles, are leading through this time of ambiguity and complexity. They have unique ways of seeing, knowing, and leading. Their time is now.

Some will wait all too patiently for a messiah with commandments etched in binary code to dispatch new rules to their laptop or PDA. They seek stability and rely on existing models. But ours is a time of disequilibrium. It calls for action and feedback. It cries out for leaders who understand dynamic and open learning systems. "I don't think I've learned this much since I was in college," said Leanne Kleinmann, a veteran newspaper and magazine editor who dropped her name from the masthead of the *Memphis Commercial Appeal* to foray into a woman's world she invented at iDivamemphis.com. "We were plodding along and wringing our hands about the future," Kleinmann said, when she decided to figure out ways to talk with women about the things that mattered to them. Her attitude: "You can't scare me by telling me this won't work." Kleinmann's sense of urgency has grown with the site, and with the steady drumbeat of potential newspaper sales. Shortly after the CFO of Scripps told investment analysts they would consider selling the newspaper division, Kleinmann said, "I need to turn up the heat on my business plan."[4]

Innovators are "those who think differently, those who act differently," said Poynter Institute president Karen Dunlap. "Those who can walk in the present but see into the future."[5] The future never announces itself. It sends faint signals to willing receptors. The not-so-faint signals are now more than a decade old. They have morphed into "Neon Signs," flashing an in-your-face reminder that changes in technology and consumer media habits that once seemed on the edge of chaos are today's baseline beliefs. Even more insistent are the *Fog-*

horns. They are the deeper cultural manifestations of Neon Signs. It is in this arena that new products and ideas are fighting for viability in the marketplace. These signals excite today's most vigorous experiments. As news organizations experiment and adapt to these signals, they gain insight from customers about what is yet to come. Then there are the *Pulsars,* high-frequency waves that elude most of us for now. These signals exist at the edge of chaos, where systems are in balance but not quite stable or turbulent. The most adventurous of innovators dwell in this arena of ambiguity and complexity. But because the Pulsars' waves cannot be easily made visible, the signals and their receptors struggle to be recognized.

Neon Signs
- The pace of media fragmentation is quickening.
- Media distribution channels are converging.
- Customers have more choice and thus more power.
- Customer response to news articles and advertising can be measured.
- Technology enables better targeting.
- Communities are forming and re-forming around information (affinity vs. geography).
- Co-learning and collaboration with customers are critical.

Foghorns
- Categorization. Users select categories that are meaningful to them. This redefines "old media" concepts of what is local. Geography lessens in importance as communities of interest explode. RSS (Really Simple Syndication) and tagging (a user organizes Internet content under a keyword) enable this.
- Personalization. Anyone can develop and share content. Self-publishing through blogs is an example. Sharing through e-mail and Web sites such as MySpace and Friendster is another one.
- Interaction. The ability to engage with content, its developers, and others in real time or anytime.
- Mobility. Increased access through a range of devices that enable connectivity from wherever you are.

Pulsars
- Velocity of information quickens. More information and responses to it are available in "real time" with consequences for political systems, economic systems, and others.
- Information has a social life and a transactional life. It is both horizontal and linear. The newspaper evolved into a bundled package that incorporated both. As the bundle is disaggregated, understanding these distinctions becomes more relevant.
- Storytelling. Cultures tell stories to transmit values, and storytelling approaches are shaped by the medium in which they are delivered.

"The future enters into us, in order to transform us, long before it happens," the German poet Rainer Maria Rilke has been quoted as saying.

Kleinmann has been absorbing these signals for some time. "I think everything is changing in media land right now, from blogs and podcasts and wikis, to the power of Myspace.com, to the increasing capabilities of cell phones and digital video. . . . I think I'm pretty close to the edge in a media world that's pushing the boundaries every day. It's scary sometimes, since there's really no one to ask about what the next step should be. But it's also wildly invigorating, being able to start something like this and see it thrive in a business that's been too full recently of gloom and doom." She recommends first that we unlearn so that we can see anew. "Journalists need to go back to school, figuratively, to learn about these new technologies and not be afraid to think about their mission in a new technological light."

Poynter's Dunlap said the most important trends to watch revolve around "how people consume information and what they are interested in. . . . The first ties into changing technology. Will people continue to seek smaller and smaller, quicker and personal, as opposed to shared consumption?" she asked.

"We are seeing the rise of open-source approaches to knowledge development as communities, not individuals, become responsible for innovations," noted Ian Davis and Elizabeth Stephenson in a McKinsey Quarterly report on ten top trends to watch in 2006. "Ubiquitous access to information is changing the economics of knowledge."[6] Knowledge is more available and at the same time more specialized. For evidence, look at the rapid rise of search engines such as Google.

Kleinmann is quickly learning with her community about this new arena of content and knowledge development. Her iDivamemphis.com solicits writing and comment from the community, as do many emerging hyper-local news sites such as Baristanet and backfence.com. But this site is intensely focused on one community: It is unabashedly for and about women. "Face it: Traditional newspaper reporting is heavy on process. Women are interested in other things: putting together a larger picture, developing relationships," said Kleinmann, who grew frustrated with the physical constraints of the daily newspaper and with longtime definitions of news she believes are too narrow. "We can't keep doing what we've been doing—covering courts, cops, and government in incremental fifteen-inch meeting stories and relegating such broad and vast topics as health, faith, and families to the back pages. Newspapers that are successful will figure out how to flip those priorities while still serving the vital watchdog/muckraker role that gave us our primacy in the first place."

So Kleinmann flipped her vision of journalism to the Internet, where it is easier to connect women to one another and build relationships that form communities. Women come to iDivamemphis.com to discuss such controversial subjects as a proposed state ban on breastfeeding in public. On the day the Associated Press reported the news, Kleinmann's blog post asked: "Is breastfeeding indecent exposure?" That, she said, is an example of how she is learning to upend years of experience as an editor and do a "complete mind reversal" to publish only on the Web. What's different about her approach? "You must be succinct, irreverent, and get your point across." Newspaper journalists "were always looking to see the whole thing before we said anything," she said. At iDivamemphis.com the community is creating the story lines and content with her. And her goal is to stimulate involvement.

Kleinmann's skeptical colleagues aren't sure she is still a practicing journalist. She says, "I think it's a new model, one that opens the discussion up to people who didn't have a voice before, and has a professional journalist sitting at the red-hot center of the conversation, looking for important topics or good stories in the flood of comments, and grabbing them as they go by."

As the Lean Plate Club grew, Sally Squires thought the burgeoning community could become a force of social change. "It's like playing chess on a four-dimension board. It is very time-consuming but very rewarding. It's a seven-day-a-week job. You have to love this or you wouldn't do it."

Even as new content producers emerge—bloggers, citizen journalists, wiki-like communities—traditional news content is rapidly being disassembled and repackaged by a variety of aggregators. These can be search engines, RSS agents, or, from the realm of social media, personalized "play lists" bundled by friends of experts.

Neil Budde, former editor in chief of Yahoo News and former publisher of wsj.com, says the dramatic shift in consumer media consumption will increase the appetite for news. "As consumption patterns change, people will look at more news and therefore the value of each individual [consumer] will become greater [to advertisers]," he said. That means building customer loyalty will be more important than ever as the lifetime value of each customer is poised to zoom. It's difficult to project what the media company of the future will look like, but Budde believes there will be plenty to be gained. "We haven't come close to achieving the economic value we can achieve with bits and pieces online," he said.[7]

With the rock-solid support of Gannett's top leadership, Jennifer Carroll is leading the company's effort to transform its news- and information-gathering processes to take advantage of the explosion in the variety of distribution platforms. Late in 2006 her team's experimental idea was unwrapped for the public and dubbed "the information center." Before rolling out the idea to all of its eighty-nine local newsrooms, the team tested and practiced the idea of collecting information using words, images, and video for distribution across multiple platforms. The tactics were piloted at eleven Gannett newspapers and implemented full-scale in three. In October, when Carroll gathered all Gannett's editors to unveil the idea, the test site editors did the talking. Because of their involvement, "It didn't feel like a launch of an initiative as much as an incredibly progressive initiative," she said. "My biggest criticism of print is that our strength is our weakness," Carroll said. "We want to hoard and vet. We have to not be top-down." Could this become the 24-7 news company of the future? "There is a very small window here to reengage with our communities in ways we never have before," Carroll said shortly after the center was unveiled.

At this time of disequilibrium, action and feedback matter more than stability and reliance on proven models. Organizations and individuals with an open learning orientation will influence the changes. In newsrooms across the country, women are leading significant cultural change that could transform newspaper companies from rule-obedient, crouch-and-defend positions to learning organizations that share power to invent with customers. Those who have been most successful are individuals who can synthesize from many disciplines and experiences, those who are open, and those who are comfortable with ambiguity and "what if" thinking.

"Women have some qualities that fit well with a constructive culture," according to a report by the Readership Institute at the Media Management Center at Northwestern University. "Their leadership style tends to be inclusive and collaborative, rather than hierarchical."[8] The 2006 "Women in Media" study follows a groundbreaking report by the institute that found that more than 80 percent of newspaper companies have "defensive" cultures. These cultures were defined as risk averse and slow to adapt to change. Fewer than 20 percent were found to have "constructive" cultures, which encourage experimentation.[9] "Women have always had to move things around in ways that are new," said Kleinmann, recalling that since her first job at *McCall's* magazine she almost always has been the only woman in the room.

Organizational cultures are built one conversation at a time in the warp and weave of getting the job done. Martha Hild at the *Dayton (Ohio) Daily News* took to heart the challenge to "lead from where you are." From her position as director of Cox Ohio Editorial Systems, Hild has led a revolution to replace the core newspaper with one that is "as reader-focused as we can make it." They didn't tinker with special sections or tweak the margins. They took dead aim at well-grooved methods and thought patterns that have endured for decades. "One trend appears to be for news media to view content as a commodity and to imagine it can be packaged in a formulaic, perhaps automated way that will be super-efficient," she said. "This approach will have a place in the media world, but I hope at least some newspapers seek alternative remedies to the downward spiral of falling circulation, eroding resources and brand X quality." Hild has an intuitive understanding of culture and a scientist's understanding of systems. She has an eclectic background, including a PhD in isotope geochemistry, stints as a freelance writer, and work in educational publishing. "Much of my work over the years has been at the interface of language and technology, whether as an academic, writer/editor or in publishing systems," she said.[10]

In their book, *Intrapreneuring in Action: A Handbook for Business Innovation*, Gifford Pinchot and Ron Pellman offer tricks of the trade for middle managers, because it is their actions that create the culture. They identify Real Intrapreneurs, as distinguished from promoters, as having the following traits:

- A vision of a better way and the need to make it happen.
- A willingness to take moderate risks.
- Persistence.
- Intuitiveness and an ability to analyze.
- Honesty.[11]

Count Martha Hild in the cadre of intrapreneurs. Throughout her career, much of her work has focused on change and transformation. "The habits of mind that make a good scientist also make a good business innovator," she said. "You're basically trying to envision something that hasn't been envisioned before (a workflow, an org chart, a product) within a 'solution space' bounded by certain parameters (customer needs, financial goals, critical success factors) and continually analyzing the outcomes (operational metrics, financial performance, customer feedback) looking for success."

Last April the *Dayton Daily News* launched a newspaper reinvention that included structural changes in the number and type of sections, design changes that were more familiar to Web designers than to newspaper folks, and a fundamental change in the mind-set of journalists who determine what is news. "We struggled the first couple of months to escape the gravitational pull of the status quo," Hild said. But escape they have, according to Mary Nesbitt of the Readership Institute. She identified the makeover as one of the industry's most exciting efforts to offer customers what they want.

Hild, with support from the top, assembled a team of employees that mirrored the demographic makeup of occasional "light readers." High-ranking managers are usually tapped for important projects, but Hild says she "made a concerted effort to sidestep and dismantle hierarchical thinking and processes, creating a project micro culture that was highly constructive." Hild and her team let readers guide their work. They initially took aim at "light readers" and focused on six of the Readership Institute's key experiences. They focused on three positive experiences (makes me smarter, gives me something to talk about, looks out for my civic and personal interests) and three inhibitors (too long/too much, discriminates, and stereotypes). But the research quickly showed that "heavy readers" overwhelmingly approved of the prototypes, too. "We hear so much about the danger of evolution versus revolution so we just came out and asked,"

Hild said. Inside the newsroom, though, resistance was high. Using the Lotus Blossom brainstorming process, Hild says, she and her team "had achieved a very high state of collective thinking." But it was difficult to transfer to others all they had learned together.

That is the challenge of any system that survives. How do we alter and replicate the genetic code? In his 1990 blockbuster book, *Bionomics: Economy as Ecosystem,* Michael Rothschild described life's challenge as "transforming information into physical substance and then back into mere information."[12]

It is too early to fully gauge results in Dayton, but it is not too soon to applaud the teams' unflinching efforts to scan the external environment for signals about how to adapt now to thrive in the future. Too many in the news business have chosen to collude with the conventional wisdom that social trends and technological breakthroughs have doomed the industry. They would have us believe that news organizations are best led by those who will gracefully manage decline, which they believe is inevitable.

Hild is convinced otherwise. "Our experience confirms for me that, at the moment, limitations on the success of newspapers originate primarily with what organizational analysts call the 'knowing-doing gap.'" The challenges exist "primarily within the culture of newspaper organizations and institutions rather than primarily within societal trends, market forces, or other external factors," she said.

Notes

1. Jennifer Carroll, interviews with Paula Ellis, February 28, 2006, and January 12, 2007.

2. Don Graham, quoted in Chris Wilson and Harry Jaffe, "*Washington Post* Chairman Says Newspapers' Future Is Not in Paper," *Washingtonian,* December 2, 2005.

3. Sally Squires, interviews with Paula Ellis, March 1, 2006, and January 10, 2007.

4. Leanne Kleinmann, interviews with Paula Ellis, March 21, 2006, and January 11, 2007.

5. Karen Dunlap, interview with Paula Ellis, February 5, 2006.

6. Ian Davis and Elizabeth Stephenson, "Ten Trends to Watch in 2006," McKinsey Quarterly online, January 2006. Available at http://www.mckinseyquarterly.com/Strategy/Globalization/Ten_trends_to_watch_in_2006_1734 (accessed January 22, 2009).

7. Neil Budde, interview with Paula Ellis, March 9, 2006.

8. Mary Nesbitt and John Lavine, "Reaching New Readers: Revolution Not Evolution," Readership Institute report, American Society of Newspaper Editors, July 2004. Available at http://www.readership.org/new_readers/data/overview.pdf (accessed January 22, 2009).

9. Mary Arnold and Mary Nesbitt, "Women in Media, 2006: Finding the Leader in You," Media Management Center, Northwestern University and McCormick Tribune

Foundation, 2006. Available at http://www.mediamanagementcenter.org/research/wim2006.pdf (accessed January 22, 2009).

10. Martha Hild, interview with Paula Ellis, February 16, 2006.

11. Gifford Pinchot and Ron Pellman, *Intrapreneuring in Action: A Handbook for Business Innovation* (San Francisco: Berrett-Koehler, 1999).

12. Michael Rothschild, *Bionomics: Economy as Ecosystem* (New York: Henry Holt, 1995).

32

The Future of Women in News
and the Business of Journalism

MARTY PETTY

Just for the Record . . .

I've rarely let the fact that I'm a woman consciously define my work or how I go about it. However, if I'm ever in doubt about the "gender" part of the equation, I refer to the framed January 5, 1998, *New York Times* clipping in our powder room, in which it is recorded for all time—in the form of a correction—that I am a woman: "Because of an editing error, an article yesterday about the appointment of an editor at the *Hartford [Conn.] Courant* referred incorrectly at one point to the newspaper's publisher. Marty Petty is a woman." My newsroom blew up the correction the next day and gave it to me on a T-shirt. I was much more amused about being referred to as "Mr. Marty Petty" in the venerable *Times* than its *Times* reporter, who had actually worked for me at the *Courant*. She was as certain of my gender when she wrote the story as the esteemed copy editor was of his presumption that the publisher had to be a man.

How I define myself most days seems to depend on the kind of day I'm having: a mom trying to organize everyone and everything, a teacher cramming for a seminar, a "retired" journalist trying to find a minute to pass a tip along to my newsroom, a trustee reviewing the performance of investment funds, a spouse eternally grateful for everything (did I say a spouse eternally grateful for everything?), a community volunteer on a fund-raising deadline, a marketer, a daughter-in-law, a hostess, a mentor, a panelist, an unlicensed shrink, a facilitator, and, oh yes—a newspaper publisher.

To "Pubble" or Not to "Pubble"

One of my former reporters once asked a colleague, "Just what does a publisher do?" That publisher responded, "We pubble." So I am a woman who began her career reporting, and now I pubble. Believe me, pubbling isn't what it used to be, but it's still my passion.

Hannah B. and Lindsay

My husband interrupts my thirty-five-thousand-foot trance and suggests I think about leading this essay with the line about "Hannah B." that I often used on the chicken dinner circuit during my *Hartford Courant* days: "I am the first woman publisher of the *Courant,* the nation's oldest continuously published newspaper (since 1764), whose husband did not die for her to get the job." Hannah B. Watson's husband, Ebenezer, died in 1777. He left her with five young children, a newspaper, a print shop, and a paper mill. Although the *Courant* was a growing and influential newspaper, the mill burned to the ground five months after Ebenezer's death in a blaze, believed to be the work of the British. However, Hannah B., as *Courant* staffers fondly referred to her, ably guided the rebuilding of the paper mill thanks to the historic vote by Connecticut's general assembly to hold a lottery to raise the needed funds.[1]

Mark and I are on an afternoon flight back from Virginia, where we've dropped off our daughter, Lindsay. She is a first-year student at the University of Richmond. The three of us navigated the college selection process together. Actually, we drove and flew her to a variety of universities, but she made the decision as to which one was right for her. When asked if she knew what she wanted to do in life, her response was, "I'm not sure, but I want to run something and help people."

It was only when we actually went through the college selection process that the point was amplified to me how very different the process is today compared with when I graduated from high school three and a half decades earlier. I chose to attend the country's oldest journalism school at the University of Missouri–Columbia. I mailed in a postcard requesting information and an application. Then I sent it back and waited for the daily mail delivery to learn if I'd been accepted.

As a kid growing up in St. Louis, Missouri, I fell asleep at night listening to Jack Buck and Harry Caray announcing Cardinal baseball games on my transistor radio. My parents had one black rotary telephone in their bedroom. Television was limited to three network stations, a public service channel, and a couple of independents. We had to physically turn the antenna (some people had to go outside to do this) when we changed from one station to another. We listened to vinyl records and eight-track tapes. Writing term papers on a typewriter with carbon paper was torture!

Fast-forward forty-plus years to 2004. The college visitation trips with Lindsay were planned online, from the information gathering about each university to reserving airline tickets and mapping our driving route on RandMcNally.com. When Lindsay made her choice, she downloaded the application and made her submission via e-mail. Lindsay's media choices are so dramatically different from mine that in the mid-nineties, when the Web emerged as a medium for the consumer, few in my industry could possibly comprehend the transformation that we are face to face with today.

Armed with her laptop and cell phone, Lindsay and her customized group of "friends" can access a mind-numbing assortment of media and channels. Anyone can create a blog or a Web site. She is not limited to Walter Cronkite and the *Post-Dispatch* (St. Louis was actually a two-newspaper city then), as I was. All rules for political campaigning were rewritten in 2008 when president-elect Barack Obama used the Web to strategically build grassroots support, raising record levels of dollars and engagement of the young electorate to what some called "rock star" heights. Former presidential hopeful John Edwards went straight to his target audience and announced his candidacy on the *Daily Show*, a faux-news program on the Comedy Central cable network. And major Hollywood studios rewrite the ends of not-yet-released movies based upon consumer versions posted on YouTube.com.

The opportunity we have for virtually unfettered access to information has created the greatest challenge our industry has yet faced. We're no longer the gatekeepers to information; we're no longer in control.

The Consumer in Control

Time magazine named "You" its Man of the Year at the end of 2006, making official for the history books what marketers and providers of news and information know only too well: The consumer has taken control.

What impact is this having on our institutions of journalism? There are at least two significant dynamics at play: (1) rapidly changing patterns of news and information consumption by consumers and (2) fundamental changes in our core advertisers' businesses. These are converging to fuel an unprecedented transformation of the media industry—and it's not isolated to newspapers. The broadcast and cable industries face similar challenges of new consumer behavior and market fragmentation. The rapid adoption of TiVo and DVR technology, which enables the viewer to skip the commercials, has pushed the industry to now offer consumers their favorite shows online whenever it suits them to watch. "Most leading-edge thinkers long ago accepted the digital revolution's transforming reality and are now engaged in what amounts to the news industry's Quest for the Holy Grail: the development of a business model that will pay for quality journalism in a digital world," writes Michael Riley, 1995 Nieman Fellow and editor of *Congressional Quarterly* (*CQ*), an affiliate company of Times Publishing.[2]

How and at what speed we reinvent our business model and our organizations will determine our success. I'm confident we'll succeed, but to what degree may depend heavily on the talent at the top and its willingness to adapt to the new digital reality.

That Brings Us to the Money

In today's environment, the advertising categories that pose the greatest risk of loss or erosion are also those that historically have been the most profitable: help wanted, real estate, national automotive, travel, and inserts. Add the increasing pressure of public ownership that requires consistent earnings growth, and publishers face an ugly equation that allows little room for error, much less doing what is right for the reader, as they race to post a number for Wall Street.

Today we're witnessing the fallout of this Wall Street squeeze: waves of consolidation and realignment of the industry's top news and information companies. I personally experienced the closing down of the Times Mirror Company (*Los Angeles Times, Newsday, Hartford Courant,* etc.) in the summer of 2000. Seven years later, its acquirer, the Tribune Company, was itself in play. The industry consolidation did not end with the demise of Knight Ridder in 2006 after McClatchy acquired it. The Chandlers, the McCormicks, the Bancrofts, and Barrons would no longer reign among the great journalistic families of our time. And what is the people impact of these ownership changes? Who falls out in these billion-dollar transactions? "As new owners take the reins, panicking newspapers are kicking diversity goals to the back of the bus," said *Editor and Publisher* in a February 2007 editorial citing post-acquisition buyout analyses done by the National Association of Black Journalists and National Association of Hispanic Journalists. "Diversity is good for business, and good for the bottom line. That's undoubtedly true. What's increasingly clear, though, is that the bottom line ain't necessarily good for diversity."[3]

It was the fallout from this very consolidation that Nelson Poynter, the owner of the *St. Petersburg Times* from 1938 until his death in 1978, feared. Poynter believed if a newspaper's leadership always made decisions based first on what was best for the reader, whether on editorial content or business matters, the rest would follow. Poynter firmly believed in the need for the newspaper to remain independent of any external business influence, and that led him to create a school for working journalists. In the ultimate gift of charity, he gave away the newspaper and its holdings to the school upon his death to ensure protection of its independent ownership status. Today the Poynter Institute for Media Studies, based in St. Petersburg, Florida, is the sole owner of Times Publishing and its subsidiaries. The newspaper company is a for-profit, tax-paying corporation. From profits after taxes, Times Publishing pays a dividend to the school and then reinvests what's left back into operations to grow the enterprise, keeping journalism excellence and service to its print and online readers at its core.

Growing an enterprise that will endure often requires making investments that will not produce short-term gains. So is it realistic to ask whether an industry that still owns powerful brands and marketing engines and produces strong margins (the 2006 average was 18 percent) can reset the expectation for lower profits during this time of historic transformation? Based on the recent investor demands that triggered the latest rounds of consolidation, it seems unlikely. Even private owners have recently been confronted with some of these difficult questions. After all, that's a respectable margin—10 percent, 12 percent.

At the close of 2008, most newspaper companies, both public and private, were faced with unprecedented debt levels and in some cases negative market capitalization due to the fallout from historic lows in advertising revenue and the worst recession since the early 1930s. The evaporation of highly profitable classified dollars began with the collapse of the falsely overheated real estate market, and was followed by the automotive manufacturers seeking government bailouts and unemployment rates climbing. The retail ad category then followed. The question of how to balance delivery of a quality news product and an acceptable operating margin is suddenly complicated by mere questions of survival for some companies.

Given that the economics of the business are so closely linked to, even dependent upon, the health of the general economy, most believe the industry will be revived as soon as the economy recovers. Newspaper companies' brands remain trusted and strong, their relationships with advertisers solid, their total audience reach powerful, and their public watchdog roles vital.

Today's emerging business model values the developing and aggregating of new audiences for our journalism and our advertisers, likely moving us from a paid print subscription model for a single mass medium to a model that will include numerous free and paid offerings, both products and services. The metrics for the new model will be defined by audience, not simply paid circulation.

In an October 2006 analysis, the Newspaper Association of America released figures showing an 8 percent increase in total newspaper audience. "Newspapers are extending their audience reach beyond the core print product by attracting new readers to their Web sites and specialty publications, redefining the traditional newspaper audience."[4]

In a February 2007 media column, *New York Times* writer Katharine Q. Seelye looks at how some newspapers are beginning to address the marketplace's changing news and information consumption patterns. She notes the newly redesigned *Wall Street Journal*'s marketing strategy, which features Sheryl Crow and other marquee names that might connect to a very specific reader.[5] The NAA is also launching phase two of its new national campaigns. As Seelye points out, the creative approaches of the two campaigns "are quite different, as they are looking for different audiences. But they both speak to the larger fact that newspapers can no longer rely on selling themselves simply by being there; rather, they have to go out into the cluttered marketplace and stand up and shout, 'Me too!' above the din of iPods, cell phones, televisions, computers, video games and assorted other gadgets."[6]

And other factors are challenging traditional newspaper organizations:

- New competitors emerging daily. (We don't always see them.)
- Risk of a talent drain of our best and brightest. (We don't move quickly enough for the Millennials.)
- Traditionalism and lack of flexibility in our organizations. (Old ways die hard.)
- Lack of common purpose and understanding of the mission throughout all levels of the organization. (We aren't telling the story in the elevator.)
- Underfunded marketing. (We aren't committing the dollars.)
- Insufficient investment in technology and training to adopt and maximize the new tools. (We're behind our competitors.)
- Lack of meaningful connections with our communities. (Top leadership chairs revolve too frequently.)
- Lack of industry standards for online ad placement and a common platform. (It's very hard for us to play nice together.)

It's All about the People

Perhaps most important, we've been too slow to build and nurture the kinds of diverse leadership we must have to guide and speed the reinvention of our business. And we have been disadvantaged by our traditional organizational structures designed to support a fading business model.

At the *Times* we've focused on both since 2000, rebuilding our executive leadership team over that period and reinventing our organizational structure. The work is far from finished. In 2007 we established an entirely new audience development department, replacing the traditional circulation and marketing departments. And since 2000, we've doubled the representation of diversity in our top sixteen executive positions from 19 percent to 44 percent.

My colleague, *CQ* editor Riley, sees a direct business correlation, and it's not just about gender, racial, and ethnic diversity. "A big part of our success," he observed, "will be tied into rethinking what type of people we hire. The premium moving forward will rest on attracting more innovators into our midst and finding ways to give them the freedom and the backing they need to experiment and help move us into a new realm in which we can preserve the journalism and make a robust business model work."[7]

In thinking back about my daughter's expressed desire to help other people and the wide range of possibilities for her, we talked about the kind of leaders our industry must attract and grow if we are to reinvent our businesses and therefore continue to fund our public service journalism for our citizens and preservation of a free society. We need visionary leaders who are:

- Proven in more than one area of business.
- Agents of change.
- Excellent communicators, able to build common purpose around a goal.
- Able to assemble and lead diverse groups.
- Knowledgeable and comfortable with new technologies, tools, and media.
- Innovators, risk takers, collaborators.
- Marketers.
- Inspiring.
- Committed to our institutions of democracy.

In her book *The First Sex: The Natural Talents of Women and How They Are Changing the World,* noted anthropologist Helen E. Fisher cites research that observes some of women's traditional strengths in the workplace.

> Women's style of management is based on sharing power, on inclusion, consultation, consensus, and collaboration. Women work interactively and swap information more freely than men do. Women managers encourage their employees by listening to, supporting, and encouraging them. Women give more praise—and praise is more valuable to women. Women also compliment, thank, and apologize more regularly. Women ask for more advice in order to include others in the decision-making process. And women tend to give suggestions instead of giving orders. In fact, women managers sometimes soften their criticisms so much that men don't realize they have been criticized.[8]

The Obstacles

So the age-old question that many of us veterans have grown weary of discussing is: Why haven't more women excelled and risen to the top jobs in our industry?

Jeffrey V. Kohler, senior vice president of circulation for the *Philadelphia Inquirer and Daily News* in the 1990s, who has been a leading recruitment executive in the newspaper industry since then, suggests several reasons:

- Social structures and mores force women to choose between family and career.
- Unspoken bias exists among superiors, making them reluctant to invest time and resources in a woman's career for fear of the risk of losing her.
- Too few "enlightened" companies and executives truly exist.
- Comparable pay for comparable jobs lags; statistically women earn less and this makes a man's job more valuable.[9]

I would add that women are very cautious about promoting themselves and their accomplishments, having been taught to be patient and good things will come. In most organizations, women must take conscious and consistent steps to advance their value to those who can influence their career paths. There are effective ways to do this, but first someone has to encourage and coach the approaches that are effective. Too often, inexperience leads women to trip in this area and become marked as too pushy or outspoken. And often the woman errs in adopting behaviors that appear to "work" in her organization.

"Years ago when I started in management, I was one of two women," said the *Times*'s director of advertising, Moya Neville, who has been instrumental in leading the reinvention of our sales division since 2004. "I found myself leaving meetings and thinking that I hadn't accomplished or communicated what I wanted . . . then I read Deborah Tannen's book *You Just Don't Understand: Men and Women in Conversation.*"[10] Neville found Tannen's message simple but powerful: "Men and women communicate differently. Men expect to solve the problem. Communications is a means to an end. Women are about connection and feelings," she said. However, as Neville's colleagues would attest, her tough-love, high-expectations style has produced legions of sales associates who would walk through fire for her.

Neville shares how she adopted a more direct approach, and although she found it to be very effective, she was careful not to change fundamentally who she was. "I try and stay conscious of being the woman I am and not becoming exactly like the men who weren't being intuitive to me when I was younger. I worry about women in leadership creating their own 'good old girls' club' full of direct, icy women," she said. As Neville has coached women who are early in their careers, she hears their concerns. They tell me "they look around at women in leadership and think, 'If I have to be like that, maybe I don't want to lead.' That is scary," Neville said.[11]

Former veteran Merrill Lynch media analyst Lauren Fine also addressed the gender style issue: "Confident women are often thought of as bitchy and men are allowed to dismiss them for that quality. Women aren't always good at promoting themselves, having been taught repeatedly not to brag. Women are often afraid to ask for promotions, as they believe their good work will speak for itself." Fine went on to say that having a "father who was a salesman, I was taught early on to ask for the order. My predecessor never had to ask for a raise; I had to repeatedly. He never asked for a promotion; I had to repeatedly. We often discussed if I was confident or pushy."[12]

Another perspective from someone who has worked in both the cable and airline industries and consulted inside many large organizations, including the *Los Angeles Times, Baltimore Sun*, my newspaper, AT&T, Pacificare, Comcast, and Kaiser Permanente, amplifies some of the obstacles women face. Randy

Luety's observations are based on more than fifteen years assisting individuals, teams, and CEOs with professional development goals for themselves and their organizations:

> I'm not sure I would classify the current environment as a "failure," but rather a slower progression than most women would prefer. From my vantage point, I see a variety of issues still blocking the path. We still see a majority of men in leadership roles in most companies. When you are outnumbered, it takes longer to align the thinking at many levels. Women on the road to the top have few mentors in similar jobs, and most men are frightened to offer their hand in mentoring and providing honest feedback. That is a key element—lack of honest feedback.
>
> Too many men in senior leadership have had no experience or interest in developing women into top jobs. Perhaps it is threatening, but I truly believe it is about lack of experience. Throughout their careers there have been few—if any—females integrated into their work experience. Now, as these same men have achieved senior levels of management, pressure is applied to bring women into like jobs, but they have nothing to model and no one to assist.

He went on to say that he "usually find[s] men unwilling to have conversations—even with other men about the situation they face. In another 10 years, I think the landscape will change."[13]

In eight years our daughter, Lindsay, will have turned thirty. How will her impressions of her mom's industry today influence her decisions for tomorrow? Today she sees that we've made little progress since her grade school days when she accompanied me on business trips. She was always the center of attention on these trips, as all my male colleagues (the dads) doted incessantly over her at meetings. Invariably they talked about how they missed spending more time with their children. Men rarely traveled with their daughters back then. However, Mary Junck, chairman and CEO of Lee Enterprises—now the country's fourth-largest media group, based on circulation—frequently joined me in bringing our daughters along on business, as did some of our women peers. We felt it was important that our daughters, in particular, knew why their moms weren't home and what our work was about.

Lindsay says she loved traveling with me as she thinks back today on those trips. "Seeing what Mom did, how she was still learning, but most of all loving her job, made me realize how excited I was for her. I have always hoped that I will find a career that I can love and pursue as deeply as she has." Lindsay goes on to say she never felt left out when I was gone. "I always missed her, of course, but in getting the chance to see where she was going and the cool things she got to do, the influential people she got to meet, I saw how happy she was, and that is most important."[14]

So How Far Have We Come?

According to Northwestern University's Media Management Center's and its "Women in Media, 2006" report, "Women are in a holding pattern." At 137 newspapers with circulations of eighty-five thousand or greater, "women publishers have leveled off at the exact same number as three years ago." Only twenty-five women (18 percent) sat in the chair of president/publisher/CEO—the same as 2003. At the executive vice president/general manager spot, only six of fifty-nine spots are held by women, down two from 2003.

The job categories where women dominate the senior ranks are predictably human resources and community affairs, but there are some promising numbers in other areas. Women hold more than half of the senior advertising executive positions, a slight increase. They outnumber men in the top marketing jobs, and 41 percent of the managing editor positions are held by women. It's significant to note that the number of women who have moved into the top operations position has doubled, moving from eight to sixteen. In contrast, representation in the top circulation job dropped, moving down from fifteen women to ten.[15]

On the one hand, our statistics aren't any better or worse than most other industries, but more important, our performance won't help differentiate us as we compete for the rising young talent. Our industry likes to think it's different, but it has struggled with this issue for years, and for many of the same reasons we see across other lines of business. One reason still ranks number one: Women struggle to balance their personal and professional lives.

"I believe that young women coming into the workforce—unmarried or married—operate with a daily assumptive cloud over their heads: is she committed to her career? Will family needs and responsibilities be such a priority that the career will be compromised?" executive recruiter Kohler said. "There are certainly stay-at-home-dads supporting their executive wives' careers, but we know this is still less common than standard. In today's society, women are the primary caregivers."[16]

Former media analyst Fine agreed, saying, "Many companies are not flexible in handling women with families who are willing to acknowledge that their family is their priority. I have been fortunate to be in a job that is a clear meritocracy; further, Merrill Lynch has always allowed me to do my job in my own way to accommodate my desire to live a balanced life. I try hard to replicate that for others, but not all women are comfortable with it nor are their bosses."[17]

Luety said, "Women get shortchanged in this area [motherhood]. To opt out to have children—even for the shortest period of time—has an impact. I think men take advantage of that situation—though not spoken. . . . Women are either forced to move to the sideline, perhaps leaving the workforce, then are chal-

lenged to return to a similar or higher level job in their former organization."[18]
"I call it work-life integration," said the *Times*'s Neville, who had her baby at age forty-two. "I tried to hold myself to the 'balance' thing and I was setting myself up for failure."[19]

"It's all a matter of priorities," said Lee CEO Junck. When her daughter, now twenty, was a child, she took off almost two years, resigning as publisher of a metropolitan newspaper with no guarantee of a future position. She resumed her professional career at an even larger newspaper two years later as publisher at the *Baltimore Sun* and continued advancing from there. Since joining Lee in 1999, she has expanded the company from twenty-three daily newspapers to fifty-six and has turned it into an industry leader in revenue, circulation, and online growth. Yet, all the while her family has remained at the center of her life. She has been a scout leader, basketball coach, and Sunday school teacher, rarely skipping a school concert, picnic, or birthday party. "I haven't missed much," Junck said. "You don't have to sacrifice either your career or your family, but striking a balance isn't always easy." She gives a recent example of when an important business transaction hinged on her availability to attend a meeting on a day that conflicted with her plans to visit college campuses with her daughter. "I handled the meeting by phone," she said. "More often, maintaining balance means leaving the office an hour early to attend a school function, followed by two hours of returning e-mails at 11 P.M. "In Lee, we try to maintain a culture that gives people opportunity for balance in their lives," Junck said. "We reschedule meetings all the time."[20]

As for my own priorities, my family comes first and I make it a point to let my colleagues know I must take a call from a child or leave to attend a soccer or golf match. It gives silent permission to others. Supporting healthy "work-life integration" in our organizations will become increasingly critical if we are to successfully compete for and recruit top talent. And increasingly, women are likely to dominate those talent pools.

According to a November 2005 article in *Monthly Labor Review,* 58.8 percent of new entrants into the workforce between 2004 and 2014 will be women and people of color.[21] And in a 2005 report the National Center for Education Studies reported that in academic year 2003–2004, women earned more bachelor's degrees (57.5 percent) and master's (58.9 percent) degrees than men, and that by 2013–2014, women holding doctorate and professional degrees will also outnumber men.[22] While women still made up only 29.7 percent of those entering the top twenty U.S. MBA programs in 2005,[23] a 2006 survey of 1,883 postgraduate women showed the top two industries they entered were finance/insurance and accounting. Marketing was third.[24] However, according to another survey of unpublished data from the Graduate Management Admissions Council that same year, 1,729 postgraduate women cited product management first and general management second when identifying the most popular industries.[25]

We are beginning to see the same dynamic within our own organizations. As a greater number of women move into the pipeline of an organization, we are bound to increase the chances that they are lifted to the top jobs for two key reasons: First, there will simply be more women in the talent pool preparing and mentoring more women. But more important, women, generally speaking, may be more likely to excel in the new business model given the kind of leadership skills that come to them more naturally.

Does Wall Street Really Weigh Diversity of Management?

Three industry analysts, who follow our industry daily, come at this question a bit differently, but each factors management diversity into assessments in some way. "The more people I know at a company, the better," Lauren Fine, formerly of Merrill Lynch, said. "I don't explicitly rate diversity, but I am very sensitized to it. I don't think I listen differently if it is a woman speaking unless I'm not impressed and then I try to analyze it. I am predisposed to wanting women to be successful so I am typically disappointed when I don't think a woman 'shows' well."[26]

"Without question, a diverse management team is viewed by 'the Street' (and investors) as a positive," said Peter Appert, media analyst for Goldman Sachs. "That said, I don't think investors have a checklist that includes management diversity as a prerequisite to investment. Rather, I think investors are focused on operating results and performance (measured quantitatively) as the key criteria for a successful investment. The view is that a strong management team has better probability of driving these results, and a diverse management team generally is a stronger management team. Therefore, management diversity should relate to superior financial results."[27]

Paul Ginocchio of Deutsche Bank Equities says he doesn't "explicitly look at diversity as a factor when evaluating companies, but I do think when I see women in senior leadership roles, it signals to me that the company is more open-minded and not stuck with a traditional mind-set. With the operating environment for newspapers so quickly changing, those companies with the ability to think non-traditionally should do better."[28]

At the Northwestern Media Management Center's 2006 Women in Media conference, thirty female newspaper leaders explored the power of their strengths in the new marketplace and reflected on their career paths. In follow-up conversations they explored the common themes. Lisa Sullivan, director of marketing at the *Austin American-Statesman*, noted, "Women face different challenges in newspapers mostly because it is an older business and things have always been done the same way. Women bring a special outlook on what the people in this country are facing. We are working mothers. We juggle and multitask more than anyone else. We are connected with our teens and young people. We are the readers and online users we're trying to reach."[29]

In the 2005 Caliper study "The Qualities That Distinguish Women Leaders," four key findings were outlined based on the research that included in-depth interviews with fifty-nine women leaders from around the globe who were compared with men in similar positions:

1. Women leaders are more persuasive than their male counterparts.
2. When they feel the sting of rejection, women learn from adversity and carry on with an "I'll show you" attitude.
3. Women value an inclusive, team-building leadership style of problem solving and decision making.
4. Women leaders are more likely to ignore rules and take risks.

The report makes other notable observations:

The strong people skills possessed by women leaders enable them to read situations accurately and take in information from all sides. This willingness to see all sides of a situation enhances their persuasive ability.

These women leaders are able to bring others around to their point of view or alter their own point of view, depending upon the circumstances and information they uncover. . . . They can do this because they genuinely understand and care about where others are coming from.

"The male leaders we've studied, on the other hand, have a tendency to start from their own point of view [explains Dr. Herb Greenberg, PhD, president and chief executive officer of Caliper]. . . . And because they are not as flexible or willing to interact with others, the male leaders may tend to force their perspective and convince through the strength of their position . . . rather than actually persuading."

The difference in leadership styles between men and women starts with the listening. Not just listening to form your answer, but really listening, learning, reflecting, then implementing a plan that incorporates the best of everyone's ideas. . . . Because women leaders are more willing to share information, they will also talk decisions through with many more people than their male counterparts.[30]

On this important point I will linger. I've been told by colleagues I've mentored that one of the most valuable things I did for them was to think aloud about plans, strategies, and possibilities. This form of mentoring may be the most valuable training we can give a colleague. I have found that women tend to be more comfortable working this way, because they are less afraid of exposing what they do or don't know. They welcome disagreement and even try to draw it out sometimes, and are often energized by being able to extract better thinking and solutions from others. This is another form of collaboration that successful women leaders seem to naturally seek, value, and foster.

I've learned that there is another very important reason for informally engaging others in one's thinking process. It provides a powerful tool for giving the organization, particularly its top lieutenants, a sense of where you are headed, the direction you want to go, and an idea of what you'll need from them. The opportunity to plant the "directional" seeds while seeking input on the best method to get there is powerful and lasting. This approach solidifies a team's ownership of a decision, and that's typically very important to the most effective leaders. Women in particular will work extra hard to achieve it. The "how" is as important to women as the "what."

Luety's organizational coaching experience confirms this notion.

> My observations of most women in senior roles and those advancing in that direction have two seemingly inherent attributes that most men do not easily align to: interpersonal communication skills and a desire for collaboration. I am not certain that these are "inherent" skills, but most successful females have sharpened and amplified these skills and apply them consistently. Most men are not comfortable with collaboration as their perception is that it is a "softer" approach to getting the job done. What I observe is that men hold back as their female counterparts push forward with collaboration. These men search for ways "behind the scenes" to gather their strength to "win" the struggle—whatever that might be.[31]

How Do We Get There from Here?

Eight years ago, when I came to the *Times,* one of my primary roles was to be the executive agent of change. My goal was to assemble a leadership team on the newspaper's business side that would rival the standard of excellence that had defined the *Times*'s journalism for so many years in the industry. Then, and now, the *Times* is often cited as one of the country's top ten newspapers. Believing that an authoritative local and regional news report still resonates with consumers, paid circulation remains a reliable measurement of our coverage commitment. For its 2007 ABC annual audit, the *Times* was one of only a very few metro newspapers to show circulation gains at a time of declining readership nationwide. As the industry moves to an audience metric that reflects more accurately a combined print and online readership, the *Times* is also the market leader among local media.

Does our independence and unique legal status afford us some special advantage that our publicly held peer companies do not enjoy? To the extent we are able to look beyond a quarterly earnings target, then perhaps yes. But having "pubbled" at publicly held newspapers, I know it is possible to grow the business and not trade off financial performance. However, one has to be willing to do the really hard work that influences those results. I believe that's the organizational work. It's about the people.

The organizational work can be torturously painstaking, because above all, it requires the patience to wait for the absolute best person when filling a position. It requires an institutional commitment to recruiting a diverse pool of finalists for all positions. It requires a total commitment to developing people. We've had top executive spots remain open for months. At one point I was searching for both a CFO and a senior circulation executive. Based on his recruitment experience, Kohler notes that "clients who emphasize the essentiality of diversity in the recruitment process have declined in the past 18 months as business conditions have tightened," although he still works to bring forward a diverse candidate pool.[32]

Each appointment of a new team member alters the dynamic of the entire team, and each new member must effectively raise the game of everyone around the table. One must assemble an executive team with that idea always being the top priority. For me, it is always critical we add to the total capacity of the team, adding not only the leadership attributes we value at the *Times* but also the expertise and voices that we're missing.

Building a diverse executive team is not just about gender, race, and ethnicity. It's about assembling a group of generalists who reflect those we seek to serve. The aim is to employ candidates with technical skills and line experience in at least two areas critical to the running of the business. When these skills and experiences combine around the table, we reap a powerful outcome. The team is able to make better decisions for the greater good of the enterprise, not just for the division a person happens to be leading at the time. Most important, this approach equips our leadership team to teach broader and more nuanced business acumen to those they are grooming.

Building high-performing leadership teams can take several years. At the *Times* we are in year eight, and I would say we're just now getting our high-speed rhythms. Because capacity building takes time, leaders who excel in this area are more comfortable balancing the relentless pressures of the changing business climate with the significant time required to get the right people into the right jobs. They are comfortable stepping in to roll up their sleeves to fill a void or delegating to less experienced managers in the interim. Women tend to more easily keep their focus on the big picture—the long-term "get"—the possibilities of the power of the ideal hire or the dream team, working in a flatter organization that values teams and not titles or positions.

For us, it's not just about getting the job done; it's about *how* the job gets done. Not unlike our peer newspapers, the *Times* has had to significantly reduce its expense base given the real estate recession in Florida and unprecedented classified declines. We've reduced full-time staff by more than 10 percent and found innovative ways to make the print product more useful while tightening newsprint consumption. Yet in-house surveys continue to show a very high employee engagement level of satisfaction.

Until recently, most organizations, and by extension the men who lead them, have relied upon hierarchical forms of management that "command from the chair" and use a rewards system that values strictly making the numbers versus building an innovative and high-performing organization. Therefore, they are often not as comfortable or adept at navigating in a rapidly changing business climate. In contrast, women more naturally seek and thrive in an environment that encourages teamwork to achieve a common goal of success for the organization.

Anthropologist Fisher refers to this as "feminine team playing." In writing about power, she notes, "[T]o men and women, power is often a different thing. Men regularly associate power with rank and status. Women more often see power as a network of vital human connections."[33] Women and men should be encouraged to work together proactively to explore their strengths and shortcomings. The potential gains for the team are powerful when the individual strengths are combined. This requires honest, candid communication and timely feedback among peers. Too often the difficult conversations are avoided and we observe women being more inclined to get them resolved up front and seeking positive and collaborative outcomes.

In her comments for the Media Management Center's "Women in Media, 2006" report, Mary Fran Gleason, former managing editor of the *Times Union* in Albany, New York, highlighted this point in talking about how she tries to lead others: "I don't allow issues or controversies to fester, and I am not afraid of hard conversations. I have often found myself initiating discussions others put off."[34]

Resolving communication issues within our organizations requires focus and commitment. It's an investment that requires concentrated amounts of time in an already impossible daily schedule. That's why it often does not happen. However, women and men who see the value of this investment will find the time and reap the enormous benefits. As stewards of our organizations, we have never faced a greater strategic imperative to build and nurture diverse executive teams and organizations.

The bottom line is this: *The consumer is in control and women are in control of consuming. We significantly weaken our long-term business prospects without more women helping to lead us.*

Today our industry has an overall talent shortage in key strategic areas: multimedia, marketing and research, sales, brand management, database marketing, and technology. These are excellent places to begin recruiting diverse players into our organizations. The hard part is providing the kind of environment where colleagues who are different from us can grow and thrive. Getting them in the door is one thing: keeping them and promoting them is quite another. Some of the ways we can speed this work are certainly not new, but here are ten worth revisiting. And whether Wall Street gives us credit for this work should not matter. Our employees and customers will.

Ten Ideas to Help Accelerate More Women to the Top Jobs and Diversify Our Leadership

1. *Name a chief diversity officer.* Tap a proven leader who has a track record of influencing change and results, who has line management experience, and who is not from human resources. This is not a human resources responsibility. Directors must own this work and be held accountable. The CDO should report directly to the top executive and be involved in all aspects of hiring and recruiting for the top management positions. There are successful models with measurable results. At the *Times* we are accountable to the staff, and we publish a progress report to them twice a year. (Our CDO has also assumed the role of human resources director.)

2. *Require at least one qualified woman and at least one person of color to be in the final candidate pool for every top management position.* Seek candidates from outside the industry, from competitors, and from the top business schools, but make certain there are support systems and commitments in the organization to help them acculturate and grow.

3. *Establish a formal process with directors to build "leadership capacity" in the organization.* Most companies call this succession planning, and it often fails because it tends to prematurely anoint individuals and raise expectations while often overlooking promising individuals deeper in the organization who would also thrive with the right development plans and sponsorship. The work needs to be iterative, collaborative, and part of the continuing performance evaluation process. It should consistently point directors to people with talent they might not have recognized in the organization and provide a mechanism for identifying talent at risk.

4. *Talk openly about your spouse and kids.* Set a tone that values family and work-life balance or "integration." Take your pick. If men and women speak freely in the workplace about their commitments to leave the office early to attend a child's play or soccer game, to take a relative to the doctor, or to step out of a meeting when a family member calls, this behavior will telegraph powerful messages to others and give others permission to do the same. Women and men face the same challenges, and they must talk about it openly in the workplace and support one another. Work-life balance programs are helpful, but getting

support from colleagues and the boss and the time off when you need it are what really counts.

5. *Tap women and people of color to lead important and visible projects.* Use the opportunity to teach and coach. Be comfortable knowing they will go about the work differently than you might have, and focus on the results you desire, acting as a resource and a sounding board. However, do ask them to share the process and strategies they intend to use to influence the outcomes. When we state that the qualitative result is as important as the quantitative, it resets the criteria for success. Many women will naturally excel in this environment.

6. *Flip the reward systems.* Modify MBO (management by objectives) and incentive programs to reward executives and managers more for building and nurturing "healthy" high-performing teams than for just delivering the numbers. This feels very foreign to most executives, but it can become a powerful management tool. This approach reinforces the belief that if you've got the right people and have created the right work environment, the results will follow. Plus there's a better chance of sustaining high performance levels and making successful course corrections when needed.

7. *Adopt the 360-degree personal development tool throughout the top levels of the organization.* (The leadership group at the *Times* consists of about eighty managers.) The top executive must take the lead, be public about it, and be genuine about the desire for feedback. Make it voluntary. Commit publicly to using the feedback tool only for the purpose of individual growth, and leave it up to participants to share it. Work with an experienced executive coach whom managers may consult voluntarily and in confidence. Women in particular will find this enormously helpful in building stronger relationships with their male colleagues. The ongoing interactions will help establish an environment of candor and honesty. Encourage individuals to use the assessment when it will be most helpful to them. There are pitfalls, so rely upon an experienced coach.

8. *Don't be afraid to ask a colleague of the opposite sex out for a drink after work or to lunch.* This has long been a challenge for men, and understandably so, but in today's hectic work world, men and women colleagues need to find more downtime to talk substantively about business challenges and opportunities. It's just not realistic to think we can find that kind of quality time in daily routines that require numerous transactional meetings. If you're truly working as a team, such meetings will not have the same connotation they had in the antiquated top-down management style.

9. *Do not promote any individual who is not clearly the best candidate.* The organization will not rally behind her or him and its antibodies will rise up against the choice. The CEO's ratings will nose-dive. However, that does not mean the candidate must possess all the technical skills and experience for the specific

position. I have often favored the strongest leader. In many cases, tapping a proven leader with a track record of establishing strong relationships throughout the organization is the ideal choice. These people know how to influence results and will achieve those best by working through and with others.

10. *Try to identify and prepare at least one diverse candidate to succeed you.*

* * *

As I think about Lindsay's options for the future, I have little doubt her choices will be limitless and ever-changing. She is majoring in leadership at the Jepson School of Leadership at the University of Richmond and will also graduate in May with a degree in psychology and a minor in women's studies and sexuality. It seems a powerful combination in today's business climate. Regardless, I'm certain that even if one of our news organizations does not succeed in wooing Lindsay to this great and rewarding profession, she'll run something important and run it with style. I can't wait. In the meantime, I'm off to pubble.

Notes

1. Eugene Smith, *One Hundred Years of Hartford's Courant* (New Haven, Conn.: Yale University Press, 1949), 14–15.

2. Michael Riley, "Newspapers and Their Quest for the Holy Grail," *Nieman Reports* (Winter 2006): 13. Available at http://www.nieman.harvard.edu/reportsitem.aspx?id=100279 (accessed January 22, 2009).

3. "Discounting Diversity," *Editor and Publisher* 140, no. 2 (2007): 19.

4. Newspaper Association of America, "NAA Analysis Shows Eight Percent Increase in Total Newspaper Audience," press release, October 30, 2006. Available at http://www.naa.org/PressCenter/SearchPressReleases/2006/NAA-ANALYSIS-SHOWS-EIGHT-PERCENT-INCREASE-IN-TOTAL-NEWSPAPER-AUDIENCE.aspx (accessed January 22, 2009).

5. Katharine Q. Seelye, "Newspaper Readers of a Different Kind," *New York Times,* February 1, 2007. Available at http://www.nytimes.com/2007/02/01/business/media/01adco.html?ref=media (accessed January 22, 2009).

6. Ibid.

7. Riley, "Newspapers," 14.

8. Helen Fisher, *The First Sex: The Natural Talents of Women and How They Are Changing the World* (New York: Ballantine Books, 1999), 32, quoted in Pamela McCorduck and Nancy Ramsey, *The Futures of Women: Scenarios for the Twenty-First Century* (New York: Addison-Wesley, 1996).

9. Jeffrey V. Kohler, e-mail communications with Marty Petty, February 2 and 7, 2007.

10. Deborah Tannen, *You Just Don't Understand: Women and Men in Conversation* (New York: William Morrow, 1990).

11. Moya Neville, e-mail communication with Marty Petty, February 21, 2007.

12. Lauren Fine, e-mail communications with Marty Petty, February 1, 3, and 13, 2007.

13. Randy Luety, e-mail communications with Marty Petty, February 3 and 4, 2007.

14. Lindsay Petty, e-mail communication with Marty Petty, February 16, 2007.

15. Mary Arnold and Mary Nesbitt, "Women in Media 2006: Finding the Leader in You," Media Management Center, Northwestern University, 2006, 26 and 27. Available at http://www.mediamanagementcenter.org/publications/data/wim2006.pdf (accessed January 22, 2009).

16. Kohler e-mail, February 2, 2007.

17. Fine e-mail, February 1, 2007.

18. Luety e-mail, February 3, 2007.

19. Neville e-mail, February 21, 2007.

20. Mary Junck, conversation with Marty Petty, February 2007.

21. Mitra Toosi, Bureau of Labor Statistics, "Labor Force Projections to 2014: Retiring Boomers," *Monthly Labor Review* (November 2005).

22. National Center for Education Statistics, *Digest of Education Statistics,* 2005.

23. Unpublished statistics, Graduate Management Admissions Council, 2006.

24. Ibid.

25. Ibid.

26. Fine e-mail, February 3, 2007.

27. Peter Appert, e-mail communication with Marty Petty, February 20, 2007.

28. Paul Ginocchio, e-mail communication with Marty Petty, February 21, 2007.

29. "Executive Powers," *Fusion* (Spring 2006): 6.

30. Caliper Corporation, "The Qualities That Distinguish Women Leaders," 2005 study executive summary. Available at http://www.caliperonline.com/womenstudy/WomenLeaderWhitePaper.pdf (accessed January 22, 2009).

31. Luety e-mail.

32. Kohler e-mail.

33. Fisher, *First Sex,* 29.

34. "Executive Powers," 6.

Interview with Gary Pruitt

MARTY PETTY

Marty Petty: As leaders of our enterprises, we focus a good part of our energy on building leadership capacity for the present and the future. What are the three or four leadership attributes you believe to be most critical for those who are leading and preparing to lead our organizations into the future?

Gary Pruitt*: Important leadership attributes for the McClatchy Company include

1. *Adaptability:* Our business is changing at a rapid pace. Successful executives need to recognize and appreciate those changes, research and develop well-thought-out solutions, and respond quickly and efficiently.
2. *Learning agility:* To be adaptable, leaders need to be smart, intuitive, innovative, and independent thinkers. They need to apply knowledge from past experiences but be willing to learn from new experiences and seek out new ideas and solutions.
3. *Integrity:* Our public service mission rests on integrity. To attract and retain quality employees, maintain the confidence of investors and customers, and successfully promote the reputation of our company for journalistic and business excellence, it is essential that our executives not only exercise great integrity, but that they nurture it in others.

MP: Have those attributes changed over the last five years? If so, how?

GP: These have always been important attributes at McClatchy, but given technological advances and a drastically changing media landscape, adaptability and agility are being tested as never before.

MP: As you guide McClatchy in navigating the new business model, do you

---

*Gary Pruitt is chairman, president, and CEO of the McClatchy Company.

feel an even greater strategic imperative to diversify your top leadership positions? If so, why?

GP: Diversity is an absolute imperative at McClatchy. Again, our business and our business models are changing rapidly. We need a collaborative group of employees at all levels of the organization with diverse ideas about growing audience, diversifying the business, and meeting the challenges of an increasingly competitive climate.

We certainly are proud of our record of women and minorities in key management positions, and we need leaders who can attract and retain a diverse group and help connect their ideas and input with the business model. However, diversity at McClatchy must go beyond just management level, gender, and race. We believe the employees we hire must reflect the communities we serve and be able to address readers at all levels. Let's face it, we should be using high-school-aged reporters to produce our teen pages, not forty-year-old veterans.

MP: According to the 2003 statistics from Northwestern's Media Management Center "Women in Media" study, 55 percent of your eleven publishers were women, putting McClatchy at the top of the pack. In 2006, you still were at the top even though the total number had dropped from six women publishers to four, or 36 percent. The average for the peer group in 2006 was 20 percent (Gannett had twenty-four women publishers out of a total of eighty-two, or 29 percent).

What specifically have you done as CEO to champion or take a lead role in building a diverse leadership team, and can you describe in business terms the impact that work has had on you and on McClatchy?

GP: With respect to our leadership team, we look at both our publisher group and our corporate senior management team. Prior to the acquisition of Knight Ridder in June 2006, five of our eleven publishers and two of our eight senior executives were women. In the last eighteen months since the acquisition, we promoted one of our female publishers to the senior management team, so women now make up one-third of the team. In addition, we now have eleven female publishers overseeing twelve of our thirty-three newspapers. In November 2007, three of these women were promoted into their current positions—two to lead larger newspapers and one into a first-time publisher role. McClatchy also has four female board members and eleven female executive editors leading newsrooms.

One way I have promoted building a diverse leadership team is to encourage offering early opportunities to internal candidates who show promise, allowing them to stretch into more senior roles before they might otherwise be ready. In other words, we are willing to take chances on smart, talented individuals. This has worked well for us, and, as a result, we tend to have a fairly diverse and young management team. This approach also builds strong loyalty to the company and inspires ongoing internal development of and opportunities for future leaders.

We also include diversity goals in every senior manager's annual bonus plan to encourage a strong focus on hiring and retaining a diverse workforce.

In addition, McClatchy's continued emphasis on quality journalism, integrity, and sound business practices allows us to attract talent from other newspapers throughout the industry.

The result of all of this, in business terms, is an ongoing evolution that builds on itself. We've developed a diverse, intelligent leadership team that is encouraged to diversify and grow the business. That, in turn, makes us an industry leader with a sound reputation for quality, integrity, strong revenue performance, and reaching audience. That, in turn, allows us to continue to develop and attract those to expand our diverse, intelligent leadership team.

MP: Has it made a difference in recruiting and retaining women throughout the company—to see women publishers, your general counsel, VP for human resources, VP of operations, et cetera? Feel free to speak about diversity in general if that's helpful as well.

GP: I think that it's not only helpful for women in the industry to see women in senior management roles, but also to see women who have children of all ages, diverse lifestyles, and a sense of balance. When your goal is to attract people from all walks of life, it's important to remember that you also have to be supportive and respectful of different lifestyles, personal demands, and choices.

MP: Do you have a specific or even anecdotal sense whether McClatchy's commitment and performance in this area has had an influence on the analysts' assessment of the company's performance? They always tell us that they pay careful attention to the strength of a management team. Do they really? Is building diverse leadership capacity at the top of McClatchy a stated goal of your board?

GP: I believe the McClatchy team and the reports from analysts speak for themselves, not to mention that our revenue outperformed our peers for most of this decade. We had the best-performing stock in the industry from 1995 through 2005. Diversity at the senior level is not a numbers game. Instead, it has to do with the quality of the individuals; their commitment to the company; their ability to be adaptable and take calculated risks; and their ability to inspire confidence in the company, working as a unified team. That being said, you can't create a dynamic team if you don't have individual thinkers who bring diverse backgrounds and ideas to the table, and who attract the talent that is key to our papers' ongoing success in our individual communities. So, yes, our commitment to diversity has paid off and our board definitely supports this.

Afterword

PAMELA J. CREEDON AND
PAMELA J. JOHNSON

The Edge of Change is important for the time in which we live. The stories and perspectives of these women journalists provide insight on how women are influencing news coverage and the media institutions that employ them. Their experiences provide an insider's view of how newsrooms work and the challenges they face. Most important, this book should influence the national commentary on how journalism and the news industry are adjusting to meet social and technological advancements and changes. Will the unparalleled ability of traditional news media to gather and provide information needed in our democracy continue?

A View of the Edge from Pam Johnson

My own career moved along the *Edge of Change*. The *Joplin (Mo.) Globe*, where I interned and later worked, introduced me to both the Linotype era and to my first computer. I got to try my hand at many newsroom jobs, the advantage of starting at smaller papers. I had my first mentor there, who, like other male bosses I had over the years, was significant to my growth and advancement from the *Globe*, to the *Kansas City Star*, and to the top newsroom jobs at the *Phoenix Gazette* and the *Arizona Republic*.

Along the way I experienced or led transitions brought about by shifting economic trends in the news business. I was an assistant managing editor at the *Star* for most of the time that it was owned by Capital Cities Communication, which eventually acquired the ABC television network and then sold everything to Disney. I saw and appreciated the inner workings of Cap Cities and its model of a decentralized parent company.

In Phoenix in the 1990s, I led a talented spunky afternoon *Gazette* staff that fought for its future every day of its existence. The *Gazette* and its morning sister paper, the *Arizona Republic,* were owned by the Pulliam family. The family-owned enterprises published two papers a day in Indianapolis and Phoenix well into the late nineties, remaining true to its desire to offer readers a choice. Then the two Phoenix newsrooms merged in 1995 and the *Gazette* folded in 1997. Those jarring changes ushered in a new era for the *Republic,* but sixty positions were eliminated, the harshest reality of change in the making. From 1997 to 2000, when Gannett bought the Pulliam papers, the *Republic* made waves of change internally that began to prepare the company and employees for the technology advancements that would soon bring even greater transformation.

The past six years of my career have been split between the Poynter Institute for Media Studies in St. Petersburg, Florida, and, more recently, heading the Donald W. Reynolds Journalism Institute at the Missouri School of Journalism, investigating new ways to provide journalistic content while upholding our highest standards.

Some History and Context

Historically, newspapers and their publishers helped lead their communities. Their businesses were lucrative. Their journalism dominated other media. Many think of those as "the good old days." Agree or disagree, those times were easier to negotiate than today's technology-driven environment, which challenges just about every stage of newspaper publishing.

Publishers and corporate CEOs—male or female—have spent recent years fighting declines in ad and circulation revenues. And those trends are exposing the weakened state of news company business models, which have affected their century-plus core purpose: journalism for their communities. Meanwhile, the news industry has lost thousands of jobs in recent years, and we are still counting job losses each day. Newspapers contributed to their problems. They were slow to react to the vastness of change outside their doors. Their business models were tied overwhelmingly to print, to Wall Street margins, and to internal bureaucracy. Meanwhile, Google and Yahoo!, craigslist, eBay, and others offered digital speed and expanse as alternative ways for people to gain information immediately and to order their lives with a few clicks at their home or business computer without waiting for newspaper delivery.

Whether led by men or women, once-powerful traditional media companies face continued decline unless they develop new business models and adopt new journalism models.

Jolt of Reality

Papers had deep roots locally, sizable staffs, and healthy businesses. Their journalism was laced with public service and their companies were good community citizens. These attributes are mostly still vital, but much has changed significantly and swiftly, as was made painfully clear by the demise of Knight Ridder and Pulitzer newspapers. The sale of thirty-two Knight Ridder papers in June 2006 to the McClatchy Company and the sale of fourteen Pulitzer papers in 2005 to Lee Newspapers shocked the industry. Equally surprising, immediately after the sale, McClatchy CEO Gary Pruitt announced that twelve of the papers were for sale because they were not a good fit for the company. Among these twelve papers was the flagship of the chain, the *Akron (Ohio) Beacon Journal,* which was sold to Black Press Ltd., a Canadian company.

Knight Ridder was admired for decades for the strong journalism its papers produced. It was an early experimenter in digital publishing and funded a test lab in Colorado. It established programs that benefited the communities the papers served. It contributed leadership at various levels in the industry. It was elevating women and minorities. The story of how and why Knight Ridder came to such a swift end remains to be told.

Newsrooms are in their own march to a different future. Print journalists have seen their newsrooms shrink and resources going to online operations. They are expected to learn new skills, arguably to save money. They know their journalistic routines are giving way to new ways of collecting and delivering the news. They know that trend lines for advertising revenue and younger readership continue to show declines. They know that citizen journalists and bloggers are laying claim to journalistic territory. They witness the strife and tension between the *Los Angeles Times* newsroom and the Tribune headquarters as two respected editors in a row—John Carroll and Dean Baquet—left their newsrooms in 2005 and 2007 over staff cuts. And, before them, Jan Leach, who was named the first female editor of the *Akron Beacon Journal* in 1998, became the first editor in more than a century of *ABJ* history to oversee a newsroom layoff. (Jan's story is found earlier in this book.) These losses, as well as others, have had a very strong impact on the newspaper business.

A View of the Edge from Pam Creedon

In the 1970s women flocked to journalism schools and found a voice on student papers. The venerable Society of Professional Journalists admitted women for the first time in 1969, and I was among the first group of women to join SPJ while in graduate school in Oregon. (Students were admitted in 1970.) My career veered into journalism education, and my view of the *Edge of Change* is shaped by what

I see in our journalism programs today. A former member of the Accrediting Council on Education in Journalism and Mass Communication, the Hearst Journalism Awards Board, and recent past president of the Association of Schools of Journalism and Mass Communication, I am familiar with trends in journalism education. Many journalism programs in higher education are rapidly integrating multimedia skills into the curriculum. Students are now becoming equipped with the skills to work across the media platforms of print, broadcast, and online. Faculty members are retooling to meet the challenge as well. But still a great deal of work lies ahead as programs adapt and prepare a new generation of journalists to cover society and lead change in the news industry.

Students jolt our reality because they expect media to be in their lives when and where they want access. "People [especially younger audiences] want to get news at different times and in different ways. Newspapers must be willing to go where people are and use multiple channels to reach them," said Nancy Green, vice president for circulation at Lee Newspapers in St. Louis and president of STL Distribution Services.[1]

Today's students move easily between media platforms. Many communicate news (and personal information) in online social communities such as Facebook or MySpace. Newspapers are no longer the main way to receive news for this key audience of eighteen-to-thirty-five-year-olds. They want their news presented as it happens and available on demand—every day, around the clock—and they are just as willing to accept interpretations from their online social communities as to read or hear it from a trained journalist.

The challenge is huge, but journalism education is adapting and has always found a way to prepare students and expand opportunities.

March to the Future

Yet for all the angst that is rightly expressed about the future of news, its audience, and its resources, awareness is growing inside the industry and out about what's at risk if journalism fails the democracy. One of the boldest steps was taken in late 2006 by the Gannett Newspaper Division. Under the direction of then division president Sue Clark-Johnson and vice president Jennifer Carroll, eighty-nine newsrooms were transformed into information centers that operate 24-7. Key functions structure the work to be done, such as how news is presented on each platform, community conversations, multimedia content, hyper-local coverage of familiar topics, and public service.

The "State of the News Media, 2008" report, published by the Project for Excellence in Journalism, reemphasized the need for innovation, new ideas, and products and underscored the need for transformation in the news industry.

Commenting on that report for the Poynter Institute's online Biz Blog, Rick Edmonds, a media business analyst, emphasized that newspapers "need to redefine themselves as local information and connection utilities."[2] He stressed the need for "a business model that capitalized on their [newspapers'] news dominance, their continued strength as an outlet for retail and national advertising, and yet-to-be-invented businesses." Edmonds noted that "news sites get high marks for innovation," but the business side of news companies remains less willing to reinvent itself. Meanwhile, in this new era of media, Edmonds noted, the overall news audience is growing when print circulation and online are combined. Newsrooms and companies are restructuring and experimenting.[3]

Women's contribution and involvement with Internet media also has positive future potential. One site was launched by some female journalists, another is accessed by a large number of media audience members, while others include blogs and comments. According to one study, women are Internet media's largest users, and its coverage includes politics, culture, reader essays, relationships, and social networks.[4]

And, J-Lab: The Institute for Interactive Journalism has a strong role in creating the future of journalism. J-Lab is defined as "an incubator for innovative news experiments that use new technologies to help people actively engage in critical public issues. Its core mission is to improve public life by transforming journalism for today and re-inventing it for tomorrow."[5] J-Lab was created and led by executive director Jan Schaffer, former business editor and a Pulitzer Prize winner for the *Philadelphia Inquirer.*

The challenge for the news industry will be to transform itself into a more modern, innovative industry that develops new news products and business models and serves vast new and changing audiences. As this book was going to press, most traditional news companies seemed endangered, with profits sinking, readers and audiences declining, and all-digital editions in place in some communities and under consideration in others. New and bold leadership is needed in the news industry as the press redefines journalism and as companies perhaps undergo fundamental structural change in the twenty-first century.

Diversifying senior leadership in newsrooms is a process that is under way and is tied to the success of news companies, as indicated earlier in this book. We know from many studies that women and people of color bring new approaches, new business models, and adaptability to the contemporary news environment. We know that we have opportunities to bring the academy and the profession closer than ever. We know that a high premium is being placed on innovation. We know that women and people of color make a difference in how newsrooms and companies are led and how news coverage is shaped. We know that women readers will be a part of the change ahead, and that new audience communities are being created. We know that journalism and its core values are central to democracy and to building a broader international society in this age of global communication.

Women in newsrooms and companies and in emerging media will help to write the next chapter of history for the press, and for citizens. The challenge and promise is for women to play even a more central role in this and future generations as journalists, executives and leaders in news and media, and in society.

Notes

1. "Nancy Green Will Head Lee Enterprises Circulation Operations in St. Louis," March 27, 2008, Reuters Online, http://www.Reuters.com/article/Press (accessed May 1, 2009).

2. Rick Edmonds, "Newspaper Next 2.0: Way Outside the Box," Biz Blog, February 25, 2008, Poynter Online, http://www.poynter.org/column.asp?id=123&aid=138140 (accessed January 22, 2009).

3. Rick Edmonds, "State of the Media, 2008: Decoupling Blues," Biz Blog, March 19, 2008, Poynter Online, http://www.poynter.org/column.asp?id=123&aid=139610 (accessed January 22, 2009).

4. Stephanie D. Smith, "Memo Pad: The Ladies Who Search," WWD Media, December 29, 2008, http://www.wwd.com/media-news/fashion-memopad/the-ladies-who-search-1904932 (accessed January 22, 2009).

5. "Mission," J-Lab: The Institute for Interactive Journalism, http://www.j-lab.org/about (accessed January 22, 2009).

Contributors

CATALINA CAMIA is a Washington editor of *USA Today*. She was president of the Asian American Journalists Association in 1999–2000 and is a former president of UNITY, an alliance of organizations for people of color in journalism. She is a former Washington correspondent for *the Dallas Morning News,* where she covered Congress and wrote a weekly column. Camia also has reported for *Congressional Quarterly* magazine, the *Dallas Times Herald,* and *the Press-Enterprise* in Riverside, California.

KATHLEEN CARROLL is the executive editor and a senior vice president of the Associated Press. She has been a leader in decision making about security issues for journalists covering stories in war zones and other dangerous places. Previously she worked for Knight Ridder, where she directed Washington and international coverage for newspapers and multimedia, for the *Dallas Morning News,* the *International Herald Tribune* (Paris bureau), and the *San Jose Mercury News.* She has served on the Pulitzer Prize Board since 2003.

PAMELA J. CREEDON is a professor and former director of the School of Journalism and Mass Communication at the University of Iowa (2002–7) and at the School of Journalism and Mass Communication at Kent State University (1994–2002). She is editor of two editions of *Women in Mass Communication* (Sage, 1989, 1993) and coedited the third edition, published in 2007. She also coedited *Seeking Equity for Women in Journalism and Mass Communication: A Thirty-Year Update* (Erlbaum, 2004). She is a member of the International Communication Association, the Society of Professional Journalists, the International Association of Media and Communication Research, and the International Association of Business Communicators, where she became an Accredited

Business Communicator (ABC). She serves on the editorial boards of *Public Relations Review* and the *Journal of Public Relations Research.*

PAULA ELLIS is the vice president for national and new initiatives at the John S. and James L. Knight Foundation, the nation's largest journalism foundation. Previously she was the vice president for operations of Knight Ridder corporate, and oversaw operations for fifteen newspapers. She also was an editor for the KR Washington bureau. Ellis served as publisher of the *Myrtle Beach (S.C.) Sun News* from 1997 to 2004, and in various roles with the *Columbia (S.C.) State* from 1990 to 1997. She is a frequent speaker and former chair of the National Advisory Board of the Poynter Institute for Media Studies in St. Petersburg, Florida.

HELEN E. FISHER, PHD, is one of the country's most prominent anthropologists and has done extensive research and written five books on gender differences in the brain, the origin of female sexuality, love, and evolution of the nuclear family. She has lectured widely in the United States and abroad about the role and impact of women in twenty-first-century business, family life, and about the future of women in society and in cultures around the world. Fisher is a research professor and member of the Center for Human Evolution Studies in the Department of Anthropology, Rutgers University. She is the author of *Why Him? Why Her? Finding Real Love by Understanding Your Personality Type* (Henry Holt, 2009); *Why We Love: The Nature and Chemistry of Romantic Love* (Henry Holt, 2004); *The First Sex: The Natural Talents of Women and How They Are Changing the World* (Random House, 1999); *Anatomy of Love: The Natural History of Monogamy, Adultery, and Divorce* (W. W. Norton, 1992; Fawcett, 1994); and *The Sex Contract: The Evolution of Human Behavior* (William Morrow, 1982; Quill, 1983). Fisher's books have been published in many languages. *The First Sex* and *The Anatomy of Love* were selected by the *New York Times* as Notable Books.

DOROTHY BUTLER GILLIAM is a former reporter, editor, columnist, and director of the Young Journalists Development Program for the *Washington Post.* She served as the Shapiro Fellow at George Washington University's School of Media and Public Affairs for the 2003–4 academic year and is the director of the school's Prime Movers Program. Gilliam has served as chair of the board of directors of the Robert Maynard Institute for Journalism Education and is a former president of the National Association of Black Journalists. Among the honors she has received are induction into the Hall of Fame for the year 2002 by the Washington, D.C., chapter of the Society of Professional Journalists; induction into the NABJ Hall of Fame in 1992; and the University of Missouri Honor Medal in Journalism in 1998. She is author of *Paul Robeson, All Ameri-*

can (New Republic Books, 1976), and her work has appeared in a number of anthologies and collections.

ELLEN GOODMAN is a columnist for the *Boston Globe,* syndicated columnist with the Washington Post Writer's Group, and one of the nation's foremost syndicated columnists, appearing in more than 450 newspapers. Her book on social change, *Turning Points,* was published by Doubleday in 1979, and five collections of her columns also have been published. In 1980 Goodman won the Pulitzer Prize for Distinguished Commentary. Her book *I Know Just What You Mean: The Power of Friendship in Women's Lives,* coauthored with Patricia O'Brien, was published by Simon and Schuster in 2000. Goodman has written for many years about women in journalism, the women's movement in the past quarter century, women's issues, and social change in society.

SHARON GRIGSBY has been the deputy editorial page editor for the *Dallas Morning News* since 2004, having been employed there since 1980. She oversees day-to-day operations of both the op-ed and editorial pages. In an innovative move, she worked to publish bloggers from across the nation and world before most papers were taking them seriously and created *Balance of Opinion,* a weekly column on both print and Web that provides readers with the best of the syndicated national columnists. From 1994 to 1998, Grigsby was founding editor of the newspaper's religion section, which won numerous national awards and was recognized as "best religion coverage in the United States" four of the five years she was editor.

CAROL GUZY has been a staff photographer for the *Washington Post* since 1988. A Pennsylvania native, Guzy was an intern and then a staff photographer at the Miami Herald, where she worked from 1980 to 1988. Along with many other awards, Guzy has won three Pulitzers for her photography: in 1995, for her coverage of the military intervention in Haiti; in 1986, sharing the award with Michel duCille, for their work during the mudslide in Armero, Colombia; and in 2000, along with two other *Washington Post* photographers, Michael Williamson and Lucian Perkins, for photographs of Kosovo refugees.

KIRSTEN SCHARNBERG HAMPTON was a national correspondent for the *Chicago Tribune* and a foreign correspondent for the *Tribune* in Iraq until August 2008. She began her career at the *Des Moines Register* and then moved to the *Baltimore Sun* before joining the *Chicago Tribune* in 1999. While at the *Tribune,* she initially focused on long-form narrative features before diving into the world of foreign reporting during the Iraq war. She crossed the berm into Iraq during the first hours of the war with the 101st Airborne Division and has returned twice to spend months reporting from that war-torn nation. She was based for more than two years in the *Tribune*'s New York City bureau. She has also reported from Africa and served as the paper's Pacific Rim and South Pacific correspondent, as well as Midwest correspondent. She married Major Bill Hampton, the Army officer she met in Iraq, in July 2007, and in 2008 left the paper to move to Italy with her husband and two children.

CATHY HENKEL was the sports editor of the *Seattle Times* from 1990 to 2008 and one of the first females to take that role at a major American newspaper. Previously she worked with the *Wichita (Kan.) Eagle-Beacon*, the *Wichita Sun*, and the *Eugene (Ore.) Register Guard*. She has won numerous honors in sports journalism. Under her direction, the *Seattle Times* earned several Associated Press Sports Editors (APSE) awards for being one of the country's best daily sports sections. Her team also won APSE's top investigative award twice. Henkel was a reporter or lead editor in fourteen Olympics and one of the founders of the Association for Women in Sports Media, which honored her with its Pioneer Award in 2005.

PAMELA J. JOHNSON is the executive director of the Donald W. Reynolds Journalism Institute at the Missouri School of Journalism. The institute exists to develop and test ways to improve journalism through new technology and improved processes. Johnson is a former member of the leadership faculty of the Poynter Institute for Media Studies. As a professional she served in executive and managing editor positions at the *Arizona Republic* and the *Phoenix Gazette* and as assistant managing editor at the *Kansas City Star*. Johnson also worked at the *Joplin Globe* and the *Binghamton (N.Y.) Evening Press*. In 2000, Johnson was awarded the Missouri Honor Medal for Distinguished Service in Journalism. Johnson also has served as president of the Associated Press Managing Editors, as a Pulitzer juror, and as a judge for the American Society of Newspaper Editors Best Writing Awards contest.

JANE KIRTLEY has been the Silha Professor of Media Ethics and Law at the School of Journalism and Mass Communication at the University of Minnesota since August 1999. Previously she was the executive director of the Reporters Committee for Freedom of the Press in Arlington, Virginia. Kirtley speaks frequently on First Amendment, freedom of information, and media ethics issues, both in the United States and abroad. She is a commentator for *Nieman Watchdog*, and wrote the "First Amendment Watch" column for *American Journalism Review* from 1995 to 2006. Kirtley serves on the board of directors for the Sigma Delta Chi Foundation and the editorial board of *Communication Law and Policy*. She has received many awards and honors, including the Edith Wortman First Amendment Matrix Foundation Award in 2004.

JAN LEACH is an assistant professor in the School of Journalism and Mass Communication at Kent State University and an Ethics Fellow at the Poynter Institute in St. Petersburg, Florida. She is also a former vice president and editor of the *Akron (Ohio) Beacon Journal*. Leach came to Akron from the *Cincinnati Enquirer*, where she had been managing editor for nearly five years. She also has been managing editor of the *Phoenix Gazette* and city editor of the *Arizona Republic*.

CAROLINE LITTLE is CEO of Guardian News & Media Limited, North America. She was the CEO and publisher of Washingtonpost.Newsweek Interactive (WPNI) from 2004 until June 2008, after serving as president, chief operating officer, and in a number of other positions with the company. Before joining WPNI, Little was a deputy general counsel at *U.S. News & World Report, Atlantic Monthly,* and *Fast Company*. She serves as a board member of the Posse Foundation and is a trustee of Grinnell College.

WANDA S. LLOYD is the executive editor of the *Montgomery (Ala.) Advertiser* and montgomeryadvertiser.com, and was the founding executive director of the Freedom Forum Diversity Institute at Vanderbilt University. A national leader in newsroom diversity, Lloyd is a former managing editor of the *Greenville (S.C.) News* and worked for ten years at *USA Today* as managing editor/administration and senior editor. She also has worked at the *Providence (R.I.) Evening Bulletin, Miami Herald, Atlanta Journal,* and the *Washington Post*. She is a founder and past chair of the National Association of Minority Media Executives and a former board member of the American Society of Newspaper Editors. Lloyd is the only double winner of the newspaper industry's most prestigious awards for diversity—the Ida B. Wells Award (1993) and the Robert G. McGruder Award (2007). She directed the landmark National Association of Black Journalists study *Muted Voices: Frustration and Fear in the Newsroom.*

ARLENE NOTORO MORGAN is associate dean for Prizes and Programs at the Columbia University Graduate School of Journalism and served as executive director of the "Let's Do It Better!" Workshop on Journalism, Race, and Ethnicity from 2000 to 2008. Morgan is an authority on "best practices" in covering diverse communities. In her role as associate dean, Morgan oversees the administration of the school's many prestigious prizes and professional development workshops. She is the coeditor of *The Authentic Voice: The Best Reporting on Race and Ethnicity* (Columbia University Press, 2006). In 2007 Morgan oversaw the launch of the new Punch Sulzberger News Media Executive Leadership Program. She is a former editor with the *Philadelphia Inquirer*. In 1995 Morgan was honored with the first Knight-Ridder Excellence in Diversity Award for her work to diversify the staff and for her leadership in fostering diversity issues throughout Knight Ridder newspapers, then corporate owner of the *Inquirer*. Morgan has been a fellow at the Freedom Forum's Media Studies Center. She serves on numerous journalism advisory boards.

JUNE O. NICHOLSON is the associate director of the School of Mass Communications at Virginia Commonwealth University, Richmond, Virginia. She was a staff writer for the *Raleigh (N.C.) News and Observer* and covered the statehouse in Virginia for a decade. Nicholson has been a leader for two decades in the national Society of Professional Journalists. She chairs the International Journalism Committee of SPJ and headed the organization's Journalism Education Committee from 2000 to 2007. Nicholson is a contributor for the third edition of *Women in Mass Communication* (Sage, 2007) and has written about diversity issues in media for *Quill* magazine and other publications. In 2008, Nicholson received the Robert P. Knight Multicultural Award from the Scholastic Division of the Association for Education in Journalism and Mass Communication, for promoting diversity in America's newsrooms. In 2007 she was named recipient of the Distinguished Service Award from VCU's College of Humanities and Sciences, for service to the journalism profession and to VCU.

GENEVA OVERHOLSER is director of the Annenberg School of Journalism at the University of Southern California. Previously she held the Curtis B. Hurley Chair in Public Affairs Reporting for the Missouri School of Journalism, in its Washington, D.C., bureau. With Kathleen Hall Jamieson, she coedited *The Press* (Oxford University Press, 2005), and she recently completed "On Behalf of Journalism: A Manifesto for Change" (http://www.annenbergpublicpolicycenter .org/Overholser/20061011_JournStudy.pdf). She is a former ombudsman for the *Washington Post*. Overholser was the editor of the *Des Moines Register* from 1988 to 1995. Under her leadership the *Register* won the 1990 Pulitzer Prize Gold Medal for Public Service. She is a member of the boards of the John S. Knight Fellowships at Stanford, the Center for Public Integrity, and the Fund for Independence in Journalism. She serves on the governing board of the Committee of Concerned Journalists and on the Journalism Advisory Committee of the Knight Foundation.

MARTY PETTY is the publisher of the *St. Petersburg Times,* Florida's largest newspaper; executive vice president of the Times Publishing Company; and former CEO and publisher of the *Hartford (Conn.) Courant,* the nation's oldest continuously published newspaper. She was a nationally recognized newspaper designer and photojournalism expert at the *Kansas City Star* and the *Kansas City Times* and was assistant managing editor at the newspapers before joining the *Courant* in 1983 as managing editor. She was a Pulitzer chair and juror for photography. When she was named publisher in 1997, Petty was the first woman to run the *Courant* in 218 years. Both papers won a combined four Pulitzers during her leadership. She is one of the founders of the Society of Newspaper Design.

DEB PRICE of the *Detroit News*'s Washington bureau writes a nationally syndicated column on gay and lesbian issues and covers Congress. She formerly was an editor at the *Washington Post*. Price has coauthored two award-winning books: *And Say Hi to Joyce: America's First Gay Column Comes Out* (Doubleday, 2005) and *Courting Justice: Gay Men and Lesbians v. the Supreme Court* (Basic Books, 2001). She has won numerous awards, including the Gay and Lesbian Alliance Against Defamation's "Outstanding Newspaper Columnist" award of 2006 and the Servicemembers Legal Defense Network's 2005 Randy Shilts Visibility Award.

DONNA M. REED is the vice president of news and multimedia strategy for Media General Inc. She was the first female vice president for news of a major newspaper group, and oversees both news and the strategic development of multimedia across MG holdings. Reed is a former managing editor of the *Tampa Tribune* and was part of the team that developed the vision for the News Center, which houses the *Tampa Tribune*, WFLA-TV News, and TBO.com, all companies of Media General Inc. She joined the *Tribune* in 1974 and has worked as a reporter, bureau chief, assistant suburban editor, suburban editor, assistant metro editor, state editor, and deputy managing editor.

SANDRA MIMS ROWE has been the editor of the *Portland Oregonian,* the largest newspaper in the Northwest, since 1993. The *Oregonian* has won five Pulitzer Prizes during her tenure, including the Public Service Gold Medal. Previously Rowe was the executive editor and vice president of the *Norfolk Virginian-Pilot,* which won a Pulitzer Prize for general news reporting during her tenure. She is a former president of ASNE and has been identified for many years with ASNE's Journalism Credibility Project. She was the National Press Foundation's "Editor of the Year" in 2003 and *Editor and Publisher*'s "Editor of the Year" in 2008.

PEGGY SIMPSON is a former reporter for the Associated Press and an early pioneer for women's rights in journalism. Simpson worked seventeen years for the Associated Press, in Texas and Washington, D.C.; covered economics and politics for the Hearst Newspapers; served as Washington bureau chief for *Ms.* magazine; and as a freelancer during the 1990s reported on Eastern Europe's transition from communism to a democratic market economy. She has taught at Indiana University, George Washington University, and the American Studies Center at Warsaw University. She currently is a freelance writer in Washington, D.C.

MARGARET SULLIVAN is the vice president and editor of the *Buffalo (N.Y.) News*. Originally hired as a reporter in 1980, in 1998 she was named managing editor, and in 1999 became the paper's first female editor and only the sixth person to edit the paper in its 120-year history. Sullivan has written for the *New York Times,* the *Washington Post,* the *American Editor, Columbia Journalism Review,* and *Washington Monthly.* She is a board member of the American Press Institute.

JULIA WALLACE is the editor of the *Atlanta Journal-Constitution* and ajc.com, directing a team of more than three hundred journalists. She was named editor in July 2002 after serving as managing editor for eighteen months. During her tenure, ajc.com has grown into one of the most popular newspaper Web sites in the country, logging more than a billion page views in 2007 and 2008. She has focused on improving the content of the newspaper—focusing on unique local content, including watchdog reporting and great storytelling. She was named "Editor of the Year" by *Editor and Publisher* in 2004. The paper was awarded Pulitzer Prizes in 2006 and 2007. Wallace began her career in Norfolk, Virginia, at the *Ledger-Star* and then moved to the *Dallas Times-Herald.* In 1982 she joined *USA Today* as a reporter and worked her way up to managing editor/special projects. She joined the *Chicago Sun-Times* in 1992 as managing editor. She left in 1996 and joined the *Salem (Ore.) Statesman Journal* as executive editor. She also is a former managing editor at the *Arizona Republic.* She was a member of the board of directors of the American Society of Newspaper Editors and is currently chairman of the national advisory board for the Poynter Institute.

KEVEN ANN WILLEY is editor of the editorial page and vice president of the *Dallas Morning News.* After beginning her career with the Associated Press in Phoenix, Willey joined the *Arizona Republic* in 1980, where she became the *Republic's* political columnist and then editorial page editor. Under Willey's direction the *Republic's* editorial pages were two-time finalists for the Pulitzer Prize. Willey became the vice president and editorial page editor at the *Dallas Morning News* in November 2002. Her editorial pages in Arizona and Texas have three times been finalists for the Pulitzer Prize. Under Willey's direction, the *Dallas Morning News* was the first in the nation to launch an editorial board blog, where editorial board members debate issues with one another in public view online and take questions/comments from readers. Willey is former president of the Texas Associated Press Managing Editors, a member of the National Conference of Editorial Writers, and a member of the Pulitzer Prize Board.

Index

The University of Illinois Press
is a founding member of the
Association of American University Presses.

Composed in 10.5/13 Adobe Minion Pro
with Meta display
by Jim Proefrock
at the University of Illinois Press
Manufactured by Thomson-Shore, Inc.

University of Illinois Press
1325 South Oak Street
Champaign, IL 61820-6903
www.press.uillinois.edu